searching for madre matiana

Diálogos Series

Kris Lane, Series Editor

Understanding Latin America demands dialogue, deep exploration, and frank discussion of key topics. Founded by Lyman L. Johnson in 1992 and edited since 2013 by Kris Lane, the Diálogos Series focuses on innovative scholarship in Latin American history and related fields. The series, the most successful of its type, includes specialist works accessible to a wide readership and a variety of thematic titles, all ideally suited for classroom adoption by university and college teachers.

Also available in the Diálogos Series:

Women Drug Traffickers: Mules, Bosses, and Organized Crime by Elaine Carey

Africans into Creoles: Slavery, Ethnicity, and Identity in Colonial Costa Rica by Russell Lohse

Emotions and Daily Life in Colonial Mexico edited by Javier Villa-Flores and Sonya Lipsett-Rivera

Native Brazil: Beyond the Convert and the Cannibal, 1500–1900 edited by Hal Langfur

The Course of Andean History by Peter V. N. Henderson

Masculinity and Sexuality in Modern Mexico edited by Anne Rubenstein and Víctor M. Macías-González

Modernizing Minds in El Salvador: Education Reform and the Cold War, 1960–1980 by Héctor Lindo-Fuentes and Erik Ching

A History of Mining in Latin America: From the Colonial Era to the Present by Kendall Brown

Slavery, Freedom, and Abolition in Latin America and the Atlantic World by Christopher Schmidt-Nowara

Cuauhtémoc's Bones: Forging National Identity in Modern Mexico by Paul Gillingham

For additional titles in the Diálogos Series, please visit unmpress.com.

searching for Madre Matiana

Prophecy and Popular Culture in Modern

Mexico

EDWARD WRIGHT-RIOS

UNIVERSITY OF NEW MEXICO PRESS • ALBUQUERQUE

© 2014 by the University of New Mexico Press
All rights reserved. Published 2014
Printed in the United States of America
19 18 17 16 15 14   1 2 3 4 5 6

Library of Congress Cataloging-in-Publication Data

Wright-Rios, Edward N. (Edward Newport), 1965–
Searching for Madre Matiana : prophecy and popular culture in modern Mexico /
Edward Wright-Rios. — First [edition].
pages cm. — (Diálogos series)
Includes bibliographical references and index.
ISBN 978-0-8263-4659-9 (pbk. : alk. paper) — ISBN 978-0-8263-4660-5 (electronic)
1. Matiana, Madre—Prophecies. 2. Catholic Church—Mexico—History.
3. Mexico—Church history—19th century. 4. Mexico—History—Prophecies.
5. Women in the Catholic Church—Mexico—History. I. Title.
BX1428.3.W75 2014
282'.72—dc23
2014007898

Cover photograph: Tineras Súplicas . . . , 1911, by José Guadalupe Posada. Jean
Charlot Collection, University of Hawaii at Manoa Library. Gift of Zohmah
Charlot, 1981. (JCC:JGP:V10)

Cover design by Lisa Tremaine
Text composition by Felicia Cedillos
Composed in Minion Pro 10.25/13.5
Display Type is Filosofia Unicase OT and LTC Ornaments Three

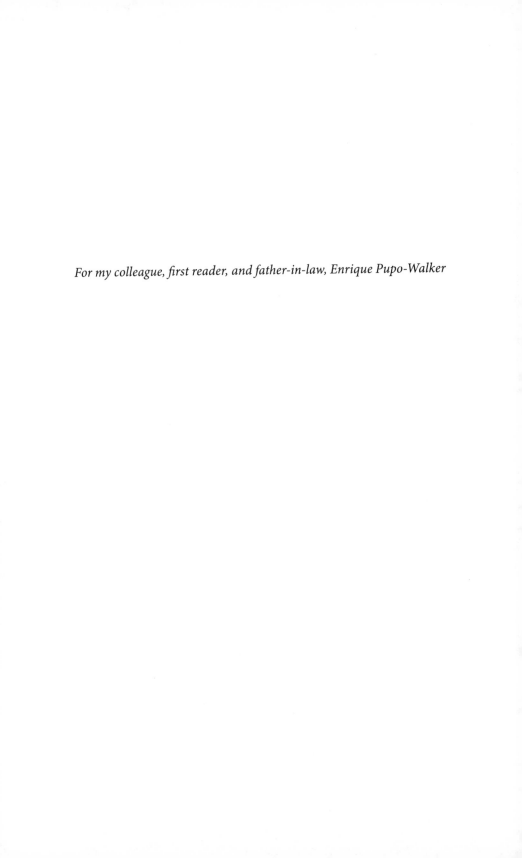

For my colleague, first reader, and father-in-law, Enrique Pupo-Walker

Contents

Illustrations

MAP

Acknowledgments

It is always a daunting task to address the balance sheet that emerges in the process of research and writing. In my case, it starts at home. My wife, Gini Pupo-Walker, and my nearly grown children, Elías and Sara, indulge my interest in old buildings, moldy books, faded photographs, and "dead people." On a different level, Enrique Pupo-Walker read drafts of each chapter, critiqued them carefully, and debated them with me at numerous breakfast meetings. My sister and colleague, Elizabeth Wright, also read and commented on chunks of the project at various junctures. (She also tracked down and secured a copy of a key source in Spain.) In Mexico I have been lucky to count on the hospitality and good company of uncles, aunts, cousins, nieces, and nephews: the Luthe Ríos and Pérez Castro clans of Guadalajara and Mexico City respectively.

As is typical, parts of this book benefited greatly from the support, encouragement, and feedback I received from colleagues in various circumstances. A trio of assistants at Vanderbilt, Francisco Flores-Cuautle, Ty West, and Lance Ingwersen, joined me in organizing and understanding my variegated sources. Likewise, Asela Reséndiz Muñoz and Beatriz Montes Rojas aided my research in Mexico. Workshops, colloquia, and discussions at conferences proved crucial. A number of graduate students at Vanderbilt read excerpts of this project at different junctures, and their insights have helped me along the way. I must also acknowledge from Vanderbilt the many friends and colleagues involved in the Mexican Studies Group, the Robert Penn Warren Center for the Humanities, and the Center for Latin American Studies. They provide the support, space, and opportunities for scholarly exchange.

I gave an early presentation at the University of Georgia's Spanish department, which helped me craft the broad outlines of this study. I also must thank Flor Salazar and Sergio Cañedo Gamboa for including me in a colloquium in San Luis Potosí where the project evolved still further. Later on Yanna Yannakakis, Jeffrey Lesser, and their graduate students at Emory University gave part of the project the rigorous workshop treatment. Chris Ehrick's insights on gender, satire, and impersonation also proved helpful as well. My analysis in chapter 6 on satirical journalism benefited greatly from their comments and the revision process that preceded its publication in *The Americas* 68, no. 2 (2011). Eric Zolov and the readers gave suggestions that were exceptionally helpful. Bill French and Bill Beezley also offered encouragement and their perspectives on facets of the Matiana tradition. In a similar vein, the entire twentieth-century portion of the project benefited from the observations offered by Margaret Chowning, Matthew O'Hara, and others at a symposium hosted by the University of California, Berkeley. Brian Connaughton also read and commented on a draft of the manuscript. At different moments, from beginning to end, he graciously shared his considerable wisdom on sources and historiography.

In less formal settings, this project would have been much different (and certainly poorer) were it not for discussions with distinguished colleagues based in Mexico: Erika Pani, John Mraz, Jean Meyer, and Laura Suárez de la Torre. Robert Curley offered insights on archival collections in Guadalajara, on Lola Álvarez Bravo's photographs, and he gamely debated Matiana's significance on several occasions. Ken Ward also shared useful insights regarding the history of printing in Mexico. I must acknowledge the feedback from Vanderbilt colleagues Paul Kramer and Joel Harrington as I put the finishing touches on the manuscript. Celso Castilho also read passages and offered useful comments at various junctures. Along these lines, I would be remiss if I did not thank other colleagues here at Vanderbilt—Marshall Eakin, Jane Landers, and Frank Robinson—whose encouragement, expertise, and friendship provide a daily reminder of the importance of intellectual community.

Naturally I owe a considerable debt to those that work in the archives and libraries. In particular, I must recognize Martha Whittaker and Haleh Motiey-Payandehjoo at the California State Library–Sutro Branch, San Francisco. The staffs of Mexico City's archdiocesan archive, Jalisco's public library, and Guadalajara's archdiocesan archive were also very helpful. It goes without saying that I am indebted to the many people working at Mexico's national archive, national library, the Federal District's historical archive, the Miguel Lerdo de Tejada library, and the national newspaper library. Tracking down old publications was a significant headache. Paula Covington, Vanderbilt's

Latin American bibliographer and collections specialist, was particularly helpful in this regard. In this I was also aided by the stewards of several other collections: the University of Sonora Library; the Jean Charlot Collection at the University of Hawaii at Manoa Library; the Center for Creative Photography at the University of Arizona; the University of Texas at Arlington Library; the University of Texas at Austin Library; the Yale Sterling Memorial University Library; the Tulane University Library; and, perhaps most crucially, the California State Library–Sutro Branch. In addition, Monte Holman helped me prepare the map included in the book.

Of course, scholarship requires funding. This project would have been impossible without the support of Vanderbilt's College of Arts and Sciences, Department of History, and Division of Sponsored Research. In addition, a pivotal portion of my research occurred thanks to a Charles A. Ryskamp Research Fellowship funded by the Andrew W. Mellon Foundation and administered by the American Council of Learned Societies.

Finally I must thank the people involved in this book's journey at the University of New Mexico Press. Lyman Johnson took an interest in the project when it was little more than an idea pitched at a conference, and then he shepherded it through the first round of revisions. John Lear read the entire second draft carefully and provided crucial insights and suggestions. In virtually the final hours of this project he also discovered the true identity of a crucial figure in this study. Lisa Tremaine patiently worked with me on cover designs, and Gianna Mosser helped me "police the text," as it were. In addition, Courtney Campbell indexed the entire manuscript. Clark Whitehorn has overseen the entire process and seen it through to publication.

Unless otherwise stated, all Spanish to English translations in the book are mine.

Introduction

MYSTIC, HEALER, AND POPULAR PALADIN, 1962

In the hardscrabble Mexican community of Tierra Santa (Holy Land), nearly all that remained of a collective will was a desperate, shared belief in the miraculous. Life, as far as residents knew, was but a harsh litany of deprivations. Farming was a desperate gamble and whatever individuals managed to nurture remained vulnerable to a local strong man's depravity. Help from beyond the blighted region was all but unfathomable: both church and state had abandoned its residents. The only thing Tierra Santa could count on was Madre Matiana (Mother Matiana)—a woman they believed could sense the secret movements of the spirits in her gnarled fingers.

No one knew how old she truly was, and some speculated that perhaps her preternatural gifts and unsettling agelessness came from dark sources. Be that as it may, her door was always open for those seeking communication with the hereafter and all manner of cures. Locals even expected Matiana to blunt weather extremes and counter Satan's relentless, soul-snatching schemes. Moreover, Mexico's Holy Land viewed the old crone as the sole agent of justice in their world, mysteriously ruling on every dubious happening. Sentencing could take years, months, or mere days, but the punishments were always exemplary. All told it was extraordinary how much power the rustic poor conferred upon Matiana. Concretely they saw her as seer, conjurer, healer, judge, and undertaker. In actuality, she was also their collective conscience and memory.

PIOUS MISFIT, 1935

Standing stiffly in a bustling public space, Madre Matiana cut an enigmatic, somewhat comical figure. Dowdy and puritanical, she commanded

1

center stage in a high lace collar, buttoned-up checkered housedress, and a flower-print scarf snugly covering her head. All around her men in modern workday attire milled about, as if an important event had just ended, or was about to begin. Although she remained still, her jarring and distinctly prudish, feminine presence drew the attention of others. In particular, four men converged upon her. The first proceeded to read Matiana a text (perhaps a poem, a prayer, or a prophecy), and another pondered the objects she held in her hands. A third individual sporting an official-looking cap gestured to the pensive fellow as if demanding payment. Madre Matiana remained impervious. As she stood the sun touched her unblemished, uniform, pale complexion and highlighted her painted eyebrows, garishly long eyelashes, and outsized nose. What she was thinking, if she was thinking at all, was anyone's guess. Deep shadows veiled a seemingly vacuous gaze, although she stole a sidelong glance at the lector to her right. The fourth individual who was hemming in Madre Matiana was a mere youth. He peered fixedly over her shoulder, uninterested in the odd woman before him—or any of the others, for that matter. Some curious undertaking was unfolding in front of Matiana and capturing the youth's full attention. So intense was his stare that he wrenched attention away from the starched oddball adrift in the sea of modern masculinity: Madre Matiana was, in fact, superfluous to the real movement, the important progress, taking place before him.

MAD TELLER OF TRUTHS, 1917

It was not so much the suffering and violent uncertainties of the Mexican Revolution that inspired Matiana to try her hand at social and political commentary. It was the rampant venality of public figures alongside increasingly perverse behaviors in the general populace that drove her to raise her cantankerous voice in the penny press. No one else, it seemed, had the courage to speak up. Madre Matiana's blood was at the proverbial boil, and in her new capacity as muckraking crusader, she was anything but prim. From her journalistic pulpit she spewed a tumult of stream-of-consciousness condemnation, superstitious nonsense, and ribald mockery. Livid, loony, and somewhat dangerous, she appeared in public as a brash man-woman in sackcloth, brandishing the sword of popular justice and promising eccentric, truthful audacity. She was fully aware that much of Mexico viewed her as a fanatical scold. Still, many conceded that her rants often evinced an eerie prescience.

Aware and unbowed by open contempt or backhanded deference, Madre Matiana deployed her unique faculties in order to see and tell all.

DIVINE MESSENGER, 1889

In truth most Mexicans simply misunderstood Madre Matiana. Her visions of a violent, turbulent future were complex and, like all truly divine prophecies, difficult to apprehend. Matiana was in fact Mexico's representative within an international pious sisterhood. Pained by Christendom's lapse into impiety, the Virgin Mary engaged a network of women to save humanity. Christ had reached the outer limits of patience and compassion, as satanic schemes and unvarnished libertinage seduced one nation after another. Outraged, he stood ready to unleash purifying retribution. Thus far only the fervor of the Virgin's most committed devotees had forestalled a harrowing reckoning.

Matiana was only doing her duty; and Mexico, likewise, was but another battleground in the war against error. The nation was, nevertheless, of particular significance: it alone bore the brunt of North American heretical contagion. As was her wont, the Virgin chose an unassuming messenger. Hence Matiana was a lowly member of society—profoundly modest, but of unimpeachable goodness. What she lacked in worldly status she made up in faith and fortitude. Selflessly answering the Virgin's call once apprised of Mexico's perilous destiny, Matiana spoke publicly of impending suffering and unrest. Few in her lifetime, lamentably, comprehended the significance of her message or embraced the remedies she proposed. Time was running out: now more than ever annihilation loomed.

MEXICO'S MATIANAS

This study, obviously, concerns a curious figure from Mexico's past. What is perhaps less evident is that this book—a history book, no less—is about a woman who probably never existed. In a nutshell, it analyzes a cultural phenomenon most likely born of "pious fraud" and a chain reaction of unforeseen responses akin to a multigenerational game of "telephone" (or in Mexico, *teléfono descompuesto*).[1] The central figure was known as Madre Matiana, and, although she clearly represented different things to different people, reliable details about her remain elusive. Her actual provenance, though, is largely unimportant. All that truly matters is that Mexicans infused her persona with a life of its own for several generations. As I intend to demonstrate, they "needed" Matiana, revisiting her story repeatedly as they probed the dissonance they encountered when pondering the authentic, the feminine, and the modern. There was something else too: rooted in this figure's idiosyncratic legacy was a peculiar, apocalyptic gender reversal—a reactionary feminism, so to say—that pervaded Catholic activism in the nineteenth century and moved certain individuals (particularly devout women). The earliest texts of the Matiana tradition spoke of an exalted, civilization-saving mission for pious women. A few of them, allegedly, were destined to achieve the same sainted status as Christ's original twelve apostles. In short, the Matiana materials portrayed pious modern women as uniquely admirable agents of Catholicism's revitalization, and even predicted that a select trio of these women would eventually crash the iconic inner circle of masculine sanctity. This may not seem that significant in present-day terms, but to devout nineteenth-century Catholics the notion of exceptionally religious women taking their place among Christ's famed disciples certainly represented a remarkable innovation.

Because the terms *reactionary* and *feminism* do not typically appear together as such, this facet of the Matiana tradition merits explication. Secular nationalism, liberalism, and anticlerical reform undermined the Catholic Church on several fronts during the nineteenth century. The ecclesiastical hierarchy in both Europe and Latin America feared that the Church's political, cultural, and economic foundations were very much at risk. In many ways, Catholicism was losing its hold on men, particularly elite individuals, to new secular social and political affiliations. Moreover, churchmen feared that emergent irreligious ideologies—especially socialism—would dissolve the bonds of belief and practice among the masses.

Ultimately the Church and its supporters responded effectively to these challenges and brought about a remarkable Catholic resurgence in the latter half of the nineteenth century. Among the pivotal ingredients of this veritable crusade was a sustained, broad-based mobilization of religious women. In part, advocates of secularization left the door open for them; despite all its egalitarian rhetoric, liberalism offered little to women. Seeking novel ways to energize the laity, the Church amplified opportunities for women and promoted new institutions where they could cultivate meaningful careers intertwined with their devotional commitments. In many instances, women secured leadership roles in these organizations. In tandem, the Church lauded devout activist women, militant Marianism, and exceptionally pious individuals as the antidote to blasphemous modern error, which they almost always gendered male. Catholic revivalism, in other words, created a new array of publically prominent roles for women as the Matiana story took hold in Mexico. Moreover, as the prophetess's legacy evolved, Mexicans witnessed a dramatic revitalization of the Church and noted women's pronounced engagement in the process as teachers, catechists, nurses, nuns, and organizers. Of course, some ironies remained: Catholic leaders championed a conservative, patriarchal social order, but out of necessity they greatly expanded the field—both social and symbolic—of female agency.

With this contextual backdrop, the jarring contrasts in the opening "vignettes" of this chapter hint at a complicated legacy, and they capture, to some degree, Madre Matiana's shifting, eclectic role in Mexican culture for more than a century. The first distills passages from Agustín Yáñez's novel, *Las tierras flacas*, published in 1962.[2] The author, a famous intellectual and politician, made Matiana the central character in a melodramatic saga of rural Mexico's flawed modernization after the Mexican Revolution. Yáñez, a figure intimately involved in the shaping of the post-Revolutionary order, had become concerned by the obvious social problems rooted in the nation's brusque transformation. Responding to mounting, vocal criticism, he made Madre Matiana the symbolic anchor of ostensibly traditional Mexico as it came face to face with abrupt change. The second vignette emerges from the camera work and darkroom craft of Lola Álvarez Bravo and an image she titled *La Madre Matiana* in 1935.[3] This artist's rendering of the enigmatic figure represented part of her wider exploration of interconnections that spanned piety, gender, and popular culture. The third scene represents a characterization of Matiana in an irreverent Revolutionary-era newspaper named in her honor (or dishonor, really).[4] In this setting she served as the edgy alter ego of a newspaper editor named Pedro Hagelstein (also known as Ángel Prieto) and his staff. Finally, the fourth portrait of Matiana comes from a nineteenth-century book that investigates her alleged prophetic visions of Mexico's bleak national history. This tome—penned by Luis G. Duarte, a well-known, staunchly conservative activist—sought to resurrect both the figure of the popular national seer and her troubling visions, as Catholic political dissidents gravely marked the centennial of the French Revolution.[5]

Additional evidence suggests that parallel popular engagements of the Matiana narrative also took shape. In fact, I first stumbled upon the prophetess while researching news of Marian apparitions in the southern state of

Oaxaca amid the volatile events of 1928.[6] There a young indigenous girl claimed that she held consultations with the Virgin Mary in a small cave above her village. A nagging question emerged during my research concerning the actors involved in the 1928 affair: a prominent local woman, Church educator, and Catholic activist—and her mostly female supporters—backed the girl's claims despite their pastor's ruling that the visions represented diabolical trickery. This brought on a classic problem of historical analysis: understanding individual motivations veiled by the passage of time. The priest and this woman had been close allies for decades. Why then would a Catholic stalwart upstage her pastor by taking the case directly to archdiocesan authorities, risking social condemnation and ecclesiastical retribution? In fact, it was only a few years until this apparition movement in Oaxaca collapsed and the one-time Church educator found herself a destitute pariah.

This woman's gamble demanded explanation. Reasoning provided by locals who knew her revealed thinly masked, gendered dismissal. Some said the devil tricked her, and others claimed that her fervent miraculous yearnings had made her mentally unstable. As luck would have it, though, I happened upon an eyewitness's unpublished writings on the apparitions. This individual labeled the episode a fraud, but chalked up support for the girl's claims to popular unease, recent natural disasters, and the "prophecies of Madre Matiana." Curious, I began gathering documentation dealing with these prognostications. Ultimately I concluded that this once-respected woman's decision makes sense within the apocalyptic feminism embedded in the prophecies. Matiana predicted that the expiatory heroics of a female vanguard would midwife a renewed Catholic order in Mexico. Thus the woman in question, I argued, probably pondered the events of her time in this light and concluded that local apparitions offered her an opportunity to help save both faith and nation, although it meant disobeying the masculine Church hierarchy.

The diverse materials I gradually amassed on Madre Matiana, however, suggested that she merited a study of her own. They revealed that the famed seer headlined nineteenth-century pamphlets, almanacs, and books, and probably stirred some young women to dedicate their lives to Catholic revitalization in the 1880s. Revolutionary satirists even commandeered her persona and voice as a vehicle for social criticism. Likewise, her reappearance in twentieth-century photography and literature suggested that this prophetess could tell *us* a thing or two about Mexico.

A PAMPHLET PROPHETESS

Even though Matiana was allegedly an eighteenth-century prophetess, she made no mark whatsoever in the historical record until 1847, a year of crippling internal strife, existential crisis, and profound disillusionment for many Mexicans. Her public emergence coincided with the occupation of the young nation by North American armies, while Mexican political factions plotted against each other instead of uniting against the invaders. The upshot was the unrecoverable loss of the territories that became the U.S. Southwest, as well as an abiding rancor and abject gloom. In keeping with the bleak tenor of public discourse, Matiana deployed the classic doomsayer repertory: society's galling impieties and excesses had enraged God and brought on celestial punishments (such as foreign invasions). Naturally the nation's suffering was destined to intensify if there was not collective repentance. In other ways, however, she broke with convention. She did not emerge from the local equivalent of the biblical outlands, nor did she channel the typical medieval street seer. Moreover, Madre Matiana deviated from Mexican traditions—she did not witness an apparition in a mountain cave or on remote hillside. In reality the prophetess first raised her voice, as it were, at Calle de las Escalerillas 2, where the very minor printing establishment of Valdés and Redondas produced pamphlets that detailed her frightening visions, which were allegedly more than seventy years old by this time. They appeared to contain eerily accurate predictions concerning the decades following Independence (for the full text see Appendix).[7] Few Mexicans, apparently, noticed Matiana in 1847. Perhaps Valdés y Redondas produced only a handful of copies, and as far as can be ascertained the shop did little to promote them. A decade later, a different printer (perhaps a relative), Luis Abadiano y Valdés, reprinted a nearly identical version of the prophecies and advertised them in one of the most prominent conservative newspapers, the *Diario de Avisos*.[8] Suddenly Mexicans took note. In other words, after a "false start" Madre Matiana strode forth from the wilds of popular print commerce and lodged herself in the national consciousness. In later years, almost all commenters on the Matiana phenomenon pointed to the late 1850s and its polarizing conflicts when discussing the seer and her visions. The prophetess's legacy, of course, would expand and evolve over the next century, and like most lasting cultural phenomena it began with a compelling story attuned to prevailing anxieties.

PROFECIAS

DE MATIANA,

SIRVIENTA

QUE FUE EN EL CONVENTO

DE

SAN GERONIMO DE MEXICO,

SOBRE

LOS SUCESOS QUE HAN DE ACONTECER

en la espresada capital.

Escritas por la madre María Josefa de la Pasion de Jesus, religiosa del mismo convento, en cumplimiento del decreto de 18 de Enero de 1837, dictado por el señor vicario de monjas.

∞

Sr. Vicario de los conventos de religiosas D. Juan Manuel Irisarri.

MARIA JOSEFA DE LA PASION DE JESUS, religiosa del convento de Ntro. P. S. Gerónimo de esta ciudad de México, y de la obediencia de V. S., pronta y gustosamente obedezco el espreso mandato de V. S. que me hizo en 18 de Enero del presente año de 1837, de que escriba toda la relacion de la noticia que tengo de las revelaciones que Sra. Matiana del Espíritu Santo tuvo en este convento, y comunicadas á mí por sus dos confidentas Doña Francisca Montes de Oca y Sra. Paula Ramirez.

Figure 1. The first Matiana pamphlet: *Profecías de Matiana* (Valdés y Redondas, 1847). Courtesy of Special Collections at the University of Texas at Arlington Library.

Matiana del Espiritu Santo, so the first pamphlets tell us, began life as a poor girl in Tepozotlán, a town some twenty miles north of Mexico City, in the mid-1700s. At a very young age she moved to the viceregal capital as the companion of an esteemed nun of the convent of San Juan de la Penitencia. There she received religious instruction from a priest of the order of San Diego, and revealed extraordinary spiritual promise. She even began to perform miracles. However, when her mistress died the devout girl found herself adrift in the capital, struggling to find a new spiritual and temporal home. She briefly moved to the convent of the Incarnation, but she remained unsettled. Finally, following miraculous directives, she entered the storied convent of San Jerónimo as a lowly servant. According to the pamphlets, "It is said, the Holy Virgin Mary ordered her to come to San Jerónimo. Immediately she obeyed and came and entered as did all the servants. Mother Catarina de San Ignacio Villajare—the one that was demented, and due to her illness ate more than was normal—took her on. Matiana sought to avoid incurring any costs for her patroness, and selflessly used her own food and salary to cover the costs of Madre Catarina. She had nothing more than the clothes she wore."[9] As the text suggests, she demonstrated exemplary humility and embraced the attendant privations. Apparently, she subsisted on stale bread given to her by fellow servants.

In the backstory provided by our sources, Matiana's exceptional piety and knack for devotional leadership began to attract attention and earn her followers when she was still quite young. First she revived a languishing religious brotherhood dedicated to charity and caring for sick and dying women. In short order it was thriving and it expanded beyond the confines of the convent. Her dedication to extreme humility inspired all those who joined regardless of their social status. Many nuns and laywomen demonstrated their own commitment, helping to sweep the convent and clean its fetid drains. Even the prioress followed Matiana's instructions, and important ladies of the era were soon coming to visit her; apparently they hoped Matiana would reveal their individual destinies.

She had her critics, naturally: "There was no shortage of the shadowy murmurs and derision that servants of God always suffer: regardless, Matiana never lost her spirit for igniting flames of divine love in all the people that knew her."[10] In fact, according to the pamphlets narrating her story, her teachings bore fruit because of her irreproachable personal comportment. Even as her fame grew Matiana remained modest, avoiding speech whenever possible, and devoting her nights to prayer.

Over time, according to the pamphlet's narrative, her exemplary piety led to greater and more troubling mystical gifts. During the prelacy of Archbishop Alonso Núñez de Haro y Peralta (1772–1800) she began to experience moments of rapture during which the Virgin Mary allowed Matiana to glimpse an unfolding satanic conspiracy destined to engulf Catholic Christendom: "Matiana also viewed a gathering in hell, and the torment suffered by the demons because of peace, a copy of which reigned among Christians in her time. Lucifer was particularly anguished. They all formed a congress, and they produced the Constitution and the Legal Code, and Lucifer ordered the demons to spread those constitutions throughout the world to pervert everyone. Then hell was emptied to make war on Christians . . ."[11] In referencing the emergence of congressional bodies, constitutionalism, and legal reforms the early Matiana pamphlets conveyed to Mexican readers that their visionary protagonist had foreseen the "Age of Revolution." Moreover, this passage framed the advent of constitutional liberalism in Mexico as part of a vast anti-Catholic conspiracy at a time when its ascendency was at the heart of bitter domestic debates in the 1840s and 1850s.

According to the prophecies, which Matiana allegedly had issued before Mexico even existed as an independent nation, decades of divisive violence and destruction would occur. The pamphlets declare that Matiana predicted the most dramatic happenings of the first half of the nineteenth century: events that the reading public had already lived through by the date of publication. They included the Wars of Independence and Mexico City's massive riots in 1828. Madre Matiana purportedly also predicted the arrival of freemasonry and Protestantism in Mexico, war with the United States, and intractable civil strife. Moreover, the erstwhile seer presaged government persecution of the Catholic Church: "She perceived the arrival of Anglo-Americans to the kingdom; she saw their sects, including their maxims and regalia, and that they would be the killers of martyrs, and how we would owe great quantities of money to them. Matiana foretold of the martyrdoms in the capital and the exit of nuns from all the convents. She even saw how the *capuchinas* would be in such poverty and need that they would beg at the gates of senators for leftovers from their meals."[12] In sum, the Matiana pamphlets suggested that the controversies and upheavals Mexicans experienced in the mid-nineteenth century had been divined in previous decades. It was all part of a vast anti-Christian plot. The penny-press visionary, the story implies, remarkably charted the instability, cultural conflict, and awaiting humiliations of nineteenth-century Mexico at a time when Spanish rule still appeared solid and Catholicism appeared firmly entrenched throughout society.

Like all accomplished prophets, though, Matiana did more than simply predict impending catastrophe—she also unveiled the path to redemption. The misery soon to beset Mexico stemmed from the nation's impending abandonment of the faith and the assault on the Church. But the Virgin Mary (hoping to avert suffering) began mobilizing her feminine phalanx, choosing Matiana as her emissary among Mexico's *religiosas* (women religious). In this capacity the humble convent servant proclaimed that in some distant future a new religious order would take shape among the nuns of San Jerónimo to assuage the righteous anger of Christ and save the nation. The pamphlets label this imagined collective the Hermanas del Desagravio de Jesús Sacramentado (Sisters of the Placation of the Sacramental Christ). An innovative aggregation of religious women, it was to be a superorder founded by three individuals from San

Jerónimo and filled out with a select forty-three nuns from other convents (making for an emblematic forty-six: the number of stars on the Virgin of Guadalupe's mantle). They would dedicate themselves to fervent expiatory piety, particularly devotion to the Blessed Sacrament (the consecrated Host) in order to counterbalance the nation's egregious impieties. The women were destined to suffer unrelenting scorn and ridicule, but God would sustain them even as he continued to punish the wayward nation. According to our pamphleteer sources, they would receive an exalted, truly glorious recompense for their pious fortitude and self-sacrifice:

> She [the Virgin Mary] told Matiana of the great benefits and good fortune that will come to the kingdom and the city with the establishment of this our order, and that it will be the last foundation in the world before the Day of Judgment. Furthermore, this new and ultimate order of the Blessed Sacrament would provide more saints for the Church than all the previous orders from their beginnings until the end, including the order of Our Father Saint Francis who has produced so many.
>
> Our Lady made great promises concerning the persons that took part in the third foundation. The founding nuns, among God's many great women, would enjoy a privilege only granted to the Holy Apostles.[13]

In other words, the new collective of holy women announced by Matiana would produce a host of Mexican saints, and its founders would surpass even many of the most celebrated "fathers of the Church." In the new order, the pamphlets proclaimed, only Christ's original followers would equal the women leading the Hermanas del Desagravio de Jesús Sacramentado.

In the short term, though, tragedy loomed. For the populace Madre Matiana promised great bloodshed and suffering, but dogma dictates that the Catholic Church always triumphs in the end. In the interim the faithful must endure the nation's penance with pious abnegation. Finally in October of some future year ending in the number eight, signaled by—the prophecies claimed—ethereal music echoing throughout the city, conflict would miraculously cease and the Catholic faithful would reestablish a Christian monarchy. Mexico and Spain, reunited in a new kingdom governed from the shrine of the Virgin of Guadalupe, would be the shining American bastion of the faith. The superorder of nuns, the Hermanas del Desagravio would subsequently take up residence there alongside the monarch. Facing a restored Catholic order, North American invaders and their heretical sects would slink out of Mexico. In addition, just as pernicious ideological influence would be cast aside, the shackling of the Mexican people with onerous loans would come to nothing. The nation's mounting debts would miraculously disappear. Throughout Mexico nuns would return to their convents and find them miraculously restored to their preexisting condition. Furthermore, impious men would repent, priests would recover the zeal of old, and all the nation's religious orders would prosper in peace.

According to the pamphlet sources, the combination of Matiana's pious reputation and her frightening visions eventually even attracted the admiration of Mexico City's Archbishop Núñez. He visited her to plumb the nature of her mystical gifts and learn the extent of her predictions first hand. Deeply perplexed, he ordered Matiana and her intimate acquaintances to submit to the Holy Office of the Inquisition and face strenuous examination. The prophetess, absolutely confident of the divine origin of her visions, apparently relished the ordeal, winning over her interrogators and her prelate. However, a few years later Matiana died because of wounds sustained during extreme self-mortifications; allegedly she cinched a penitential belt so tightly around her waist that its spikes mortally wounded her. In the wake of her passing the archbishop ordered the nuns of San Jerónimo to keep her prophecies secret because of their deeply disturbing portents.

This, more or less, is how Mexicans first encountered Madre Matiana. Particularly after the 1857 pamphlet's publication and promotion in the summer and fall of that year, she represented a scolding political critique and a strident expression of a heated reactionary feminism in the public record. Other versions emerged shortly afterward. Within months the entire text of the prophetic story reappeared in a popular almanac, alongside the typical seasonal and liturgical information much of the populace sought out each year.[14] In 1861 a wholly different printer issued yet another, essentially identical, pamphlet version of the Matiana prophesies.[15]

It is important to stress, though, that these publications approximated a particular genre of Mexican writing. The pamphlets do not offer a transcription of prophetic speech or a straightforward third-person narration of Matiana's life and visions. Instead, they claim to be a faithful rendering of an official report composed by a nun from San Jerónimo several decades after Matiana's death. According to the texts, Madre María Josefa de la Pasión de Jesús (also known as Madre Guerra) actually put pen to paper in 1837 (the date is listed as part of the subtitle). The pamphlets, then, claim to be a rediscovered testament outlining Mexico's star-crossed emergence as an independent nation. As the story unfolds, Madre Guerra describes how she learned about the prophecies and Matiana from the seer's two closest confidants before they too passed away. Decades later, at the explicit behest of a new male superior, the pamphlets suggest this particular Jeronymite broke her silence.

The text reads as if an earnest, common religiosa listed everything she could remember about a complex history that she had heard many times, but which had never been arranged as a coherent linear narrative. The narrator seems to recover her disparate memories—and those of her alleged informants—as she records her testimony, producing a rambling story marked by digressions. Some information appears spliced into the narrative with footnotes at a later date. For long periods, particulars that only a member of a traditional religious order would recall dominate the text. For example, Madre Guerra details internal debates on the color of the imagined Hermanas del Desagravio's vestments and other minutiae of institutional bureaucracy. A strong undercurrent of gendered, Catholic anger carries the story. At numerous points the text acknowledges the tendency to mock women as fanatical and delusionary, while stressing that the nation's very fate resided in the hands of devout women who would counter male error. The pamphlets essentially pose the unspoken rhetorical question: What kind of society attacks venerable female religious institutions, and forces previously cloistered nuns out onto the scandalously profane streets of Mexico City? The answer is obvious, by implication—only a perverse and iniquitous order inviting annihilation would even contemplate such measures.

WOMEN, NATION, AND MYSTICAL NARRATIVE

At first glance, analyzing the trajectory of fantastical prophecies may seem like little more than an entertaining foray in historical folklore. The issues embedded in Matiana's visions and their interpretations, however, are absolutely central in Mexican history. During the nineteenth and twentieth centuries, Mexicans of all stripes took part in complex and conflicting efforts to create a modern nation-state and fashion a national identity and culture. Writers tried to rhetorically call the nation into being and define or conjure a distinct and unique "Mexican-ness." Lithographers, mapmakers, and painters etched, delineated, and colored an iconography and geography of national types, settings, and spaces. All manner of social actors served as the market for their labors, and thus exerted considerable influence over the outcomes. Scholars have long debated the legacy of this process in terms of race and ethnicity; however, the overlapping and equally crucial issues of religion and gender have attracted less attention. Throughout this period Mexicans hotly debated the role of Catholicism and women, particularly religious women, in society. A strong current in Mexican thought has long conflated Church-centered social identity and femininity. In fact, modernizing reformers throughout Latin America, usually Hispanic men, tended to analyze the nation's "problems" from an elite, masculine perspective. Whatever they judged as backward they feminized: for example, indigenous populations, Catholic practice, and popular culture in general.[16] Examining the ideas and endeavors of historical actors and groups that engaged the Matiana prophecies, then, helps us probe complex currents in Mexico's history.

Some historians have touched on the Matiana legacy, but they have approached pamphlet sources as straightforward accounts of colonial mysticism.[17] What follows then is a tracking of Matiana and her interpreters through the years where the prophecies and the seer's persona bridge different historical periods. This study delves into the lives of individuals who drew inspiration from the narrative's construction of duties appropriate for the faithful and of Mexico's identity and destiny. People also appropriated the visionary persona and story for their own purposes. For some this meant addressing Madre Matiana's legacy with devout sincerity, imputing personal and political meaning to her visions. These interpreters tended to deploy notions of female mysticism as if they opened a special window on the nation's collective soul and conscience. For others the prophetess functioned as a symbol of deeply rooted fanatical ignorance; and hence the Matiana narrative's invocation of divine intervention and restored pious order served as the target of scorn. For still others, she represented a symptom of the nation's stubbornly irrational popular culture. In this vein, Matiana inspired both irreverent satirists and reformist handwringing.

Due to the nature of available documentation, this work must be a hybrid of literary and historical scholarship. A search of the Mexican National Archive's catalog turns up a tantalizing reference to Matiana's prophecies amid early nineteenth-century correspondence (1824–1847) belonging to the convent of San Jerónimo. However, the folder mentioned therein contains a different religious order's papers.[18] Rifling through the entire box where this folder resides, in addition to the boxes preceding and succeeding it, yielded nothing about the visions either. Inquisitorial documents from the colonial era are also silent on Madre Matiana, even though she allegedly submitted to a rigorous examination at the Holy Office.[19] Quite simply, Madre Matiana comes to us solely from nineteenth-century Mexican polemics and attendant penny-press commerce.

Given the absence of evidence, it is most likely that Matiana is a fiction—a popular figure invented amid the conflicts that she ostensibly foresaw. This conclusion is compelling for an additional reason. The visionary narrative fits longstanding strategies prevalent in both Spanish and Latin American literature.[20] Writers from the region often bolstered the authority of their texts by structuring them as historical documents: as with novels in the form of judicial findings or essays that appropriated the structure and language of scientific treatises. In truth, both the veil of anonymous authorship and the official report format (*carta de relación*, or just *relación*) represent crucial features of the foundational novel of the picaresque literary genre, *El Lazarillo de Tormes* (1554).[21] As in the Matiana pamphlets, the plot emerges from an alleged deposition demanded by authorities. On a related note, the published, widely read cartas de relación originally sent by Hernán Cortés to Emperor Charles V in the 1520s represent the first works of Spanish American literature. In them the savvy conquistador attempts to establish the historical "truth" regarding his subjugation of the Mexica (i.e., Aztec) empire. Ironically even in this instance questions about a lost, mysteriously suppressed, or possibly apocryphal initial relación (to which Cortés and others referred) remains an abiding mystery.[22]

Thus the long-lost report and found archival document trope was in fact a classic, if not cliché, device. In a sense Latin American authors repeatedly produced literature in the bureaucratic, evidentiary idioms of the scribal elite to give them the aura of "reality" and the authorial gravitas of official writing.[23] In this light, our visionary protagonist was probably a mere character crafted to stir a collective memory of baroque female mysticism and an idealized time of pious purity, as a means of criticizing the alleged rampant irreverence and secularizing political reforms of the mid-nineteenth century.

Again, Matiana's origins, though interesting, are not that important. As Antonio Rubial García reminds us, it is crucial to focus on the social history of interpretation when dealing with mystical narratives.[24] The lives of seers were not written to depict historical reality, but rather to fashion mythic narratives. What "happened" is of distant, secondary importance; what matters is the rendering of the exemplary. Hence, present-day readers often note the

contrived nature of hagiography, prophecy, and popular devotional literature: character traits, plots, social situations, and actions seem to "float" from
one text to the next. First and foremost, visionary narratives seek to inspire
adherence to specific religious norms and boost pious zeal. They are much
less concerned with documenting past events, even though they typically
resonate in particular historical contexts.

In any case, someone (or some group) brought Madre Matiana and her
visions to the attention of the populace in the mid-nineteenth century. Essays
and sermons of the time blamed foreign ideas and impious policies for creating instability. Numerous individuals argued that Mexican society functioned best when it cleaved to Hispanic tradition and avoided the secularizing,
democratic currents in vogue elsewhere. For example, historian Lucas
Alamán (1792–1853) argued in the late 1840s that although Independence had
been necessary, it was foolhardy to abandon the unifying foundations of colonial order, which included hierarchy, a protected Church, state-sanctioned
religious practice, and social foundations anchored in Catholic institutions.[25]
Deviating from the only tradition Mexicans understood, Alamán contended,
only invited disorder. This argument won many adherents at the time, and it
has been echoed in more recent historical analysis.[26] The Matiana prophecies
went even further, claiming that Mexico's calamitous problems stemmed
from society's provocation of divine fury.

The seer's story, crucially, unfolds in a format that Mexican readers recognized as the appropriate arena for establishing legitimacy in religious matters, the ecclesiastical relación. Essentially the reader is left to presume that
Church authorities followed standard bureaucratic procedures: they heard
about troubling portents, noted their concordance with recent occurrences
(post-Independence instability), and launched the inquiry leading to Madre
Guerra's deposition. Religious teachings and folklore of the time offered numerous examples of harsh providential punishments visited upon nations
deemed wanton by heaven. Thus the discovery of a pious woman's visionary
testimony—revealing a vast diabolical conspiracy and collective dissipation—reaches for a unique emotional register.

As with most prophetic narratives, once the basic story became embedded
in local memory, meaning and content were subject to embellishment and
outright fabrication. In other words, successive interpreters fashioned their
own Matianas. By all appearances the seer and her visions served as a sound-
ing board in debates about the nature of Mexican society, particularly regarding how political, social, and moral order could (or should) be sustained,

constructed, or revived at particularly divisive moments. In addition, and perhaps more interestingly, this prophetic tradition reveals a lasting, convoluted relationship between pious femininity and national identity in Mexico. Matiana ultimately became a symbol of a particular kind of womanhood: one freighted with gendered notions of innate piety, irrational fanaticism, sclerotic traditionalism, mystical wisdom, farcical ignorance, and cultural authenticity—all at the same time. Cloaked in this paradoxical guise the prophetess haunted the nation, because she simultaneously embodied the nature of popular culture for many observers while clashing with understandings of modern nationhood. In other words, Madre Matiana has endured because Mexicans could neither wholly expunge nor assimilate public devout femininity—and the widespread beliefs and practices associated with it—in the emerging national imaginary.

Indeed, despite the colonial backdrop, Madre Matiana's visions truly put into play post-Independence issues refracted through the prism of an idealized "usable past" of social harmony, all-encompassing religiosity, and feminine purity. For those inclined to believe in a historical Matiana and the divinely inspired nature of her prophecies, the narrative summoned a conservative utopia: a lost saint-producing social world of ubiquitous godly propriety. Like so many historical engagements of religious faith and practice in Mexico, Matiana's visions activated common assumptions that conflated religiosity and social solidarity, concerns about modernity's corrosion of gender relations, and uncertainties relating to cultural legitimacy. In doing so she stoked the presumption that piety could inspire collective actions of nation-forging import, and fueled notions that coordinated devotion could secure divine favor and set the stage for "true" Christian order. Naturally not all Mexicans embraced this devout brand of nationalism or viewed the alleged colonial visionary in a positive light. Among skeptics she quickly became symbolic of foundational problems, ideological and social, which they felt duty bound to address.

In sum much can be learned about Mexico by scrutinizing the prophecies' cycles of reinterpretation. First, three overlapping spheres demand attention: the deep intertwined legacies of mystical prophecy and female piety; the complexities of nineteenth-century print commerce and culture; and the immediate context of popular literary production, nationalist expression, and the marketing of Matiana's prophecies. The first three chapters address these topics. Chapter 1 ventures into an inquisitorial investigation of seditious female prophesy from the mid-1700s, before exploring the enduring significance of mysticism and devotional practices associated with femininity.

Chapter 2 proceeds with a careful examination of nineteenth-century print-ing, particularly the role of the Librería Abadiano, the publisher and pro-moter of the 1857 Matiana pamphlet. Chapter 3 explores the seldom-analyzed world of popular almanac production and how the prophetess's emergence in this medium placed her in the thick of Mexican identity making and mar-keting. Chapter 4 focuses on intensely conservative Catholic activists, like Luis G. Duarte, and their ambitious reinterpretation of the visions between 1880 and 1910. These figures, it turns out, worked to merge the Matiana nar-rative with the right-wing European militancy of the late nineteenth century and keep the visionary figure alive in Mexican memory. Ironically they be-queathed a sharply political, deeply reactionary Madre Matiana to subse-quent generations who made use of her in a decidedly less-reverent fashion.

The subsequent chapters analyze this very distinct twentieth-century phase of Matiana's "life and times," characterized by outright appropriations of the seer's persona. Chapter 5 details how the satirical journalist Pedro Hagelstein and his staff effectively hijacked Matiana to voice impertinent criticism and nation-building derision as the dust settled following the Mexican Revolution. These individuals built their commentary on the prophetic protagonist's color-ful past, initially structuring their newspaper as a veritable mock almanac and playing up Matiana's fanatical reputation. Finally, chapters 6 and 7 examine the distinct artistic engagements of the prophetess's legacy. The former ex-plores photographer Lola Álvarez Bravo's arresting visualizations of ethnicity, religiosity, and gender, as well as her unique contribution to the Matiana phe-nomenon. The latter details Agustín Yáñez and his early-1960s novelistic rep-resentation of the legendary seer as a quintessentially problematic national figure.

Obviously this kind of analysis requires a certain amount of intellectual and evidentiary hopscotch (*rayuela histórica*, if you will). The fresh perspec-tive gained by tracking the visionary narrative's varied incarnations and the Matiana persona's divergent use over time, however, makes the venture worthwhile. In a sense *Searching for Madre Matiana* is a quest, and, as befits the metaphor, it is the journey that matters.

PART I
A National Seer

CHAPTER 1

Mystical Matters, Mystical Madres

The Legacy of Female Piety in Mexico

WHY WOULD THE APPEARANCE OF PROPHETIC PRINTINGS CAUSE A stir in mid-nineteenth-century Mexico? Why were some Mexicans prone to believe that God was indeed punishing them and trying to communicate with society via a seer? In addition, why did it *matter* if the visions in question had been experienced by a humble, pious woman? Perhaps the best way to develop a nuanced appreciation for Madre Matiana's impact in the nineteenth century is to plunge into the polemics surrounding female mysticism some eighty years prior to the appearance of her pamphlets, ironically around the time when Matiana allegedly foresaw the nation's troubled future.

In early 1767 the Bourbon monarchy, following the lead of the Portuguese in 1759, decreed the expulsion of the Jesuit order from its domains. In the Spanish colonies officials rounded up over two thousand members of the Company of Jesus and marched them off to exile.[1] News of pro-Jesuit miracles and prophecies followed hot on the heels of royal action. For example, inquisitors in Mexico fretted about circulating broadsheets, which described the alleged visions of a Capuchin nun in Spain. According to these publications, a purple-robed, plaintive Christ with blood gushing from the wound in his side had appeared to the young woman. She reverently inquired about the Savior's pitiful state, and he blamed, "those that are presently persecuting the beloved sons of my Compañía (the Jesuits)."[2] Christ, however, alerted the capuchina to an imminent, miraculous revival. He reminded her of a terebinth, a Mediterranean evergreen associated with divine revelation in the

Old Testament, that had once flourished where Jesuit confessors ministered to the nuns of her order.[3] According to the broadside, the tree had recently died and been chopped for firewood, but Christ assured his visionary that both the tree and his Company would blossom anew. The woman would see twelve flowers symbolizing the tribes of Israel, which would unfold and flourish before her eyes. Just as God had freed the chosen people, he would liberate the Jesuits. The religiosa waited until the dismembered terebinth burst into full flower as foretold before she recounted her vision to her astounded sisters.[4]

News of Mexican miracles and prophecies also emerged.[5] Stories circulated widely of a crippled boy's encounter with an enigmatic man dressed like a Jesuit. Upon their meeting, the man told the youth of two immanent marvels: the missionary order's revival and the miraculous cure of his deformity. The youngster's father, a Puebla merchant, assured investigators that his son twice walked normally when describing his revelation.[6] At roughly the same time, Mexico City residents discussed stories of a deceased Jesuit's prophetic writings, which likened the order's troubles to a solar eclipse: the expulsion would only temporarily dim their fortunes before a glorious revival.[7] Reports also circulated of a Jesuit who miraculously tamed an indomitable horse and rode all the way to Veracruz to join his brethren in exile.[8] Locals in the port city also shared the tale of a church painting of Saint Ignatius, the founder of the Jesuit order, which mysteriously fell onto a renowned local critic of the black-robed missionaries.[9]

The most dramatic Jesuit restoration prophecy, however, featured a girl's powerful allegorical revelations.[10] During a moment of pious ecstasy, this unnamed seer beheld a church lit by scores of lamps, which one by one succumbed to a small, malevolent whirlwind that churned around the sanctuary. Ultimately only a single beacon flickered on the main altar. Suddenly, she saw a small ball of fire, "God's loving Providence," zoom around the temple to reignite each and every smoldering wick. In short order, the entire church was alight despite the "hurricane of persecution." The astounded mística understood immediately that this vision symbolized the hounding and subsequent resurgence of the Jesuit order: they would be reduced to the single province of Rome, only to achieve even greater splendor after a miraculous revival.

The rapid emergence and circulation of these prophecies suggests that the Jesuits' suppression struck a vibrant chord in Mexico, a chord that allegedly vibrated most strongly among religious women.[11] Of course, there were other ways to articulate such feelings. Some regions experienced full-blown riots, which José de Gálvez (1720–1787)—New Spain's powerful visitor general—suppressed with infamous brutality.[12] Dominican priests reported that some Mexicans viewed them as complicit in their rival's demise and hence shunned their services. Rumors even circulated that the king and his ministers had succumbed to heresy. Holy cards (small images of saintly figures) passed from hand to hand, some featuring an image of Saint Josaphat flanked by the pope and Saint Ignatius, with an accompanying caption that questioned the orthodoxy of Jesuit critics.[13]

A sample of inquisitorial rhetoric that responds to the pro-Jesuit visions is also instructive. Although infamous in present-day estimation, the Inquisition functioned as a widely accepted institution charged with protecting orthodoxy: it steered deviants back to official belief and practice when possible, and it assured fidelity to established authority in both religious and political matters.[14] As well-trained Church *funcionarios*, the inquisitors may have simply been trying to intimidate Jesuit sympathizers, but they wrote as if they truly feared subversive prophecies would spread like a disease. The vectors of infection, they presumed, were female religious orders historically served by Jesuit confessors. According to the theories, La Compañía began inculcating their *hijas espirituales* (spiritual daughters) with "false prophecies" and "fanatical revelations" well before the expulsion order in April 1767. They purportedly chose women because of their credulity, seeking to drag them into "issues of governance, completely at odds with the frailties of their sex and the reserve required by monastic profession." Furthermore, these machinations represented "an astute means to disseminate ideas among the population contrary to public tranquility because nobody could be easily persuaded . . . that evangelical ministers would propagate sedition among their penitents."[15]

Echoing these claims, the Franciscan commissary general, Fray Manuel de Náxera, issued a particularly detailed condemnation. In the process he revealed a great deal about negative attitudes toward female piety and real fears of its political potential.[16] First, he claimed that Jesuits propagated sinister maxims internally, and they also induced members to abuse their ministry. As he put it, Jesuits had blasphemously seduced "brides of Christ." with their perfidious teachings. Even where no evidence of prophetic subversion appeared, de Náxera cautioned, nuns with ties to La Compañía harbored anguished longings for their banished confessors. The sisters remained fertile ground for seditious fanaticism: they had internalized a set of specious doctrines beyond the offending prophecies that exacerbated innate female inclinations toward visionary self-indulgence.

In short, to explain the prophecies' propagation, officials deployed stereotypes: women were weak-minded, gullible, and prone to vain, delusional excess.[17] In de Náxera's view, because of "the fantasies alive with excess, which tend to those of their sex, colored by their natural piety, they [women] easily succumb to illusions, and they convince themselves that they see visions and revelations." In reality, he argued, "[The Prophecies] are only figments of their imagination forged with the vehemence of their affections and passions, which, since they believe them to be pious, they do not restrain, and allow to accumulate until their imaginations are deeply confused and they believe they see what does not exist." Once deluded, religiosas become dangerous *ilusas* (false mystics), potentially corrupting the public.[18]

It was a classic ruse, de Náxera claimed. Heretics throughout history had targeted nuns and beatas (devout laywomen).[19] *Fascinadores* (charlatans) bolster their falsehoods with invented miracles among women, and to many outsiders the "false" revelations appear to be harmless, female vanities. Therefore all Mexican Church authorities, he commanded, were obliged to report Jesuit-inspired ilusas and their followers. He pleaded with abbesses to recognize the diabolical assault the prophecies represented, but he issued threats as well. Anyone who withheld information or was slow to report seditious portents faced a loss of their office and unnamed additional punishments.[20]

In the end, not a single religiosa appears among those deposed. Were there no convent prophecies to begin with? Had timely inquisitorial action blocked their progress? Perhaps abbesses dealt with mystical claims internally, beyond the prying eyes of de Náxera and his colleagues. We may never know, but this case reveals the substantial power ascribed to female visionary narratives. The potential impact attributed to women's prophetic expression—and the legacy of debunking discourse accompanying it—indicate that mystical women occupied an iconic, albeit often contested, social niche long before the nineteenth century. Indeed, male authority figures clearly feared the ability of female prophets to sway public opinion and stoke sedition.

THE PIOUS SEX

As in the Jesuit restoration prophecies, the legacy of female mysticism represents perhaps the most complicated component of Matiana's legacy. Attempting to flesh out the complex symbolism associated with femininity at times requires reaching back to the Middle Ages. Matiana's visions, the story woven around them, and the religious traditions invoked within the narrative tap into deeply intertwined cultural assumptions and practices. For lack of a better term, scholars group these issues under the umbrella of female piety, but the implications regarding how Mexican society produced and consumed stories about itself reaches well beyond the realm of female religiosity. The multifaceted symbolism surrounding expiation, Eucharistic devotion, and asceticism play key roles in the Matiana prophecies. Together these factors gave the story its staying power and put into play conceptions of feminine sensitivity to the prevailing moral character of society and the will of God. Another way to put this is that Matiana's story gained traction in the nineteenth century because she echoed historical models and traditional notions of women's unique aptitude for visionary grace.

Prior to the twentieth century the prevailing exemplars offered in Mexican society for popular emulation were Catholic saints and local historical figures of renowned saintly reputation.[21] Indeed, these were the models that secular nationalists labored to replace with new civic santos of liberal patriotism after the mid-nineteenth century. The reigning male ideals were the martyrs, the founders of religious orders, theologians, and saints. These figures modeled intellect, agency, reason, and pious wisdom—the architects of Christian order. Standards of female religious virtue and accomplishment were another story. As scholars of the Middle Ages have shown, Catholics have historically associated women with the human body, passivity, irrationality, emotion, lust, mercy, and disorder.[22]

When pondering Madre Matiana, Mexican readers could call up various categories of supernaturally adept women. In some cases these were official saints, but many other figures enjoyed saintly reputations without official sanction. Female spiritual power, however, also bore negative associations. Enduring notions of sinister sexual deviance and witchcraft populated the Mexican consciousness with stories of dangerous women and fear of seductive deception.[23] In addition, assumptions of elemental feminine irrationality and vanity undergirded the occasional dismissals of female religiosity as fanatical excess, attention-seeking fakery, or blind superstition. In sum, a profound ambivalence pervaded conceptions of devout women. This comes through clearly in a famous fifteenth-century inquisitorial treatise on witchcraft: "[Women] reach the greatest heights and the lowest depths of goodness and vice. Where they are governed by a good spirit, they are most excellent in virtue; but when they are governed by an evil spirit, they indulge in the worst possible vices."[24]

To the scholar today these dualities seem clichéd reflections of patriarchal insecurities: saint or succubus, nun or witch, and humble beata or vainglorious ilusa. But there is also an underlying conception of uniquely female, innate, spiritual sensitivity that bolsters these characterizations. They depend upon assumptions of women's natural openness and visceral, emotional acceptance of the supernatural, as well as their greater ability to embrace humility and self-sacrifice. These ideas have deep roots, but much of their elaboration emerged from medieval thought, which came to Mexico after the conquest via Spanish Catholicism. As the thinking goes, men seek wealth, intellectual mastery, and prestige, but they often come up short in their spiritual development. Masculine strength helps them resist temptation and uphold the faith, but it also impedes the self-effacement required to achieve spiritual union with God. The flip side of these gendered assumptions is that women, in very special cases, could draw exceptional spiritual strength from feminine weakness. In fact, some men who trod the mystic's path spoke in terms of gender transformation—approaching oneness with Christ involved embracing a reconception of the self as a submissive woman before the masculine divinity.[25]

Devotional materials published in Mexico City in the 1850s reveal this conception of mystical union in practice at the time when the first Madre Matiana pamphlets were in circulation. In fact, one of the early prophecy printers, the Librería Abadiano, also published a 200-page dialogue between Christ and "his wife," the human soul, in 1851 detailing the extremes of humility and obedience required to achieve union with God.[26] For the present-day reader the didactic booklet is distinctly unsettling, as it gradually presents what seems like the ultimate male fantasy of adulation and control. The Christ figure emerges as simultaneously a husband, father, teacher, confessor, and judge with unfettered access to the soul's innermost insecurities and feelings. His interlocutor, the soul, is an eager female pupil-daughter trying desperately to please, and as Christ puts it, "*matar su amor propio*" ("kill your self-love"). In the climactic final section on achieving ultimate spiritual unity, he promises to be the eternally loving and supremely powerful ideal husband, provided that the female soul has no thoughts or desires beyond his constant, utter gratification. In response the soul testifies her passionate love for her divine partner and pleads fervently for his help in meeting his standards.[27] This dialogue is so strongly gendered in terms of divine patriarchal supremacy, utter female submission, and self-effacement that it is difficult to imagine its production for anything other than a young, feminine audience. However, hypothetically both men and women seeking

Figure 2. Dialogue between Christ and His Wife the Soul. The long subtitle of this work stresses the sensual: the soul, gendered female, "yearns to please and serve Him, and anxiously seeks to love, and savor Christ in their divine union." From *El Camino Verdadero*, Mexico City: Imprenta de Luis Abadiano y Valdés, 1851. Courtesy of the California State Library–Sutro Branch, San Francisco.

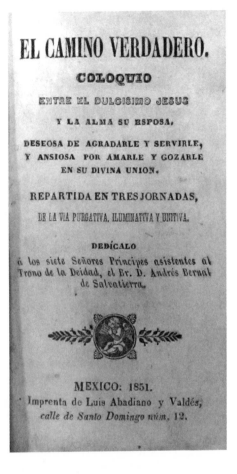

EL CAMINO VERDADERO.

COLOQUIO

ENTRE EL DULCISIMO JESUS

Y LA ALMA SU ESPOSA,

DESEOSA DE AGRADARLE Y SERVIRLE,
Y ANSIOSA POR AMARLE Y GOZARLE
EN SU DIVINA UNION.

REPARTIDA EN TRES JORNADAS,

DE LA VIA PURGATIVA, ILUMINATIVA Y UNITIVA.

DEDÍCALO

á los siete Señores Príncipes asistentes al
Trono de la Deidad, el Br. D. Andrés Bernal
de Salvatierra.

MEXICO: 1851.
Imprenta de Luis Abadiano y Valdés,
calle de Santo Domingo núm. 12.

mystical union with God would also have to humble themselves in this definitive manner in order to cede their most intimate desires, thoughts, and feelings to the über-male Christ.

Thus a paradox rested at the center of prevailing notions of female piety, which may seem simple and even simpleminded in present-day estimation, but the beliefs proved remarkably durable and influential well into the modern era. On the one hand, doctrine stressed women's openness to deception, error, and sin. On the other hand, if a woman dedicated herself to meticulous religious development under male spiritual directors, she could fully subjugate her vain tendencies and carnal appetites. Then her passive, emotional temperament would make it easier for her to cultivate the extreme humility that opened the soul to the Divine Spirit.

Not surprisingly this tension marked female spirituality in the eyes of the Catholic Church and many believers. Here the so-called Pauline Silence is also at work: the apostle Paul's prohibition on women as figures of authority vis-à-vis men and proscription of female speech in religious settings.[28] This cornerstone of gender bias, however, ran against the long Christian tradition of underscoring God's predilection for the lowly and those whose faith was more instinctive than intellectual. For centuries Christian visionary movements countered skeptics with the argument that God chooses the most disparaged to speak for him. The Matiana narrative, for one, explicitly reminds readers of this tradition in celebration of female revelation.

Still, cleavages in patriarchal structures provided a very limited sphere of action for religious women. The Church essentially banished them from the realm of rationality, but in doing so it also delineated a female sphere beyond rationality—the mystical.[29] Even the most privileged women in places like colonial Mexico enjoyed very limited educational opportunities; however, society encouraged their limitless pious development.[30] Confined thus, but seeking to express themselves within Catholic tradition, some women excelled and in the process turned mysticism into the paradigmatic locus of the female "voice."[31] It is important, though, not to romanticize female piety: men often controlled mystical women and policed female religious expression. Indeed, colonial women's spiritual experience frequently served as "raw material" for priestly editors, who shaped its written meaning. Of the few known texts pertaining to female mystics, most are found in the writings of male spiritual directors. In many instances the only surviving evidence of a particular mística's life is the narration residing in such documents.

Despite male filtering, and even outright fabrication, the strong identification of mystical grace with female piety is of vital importance in Catholicism. Increasingly, notions of female erotic experience, childbirth, and marriage became the prevailing metaphors of spiritual union with the divine.[32] Regardless of rhetoric that belittled female piety, the idea that the emotional path to God represented the surest means of spiritual enlightenment took root. In a nutshell, elite men largely ceded the affective register of religious understanding to devout women. Since the realm of feeling and sentiment is where a great number of believers experience their faith, this explains the extraordinary popularity of famous female mystics and their approach to spirituality. Both Church leaders and the common laity looked to them. The periodic emergence of uniquely graced figures from among the faithful is absolutely essential to sustain commitments to the "Church Universal" and its myriad institutions. To put it bluntly, throughout its history the Church has employed exemplars of exceptional pious achievement to make Catholicism feel intensely meaningful and make sanctity seem within reach of the intensely devout.[33] In addition, these figures model exceptional practice and ideal behaviors.[34] For common believers the emergence of sainted individuals from within their midst represents evidence of the collective merit. Local affinities for holy women were often particularly strong, since they were much more likely to have been born and raised in the region where their pious fame took shape.[35]

Again, the tight braiding of female piety and mysticism became a prominent feature of Catholicism in the Middle Ages, and it remained profoundly influential afterward. Visions became the centerpiece of most claims of sanctity for women, such as Saint Catherine of Siena (1347–1380). As a result scholars identify affective, expressive, lyrical, and image-centered practice with women, but to focus entirely on modes of religious expression misses the deeper linkage of female piety to the humanity of Christ. Too often scholars assume that women focused their devotional energies on overtly feminine images, such as the Virgin Mary, but in actuality the imitation of Christ represented the core of female mysticism. One of the more significant outgrowths of this phenomenon was the dramatic expansion of devotion to the Eucharist (also known as the Blessed Sacrament), elaborated almost exclusively by women.[36] According to Catholic teaching, the Eucharist is both the ritual bread, which dogma dictates becomes the actual Body of Christ through priestly consecration during Mass, and the sacrament of Communion. The latter represents the central moment of the liturgy when the faithful consume this miraculously "transubstantiated" bread—typically called the Host. For Catholics it is an exceptionally solemn ritual understood simultaneously as the moment of most intimate proximity to God, a celebration of collective Christian commitment, and an act of pious thanksgiving.

Since the Matiana prophecy calls for an expiatory crusade centered on coordinated female Eucharistic piety, this realm of devotion is especially relevant. It fits within a broader cluster of practices associated with women that revolve around notions of eating, fasting, serving, and feeding. The gendered origin of these associations is obvious, but the metaphorical and symbolic extrapolations on sustenance (e.g., consuming, hungering, producing, nourishing, and even being food) are extensive.[37] In the early Church, celebrating the sacred meal of the Eucharist was less emphasized and more straightforward in Christian thought. For the most part, it represented the bond between Christians and their coming together in Christ. However, during the twelfth and thirteenth centuries the Eucharist, the Body of Christ present in the consecrated Host, emerged as an object of adoration in its own right and transformed the liturgy and devotion.

Focusing on the Eucharist involved a heightened emphasis on the human body of Jesus Christ. In Catholic teaching consecration is the moment when, dogma dictates, God descends and becomes flesh. Essentially it gained importance as a reenactment of the mystery of the Incarnation. For the devout it was a very powerful experience. First, they witnessed transubstantiation: the bread and wine becoming body and blood in the hands of the officiating priest. Second, they personally encountered Christ when they consumed the Host. The emphasis shifted to the individual seeing a recapitulation of Christ's embrace of humanity and personal suffering. In 1264 Rome decreed the official institution of Corpus Christi (the feast celebrating belief in Christ's real presence in the Host), and by the fourteenth century this practice had been widely adopted. It also proved to be one of the most elaborate, popular festivals in colonial Mexico.[38] As it gained importance practices emerged that proved central to Matiana's prophecies in the nineteenth century: in particular, ritual visitation and prayerful vigil before the Blessed Sacrament. Indeed, it is also probably not a coincidence that a few years before the Matiana prophecies' initial publication an innovative devotional organization led by women (the Vela Perpetua) was established and began to spread rapidly in Mexican cities and towns.[39]

As with so many aspects of devotional practice, the array of meanings linked to Eucharistic piety multiplied over time. As a result a chorus of understandings took shape amid burgeoning veneration of the Blessed Sacrament. For the clergy, it bolstered the power of the consecrating priest who reenacted the moment of Christian sacrifice. This rite stood for a crucial moment in the struggle between good and evil: Christ's assumption of human form in order to vanquish sin. As a result it also became a powerful symbol of the Christian sociopolitical body and gained symbolic associations with Catholic unity in the face of the Church's enemies. Ultimately this powerful array of meanings, as well as attendant practices, gained even greater importance during Catholicism's nineteenth-century struggles. The champions of this mode of Catholic piety and the flesh-and-blood witnesses to the increasing number of Eucharistic miracles were female mystics. They became known for the visions they reported, such as seeing the Host flying, bleeding because of alleged profanations, or transforming itself miraculously into the Christ Child. According to the pious biographies penned about these women these experiences were quite visceral. For example, Saint Catherine of Siena, and many of her sister mystics, distinguished the distinct flavor of blood in her mouth when she took the Host.[40] Saint Colette of Corbie (1381–1447), according to her followers, was extraordinarily committed to the Eucharist; she heard Mass daily and took Communion frequently. She, however, did so in private as much as possible, because she could not control weeping and slipping into ecstatic trances. On many occasions she saw visions at the moment of consecration. Colette once envisioned the Christ Child carved like a piece of meat on a plate, and she understood that this symbolized his bodily suffering and sacrifice for humanity's sins. Inspired by such experiences, according to her biographers, she unflinchingly punished her own flesh and miraculously displayed the wounds of the Christ's passion on her own body for brief periods. Like many other famous female mystics in Catholic lore, Saint Colette frequently remained in the grip of devout ecstasy and refused all food for hours after Communion because the Host miraculously sated her completely.[41]

Given this legacy it follows that Catholic women in general became the recognized virtuosos of Eucharistic devotion through marathon vigils, frequent communion, and elaborate practices warding off the Host's profanation. In their focus on the Body of Christ, pious women often glorified Christ's human suffering; their focus on these themes makes sense. Blocked from intellectual exploration and leadership, many religious women turned inward and became specialists in the ritual enactment and bodily experience of the highest goal of the faith, full union with God—the One believed physically present in the Host. In Catholic thought Christ's physicality, his human body, came from the Virgin Mary, and as we have seen, women were associated with carnality. Not surprisingly, female mystics tended to conflate themselves, and women in general, with humanity. To focus on Christ's body and the Blessed Sacrament asserted an essential affinity between woman and Savior. By extension the penitential extremes and emotive intensity in female mysticism stemmed from the fervent attempt to secure union with Christ—often expressed in terms of conjugal bliss—by embracing levels of human suffering approaching crucifixion.[42]

The success of female mystics in the late Middle Ages and the increased number of female saints brought with it a backlash. Many of the texts produced as manuals for eradicating heresies and heterodoxy at this time targeted women who engaged in ecstatic visionary piety. For Catholic authorities the whole notion of mystical union wandered perilously close to the heretical realm of unmediated communication with God. Hence as the Early Modern period took shape, and particularly with the Counter-Reformation's amplified suspicion of deviation, religious women ran greater risks. The fervent and intrepid, nonetheless, continued to practice mystical piety. Among the most famous was Teresa of Avila (1515–1582), a Spanish Carmelite nun.[43] In many ways she represents a pivotal inheritor of medieval traditions, which she reworked to some degree. Her life also serves as a case study of the challenges that faced religious women in the male-dominated Catholic culture that came to the Americas. She wrote several works outlining a methodology of mystical practice and personal religious fulfillment that barely escaped the flames of inquisitorial censorship. This combined with the accessible nature of her spiritual exercises and her posthumous assent to favor within Spain's royal family, and eventual sainthood made her the most important model for subsequent female mystics. Her writings, sermons extolling her virtues, and hagiographic works about her became "classics" of devotional literature reproduced and sold by printers and booksellers throughout the Catholic world. In Mexico, the same presses that produced the Matiana prophecies were no exception.[44]

According to literary scholar Alison Weber, the key reason for Teresa's success proved to be her deft deployment of the "rhetoric of femininity."[45] Teresa of Avila wrote as society expected pious women to speak, while simultaneously, albeit subtly, asserting the superiority of her methods and personal revelations acquired in mystical practice. It was perhaps inevitable that such a sainted controversial woman inspired feminist scholarship. Her legacy, however, should not be confused with simple resistance to male-dominated orthodoxy. She did not so much overthrow the misogynist strictures of her time as carve out a space within them, and establish an accepted, mystical personality for women. Thus she avoided the language of theological debate and embraced the informality of private discourse and the language of lower social groups. Her style was more familiar, and seized a different kind of authority rooted in a female, less formal, authenticity. In a sense, Saint Teresa taught without being didactic. In her writings she was careful to stress her orthodoxy and obedience to male superiors, and she also cultivated a self-deprecating authorial persona. For example, she commonly referred to herself as a *mujercilla* (little woman). For some present-day scholars, Saint Teresa essentially showed women how to survive in the Counter-Reformation Church.[46] For others, her key legacy was crafting the touchstone works of heroic autohagiography.[47] Devout women in Latin America centuries later continued to do much the same when they wrote about their lives. Essentially they created autobiographical myths to narrate personal religious fulfillment.[48]

Alongside this legacy, nostalgic yearnings for an imagined golden age of colonial stability also pervaded the Matiana narrative. Central to these notions was an assumption of a foundational culture of intense Catholic belief and practice, which secured divine favor. The text invoked an idealized, baroque world where a miraculously gifted servant girl could gain prominence in one of Mexico City's most storied convents and renown in wider society. There is a certain irony in this sugarcoated depiction of the late colonial period, since reformers and inquisitors at the time—such as those investigating Jesuit restoration prophecies—censored expressive devotional traditions and claims of supernatural revelation. Although the Matiana text speaks explicitly of the mid-1700s, it invokes a much deeper history. Catholics in Mexico inherited both the older traditions of female mystical piety and the more recent legacy of pointed criticism regarding this particularly emotive mode of religious expression. These fine points were of little consequence to individuals pining for conservative religious renewal in the mid-nineteenth century. If much of Matiana's original audience embraced a romanticized historical memory of viceregal Mexico, the importance placed upon female piety during the nation's colonial period necessitates a still closer look.

MEXICAN MYSTICS

In terms of understanding Matiana's complex legacy, the era spanning the late 1500s and early 1800s, when baroque Catholicism flourished in places like Mexico City and Puebla, is of central importance. These urban settings developed an extensive complement of religious institutions and sustained the full array of pious practices associated with them. In addition, larger cities possessed printing presses, a crucial ingredient in baroque devotional culture. These conditions came together between 1550 and 1620. In Mexico, Counter-Reformation concerns with such things as Judaizers and Protestants were of secondary importance, but fears of local heterodoxy weighed on churchmen. More or less simultaneously, the Holy Office of the Inquisition took root and female convents expanded to accommodate growing criollo (Mexican-born, but of European origin—Creole) populations, and an educated Mexican priesthood grew quickly. Likewise, a diverse

collection of brotherhoods and affiliated institutions for the laity targeted
distinct social niches, and they gradually incorporated much of the populace, male and female. It is also at this time that the Jesuits secured a foot-
hold in the Americas and brought with them their more emotive brand of
spirituality; urban preaching orders, like the *dieguinos* (barefoot Franciscans) who appear in the Matiana prophecy story, established themselves as
well.[49] The Church was very aware that multiethnic colonial realities represented a new kind of society, and this led to an openness toward exemplary
life stories set in the New World and the emergence of new sacred sites.
Many shrines and apparition narratives date from this period. Saint Rose of
Lima (1586–1617) established her reputation amid a mystical fluorescence in
seventeenth-century Peru and inspired longing in many viceregal cities for
their own local saint.[50] In New Spain, individuals like the hermit Gregorio
López (1542–1596) achieved considerable fame as well.

The elevation of these and other models of piety, however, gained greater
momentum during the peak of baroque piety, from roughly 1620 to 1750.
Colonial Catholics became distinctly self-aware as a surging criollo identity
inspired exaltations of the landscape, local Church history, and idealized
renderings of pre-Hispanic civilization.[51] It was during this period that the
largely criollo-staffed Church began depicting Mexico as a chosen religious
community: they asserted that the Americas had come of age spiritually and
proclaimed religious parity with Europe. In other words, Mexican-born
Catholics began to see themselves as equally deserving of divine favor as
their brethren in Spain. This development brought with it the expectation
that saints would emerge from local society. As a result, New Spain's printing
presses found an eager and expanding market for new narratives of exemplary piety. In many ways, the surge of biographical writings about presumptive Mexican saints from this period emerged from Creole efforts to craft a
unique and devout local identity. Historians today point to incipient pious
criollismo (roughly, Americanism) as the seedbed of Mexican nationalism.[52]
Indeed, notions of a unique Mexican Catholic culture depended on an abiding belief in a special God-given destiny as the bulwark of the faith in
America. Regional identities proved very important too; much of the support
for various canonization campaigns emerged from specific cities' efforts to
glorify favorite sons and daughters. Outside of the elite, few enjoyed literacy,
but sermons, confession, and popular retellings spread pious life stories
throughout society.[53] The ideas and practices celebrated in these texts were
not new, but it made all the difference to devout Mexicans that saintly

narratives unfolded in their own social world. In many cases, the *vida* (biography) simply followed shopworn patterns; however, realistic depictions of colonial society surrounded the presumptive Mexican saints.

Evidence of this dynamic appears in the famed criollo chronicler Carlos Sigüenza y Góngora's *Parayso occidental* (1694), a book recounting the Mexican establishment of the Royal Convent of Jesús María (1616).[54] Based on archival documents and interviews with nuns, the author composed a first-person narrative of the religious lives and miraculous experiences of two exceptional nuns, Madre Marina de la Cruz and Madre Inés de la Cruz, leading up to their founding of the convent. Much more than simple life stories of religious women, the author uses their story to make his case for the securing of "paradise" in the Americas (as in a spiritual conquest of pagan lands and a pristine establishment of the "true" faith in all its mystical complexity), epitomized by the pious purity of these exemplary women. In other words, the presence of paradigmatic female virtues, and the proof of their exceptional nature in divine mystical graces, allowed Sigüenza y Góngora to proclaim the Christian bona fides of his American birthplace. Like the Madre Matiana narrative, although much more artfully realized, *Parayso occidental* works within the genre-bending relación (official report) tradition: this book is simultaneously a historical legal document and vida.[55]

The visionary narratives within this text offer glimpses of baroque culture, as evidenced by Sigüenza y Góngora's transcription of Madre Inés's troubling visions of Mexico City's presumptive divine destruction:

> Imploring God a great deal in those days about the news from the city, seeing as this was my main concern, it occurred that while I was in prayer I perceived that the buildings were crashing into each other as if everything was about to fall apart. Later I saw clouds descending and almost engulfing the Earth, and I understood that God was angry with the city, and wanted to destroy it. I called the nuns saying, "Can't you see this?" They all came together, and looking off with my eyes I saw what appeared to be a chapel, and inside it our Lord Jesus Christ and his Blessed Mother on her knees. It was manifested to me that she was pleading with him to have mercy on this city. All of us went to the chapel [of the convent] and kneeled together, and I was right next to Our Lady, who turned her tender face to me and placed her hand on my head, letting me know that I had gotten Our Lord to grant her request.[56]

This passage is significant in terms of style and content: it reveals the deep, expressive tradition of feminine prophetic warning and the call to collective atonement at work in viceregal Mexico. Simultaneously it also testifies to longstanding notions of devout women as the stewards of the public's relationship with God. As in the Matiana narrative, *Parayso occidental* portrayed pious local women saving society from destruction through visionary foresight and organized expiation.

These linkages may seem esoteric, or simply quaint, from present-day perspectives, but miraculous thinking and public piety suffused colonial society. The rejection of presumed divine agency in human affairs was much more aberrant than heeding local visionaries. Doubts regarding mystics, for the most part, centered on issues of authenticity. Were they the real thing or were they "false mystics"? As we have seen, ecclesiastical suspicions of heresy, fraud, and religious entrepreneurship made religious fame dangerous. The bipolar understanding of female piety ensured close scrutiny by Church authorities. Thus alongside baroque culture's veneration of local mystics a set of practices and ideas evolved to undermine revelations and discredit emergent holy figures. Dead, sainted women could be safely admired and idealized; but living practitioners of mystical traditions, particularly those with numerous followers, represented a threat to institutional control. Recent historical scholarship indicates that cities like Mexico City, Puebla, and Querétaro sustained vibrant mystical practices throughout the 1600s, 1700s, and early 1800s. These traditions, the moral value placed upon them, and a historical memory of pious social unity remained quite strong even when rationalism and scientific thought made them seem backward in some circles.[57]

The Church policed mystical culture in a variety of ways. For elite women, confessors monitored their charges' religious and personal lives. In this context women produced the documents that serve as the basis of our understanding of colonial mysticism.[58] Poor indigenous and mestiza women incorporated mystical piety within other popular practices (like magic and healing), but they only drew the attention of authorities if they were implicated in witchcraft or began to develop outsized reputations. Middling or poor Spanish and Creole laywomen had the most to gain (and lose) in baroque mysticism. They could significantly improve their social standing if they earned renown for their ability to communicate with souls in purgatory, to mediate supplications for divine favor, and to foresee future events. Trouble with authorities, though, was likely to emerge if they strayed from simple pious ideas—such as calls for repentance—and began to expound on doctrine, direct the pious practices of others, or assert independent interpretations of their miraculous experiences. Prophecies infused with thinly veiled political critique, naturally, invited trouble. Investigations could lead to torture, imprisonment, and severe sentences if inquisitors determined them to be *alumbradas, endemoniadas,* or ilusas. The first term marked those accused as practitioners of heretical mysticism. The second category referred to those who had reputedly succumbed to satanic deception and seduction. The latter described individuals who had been tricked by the devil into believing they experienced "authentic" mysticism, sustained delusions of pious self-importance, or simply faked visionary experiences in hopes of personal gain. According to historian Nora E. Jaffary, the irony of the one hundred or so inquisitorial investigations for which we have documentation is that most of the mystics under scrutiny remained convinced that they practiced the faith within the bounds of orthodoxy.[59]

As the eighteenth century wore on, new ideas emerging from the Enlightenment undercut baroque piety, but traditional practices endured despite their fading cachet. This is evident in both the dismissive response to Jesuit restoration prophecies and the fears inquisitors expressed concerning their potential seditious impact. Particularly after 1750, Bourbon reformers and churchmen grew increasingly critical of pious excess and miracle-centered religiosity. They encouraged a staid, personal, intellectual interior piety, and rejected the baroque emphasis on miraculous experience and flamboyant public display.[60] Seeking to bring about greater order, authorities moved to restrict male and female religious orders, limit lay brotherhoods, curtail feasts, silence visionaries and self-proclaimed prophets, and dampen celebratory fervor. Not surprisingly official documentation reveals that accusations of diabolism and heresy faded, but inquisitors branded an increasing number of women ilusas. The small late-colonial elite essentially challenged cherished belief and practice, and hence their efforts amounted to a struggle against the tide. Decades later, liberal reformers would essentially take up the same mission without much more success. The task was, in truth, daunting. Alongside enduring pious traditions in everyday life, myriad official and unofficial hagiographies, as well as devotional texts, made up a hefty chunk of eighteenth- and nineteenth-century print culture. Biographical treatments of venerable nuns and churchmen were also common. In addition, many religious orders produced stories that lionized famed late members who enjoyed saintly reputations. Moreover, popular stories, often cribbed from these sources, appeared in pamphlets and almanacs; preachers, likewise, often worked these stories into their sermons.

A sample of women's mystical writings offers a more detailed understanding for this corner of baroque culture that would be idealized a century later. María Josefa de la Peña was a beata affiliated with the Carmelite order in her hometown of Toluca. Born in 1759, she developed a reputation for exceptional piety, vivid visionary experiences, and miraculous gifts by the early 1780s.[61] Witnesses, including clergymen, described how she miraculously received Communion on some occasions, interceded for souls in purgatory, predicted deaths, and cured the sick. Her growing fame drew the attention of inquisitors, although she did not face trial. Nonetheless, she died unexpectedly of a fever amid an investigation ordered by the Holy Office in 1783; authorities eventually recognized her as an ilusa posthumously. The central problem was not her religious practices, which were rather typical. Instead, what disturbed authorities was the fact that she had begun to direct the spiritual development of others. This assumption of patriarchal functions contradicted tradition and Church law, but de la Peña, allegedly, claimed that her Franciscan confessors approved. Regardless of the Inquisition's after-the-fact conclusions, she must have been very convincing because the priests monitoring her spiritual development stayed by her side as illness took its toll and prostrated themselves before her corpse, reverentially kissing her hands, feet, and the floor around her body after she expired. Apparently they even took up her personal effects and distributed them as relics. These acts of unsanctioned veneration scandalized the Holy Office; eventually these priests found themselves branded false mystics as well.[62]

Like so many women engaged in this kind of spirituality, de la Peña recorded her experiences at the behest of her male spiritual director, and thanks to the Inquisition we can consult them. The Mexican beata patterned her testimony on Saint Teresa's officially approved mystical writings, both in terms of devotional practices and expressive style. In fact, one of her confessors, arguably trying to distance himself from the dead ilusa, claimed that she plagiarized the famous Spanish visionary.[63] Following tradition, she complained of her womanly ignorance and questioned the value of her testimony, but agreed to write only out of respect for her priestly confessor:

> The truth is my father, that if my obedience was not so complete, I believe that I would say nothing. . . . Because I think I will not know how to say much, nor [have] the understanding to know how to understand

and moreover [express] that [which comes from] a bumbling, uncouth woman. . . . My God, my husband, most amorous envoy, loving master, send rays of light to the understanding so that I can shed some [light] on other souls and you would be served that they enjoy with frequency these gifts and not be tricked by the Devil transfiguring himself into an angel of light.[64]

These kinds of statements, while derivative, were important. They made a show of submission, but simultaneously they imply that de la Peña had received a unique miraculous wisdom, which God, her adoring husband, called her to share. To the present day reader a self-serving conceit seems obvious: Peña asserts no personal interest in sharing her spiritual knowledge, but she proclaims that both her confessor and (most importantly) Christ demand that she describe her experiences. At the time, however, prevailing norms required this seemingly over-the-top humility of mystical women, and they, somewhat ritualistically, met these expectations. Anything else aroused suspicion.

De la Peña spent considerable energy trying to explain to her spiritual director precisely how she experienced trance-like states. It was during these moments, she assured him, when Christ appeared to her, usually as the resplendent Lord of the Resurrection, and he imparted flashes of divine insight. Typically these occurred during moments of intensely devout *recogimiento* (contemplation), but sometimes they surprised her during everyday tasks. In each case, de la Peña claimed she could feel the visions coming, but she was powerless to control them:

> The first thing I do before I pray is read some portion of the passion, or of the life of Christ; after reading the excerpt I always make sure to begin to meditate, but, at the most these meditations last one station [of the Cross] . . . because soon these powerful impulses commence where it seems like the soul is about to escape the body. . . . After this, rapidly I perceive a powerful light that is inexplicable because it seizes the soul as if by surprise. And later, with this light comes a great clarity and understanding with which one can comprehend and know what the Lord has decided to reveal.[65]

The visions, according to de la Peña, often lasted fifteen or thirty minutes, but they typically left her exhausted and in a pained state of heightened anxiety. During such times, which could last hours or even an entire day, she was unable to speak or understand those that spoke to her. In some of her visions, she experienced a kind of delirious love for Christ, "I felt I was melting in his divine love."[66] Christ, in turn, offered to reward de la Peña for her unflinching adoration. On one occasion, she asked him to free a woman who she knew was suffering in purgatory: "Then he said to me, 'My daughter, look at her escape from the suffering she endured [and] come to enjoy me completely,' and I saw her extraordinary beauty as she rose to delight in God."[67]

Aside from such cheery revelations, de la Peña also described more ominous visions, echoing the warnings of mounting impiety and impending divine retribution in both *Parayso occidental* and the Matiana pamphlets:

> I saw a very great house, and inside it a multitude of persons, and in the middle of those people their Lord appeared very aggrieved because each one of those present was torturing his Holy Majesty imparting distinct torments like on the night and day of his Passion. . . . It greatly wounded me to see my Lord suffer and his Majesty turned to me and said, "Look my daughter, these people are those that in these times of deviations through the sins they commit make me suffer and crucify me anew, but just as my mercy is infinite, so too is my justice."[68]

Again, in many ways, narratives such as these are little more the pious boilerplate. Similar vague warnings of collective depravity and approaching punishment repeatedly crop up in Christian visionary tradition. However, it is precisely their commonplace nature that makes them noteworthy. In the manner of previous mystics, María Josefa de la Peña essentially worked from a script. In other words, she reenacted a longstanding cautionary performance regarding collective irreverence and the need to practice exceptional piety. Naturally, blasphemous transgressions were (and are) always in evidence; the point was to inspire renewal.

This legacy served as the complex cultural milieu surrounding the Matiana narrative, and the evidence reveals that a collective memory of mystical piety burrowed deep into Mexican folklore. Viceregal culture's development was inseparable from these religious sensibilities. Its very foundations were built on notions that the supernatural was always close at hand. Furthermore, the most admirable figures were those who practiced intense penitential self-denial and "mental prayer" (rigorous nonverbal, even subconscious, contemplation of God's love as championed by Saint Teresa). In both instances the goal was to escape the earthbound self and transcend the rational mind.[69] For women perceived in this august company, mystical graces, such as visions, levitation, divine illnesses, and prophecy represented standard expectations.[70] Moreover, much of society accepted the reality of these experiences as an article of faith. Crucially the female mystics who wrote autobiographies often did so with the express purpose of passing on their methods and experiences to kindred souls. Evidence suggests that nineteenth-century nuns sought out texts composed by their colonial predecessors, even those from different orders.[71] In sum, the cultural foundations of baroque mystical expression remained accessible in the nineteenth century.

The Matiana pamphlets we can consult today not only invoke this history of mystical effervescence and inquisitorial inquiry, but they also nestle the entire prophetic story in the memory of Mexican baroque culture. In the printed pamphlet's preamble the narrator, Madre Guerra, tries to allay suspicions of mystical femininity: "*Parecen cuentos de viejas é ilusiones de mugeres [sic] dementes, ó sueños . . .*" ("They may seem the stories of crones and the illusions of demented women, or dreams . . .").[72] She also acknowledges the tradition of discrediting visionaries as ilusas when she spoke of the woman destined to lead the new expiatory order of nuns: "*La tendrán por simple, ilusa, loca, mentirosa y fanática*" ("They will judge her simple, a false mystic, insane, a liar, and a fanatic").[73] Here the text essentially redeployed the colonial-era vocabulary embedded in the inquisitorial critique of Jesuit restoration prophecies and mystical narratives like de la Peña's. Finally, toward the end of the Matiana narrative, we learn how the seer and her two confidants ended up before the Holy Office. The text implies that they faced torture ("*la maltrataban mucho*"—"they mistreated her extensively"), and yet Matiana met physical torment with a pious elation grounded in devout certainty.[74] In sum, the Matiana narrative not only invoked the dramas that historical mystics faced, but it also commemorated colonial piety—particularly the piety of humble Mexican women.

MODELS OF REVERENCE AND IRREVERENCE

Like her mythic forbearers, Madre Matiana evolved into an archetypal figure, but her story worked from an array of spiritually powerful stock characters: the *monja*, beata, and bruja or *curandera* (the nun, devout laywoman, and witch or healer). The pious nun figure, often in Mexico simply called religiosas, featured classic subtypes, such as the institution-founding abbess, the reformer and champion of strict observance, the cloistered ascetic, and the visionary. As the nineteenth century progressed, the selfless nun dedicated to teaching or nursing joined this list. For centuries, though, the prevailing understanding of nuns centered on convents as repositories of female purity where the most accomplished nuns could approach pious perfection in cloistered solitude.[75] Religiosas, ideally, embodied local society's most devout sentiments, and they served as intermediaries between the larger population and the divine. They sought heavenly relief for the community facing hardship, and if necessary they offered their own bodies to assuage celestial anger. In their idealized selflessness they embodied an important complex role in the Catholic "economy of salvation."[76] In part, they represented innocent victims sacrificed to atone for society's sins. Still they were not without critics. Particularly as the eighteenth century matured, reformers complained of the luxuries, laxities, and the general wastefulness of traditional convent life. As modern notions of social utility gained ground, the value placed on reclusion and dedication to a life of prayer and asceticism lost some of its luster. Still nineteenth-century Mexican Catholics continued to value cloistered piety. New ideas nudged traditional ways of thinking, but they fell well short of replacing them.

Women seeking religious self-actualization, however, often could not enter convents for a variety of reasons, such as wealth, ethnicity, and class origin. Many of them embraced publicly pious lives outside of religious orders. This too had a long history in the Catholic world. In Spain and Spanish America they were known as beatas, but due to their relative independence, and generally more humble origins, they often inspired skepticism. The label is remarkably plastic. It applied to laywomen who made personal vows of chastity and joined third orders (lay organizations affiliated with monastic orders that lacked strict cloistered observance but shared some of their devotional practices). In some cases, it also referred to those who lived together in special houses known as *beaterios*—collectives of unprofessed laywomen committed to particular spiritual practices and communal rules. It also served to describe women who took part in, and sometimes led, less formal groups devoted to Catholic mysticism; these included likeminded men and women. In addition, women who simply enjoyed particularly devout reputations or projected devout public identities were at times labeled beatas.

Establishing a reputation as a deeply religious person was a very important life goal for many Mexican women. It was often the most important standard of a woman's character. Some achieved a real social ascendancy if they developed reputations as gifted mystics, often with a specialty such as prophecy. With the same goal as nuns (that of mystical union with God), devout laywomen used the same techniques as their cloistered counterparts. They maintained elaborate regimes of pious exercises, embraced extreme penitence and fasting, and practiced the mental prayer and rigorous self-examination methods outlined in mystical literature. In the most famous cases there was a certain slippage between the saintly nun and beata. Renowned laywomen sometimes gained the honorific *madre*.[77] We see this in the Matiana text, where the visionary protagonist was an unprofessed convent servant and yet labeled thus.

Again, there were considerable risks for mystics and devout laywomen. They lacked the institutional protections of nuns. Professed religiosas were typically of higher social standing and some of them enjoyed family ties to influential figures that could partly shield them if they aroused suspicion. Moreover, cloistered orders commanded considerable respect and could prove formidable in protecting their members. In the first place they jealously guarded their right to address religious and moral discipline internally, so they worked to keep news of irregularities from emerging beyond the convent. Secondly, inaugurating an investigation of a particular nun could create clashes with the abbess and her allies in the clergy and secular society. Devout laywomen, particularly lower-class beatas, were much more open to scrutiny.

Mere hints of heterodoxy or misbehavior, and attempts to lead likeminded believers, could draw the ire of authorities. Sometimes a beata simply fell afoul of strict gender norms and class stereotypes, such as accusations of less-than-saintly personal lives. Women who were of lower social origins were especially at risk of character assassination.[78] The defaming of beatas as closet strumpets, or more subtly as women with hidden histories, endured well beyond the colonial period. Hence they appeared as the target off-color songs alluding to sexual and religious deviance, such as the infamously bawdy eighteenth-century "Chuchumbe," a song and dance which caught the attention of inquisitors:

Una vieja santularia	An old saintlet
que va y viene a San Francisco	who comes and goes to San Francisco
toma el padre, daca el padre	she takes the padre, seizes the padre
y es el padre de sus hijos	and he's the father of her children
Eres Marta, la piadosa,	You are Marta, the pious one,

en cuanto a tu caridad,	because of your charity,
que no llega peregrino	not a pilgrim arrives
que socorrido no va.[79]	that does not leave succored.

Here in the first stanza, an elderly woman is derided as an oversexed *"santularia"* (roughly a saintlet, like starlet) who comes and goes from the church of San Francisco. She takes or seizes the padre, and she even bears his children. In the second stanza, Marta, "the pious one," makes sure that every pilgrim enjoys her charity. This counterpious satirical tradition remained healthy in the nineteenth century too. For example, the famous Mexican geographer Antonio García Cubas's 1904 memoir includes a transcription of a drunken, urban, low-life's singing:

Que estoy borracho dice la gente	That I am a drunk, that's what they say
Que estoy borracho de agua ardiente	That I am drunk with agua ardiente[80]
Me enamore de una beata	I fell in love with a beata
Ay si!	Oh yes!
Por tener amor bendito	To have holy love
Ay no!	Oh no!
La beata se condenó	The beata was condemned
Ay si!	Oh yes!
Y a mi me faltó un poquito	And I missed it a bit
Ay no!	Oh no!
Ah! que susto tenia yo	Ah, what a scare I had
Ay si!	Oh yes!
Sentado en un rinconcito [81]	Sitting in a little corner

Clearly blasphemous innuendo remained an effective, even timeless, attention-getting device. Piety (and sanctimony), among other things, invites satire, and the self-important beata remains a stock figure of Mexican culture. But it is also true that religious, nonelite women represented easy targets of misogynist mockery. Here the singer jokes about his amorous longing for a beata and her "holy love." Then he deploys the double meaning of her condemnation, which nearly brings on his own and leaves him without blessed love. Providentially, then, in this street ditty there is evidence of both the ribald derision aimed at pious women and the historical memory of beatas' persecution.

Deeply religious women, evidently, had to face irreverent taunts. In reality this is just as much part of the context of the Matiana phenomenon as mystical religious practice and the devout femininity of its sainted exemplars. Indeed, to this day Mexican women of the Vela Perpetua (those committed to organize vigils of the Blessed Sacrament) remain an easy target of scorn for those mocking and feminizing "traditional" Catholicism.[82] Most religious women, though, never approached mystical fame or infamy, although they sought to emulate the religiosas and beatas celebrated in folklore. Particularly as the nineteenth century advanced, another pejorative characterization of the beata became prominent. Secularists applied the label to female supporters of the clergy and the Catholic Church. To a certain degree the term could identify any woman with close ties to the clergy or a reputation for putting on pious airs. It essentially cast all female supporters of the Church as mindless priestly toadies and sustainers of "useless" practices. This usage recycled older stereotypes of female religiosity in general and assumptions about women's intellectual deficiencies and innate fanaticism. At times such critics even insinuated that beatas' true motivations regarding the male clergy stemmed from repressed sexual desires.[83]

The final figure of female spiritual prowess in play was the bruja or curandera (witch or popular curer). Although this figure did not enter the original Matiana narrative, the depiction of the prophetess and popular healers merged in the twentieth-century fiction of Agustín Yáñez. Hence it pays to outline this classic character at least briefly. From Christian tradition the witch embodied the mirror image of the female saint: both figures were possessed by supernatural entities—the devil and God, respectively.[84] For the poor, the curandera represented an accessible combination of local spiritual savant and curer, and a potentially powerful local person. Colonial authorities saw it differently: notions of witchcraft were inseparable from the paranoia of male officials who contemplated the nonwhite masses beyond their control, especially indigenous women.[85] They viewed the women employing the local knowledge of curing and the sacred as savages engaged in dark arts to undermine patriarchal authority or attack personal enemies—hence the bruja label. In essence they represented the darkest extreme of evil in a polarized, race-obsessed conception of the supernatural and the social world. Witchcraft simultaneously activated fears of indigenous cultural independence, female weakness before the seductive arts of Satan, and nonwhite depravity. Much of this remained grounded in the assumption that women, left to their own devices, gravitated towards deviance. The linkage of popular healers to the devil weakened in the eighteenth century and nineteenth

century; the shift in terminology from *bruja* to *curandera* more or less re-
flects this development. Increasingly this figure became a symbol of stubborn popular culture. It is hardly surprising that healing and health concerns
of the poor should remain within the realm of curing and magic. In the
twentieth-century, *indigenista* (indigenist) nationalism celebrated local cur-
ers. For them the native curandera became a salt-of-the-earth, definitively
authentic figure. In fact, her healing arts represented "surviving" indigenous
wisdom for some. In this light, however, ambivalence endured: the curandera simultaneously served as an icon of folk authenticity and a symptom of
primitive backwardness.

MATIANA'S FORESIGHT IN HISTORICAL PERSPECTIVE

Although it seems exaggerated in hindsight, inquisitors tracking the Jesuit
restoration prophecies had good reason to proceed carefully: mystical narrative was part of a tradition that authorities took very seriously. Quite
simply, visionary stories deployed archetypal figures and conveyed religious standards of judgment that could help or hurt political regimes. The
Spanish monarchy made frequent use of them over several centuries.
Legends touted miraculous predictions of Spain's victory over their
Moorish enemies, and Crown-patronized seers delivered "fulfillment
prophecies" that spoke of the king's glorious destiny. Critics, however,
could also don the prophet's robes. They often faulted the moral character
of the establishment during crises, and they raised the specter of apocalyptic punishment (typically, the "loss of the kingdom"). In this way prophecy
represented a classic medium of dissident expression, a distancing device
for individuals to propose new ideas, and sometimes a group's attempt to
seize greater influence. In many cases the underlying political projects were
patently obvious, but they could prove difficult to disarm without recourse
to counterprophecy. Intellectuals and rulers could defend themselves with
biblical and legal arguments, but by definition divine revelation trumps all
precedent. Thus prophecy sometimes served as a means of short-circuiting
elite discourse, which invariably excluded much of the population.[86] Of
course, its reputation as the quintessential barometer of popular opinion
also made it attractive to dissidents.

Imperial Spain experienced a veritable fluorescence of doom-and-gloom
visionary activity. For much of the period, astrological predictions served as
the mainstay of popular almanacs. More polemically, though, as the empire

faced a series of setbacks in the late 1500s, social figures patterned after John the Baptist held forth on topics such as the nation's dissipation and corruption within the Church.[87] One of the more interesting predecessors of Madre Matiana was a Spanish laywoman, Lucrecia de León, who gained fame with elaborate prophetic dreams that criticized the royal government. According to historian Richard L. Kagan, from the very beginning a group of important clerics coached her, although she played the part of the simple conduit of divine wisdom drawn unwittingly into the limelight. In reality she was an intelligent young woman from an ambitious family. Explicitly citing previous prophecies critical of the Crown, she also spoke of a doomed kingdom and sketched a more equitable social world that probably reflected wider sentiments. Her predictions gained a sharp immediacy with the Spanish Armada's ignominious defeat in 1588, earning her inquisitorial persecution. Her prophetic career thus ended in torture, confession, and punitive labor. In essence, fame put Lucrecia before specialists trained to discredit presumptive mystics, and she faced the full range of delegitimizing strategies used against visionary women.[88]

The sad saga of Lucrecia de León also reveals a crucially important fact about prophetic and visionary endeavors. Despite folkloric portrayals to the contrary, they are usually collective, public pronouncements linked to groups with recognizable agendas. The solitary prophet of legend is, for the most part, only a mythic figure. Prophetic movements are typically framed in terms of an inspirational private experience, but visionary narratives represent mediating discourses that articulate a specific cause within society.[89] Typically the contributions of the invested social group surrounding the visionary were as important as the stories of foresight and the charismatic talents of seers.[90] This dynamic was undoubtedly in play in the emergence of the Matiana prophecies.

It is crucial, though, not to pigeonhole alleged visionary clairvoyance as a mere partisan smokescreen. To begin with the political prophecies are the most well known, thanks to the documentation generated in the conflicts surrounding them. Still it is important to keep in mind that historically Catholic countries remained deeply religious environments in the eighteenth and nineteenth centuries. Mexicans, for example, largely believed in a God determined to shape human affairs and revelation by communicating his divine plan. For the believing population, mystical prophecies forged a cognitive framework that linked the past and future: visions served as means to place lived experiences within the shared understandings of sacred history.

They also conveyed notions of morality and judgment, as well as standards of the divine and the damned. Through prophecy the faithful ascribed meaning to happenings and created order from experience, memory, and aspirations that they could project into the future. It was a tradition long admired and feared by the Catholic Church and nation-states because it could focus popular understandings but also frame sentiments against these institutions. Economic crisis, natural disaster, and political turmoil heightened the salience of prophetic narratives, but they did not evaporate during more stable times.[91]

Alas, there was no mid-nineteenth-century equivalent of the Holy Office of the Inquisition to investigate Madre Matiana's visions. No one compelled the abbess of San Jerónimo to come forward or convinced nuns to testify; nor did anyone depose the printers who marketed the prophecies. Ironically, inquisitorial interrogations concerning the Jesuit restoration prophecies took place in the Dominican convent a few blocks from the shops that printed and sold Matiana pamphlets several decades later. Lacking such nosy investigators, we must piece together Matiana's legacy from more disparate sources.

CHAPTER 2

The Protagonists of Print

OUTSIDE MEXICO'S GENDERED LEGACIES OF MYSTICAL PIETY AND prophecy, and the ever-latent political ramifications of both traditions, exploring the Matiana phenomenon entails scrutiny of a tumultuous twenty-year period (1847–1867). It was during this time span that the prophecies secured an emblematic niche in Mexican culture. Aside from the violent upheavals taking place between 1910 and 1930, there could hardly be a more volatile pair of decades in the nation's modern history. At present only three pamphlets and two almanacs where the prophecies of Madre Matiana appeared in their entirety seem to have survived from this era. While there may have been others, these texts from different publishers currently represent the pamphlet seer's evidentiary foundations. The pamphlets appeared in 1847, 1857, and 1861. The Matiana almanacs, the *Calendario nigromántico para el año 1858* and the *Calendario de la Madre Matiana para el año 1867*, were available for purchase in the last few months of 1857 and 1866.[1]

They may not seem to form a pattern at first, but to even the casual scholar of Mexican history the dates associated with these publications signal critical years in the nation's difficult nineteenth century. The first period marks when U.S. invasion made Mexicans fully and painfully aware of the depths of national disunity, as the government failed to organize an effective response. That shocking experience sparked anxious introspection and desperate actions across Mexico's ideological spectrum. The second pamphlet and the first almanac appeared amid the contentious promulgation of a new constitution in 1857, a year of previously unknown levels of polarization. As the prophecies circulated, conspiracies unfolded and Mexicans talked openly of civil war. Then, only days before the start of 1858, the nation plunged into a bloody three-year struggle. The rancor within this conflict stemmed from polemical reforms, which anchored the new national charter. In brief, the Constitution of 1857 sought to definitively subordinate the Catholic Church to the secular nation-state by curtailing Church wealth, limiting the political influence of clerics, and diminishing religion's salience in public life. The third pamphlet emerged during the fateful year of 1861, as liberal forces briefly held national power before French military intervention inaugurated yet another phase of warfare and the brief establishment of Maximilian of Habsburg's ill-fated Mexican empire. Not surprisingly, renewed violence further hardened ideological conflicts. Lastly the eponymous Matiana almanac appeared in the fall of 1866 as French troops withdrew and the emperor's regime disintegrated. Ironically, this publication's calendar listed Maximilian's saint day in bold type during the month of October, but by that date he had been dead for months, executed by a Mexican firing squad. Moreover, liberals had reinstated the Constitution of 1857, the secularizing charter alluded to by the Matiana prophecies. In sum, the seer's politically charged visions of violent strife were by no means simply eccentric penny-press stories. They were part and parcel of the intense ferment that epitomized these critical decades.

While presented as a colonial-era seer, Matiana was very much a creature of this more recent period of crisis. Her emergence just as internal strife, foreign invasion, and domestic polarization racked Mexican society suggests that these factors inspired the presumed authors of the Matiana narrative. Given the context, among the prime suspects for their fabrication are the pamphlet publishers themselves, perhaps in league with conservative ideologues and writers who had been publishing with these very same entrepreneurs for years. In fact, given how most prophecy narratives have roots in specific social groups (not simply a lone individual's mystical inspiration), this aggregation of actors represents the party most likely to deploy a visionary narrative for their cause. Alas, there is no "smoking gun," but the nineteenth-century printings and actions of one particular Matiana publicist, the Librería Abadiano, are available thanks to the fortuitous preservation of their holdings and records. The basic linkages between the prophecy narrative and nineteenth-century events are relatively obvious. Furthermore the seer's vilification of liberal reform and anticlericalism essentially rephrases the era's conservative talking points in a heated apocalyptic register. The evidence marshaled here suggests that the Abadiano family had both economic and ideological motives that may have been served by Madre Matiana's "timely emergence." The press and bookstore was a business still cast in the mold of colonial print commerce: Don Luis and his sons supplied religious and scholarly books for a relatively elite readership, printed devotional pamphlets for broader consumption, and offered printing services for Catholic institutions. Liberal reform, therefore, threatened their livelihood. In order to make this case, this chapter first provides a sketch of the historical context surrounding Matiana's emergence, and it subsequently analyzes the evidence surrounding the production and sale of the pamphlet prophecies. The almanacs, although equally important, were a different matter, as will be taken up in detail in chapter 3.

MEXICO'S FRAUGHT BEGINNINGS

Lurking in nearly every paragraph of the Matiana prophecies are a pair of specters that haunted nineteenth-century Mexico: endemic instability and a profound crisis of legitimacy. This does not mean that these issues necessarily caused the populace to embrace narratives of miraculous visionary foresight. In a country like Mexico where mysticism represented a time-honored and widely accepted cultural practice, it was natural for the nagging challenges of the day to emerge in prophetic narrative. What Matiana's alleged visions rub up against, therefore, are fundamental questions that confounded nineteenth-century Latin Americans, particularly in regard to the region's sustained instability after Independence. As we know, Madre Matiana offered a divine punishment theory of enduring volatility. Scholars, naturally, have proposed a set of earthly factors to explain Mexico's predicament.

The protracted struggle for independence indeed set the stage for the nation's tribulations. As historians have shown, the varied opponents of Spanish rule lacked shared ideological goals.[2] In reality Mexico experienced a divisive multifaceted struggle. In simplest terms, a relatively radical, but unfocused agrarian rebellion initially faced effective opposition from moderate and conservative Mexican-born elements allied with the Spanish Crown. With the exception of a small group of creole plotters, evidence suggests that few insurgents took up arms with the intention of independent nation-building. Deep colonial grievances and mounting local economic tensions fueled an explosion of violence grounded in very immediate concerns of basic subsistence and community cultural conflicts. Rebels, by and large, attacked colonial rule in hopes of reestablishing an imagined, just, local order, often somewhat utopian in nature. Evidence of an emergent national consciousness, shared political blueprint, or social consensus remains skeletal at best. In any case, the royalists crushed the first wave of revolution.

Once the threat of popular insurgency had been brutally neutralized, these same forces eventually turned against Spain, forged a tenuous agreement with remaining rebels, and proclaimed independence with essentially conservative objectives. A deliberately vague platform sought to limit fundamental change, as it proclaimed national sovereignty in the name of unity, religion, and customary corporate rights (i.e., special privileges enjoyed by groups like the clergy and military). In essence, what took place was a conservative coup that removed Mexico from Spain's perennial crises, while maintaining colonial social hierarchies and institutions. This arrangement put Mexican-born elites in power without addressing deep social grievances. Intellectuals and political leaders of the early 1820s were optimistic about the nation's fortunes even though unresolved tensions simmered barely below the surface. They viewed themselves as civic leaders well suited to enlightened governance. Furthermore, they considered their country a rich land of opportunity destined for prosperity. With a new constitution in 1824 that enshrined moderate republicanism and elite stewardship, few doubted that Mexico would emerge as a thriving and stable nation.[3]

The hope, which appears naïve in retrospect, was that with the distinctly nonwhite social rebellion suppressed and Spanish rule terminated, Mexico would quickly attain prosperity rooted in domestic control of the same resources that had made New Spain an important colony. Few understood how difficult it would be to revive the war-torn economy, mend a society scarred by counterinsurgency, or establish a new broadly legitimate, nation-state. In addition, deeper issues embedded in the era's political culture also hampered unity and stability.[4] Before Independence, much of Mexican society viewed governance with a jaundiced eye. Many experienced colonial rule as capricious, exclusionary, and corrupt. Established norms entailed gaming the system, securing preferential treatment whenever possible, and evading rulings when necessary. As a result the new nation could not count on a tradition of respect in regard to officeholders, institutions, or laws. Cynicism prevailed within the general populace and even among functionaries. Compounding this issue, widely held understandings of political philosophy undermined the legitimacy of the central government. Reaching back to Spanish tradition and fueled by pronounced regionalism, many Mexicans believed that sovereignty ultimately resided in municipal councils and elected local bodies rather than the nation-state.[5] As such states, cities, and sometimes even very small communities behaved as if they were countries in their own right. They often refused to cooperate with baseline national initiatives like coordinating national defense, regulating commerce, and collecting taxes. In addition to issues of competing sovereignties, many Mexicans remained committed to colonial-era corporate privileges, so they failed to embrace broader notions of collective responsibility.[6] In other words, colonial attitudes endured and shaped outcomes. Although often discussed in the abstract, many actors across the political spectrum did not internalize democratic, sociopolitical norms and notions of equality.[7] Finally the nineteenth-century Mexican elite were simply too divided in terms of social origin, ideology, and regionalist allegiances to forge a stable political system. Division at the top, not surprisingly, created opportunities for popular revolts fueled by unresolved grievances.[8] Complicating matters still further were the ambitions of foreign nations, such as the United States and France.

It is best to think of all of these factors simultaneously at work. This situation also coincided with the emergence of a diverse, combative press, which claimed to speak for the populace despite only incipient means of gauging public opinion. Governments were chronically insecure about their status relative to changing public sentiment, and anxious about important groups (such as the clergy) deemed potentially capable of shaping popular attitudes. In this context, state actors often clumsily sought to control opinion while their opponents labored to sow discord.[9] This often led to a political climate where governments lashed out at perceived threats, conspiracy theory was essentially endemic, and actual sedition was intermittently in the works. Together these factors created fertile conditions for all manner of political rumor and innuendo.[10]

In fact, a standard subversive tactic was to exaggerate reports of uprisings and impending regime collapse. Naturally governments downplayed the seriousness of revolts, as they sought to suppress claims to the contrary. In fact, one way to categorize the prophecies of Madre Matiana is as a kind of antigovernment rumor, or in the Mexican argot of the era, a *borrego*. Literally this term means "sheep," but figuratively it referred to an unsubstantiated story loose in society, and by implication hard to apprehend or contain. Hence pithy phrases like "*soltar un borrego*" ("let loose a rumor") and "*soltar un borrego lanudo*" ("let loose a wooly sheep," or really outlandish rumor) appeared with some frequency during the era.[11] Moreover, in 1870 the satirists at *El Boquiflojo* used the dismissive phrase "*salió borrego*" (denoting what was once considered true and since proven false) explicitly in reference to Madre Matiana's prophecies.[12] Given the rudimentary means of communication and the general skepticism afforded the press, Mexican

communities were awash in political gossip, troubling hearsay, and conflicting speculation. Feeding the cycle was the knowledge that every so often a
seemingly outrageous borrego proved correct.

To approach the more immediate context of Matiana's publication, a pair
of provisos is in order. There are two interrelated misconceptions that remain
difficult to dispel and thus cloud the understanding of nineteenth-century
Mexico. The first is a tendency to depict the nation's experience of instability
as simply chaotic.[13] The second, and perhaps even more stubborn, misconcep-
tion emerges from the scholarly propensity to take the liberal-conservative
conflict of the mid-1850s and anachronistically project it onto the previous
generations.[14] This leads to deterministic depictions of a two-sided sectarian
conflict culminating in civil war and the defeat of conservatism in 1867. In
reality it was a much more complex, agonizing process.[15]

In truth most influential Mexican political actors prior to 1846 occupied
an amorphous ideological center characterized by many small factions. Very
few sought the wholesale abandonment of the colonial order, and most embraced essentially "conservative" social ideas.[16] In general terms this group
loosely adhered to a very moderate liberalism in the realm of economics and
political philosophy, as well as a foundational conservatism in regard to social norms. Instead of viewing Mexico's volatility as the result of petty war-
lord chaos or the product of two discrete ideological camps locked in
decades-long combat, it is more useful to think in terms of an intricate multi-
stranded instability, which gradually stoked polarization and a drift toward
more extreme solutions.

In other words, before going to war with the United States, Mexico featured
a loosely defined, small elite that was searching for a formula of stable governance and development. For the most part, this was a group numbering only
a few thousand individuals in the 1830s.[17] Known at the time as *hombres de
bien* (men of rank), they viewed themselves as the appropriate stewards of society, and they shared rather modest goals. These men wanted to keep pace
with political and economic innovations elsewhere but dreaded fundamental
social change. Mexico, most of them assumed, was a Catholic nation with laws
and customs grounded in Hispanic tradition. Furthermore, most political actors felt the Church should be protected by the state in some fashion, although
they debated the degree of control that government should exercise. In general
they had internalized Spanish liberalism and its elitist framing of representative government. Finally, nearly all of Mexico's elite believed it was important
to protect property rights and support capitalist development. To be sure there

were vocal minorities on the fringes who cultivated intransigence of one stripe or another. There was no shortage of opportunists and profiteers either. In addition, popular movements undermined elite calculations, championing their own ideas concerning property, power, citizenship, and governance. Periodically such groups took up arms and became part of the matrix of challenges that occasionally spelled doom for particular administrations.[18]

These factors, however, do not amount to aimless anarchy or to a bipartite factional endgame. In reality most groups longed for a government strong enough to coordinate administration, organize economic development, and carry out cogent fiscal management. But regardless of ideological formulae, or policies employed, central control remained a fiction: the rule of law was largely symbolic, and national power remained theoretical. To put it bluntly, the Mexican nation-state appeared trapped in an embryonic stage. Successive governments almost immediately found themselves plagued by opposing factions and their basic legitimacy under assault. Frequently, administrative paralysis ensued. As a result autocratic solutions became increasingly alluring across the ideological spectrum, and most political actors were willing to sacrifice their principles for the promise of secure control.[19] Given this context, by the time Madre Matiana's prophecies appeared in 1847 the optimism of 1824 had been replaced by a general malaise, if not outright despair.[20] And despair, it turns out, only fed polarization.

In truth it is very difficult to disentangle the ideological currents of the time. Reaching back to the eighteenth century, historians have detailed the inseparable nature of Catholicism and Mexican political thought during the era. Influential clerics and devout laymen were instrumental participants in colonial reform debates and nineteenth-century liberalism's evolution. Moreover, religious ideologies grounded debate across society.[21] Likewise, evidence suggests that the nation's conservative movement emerged from within evolving liberalism only after disillusionment set in. Still it did not achieve a distinct political identity until the late 1840s, when U.S. invasion and annexation of half the national territory shook Mexican society to its core.[22] As this movement gained adherents in the wake of catastrophe, it claimed the mantle of pragmatism and argued that given disunity and the nation's existential vulnerability it was time to abandon abstract theories and utopian reformism. Instead emergent conservatives called for a politics attuned to the "true" character and historical experience of the populace. More than deep ideological consensus or antirepublican conviction, it was a profound fear of deeper social unrest and further American expansionism that inspired calls for strictly limited

democracy, dictatorship, and Catholic monarchy among various conservatives.[23] These same acute apprehensions ultimately bolstered a broad willingness among moderate liberals as well as conservatives to collaborate with
French-backed imperialism in the 1860s.[24]

In a similarly paradigm-muddying development, research also shows that
the most prominent radical liberal of the 1830s and 1840s, Valentín Gómez
Farías (1781–1858), was in fact rather moderate. Even though opponents
tarred him as a Jacobin firebrand, he actually sought gradual change and
compromise.[25] In truth he never held power for long enough to enact his vision for the nation, but when given a chance he pressed for federalism, equality before the law, broader political participation, and limits on the Catholic
clergy's power and religious institutions' ability to hold property. As with the
term "conservative," the label "moderate liberal" emerged rather late, in 1838.
Moreover, during the early 1840s this group differed little in terms of policy
stance from avowed centralists (those who later became known as conservatives) or the followers of General Antonio López de Santa Anna (1794–1876).
Most liberals generally sought order first and foremost while theoretically
supporting democratizing reforms in a vaguely defined future.[26] As was the
case with conservatives, scholars point to 1846 as the pivotal moment when
a new generation of "radical" liberals (the so-called *puros*) began to coalesce
around notions of fundamental transformation.[27]

In sum, the late 1840s represents the watershed moment when Mexico
began heading toward the clash of two bellicose camps that would characterize the 1850s. Mexico's social fabric had suffered considerable stress, but it
was during the U.S.–Mexican War that it truly began to disintegrate. Even so
compromise still seemed possible, and even desirable, for many conservatives until 1854. Between 1854 and 1857 conservatives (particularly religious
conservatives) became increasingly alarmed at the ascendency of radical liberalism and turned against conciliation.[28] Thus Madre Matiana was "born"
at a historical juncture when the post-Independence political class's ambigu-
ous cohesion became untenable, and mounting intransigence began carrying
Mexico toward civil war.

PROFITS AND THE PROPHETESS

Documentation related to the prophecies points to the street directly behind
Mexico City's cathedral. Calle de las Escalerillas (today the Avenida República
de Guatemala) had long sheltered a concentration of down-market printing

establishments. The most renowned printer-booksellers preferred the tony arcades located a few blocks away at the southwest corner of the *zócalo* (main square).[29] In a sense Escalerillas was a perfect locale for the seer's emergence: only steps from the nation's colossal "mother church," the prophetess elbowed her way into the public sphere as she predicted the triumph of Catholicism over modern error. In this veritable thicket of fellow wordsmiths, the earliest Matiana pamphlet producers worked within shouting distance of each other. From Escalerillas 2, the presses of Valdés y Redondas unleashed Madre Matiana in 1847, amid U.S. invasion and an urban uprising in the streets of Mexico City. Down the street at number 13, Luis Abadiano y Valdés subsequently issued a nearly identical pamphlet in 1857, as a truly national civil war appeared inevitable. We know next to nothing about the former pamphlet, although it is quite possible that it emerged from a brief partnership between Leandro J. Valdés and Manuel Fernández Redondas, two active mid-nineteenth-century printers.[30] The latter, however, represents a well-heeled resident of this printer's alley. Abadiano, as noted previously, actually purchased newspaper advertisements to announce the availability of the prophecies, entrenched as they were in the sabre rattling and scheming that dominated the summer and fall of 1857.[31] Like other successful printers, he maintained a separate bookstore. In fact, his store had been a fixture of Mexican print commerce for decades. Don Luis's uncle, Alejandro Valdés—the one-time official printer of Agustín de Iturbide's administration (1821–1822)—founded his own shop in the waning days of Spanish rule.[32] The bookstore, initially known as the Librería de Valdés and eventually renamed the Librería Abadiano, stood around the corner from Escalerillas 13 at Santo Domingo 12.[33] It was there that Mexicans could purchase a copy of the prophecies for 1 real (one-eighth of a peso). Looking back it is impossible to pinpoint with absolute certainty what set the pamphlet prophetess on the road to notoriety. However, like many ordinary happenings that later accrue historical significance, it probably had much to do with the unique context of the moment. The Abadiano's republication of the prophecies in mid-1857 coincided with swelling crisis and uncertainty—conditions that seem in retrospect tailor-made for doom-and-gloom visionary expression. Instability alone, though, was clearly not enough. If so, Madre Matiana and her predictions would have garnered much more attention in 1847. As any purveyor of media knows (both then and now), marketing matters. Someone at the Librería Abadiano recognized the auspicious nature of the moment and took action. In sum, credit should probably go to the synergy of acute social crisis and energetic commercial promotion with the inauguration of Matiana's enduring legacy.

Peddling the printed word was a growing but risky economic venture in mid-nineteenth-century Mexico. The viceregal seat turned national capital had long been a center of printing in the Americas, but the new century saw Mexico increasingly take part in the expansion and diversification of print capitalism. In the colonial period religious institutions served as the primary consumers of printed material. The first half of the nineteenth century stands out as a crucial period of experimentation. New technologies, markets, products, and reading spaces facilitated the spread of ideas and the gradual establishment of a modernized, shared culture in Mexico. However, it was hardly a straightforward process. Independence did indeed bring a period of innovation, but older ideas and forms of expression endured. Indicative of attitudes at the time, the era's print capitalists simultaneously spurred the emergence of a secular public culture while preserving longstanding religious printing traditions. This was simply a matter of basic business sense at the time—such was the Mexican market.

Moreover, as historians of the press in Mexico have stressed, pamphleteering, book publication, and journalism often proved controversial and printers struggled amid turmoil.[34] Press freedoms waxed and waned during the period. Phases of wide open, combative expression gave way to periods of stifling government censorship.[35] Many publishers experienced harassment, incarceration, and/or exile during the period. Nonetheless, the broader processes of change remained largely market driven. Political administrations in Mexico were often short-lived and weak. Although governments tried to dictate public opinion, the state never established sustained control over expression. Instead a loose-knit collection of individuals, mostly ensconced within a handful of blocks around the zócalo, shaped Mexican print culture while trying to secure profits, outflank rivals, and settle political scores. Though they competed fiercely, on the whole the publishers' goals remained broadly nationalist. Borrowing freely—in terms of style, content, and technology—from North American and European publications, they endeavored to simultaneously invent the nation, promote traditional materials, and create new products that the diverse people now called Mexicans would purchase.[36]

In a statistical analysis of nineteenth-century printing, historian Nicole Girón estimated that Valdés y Redondas published only seven pamphlets or so per year, although they surely engaged in other kinds of print business.[37] In contrast, the Abadianos (Don Luis and his sons) produced approximately

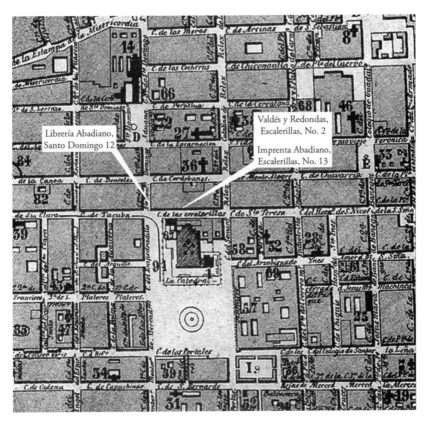

Map 1. Mexico City, 1851. The streets near the *zócalo* (central plaza) were thick with printers during the 1800s. Escalerillas, where the Abadianos' workshop resided behind the cathedral, was the low-budget "printers' alley." Their bookshop was around the corner on Santo Domingo. Many other printers clustered around the Santo Domingo plaza a block to the north. The most prestigious print entrepreneurs maintained stores in and around the arcades in the southwestern corner of the *zócalo*. Their presses were often located in the blocks to the south and west of their shops. Courtesy of the Archivo Histórico del Distrito Federal.

190 pamphlets per year. Larger ventures such as theirs were much more than just printers and book dealers.[38] Archival documents related to the Librería Abadiano's business practices reveal that they produced the entire gamut of custom-made invitations, announcements, forms, and flyers. They also manufactured almanacs, bibles, political tracts, devotional manuals, government bulletins, and literature (often serialized). In addition, printers marketed engravings and prints, and they offered bindery services.[39] Beyond on-site

production and sales, they also imported books, purchased and resold local collections, and maintained large holdings for consultation.[40] Additionally Mexico City's printers owned, edited, and produced the capital's newspapers and imported foreign periodicals. These multifaceted commercial interests, and the nature of their work as information clearinghouses, made the capital's printing businesses nodes of intellectual ferment. In many ways they were simultaneously publishers, libraries, salons, and newsrooms where important figures gathered. As recent scholarship shows, they brought together politicians, ideologues, writers, and prominent churchmen.[41] In these environs important individuals developed friendships and cultivated enmities. Not surprisingly different shops established reputations based on the materials they published and their perceived ideological leanings. Often competitors, both political and commercial, worked only a handful of blocks, or just a few buildings, away from each other.

The period from 1810 to 1867, then, proved a dynamic time for print entrepreneurs. Instability and changing press laws brought a real risk of economic ruin and persecution. However, these factors also served to focus the writing and printing on the nation's alleged problems. Moreover, as the present and the following chapter will demonstrate, authors and editors believed they could inspire cohesion and convince Mexicans to unite around their respective visions of political and social order.

The period truly appears, from a present-day vantage point, as fertile ground for political prophecy, and naturally there had been precursory rumblings. According to historian Donald F. Stevens, voices within the Catholic Church invoked the specter of divine punishment when Gómez Farías's first attempts at liberal reform coincided with the cholera epidemic of 1833.[42] In a similar vein, Mexicans could purchase a pamphlet in 1841 that relayed a French priest's calculations that predicted the world would come to an end in 1860; naturally, the text alluded to an Anti-Christ-dominated time of troubles leading up to the ominous date.[43] Among more committed traditionalists rancorous anxieties clearly intensified from the 1830s onward. This is palpable in a pamphlet produced by Alejandro Valdés's press in 1834 (precisely as Luis Abadiano y Valdés was taking charge of his recently deceased uncle's business), which testifies to the emergent fault lines. In this particular publication, the author—protected by the pseudonym "*Uno de Tantos*" ("One of Many")—lashes out at the state of Veracruz's new laws. These reforms aimed to curtail monastic orders because of the alleged irrationality of monastic celibacy, as well as accusations of indolence and subversion on the part of friars in general. Allowing that some monks were indeed shiftless and immoral, the pamphlet argued that the real motivation behind new anticlerical laws was greed and veiled, spiteful atheism: "Let us, then, [call] out the impious, because all the arguments of the rabid *fratima-niacos* are little more than patent absurdities, ineptitudes, lies, and ridiculousness. What in actual truth enflames them against the friars, and what they try very hard not to show, is a wicked desire to gain control of their property, a rabid atheism that hates all that belongs to God and to religion, and a damning and devouring jealousy that eats away at their insides and dismantles their hearts."[44]

On the national level, the successful bid for independence in Texas in 1836 also caused a stir, but invasion by the United States from 1846 to 1848 and the humiliating alienation of approximately half the national territory caused broad disillusionment. Equally galling was the fact that Mexicans proved unable to set aside their partisan squabbles in the face of national crisis. For example, in January 1847, as U.S. troops advanced into Mexican territory, National Guard units in Mexico City rose up against the acting president, the liberal Gómez Farías. The committed reformer had returned to power alongside General Santa Anna and moved to expropriate funds from Church institutions to finance the nation's defense, enraging the Church and its supporters.[45] Funded surreptitiously by high-level clergymen, this uprising—known as the Revolt of the Polkos—led to intense street fighting in the capital. Eventually Santa Anna obliged the mutineers and deposed Gómez Farías, but he could not undo the harm done to the war effort. Events such as this left many Mexicans at the time exasperated by the state of political dysfunction; many wondered if the nation could endure.[46] On the one hand, disunity plagued the capital, but also regional separatism in such places like Tabasco and Yucatán threatened further fragmentation.[47] Moreover, many Mexicans believed that the United States remained intent on seizing still more territory after 1848.[48]

Beyond the loss of territory and troops, the U.S.–Mexican War truly catalyzed intellectual ferment.[49] Previous ideological commitments had been fluid, and deep critical thinking about the state and its relationship to society had been limited. The crushing defeat led to a rethinking of Mexico's predicament and sharper distinctions. In short order an array of newspapers took up a particularly intense and pointed revival of perennial debates centered on precisely which government structures, ideological bases, and sociocultural order would foster national unity and prosperity.

It was in this context that a formally organized conservative party first emerged in 1848. In simplest terms the coalescing movement repudiated the nation's experiment in liberal governance, which critics defined as foreign inspired and hopelessly ill-suited to Mexican society and culture. They held that the weakening of traditional authority since Independence, glib talk of liberties and social equality, and steps toward mass political participation only encouraged disorder among the uncivilized rabble and opportunism among arriviste demagogues. The spreading of liberal ideas, conservatives argued, was catalyzing an individualist free-for-all and rampant disregard for faith and authority. The result was a debilitating spiral of moral decay and disorder that left the nation vulnerable to North American depredation. The only means to rally the nation, conservatives claimed, was a return to Hispanic traditions of strong central authority, state protection of existing hierarchies, and fervent Catholicism. Religion and vigilant priestly guidance, they contended, was the surest means to hold the diverse populace together and keep them in check.

The period after the U.S.–Mexican War also featured an ascendant generation of more radical liberals. They blamed an imagined traitorous nexus within the Mexican polity, arguing that reactionary elites, particularly the high clergy and elements of the military, remained bent on sustaining aristocracy, protecting ill-gotten wealth, and safeguarding the means to exploit society. In short, they accused opponents of seeking to maintain the colonial order at all costs, even if it required them to undermine the nation's defenses. According to this viewpoint, conservatives schemed against the government during the U.S. invasion in order to achieve narrow self-interests. Moreover, puros alleged, the Church cultivated superstitious beliefs among the masses to blunt social change and keep the ignorant in thrall. For radicals embracing this analysis, it was imperative to definitely humble the Church and the army with unflinching reform. This alone, they argued, would establish conditions under which unity and stability would take hold.

In sum, each group blamed the other for the nation's defeat at the hands of the United States and for abiding turmoil. Likewise, these factions pressed for unmitigated authority to impose their vision on the nation, and each side crafted a skewed national history to ground their claims. Political shelter for those that favored conciliation and flexibility shrank steadily as liberals gained the upper hand in the mid-1850s; by 1857 it disappeared altogether.[50]

In a sense the prophecies of Madre Matiana appeared a little too soon, and as a result the 1847 pamphlet inspired little or no response. (I have not been able to find even a single mention of the prophecies between 1847 and 1857). Perhaps Valdés y Redondas printed too few, or quite likely a "coalition" of prophecy promoters had yet to take shape. Affinities, however, suggest that the Revolt of the Polkos may have inspired the first pamphlet printing. Although never mentioned in the Matiana texts, a set of factors suggest some degree of correlation between the insurrection and the seer's message. First, there is the obvious fact that the revolt and the pamphlet's initial publication occurred in 1847. Second, they share a certain thematic overlap as both the prophecies and the plotters attacked government attempts to confiscate Church property. Third, the visions described fighting in the streets of the capital, perhaps alluding to what Mexico City witnessed in early 1847. Finally, as historian Michael P. Costeloe has shown, the insurrectionists were linked to individuals who sought to protect female religious orders: the churchmen who orchestrated fundraising efforts for the mutinous guardsmen were convent administrators.[51] These individuals, in turn, enjoyed the support of the archdiocese's capitular vicar, Juan Manuel Irissari—the very same official named in the Matiana pamphlets. Nonetheless, these connections do not rise beyond circumstantial evidence.

In any case, the consequences of the U.S.–Mexican War were not yet fully manifest in 1847. Most likely the reality of territorial loss and the newly intense partisanship following defeat had yet to set the conditions that later vaulted Madre Matiana to fame. Nonetheless, it is telling that her narrative of celestial punishment surfaced as U.S. armies marched on the capital. The first Matiana decade, then, coincides with a wholly new era of accelerating polarization, which featured four distinct phases: first, a period of intense debate from 1847 to 1853 as moderates attempted to reestablish political calm amid puro and conservative criticism; second, Santa Anna's last military coup and presidency (1853–1854), which featured an attempt to inaugurate a conservative autocracy; third, a period of broad liberal uprising in 1854 and 1855 that deposed the dictatorial general. Victory, however, immediately revealed rifts between moderate and radical liberals. The former, represented by Ignacio Comonfort (1812–1863), secured the executive branch. For a time conservatives were willing to abide his government under the assumption that Comonfort would restrain the radicals, but this calculation proved erroneous. Committed puros shaped the legislation that emerged from the new congress—which excluded conservatives—and brought on the highly contentious fourth phase spanning from 1855 to 1857. During this time liberals issued their Laws of the Reform, as they were known, which sketched a restructuring of the institutional bases of Mexican society. The culminating moment for the puro reformers was the promulgation of a secularizing constitution on 5 February 1857; it incorporated the polemical laws to separate church and state definitively and codified the curtailment of Church wealth. Conservative Catholics looked on in anger and growing frustration. They upbraided Comonfort for failing to rein in radicals and branded the constitution a wildly irrational and impious act of self-destructive madness. Loudly they warned that it fatally undermined the cultural and moral foundations of Mexican society.

The next decade provided a bleak fulfillment of the widely acknowledged fears of a new round of intense social strife. First Comonfort overthrew his own government on 17 December 1857, with moderate liberal and conservative support, claiming that the new constitution was unworkable and too destabilizing. Within weeks, though, conservative forces deposed him and war began in earnest.[52] The Three Years War, as it came to be known, would prove to be the most intense civil conflict that Mexico had experienced since the Wars of Independence. Liberals achieved a brief victory in 1861, only to return to years of battle within months when French armies invaded. Emperor Napoleon III, at the time seeking to establish a new imperial sphere of influence in the Americas, took advantage of Mexico's weakness to oust the liberals and form a monarchy in alliance with Mexican conservatives. After three years of warfare, Napoleon's armies controlled most of Mexico and offered the crown to Austrian Archduke Maximilian of Habsburg in 1864. Subsequently many conservatives and moderate liberals accepted posts in the new government. However, France's military entanglements in Europe led to Napoleon's withdrawal of troops in 1865, which allowed liberal militias to gradually regain power. When the militias finally captured Maximilian in 1867, the violence and resentment had reached unprecedented levels. The emperor had decreed that liberal combatants were mere bandits subject to summary execution, and in retaliation, numerous conservative fighters and eventually the Archduke himself faced the firing squad.[53] Surviving conservatives and other collaborators bore the stigma of treason for decades.[54] Furthermore, many liberal commanders spitefully targeted the Catholic Church as never before, hoping to terminate the clergy's ability to support the conservative cause. Often they brusquely expropriated and sold off the holdings of religious institutions when occupying a region. Willing speculators typically purchased said properties at well below market rates, while commanders gave little thought to the potential local impact of these sales.[55]

Mexicans, in reality, did not need Matiana's prophecies to announce the coming of civil war in 1857. Well before Comonfort's fateful overthrow of his own government, newspapers openly discussed the inevitability of armed violence.[56] The thinly veiled threats, rumored uprisings, and conspiratorial plotting truly formed the backdrop of the Librería Abadiano's marketing of Matiana pamphlets, and it probably fueled sales. Undoubtedly the printer took into account the prophecies' predictions about a future year ending in the number eight when they decided to produce the pamphlets, but they did not alter the first printing in any way. Given that various versions of the prophecies and references to the prophetess in the press followed on the heels of this publication, it likely marks the moment when Madre Matiana made her first indelible mark in Mexican popular culture. Subsequently the brutal warfare from 1857 to 1867 did much to secure her reputation. In sum, in terms of attacks on the Church and clergy and the sheer volume of bloodshed, the prophecies indeed appeared prescient.

THE LIBRERÍA ABADIANO

The basic motive behind the prophecies—to dampen the advance of liberalism and undermine the legitimacy of reformist government—is transparent. However, the pamphlet's conceptualization remains a mystery. Without going too far out on a limb, it is safe to assume that the target audience was the devout public, both humble and affluent—in brief, those most inclined to seriously absorb mystical narratives. Considering the profoundly religious culture of the era and its deep mystical traditions, the potential audience for the prophecies, as reading material or in the retelling, was probably larger than those who routinely purchased newspapers.[57] It is quite possible that the printers were complicit in the fabrication of Matiana's visions, but publishing the pamphlets alone is not sufficient evidence of deeper involvement. Again, there is a lack of correspondence, receipts, or institutional documentation concerning the prophecies' actual production, but a wealth of newspapers and publications from the era allow us to gauge printing patterns related to them. Moreover, archival documents preserved by the Librería Abadiano's 1889 liquidation and sale to a North American collector confirm that Matiana's message corresponded with the printer's politics.[58]

When considering the post-Enlightenment surge in print capitalism worldwide, scholars generally assume it brought with it the secularization of print commerce. Indeed, it is true that much of the expansion took place in nominally secular writing such as political journalism, scientific texts, commercial printing, and literature. In Mexico, devotional publications and Church-affiliated patronage of printers' services changed little before 1820. At the Librería Abadiano and its predecessor, the Librería Valdés, religious tracts dominated production. In fact the bookstore at Santo Domingo 12 was perhaps the most important purveyor of textual materials for clergymen during the two generations previous, and probably much longer. The printing business that Luis Abadiano took over had endured almost as if it had been a landed estate, passed down over generations and occasionally merged with others. Its lineage reaches back to a bookstore and press established in 1631.[59] In the 1700s María de Rivera, a descendent of the original founder, took ownership and secured an exclusive license to produce official prayer materials, such as missals, breviaries, and a range of other liturgical supplies. In the late 1760s an enterprising print entrepreneur named José de Jáuregui (a nephew of Rivera's) purchased and merged the Imprenta de la Bibliotheca Mexicana (founded in 1753 by Juan José de Eguiara y Eguren) with his aunt's establishment.[60] Years later one of his heirs, the clergyman José Fernández de Jáuregui, ran the business. After his death in 1800, his sister María Fernández de Jáuregui took over until her own passing in 1815. The Jáureguis were still publishing devotional materials, although it was no longer a monopoly. In any case, the bookstore remained a veritable center of Church-affiliated print commerce. Before 1817 when he purchased the store and press from doña María's heirs, Alejandro Valdés worked with his father, the famed printer Manuel Antonio Valdés y Munguía, a Jáuregui competitor.[61] The younger Valdés secured the bookstore, all the equipment, and a vast stock of merchandise. The remarkable inventory from this transfer lists hundreds of books and thousands of novenas, printed religious images, and devotional pamphlets. All told, assessors valued this haul at about 31,000 pesos.[62]

Even without the official monopoly of the colonial era, it seems likely that Alejandro Valdés also inherited much of the clientele accustomed to doing business at the bookstore on Calle de Santo Domingo, as well as the prestige he enjoyed thanks to his father's reputation. As the inventory reveals, he certainly had an impressive storehouse of religious writings, and his role as the official printer of the government of Emperor Agustín de Iturbide (1821–1823) attests to his stature. Valdés died in 1831 leaving his nephew, Don Luis, and two subsequent generations of Abadianos to sustain the bookshop and printing press after a seven-year period of transition.[63] Over two hundred extant receipts from 1835 through 1844 reveal that 79 percent of them were for explicitly religious texts or printing jobs commissioned by Catholic institutions. In most years it was over 80 percent of the total business, but in 1837 only 57 percent of the documented print jobs were Church related.[64] During that year Don Luis Abadiano may have enjoyed particularly good connections inside the government, because more commissions from state entities appear than in other years.[65]

Of course, there is no way to know for certain if these receipts are representative of the shop's total production, because some records were probably lost. However, these slips of paper and other documents suggest that the Librería Abadiano was following in the footsteps of their colonial predecessors, as they focused their efforts on the traditional market niches: religious books for the educated elite, cheaper devotional materials for the wider populace, and general printing services for religious orders. Some of their competitors, most famously Ignacio Cumplido, were betting on innovation and new kinds of merchandise, such as literary magazines, lithographed picture books, and encyclopedia-like collections.[66] This does not mean that the Abadianos were stubborn or foolish. In fact, the more innovative products their competitors favored were often risky investments, whereas the market for "traditional" printed materials was steady, although not always lucrative, throughout the century.

Aside from receipts for specific orders, costs and revenue for various weeks were noted on thick wads of index card–sized slips. Although the value of Mexico's currency undoubtedly fluctuated—with the general economic turmoil caused by political instability making any comparisons impressionistic at best—these records indicate that liberal reforms damaged the Abadianos' livelihood. Tallies from 1839 and 1840 show the press frequently netted profits of 60 to 80 pesos a week, and occasionally over 100.[67] Income then declined in the 1850s. After accounting for costs and worker's salaries during several weeks in 1853 the Abadianos typically made only 37 to 49 pesos, although on at least one occasion they cleared only 21 pesos and on another they surpassed 50.[68] In 1854 more or less typical profits varied between 25 and 45 pesos, with occasional stronger weeks. In the spring and summer of 1856 the printer's income fell off considerably, probably due to mounting certainty that civil war was immanent amid the implementation of the Laws of the Reform. By 1858 hostilities had broken out and meager profits of 10 pesos a week had become the norm.[69] The steadiest source of income for the Librería Abadiano seems to have been the printing of lottery tickets for the government. (War, apparently, did not curb the urge to gamble.) The unrest weathered by all Mexicans must have been a main factor. Still the expropriations of Church wealth by both conservatives and liberals and the suppression of religious orders would have hit the Abadianos particularly hard. Did these patterns influence the printer's decision to publish and advertise Madre Matiana's prophecies? It is impossible to know for sure, but it appears that liberal reform was altering the marketplace. Given the patterns of economic contraction revealed by receipts of the 1830s and 1840s, laws that weakened religious orders must have adversely impacted printers like the Abadianos. At the very least hawking doom-and-gloom prophecies as the nation lurched towards war in 1857 would have brought in crucial income. If by some means the pamphlets bolstered conservative chances of victory and the restoration of traditional Catholic institutions, the Adadianos would have likely been pleased.

The book marketing and publishing legacy of the Abadianos is replete with religious titles, but this is true of many printers at the time. Quite simply, Mexico's reading culture remained closely tied to Catholic education and devotional practice. Still, one is hard pressed to find liberal political tracts produced by the Abadianos' presses. More importantly, other kinds of documents reveal a commitment to conservative causes. First, both Don Luis and his son, Francisco Abadiano, appear among the Mexicans who actively lobbied for the reestablishment of the Jesuit order after its colonial-era expulsion. In many ways La Compañía served as the nerve center of the Church's revitalization internationally during this period. Jesuits represented the intellectual vanguard, who were reshaping social thought and religious practice to align with the swelling Ultramontane revivalism throughout the Catholic world at the time.[70] After Independence, restoring the Jesuits became a cause célèbre among activist Catholics in Mexico. At a deeper level it also represented an attempt to roll back precedent-setting exertions of state power over the Church that had begun before Independence.[71]

The Abadianos, evidence shows, took part in these efforts. Curiously, this advocacy hints at the possibility of deeper historical family ties to the black-robed fathers. Their ancestor, Manuel Antonio Valdés (the father of Alejandro Valdés), had been educated by the Jesuits and administered the order's printing press at the time of the order's expulsion in 1767.[72] In the early 1850s, the Abadianos printed two lengthy publications aimed at different audiences. The first was a 175-page treatise in support of the Jesuit restoration with an intended audience of politicians and intellectuals versed in law and constitutional theory.[73] The second adopted the fallback format of nineteenth-century pamphleteers hoping to engage a more humble audience, the popular dialogue. In this case it featured a 126-page discussion between a barber and one of his patrons, where they aired and refuted criticisms of the Jesuits. Ironically by making the text so long and detailed they probably nullified any popular impact they hoped to achieve.[74] Regardless the text documents an attempt to change the public's ideas about the Jesuits. Finally, the best evidence of the Abadianos' pro-Church commitment resides in an open letter published in September 1853, thanking then-president Santa Anna for allowing La Compañía to return. Both father and son appear among the many signatories and the Abadianos published this document.[75] In other words, Don Luis and Don Francisco publically affirmed their support for the institutional champions of conservative Catholic revival.

It is also tempting to impute a real political fervor to the Abadianos given some of the publications they produced during civil unrest. One such printing was a February 1859 sermon that simultaneously celebrated the Virgin Mary and recent conservative military victories. It also taunted liberals at a moment when conservatives controlled Mexico City and gives us a glimpse of the conservative mindset. As the preacher Father José Sánchez inveighed: "And you libertines listening, what say you? You accuse us of being fanatics; is that not true? Maybe our acts of piety inspire mirth. . . . And if you long for the recent era that we just left behind, your memories are repulsive. Because at that time, by lamentable disgrace, the magistrates perpetrated the most sacrilegious attacks that shocked even the most depraved hearts. . . . Have shame, vile followers of Satan! You say you have no need of Mary's aid, and because of this the only thing covering you is reproach."[76] At the climax of this homily, Sánchez, seemingly echoing Madre Matiana's prophecies, placed the blame for the nation's troubles on appalling anticlerical impieties. In addition, he implied that Mexico was facing divine punishments while proclaiming that Marian intercession had kept the nation from absolute calamity: "Is it not true that in the past attempts were made to disappear from this temple this [image of our] graceful Lady? And also did not public officials with despicable hypocrisy, tricking this sanctuary, abusing the good faith of the bishops, become hostile to Religion to such a degree as to apprehend the ministers of God and exile the shepherds of Jesus Christ's flock? Then our sufferings are nothing but the daughters of insolence, because if it were not for Mary as intercessor, Mexico would have drowned already due to incalculable misfortune."[77]

LIBRERIA

DE FRANCISCO ABADIANO.

1ª calle de Santo Domingo n. 12.

En esta librería, que cuenta de existencia desde principios del siglo pasado, tiene un gran surtido de obras anti-
guas y modernas sobre Historia y lenguas del país, exposi-
tores de escritura, Santos Padres, obras predicables y otras
eclesiásticas, rezos y novenas de toda la corte celestial, en
fin, cuanto puede necesitar un buen católico y un hombre
instruido,

Se compran libros y se hacen avalúos.

Se reciben suscriciones á "la Religion y la Sociedad,"
que se publica en Guadalajara, y á "la Ilustracion Ame-
ricana."

Figure 3. An advertisement for the Librería Abadiano, 1866. This ad conveys the Abadiano's specialization in gentleman's Catholic printed materials. It reads: "This bookstore . . . has an extensive selection of ancient and modern works about the history and languages of the nation, interpretations of scripture, [and the] Holy Fathers; preaching texts and other ecclesiastical works, prayers and novenas of all celestial types, in short, all that could be needed by a good Catholic and educated man." It also notes that customers could arrange for subscriptions to Catholic periodicals at the bookstore. From *Calendario del Gran Avisador para el año 1867*, Imprenta Literaria. Courtesy of the California State Library–Sutro Branch, San Francisco.

Additional documents produced by the Abadianos in subsequent decades suggest that the family remained politically aligned with the Catholic Church for many years. In fact, it seems that their business, politics, and religious sentiments were inextricably intertwined. Francisco Abadiano's personal records show that he managed the accounts of the Sociedad Católica in the late 1860s and early 1870s, and a copy of this organization's official bulletin noted that subscriptions could be arranged at the Librería Abadiano.[78] This was one of the first Catholic organizations founded in the wake of conservatism's definitive defeat in 1867. Established for men in 1868 and for women in 1869, it proclaimed exclusively doctrinal and devotional goals.[79] Still it served as a key space where Catholic conservatism endured and activists regrouped.[80] In the Sociedad Católica's newsletter, the Abadianos were also important advertisers.[81] Don Francisco's records also reveal that Bishop Clemente de Jesús Munguía, the well-known conservative ideologue, maintained an account with the Abadianos. Finally, the Catholic activist, pedagogue, and author of the most ambitious Madre Matiana text—an 1889 book reinterpreting the prophecies (as discussed further in chapter 4)—Luis G. Duarte also did business at the bookshop in the 1860s.[82] In sum, these documents suggest that Francisco Abadiano, like his father before him, occupied an important position within Mexico City's conservative Catholic network. Moreover, at some point Don Francisco, who died in 1883, or perhaps his heirs, rechristened their store the "Antigua Librería Católica de Abadiano."[83] It appears that the enterprise's conservative Catholic identity was well known and enduring.

A PUBLISHING CAMPAIGN

Beyond what the Librería Abadiano manufactured, a wider array of publications from the era provides the broader context for their production of *Profecías de la Madre Matiana*. If we contemplate the range of conservative publications during the period it is clear that a feverish printing crusade to halt liberalism's ascendency took shape from 1855 to 1858. In many ways it was a remarkable blitz that targeted multiple social niches. It amounted to a saturation strategy of sorts, whereby conservatives marshaled different rhetorical formats, voicing strategies, and vocabularies to convince as many Mexicans as possible to reject liberal reform. There are texts crafted for intellectual polemics, pleas to pragmatic leaders, emotional appeals, gendered sympathy ploys, devout calls on Catholic identity, and—as with the Matiana prophecies—mystical warnings. The arguments were not really new, but the intensity was novel. In the aggregate this was an attempt not only to reach a diverse public, but also to create the impression that a broad constituency was rising up to defend the faith.

Like so much related to the Madre Matiana phenomenon, the surge in conservative publications began in earnest after the U.S.–Mexican War. The multivolume history published between 1849 and 1852 by the doyen of Mexican conservatism, Lucas Alamán, provided a thorough conservative interpretation of the nation's difficult beginnings.[84] Alamán faulted the an-archic tendencies he saw emanating from liberalism's corrosive impact on the traditional structures of authority. He was particularly critical of what he viewed as the lawless tendencies of Mexico's uneducated masses. He believed that liberalism, with its talk of democracy and individual rights, simply en-couraged them to challenge the established order. Second, he argued that Mexico's true foundations resided in Hispanic culture and Catholicism.[85]

If Alamán served as the thinking layman's conservative voice, Bishop Clemente de Jesús Munguía offered a prelate's authoritative intervention.[86] Raised in Michoacán and trained in law, he briefly sought a secular career in Mexico City before leaving in disgust. Convinced of the need to protect the Church, he returned to Morelia and became a priest in the early 1840s. Munguía quickly gained prominence within the Church after he published a series of treatises that defended an exclusively Catholic nation-state. For the rest of his career he would essentially recycle these arguments, although with greater passion as polarization mounted.[87]

First and foremost, Munguía began with the premise that mankind was prone to disorderly passions, which if unchecked brought on chaotic social violence. Mexico, he proclaimed, like a profligate adolescent, had proven un-able to master its unruly impulses. The solution resided in religion, which tempered passions and created the interlocking social bonds that made civi-lization possible. The Catholic Church, he argued, was a sovereign "perfect society." By this he meant it was a divinely ordained social body whose na-ture and internal workings remained outside the control of any earthly po-litical order. Thus, any legal infringement of its rights, including the Church's ability to hold property, represented a violation of divine prerogative and the entire Catholic population's rights. Munguía was not a knee-jerk monarchist: for him, the form of government was less important than its moral founda-tions and policies. As a Catholic people, he contended, Mexicans needed a government that was willing to defend the Church and uphold orthodoxy. Accepting the presence of different religions, weakening the Church's eco-nomic foundations, or limiting the clergy's influence only weakened reli-gion's ability to tame human passions. Thus the Constitution of 1857, in his view, violated the basic tenets of legitimacy and actually promoted disorder. He proclaimed that all Catholics should oppose the new order and refuse to take part in irreverent governance. Munguía did not openly advocate armed resistance, but those inclined to agree with him imputed this indictment of the constitution as "just cause." Stoking tensions further, the bishop also contended that priests should refuse to minister to liberals and their collaborators.[88]

Munguía's treatise *Del derecho natural* (1849) served as the basis of conservative dissent, but his most impassioned writings appeared in editorials, pastoral instructions, and pamphlets.[89] These increased in both volume and vehemence as 1857 approached, and the Librería Abadiano's holdings included several of them.[90] In some instances, Munguía verged on the millenarian, suggesting that conditions in Mexico echoed biblical descriptions of the "last days." He also spoke fearfully of modern processes that would bring on the reign of Satan.[91]

Perhaps sensing the need for broader dissemination of his ideas, Munguía joined poet José Joaquín Pesado and novelist José María Roa Bárcena to produce a weekly newspaper dedicated to religious polemics.[92] Many conservatives grounded their ideological affiliation in terms of political beliefs, but Munguía, Pesado, and Roa Bárcena stressed liberal reform's violation of Catholic doctrine. In service of this trio, renowned conservative printer José María Andrade published and edited the new periodical.[93] This group called their publication *La Cruz* (*The Cross*), and framed their stance as a militant defense of Catholicism in the face of a blasphemous antireligious assault. It proved perhaps the most influential conservative publication of the era. As a result *La Cruz* offers a window on conservative sentiments during the Reforma era and spotlights the progressive recourse to the kind of apocalyptic language and militant symbolism pervading Madre Matiana's prophecies.

In the first weekly issue published on 1 November 1855, the editors outlined what they saw as the timely importance of their crusade. Liberals had taken over the government a few months earlier, and they had further outlined their agenda at a convention in October. According to *La Cruz*, their proposals threatened to cripple the Catholic Church and make religion irrelevant. The editors adamantly asserted that neither peace nor civilization was possible without Catholicism, and hence they felt compelled to protest.[94] Each issue included serialized essays that predicted the negative consequences of reform legislation and attacked liberal political theory. Thus a critique of the new constitution commenced in May 1857, and another addressing church-state relations began in early July.[95] Generally these writings presented standard conservative arguments, but *La Cruz* also issued more pointed accusations. For example, when he discussed church-state issues, Pesado placed the liberals alongside history's infamous heretics. Like them,

he argued, they dared to rebel against God and thus faced certain catastrophic failure.[96]

Shorter, more literary pieces often ventured into expressive territory akin
to the Matiana prophecies. For example, a poetic story alludes to the irreverence permeating society. The text, not unlike a prayer, begs for mercy before
a duly livid God, rejects worldly society, and ultimately confronts lapsed
believers:

Huyan, huyan de mí confundidos,	Flee, flee from me addled ones,
y al verme entre ellos triunfante,	and seeing me triumphant among them,
Se averguencen, Señor, y al instante	Shame overtakes them, Lord, and in that instant
Reconozcan tú excelso poder.	They recognize your exalted power.[97]

Another article spoke to the symbolic importance of the Blessed Sacrament
(the devotion anchoring renewal in the Matiana prophecies) in June 1857. Its
author, José Mariano Dávila, juxtaposes irreverent disobedience, "the bitter
leavening agent of original sin," and the ultimate symbol of unity with God
and harmony among humans, celebrating the Body of Christ.[98] The
Eucharistic miracle, devotion to the Host, and the individual consumption
of the Blessed Sacrament, he crows, mystically joins the Divinity, the Holy
Mother Church, and the communion of Christians. The patriarchal family
metaphor of order anchors this essay: father-God, mother-Church, and
childlike humankind held together by this miraculous "*lazo de unión*" ("rope
[or bond] of unity"). It alone, Dávila maintained, held back the "empire of
passions."[99]

As the summer of 1857 advanced, with the much-vilified national charter
theoretically in force and many conservatives seeing revolt as the only way to
block its implementation, the Mexican press openly discussed looming war.
It was precisely at this juncture that the Librería Abadiano began publicizing
the prophecies of Madre Matiana, and *La Cruz* edged ever closer to apocalyptic prediction in an essay titled "¿Para que hay revoluciones?" ("Why Are
There Revolutions?").[100] There is a shift of sorts here: violence between liberals
and conservatives now seemed unavoidable and the weekly publication
changed focus. It now sought to explain imminent violence and hardship. *La
Cruz* couched this particular essay from 6 August 1857, in grand biblical and
historical terms, but the allusions to local current events are obvious. In a

nutshell, the article describes how revolutions function as God's means of chastising impious nations. The size and frequency of such conflicts, the essay asserts, correspond to the level of sacrilegious behavior; moreover, by design they represent exemplary punishments. Throughout history, *La Cruz* clarified, the horrors of revolution are providence's means of rousing indifferent nations when exhortation has failed. God simply allows blasphemous ideas to unhinge the political world and bring on violence and mass suffering. Ultimately, the newspaper lectured, chastened survivors repent and reestablish Christian order and the harrowing experience typically serves as a cautionary reminder.

A week later *La Cruz* returned to these themes but cast them in terms of a global crisis. Europe, the paper proclaimed, also faced class conflict and dangerous new doctrines; Spanish America remained trapped in a vicious cycle of reformist hysteria and revolution; and anticlericalism, allegedly, knew no frontiers. On the sidelines, an ever-smug Protestant North America quietly plotted against "true" faith and amassed riches. *La Cruz* thought it obvious that societies flirted with ruin and many nations faced destruction. According to the editors, the signs of terminal moral decrepitude were everywhere, and the paradigmatic processes of civilizational extinction advanced apace: "The present, despite its arrogance and hopes, resides much closer to its end that she herself imagines."[101] Toward the end though, *La Cruz* shifted to prophetic assurances. All suffering, they stressed, ultimately brought greater Catholic unity and splendor. As the poet Pesado explained on 8 October 1857 in seer-like, paradox-speak: horrible persecutions represent marvelous tests visited upon the faithful. Great evils, he assured his readers, bring great benefits because they deepen devotion and underscore the magnificent truths of the faith.[102]

La Cruz did not carry the conservative banner alone. Conventional newspapers expressed similar views, but they often targeted the urban political class rather than the Catholic faithful. There was undoubtedly considerable overlap in readership, but these other publications also spoke to individuals less inclined toward the pietistic approach. They still, nonetheless, also convey escalating conservative anxiety in the mid-1850s.[103] Among the key players was a newspaper called *La Sociedad*. Like *La Cruz*, it emerged from the presses of José María Andrade, and, with the exception of Bishop Munguía, the same conservative brain trust was at the helm. Andrade served as editor in chief. Roa Bárcena contributed opinion pieces and literary works in his own name and under his pseudonym (Antenor); eventually he also took over as editor-in-chief. Pesado, the other *La Cruz* stalwart, was also a frequent contributor.[104] Edited and printed virtually side by side, these publications represent two faces of the same movement: *La Cruz* served as the ideological forum and *La Sociedad* functioned as the discursive combat arm.[105] The latter worked with the same themes, but it wove them into everyday coverage of reform-era politics and achieved relatively wide circulation in 1857, listing sales representatives in ninety-two different Mexican towns. This was still well short of the figures offered by liberal newspaper *El Siglo Diez y Nueve*, which listed 150 such agents selling their publication throughout the republic, but nonetheless quite respectable.[106]

In a way, *La Sociedad* feigned flexibility. The newspaper accepted moderate liberalism in theory but warned that in practice it opened the door to mob rule. By December 1855, the editors argued, this was exactly what was taking place, as the administration was cobbled together after the liberal overthrow of Santa Anna. *La Sociedad* stressed that many concerned citizens initially trusted the moderate President Comonfort, but within weeks they became disillusioned.[107] The *demagogos* (a conservative slur for the radical *puros*), they fumed, were taking over and implementing "fanaticism for the new." Blind to history they offended upstanding individuals with their anticlericalism, while inciting *la turba* (the horde) with their twisted concept of liberty (i.e., promises of libertinage and plunder). Moreover, they spat, *puros* cloaked their authoritarian plans in democratic verbiage.[108] Exasperated, the *La Sociedad* remarked: "We do not know, and we do not wish to prophesy what may happen . . ."[109]

In subsequent coverage *La Sociedad*'s desperation mounted. The anxiety is readily apparent in a series of columns by Francisco Vera, one of the newspaper's founders.[110] Vera channels the mounting conservative anger in a particularly acute essay from 8 March 1856, spurred by the Comonfort administration's new curbs on press freedoms, which were intended to dampen incitement and alarmism. In many ways the law appears to have been crafted in order to squelch publications like the Matiana prophecies.[111] In a very concrete sense, though, repressive press laws represented a real threat to conservative journalists.[112] *La Sociedad*'s stock and trade at the time, arguably, was indeed alarmism. If his newspaper had been shy about prophecies before, Vera stepped up to the task now. He railed that religion and property, the twin foundations of the "social edifice," were now in grave danger. All sacred traditions, he warned, were to be expunged in order to form a fantastical society grounded in absurd ultrademocratic theory. Vera predicts: "All will be useless for saving us from the ultimate ruin, while the wicked preach reform, while the most ignorant preach enlightenment, while we concede the mantle of reform to those who only know how to destroy."[113]

Other journalists noted Vera's anger and sympathized to a degree. *La Patria*, a moderate liberal publication, cited the author at length as it tried to embody the voice of reason amid the vitriol emanating from *La Sociedad* and its archrival, *El Monitor Repúblicano*. They conceded that his characterization of the most radical initiatives had merit. Some of the proposed reforms could indeed prove destabilizing, but *La Patria* also faulted *La Sociedad's* exaggerations.[114] One of its columnists, Luis Villard, also took to task liberal colleagues at *El Siglo* and *El Monitor*. For example, noting the former's claims that conservatives cloaked their reactionary goals with pious objections, he stressed that the new laws undeniably impinged on real religious interests.[115] *La Patria* also criticized *El Monitor's* attempts to conflate its policy preferences with an imagined global struggle against religious fanaticism.[116] At the same time the moderate periodical faulted conservatives' undifferentiated accusations of liberal impiety. Indeed, both *La Patria* and *El Monitor* covered Holy Week festivities with exhaustive devout attention in what was arguably an attempt to counter such attacks.[117]

Ultimately, Villard vented his own frustrations: "All the parties say the same thing today . . . all of them talk about union, but all of them want union exclusively under their ideas."[118] Looking back a few years later, Manuel Payno, a moderate liberal and Comonfort's Minister of Hacienda, described a feeling of abject dread as polarization peaked in 1856 and 1857: "At this time, one [radical liberals] appeared to me threatening, tyrannical, impatient, and ready to destroy everything; the other [conservatives], obstinate, cold, resolved to enclose itself in its ancient practices, without ceding anything, not even to time."[119] Sadly, he noted, for those in the middle death and destruction awaited all the same.

As insecurity mounted in 1856 the liberal government cracked down on critical expression, but many observers complained that these measures proved counterproductive. Within mere days of penning his criticisms of both camps the moderate Villard faced prosecution under the new press laws.[120] Seconding the measured analysis of *El Pensamiento Nacional*, *La Patria* editor G. Alfaro blamed draconian legislation for the raging epidemic of seditious rumor and reactionary falsehoods coursing through the *populacho* (riffraff). Overly harsh curbs on the press, he argued, only left the field to anonymous rumormongers as reputable journalists like Villard were silenced. In other words, heavy-handed censorship was unwittingly fanning the flames of malicious misinformation, much of it couched in ominous religious rhetoric.[121]

Evidence suggests Alfaro's analysis was accurate. Despite the harsh laws, narratives of murky provenance became particularly prominent as 1857 went on. In January *El Monitor* argued that interminable seditious rumors had inspired businessmen to withdraw from commerce, thus undermining public order.[122] By the fall several newspapers were predicting immanent civil war.[123] During the last months of 1857, liberal papers seemed to avoid even the mere mention of Madre Matiana even though her prophecies were in wide circulation, both in pamphlet and almanac form. It is possible the complaints about seditious gossip and falsehoods were at least in part inspired by "her" appearance. Some alternative end-of-the-world narratives did appear in the liberal press. Hidden on the back page of its 2 July 1857 issue, *El Siglo* mentioned the prophecies of a German friar that had been allegedly pronounced some five hundred years previous. Apparently he had stated that the Anti-Christ would be born in 1856 and live a symbolic thirty-three years before inaugurating the end times. In other words, by this prediction apocalyptic events were destined to culminate in 1889 (the hundredth anniversary of the French Revolution).[124] Were editors at the liberal paper of record getting nervous about divine retribution? The issue of sedition via rumor and whisper campaign remained current in 1861 (a year when Matiana's prophecies appeared yet again in pamphlet form). Manuel de Zamacona, a columnist at *El Siglo*, poetically captured profound anxieties about antiliberal hearsay and revealed prevailing characterizations of the popular mindset among intellectuals. Mexicans, he asserted, were a particularly sensitive lot: the people's "heart is soft wax and impressionable paste, and their spirit is like water, not only in its mobility [fickleness], but also in terms of its faithful reflection of even passing small clouds."[125]

DEPLOYING FEMININITY

Opinion journalism, though influential, did not reach everyone. On one level, literacy rates were very low. Historian Michael P. Costeloe estimated that only 5 percent of the population could read in 1840, but he argued that those that could were avid consumers of print journalism. The most widely read newspaper, *El Siglo*, produced on the order of 2,200 papers per day at this time.[126] Figures from the first census carried out in independent Mexico suggest that only 14 percent of the population could read in 1895; by 1920 the number had only risen to 20 percent. These general statistics, however, do not reveal the regional disparities. Apparently 38 percent of all literate Mexicans resided in the nation's capital, where the lion's share of newspaper and pamphlet publishing occurred.[127] Of course, these figures tell us nothing about practices such as reading out loud or the oral transmission of news and narrative. By the same token those who could read did not necessarily enjoy political reportage. Conservatives and liberals were undoubtedly aware of these issues and hence presented their arguments in a range of formats. In different kinds of texts the gendered dimensions of conservative discourse, which emerge so emphatically in the Matiana prophecies, come to the fore most clearly. *La Cruz* tacitly acknowledged the need for alternative tactics in its publication of serialized stories, like the satirical short novel by Roa Bárcena called *La quinta modelo*.[128] Appearing in installments during the pivotal year of 1857, it tells the story of a maniacal liberal landowner who creates a utopian community on his hacienda by banishing the clergy and military authorities and giving free reign to his radical ideals. The model republic, predictably, descends into chaos. Due to the intensely partisan moment and the story's spirited mocking tone, *La quinta modelo* attracted considerable attention.[129]

Historian Erika Pani astutely points out the patterns of gendered argumentation grounding this novel in particular and nineteenth-century conservative writing in general.[130] She notes how these texts frequently deployed the shallow, young male libertine as the personification of liberal error. Convinced that new ideas absolve him of all moral obligations, he mocks tradition and indulges his basest instincts. In *La quinta modelo* the liberal landowner's son plays this part and comes to a sticky, well-deserved end; the cynical agitators he calls friends remorselessly murder him. More directly relevant to the Matiana narrative, Roa Bárcena and other conservative writers juxtaposed the foolhardy libertine with archetypal women: the wise, pious Mexican mother and the sensible devout girl. These paragons of practical, devout femininity sense the inherent folly in radical thought and naïve reformism. Saddened but resolute, they sustain the faith and serve as self-sacrificing witnesses to the resultant calamities. Furthermore, in Roa Bárcena's cautionary tale, it is around these pillars of purity that society is rebuilt in the wake of liberal misrule. In this manner conservatives made devout women the guardians of a deep Catholic national culture. In contrast to the liberal characters, they speak in plain language and voice pragmatic support for tradition within accepted gender norms.

Conservatives used this construction of Mexican femininity in the political arena to great effect in their efforts to block specific liberal initiatives, such as religious tolerance. Figures like Bishop Munguía and the conservative press spoke out frequently against welcoming Protestantism in Mexico. But these arguments tended to remain in the realm of intellectual debate. Novels carried conservative sentiments by other means. However, among the most effective expressions of conservative dissent appear in petitions with hundreds of female signatories. Not only were these delivered to the government through official channels, but they also appeared in pamphlet form. Women could not vote, and across the political spectrum men recoiled from the notion of female political participation. But the time-honored maternal plea for consideration reached a unique emotional register, and hence offered a potent means of indirect participation. The signatories proclaim a profound reluctance to enter public debates and invoke prevailing assumptions about the unseemliness of women in the political arena. Simultaneously they assert that an innate understanding of the Mexican family, the education of children, and the hierarchy of household stability forces them to speak out. The petitions typically enunciate a plea for masculine protection instead of a straightforward critique of liberalism. Women, they assert, are weak and must depend on their husbands and male relatives. They predict Protestantism will have a corrosive impact on Mexican society, because it allows men to cast their wives aside at whim. Only Catholicism truly protects women and children, they argue, because it safeguards the sanctity of marriage. Hence they beg the congress to defend this institution. In addition, they argue that without Roman Catholic exclusivity women would be unable to inculcate firm moral principles in the youth.[131]

These petitions did not impart new information, but they were part of a shrewd, coordinated public relations campaign to feature similar pleas from men and women from all walks of life. For a time they allowed conservatives to shape the debate as a straightforward clash between faith and home, on one side, and heresy and dissipation, on the other. Each pamphlet features a different group of women from a distinct locale—such as the capital, provincial cities, and rural communities—making essentially the same argument. In the aggregate they represent a clever strategy to convey widespread feminine sentiment.[132]

Figure 4. *La Sociedad* organizes a petition of concerned Catholic ladies. In addition to political satire, the image also offers a glimpse of the life of wordsmiths and letter writers. To the left on a column are the words "Portal de Sto. Domingo." The flustered scribe (called an *evangelista* in the costumbrista texts of the era) is at Mexico City's epicenter for all things printed. Even today printers and letter writers ply their trade at this very spot. The Librería Abadiano storefront was only a block and a half away. From a framed clipping at the Museo del Estanquillo, Mexico City, unknown newspaper, 1855.

Liberal journalists, in response, complained bitterly that their conservative rivals duped credulous women into this distasteful intrusion.[133] For example, a cartoon from 1855 shows a man wearing a clerical three-pointed hat labeled "*La Sociedad*" concocting one of these petitions. The dialogue printed below the bewildered scribe complains: "But Mister Journalist how can you want me to put down 500,000 signatures when there are barely 40 ladies here." The unscrupulous newspaperman replies: "That does not matter Mister Scribe the ladies can multiply the signatures as they please because these *señoritas* are signing for generations of the past, present, and future." Behind him a crowd of dowdy matrons mill about as their political intrusion is arranged. In short, the cartoon challenges notions that these petitions

Figure 5. "The Mexican fair sex inspired by their religious zeal, craft a petition." Lest there be any doubt about who was truly responsible for women's entrance into the political arena via petition writing, Archbishop Labastida y Dávalos is front and center in his prelate's vestments eying the viewer. From *El Buscapié*, 9 February 1865.

represented a true mobilization of Mexican femininity. Nonetheless, the tactic clearly remained useful because similar critiques also appeared during Maximilian's empire. In a caricature from 1865, *El Buscapié* depicted conservative politicians and the archbishop hiding behind a trio of elite ladies, who mindlessly perched on their laps. Despite their ridiculous attempt at deception, the men's invention of the petition is patently obvious as they reach under the doñas' arms to lobby Emperor Maximilian behind a façade of female pious concern.

Despite these criticisms, additional evidence suggests the petition process represented an effective means of women's political participation. Their voices certainly reached members of the Comonfort administration: Secretary of Finance Manuel Payno stressed that broad female mobilization against liberal reform reached critical, unprecedented levels in December 1857.[134] Moreover, scholars specifically credit the petitions in forestalling religious tolerance laws. Legislators waited until liberal militias had secured clear supremacy in 1859 before implementing the offending reforms.[135] Not surprisingly, Librería Abadiano held, and undoubtedly sold, numerous pamphlets that criticized religious toleration.[136]

What then can we conclude about Madre Matiana's emergence and the factors influencing her subsequent lasting career? Looking back over Mexico's difficult beginnings, it would seem that Matiana's visions materialized thanks to three "authorial" impetuses. First, the nagging legacy of political instability troubled all political factions. Second, the U.S.–Mexican War's shocking outcomes sparked unprecedented levels of introspection and debate, which in turn inspired more radical responses and vehement rhetoric from both liberals and conservatives. Third, this new combative political milieu fomented a mounting intransigence within Mexican politics that would ultimately ignite civil war in 1857. Alongside this third factor, circumstantial evidence suggests that the Matiana pamphlets were part of a conservative publication campaign designed to turn Mexicans against liberalism. Given the patterns observed in the wider arena of conservative printing and journalism, the pivotal years for the Matiana phenomenon were 1854–1857. It was during this time that antiliberal publications appeared to saturate Mexican print culture. But clearly political argumentation was not enough. Some targeted intellectual and legal debates; others made the conservative case in terms of theology and dogma; and still others spoke to pragmatism and gendered stereotypes in what amounted to morality tales. Among them we find histories, sermons, petitions, essays, novels, editorials, dialogues, and legal disquisitions. Given Mexican culture at the time, it is hardly surprising that the same argument would also emerge in mystical narrative.

In sum, the first publications of Madre Matiana's prophecies are best understood as part of an array of publications animated by increasingly fearful and angry conservative activism. To put it in present-day terms, particularly in the late 1850s, Matiana's visions circulated as part of a multifaceted public-relations campaign as radical liberal reform gained ground and secured concrete expression in the Constitution of 1857. At the risk of dabbling in speculation, it is quite likely that individuals working in, or with, the second-tier printers located behind the cathedral collaborated in the fabrication of the prophetess and her visions. Even if the prophecies were simply transcriptions of historical documents, as they claimed, somebody from within this group would have been responsible for editing this material and arranging for its publication. In the end, though, authorship matters little in terms of what Matiana and her visions came to symbolize. The pamphlet seer became a mirror of sorts for Mexicans of the nineteenth century in a fashion similar to how Juan Diego, the fabled colonial-era seer of the Virgin of Guadalupe narrative, became a founder-like figure for Mexican criollos of the 1600s and the 1700s.[137] The Guadalupe legend has had a much higher profile in Mexican history, but additional parallels merit mention. In both instances the seers at the center of the respective visionary narratives are quite likely apocryphal, and yet the impact of the mystical stories surrounding them was real and powerful. Juan Diego's visionary legend proved crucial to the construction of creole identities in the colonial period and a broader Mexican identity afterward. Matiana's visions offered nineteenth- and twentieth-century Mexicans a different kind of reflection on who they were—or who they should be.

The polemics and mounting social tensions that led up to the fateful year of 1857 certainly had much to do with Matiana's ability to secure a niche within Mexican culture. Conservative rhetoric suggests that some Mexicans indeed expected divine intervention, as they judged changing cultural norms to be arrogantly blasphemous. In fact, a recent study of the nuns of La Purísima Concepción in Guanajuato notes that the women there were shocked when 1500 liberal troops actually evicted them from their convent in 1863. Despite the fact that laws stipulating the convent's closure had already been enacted, the religiosas expected divine interven-tion to halt expropriation.[138] This suggests that at least within devout cir-cles, Matiana's prophecies were not in the least farfetched. Some Mexicans, it appears, assumed that God simply would not let secularizing reform take place. On another level, both liberal and conservative writings indicate that an important reason for Matiana's endurance resides in the manner that Mexicans deployed gender in debates about the nature of society, culture, and the nation. As subsequent chapters reveal, the pamphlet seer eventu-ally became both the personification of irrational religiosity and the cau-tionary icon of women's supposedly aberrant presence in political debates. She even encapsulated liberal patriarchal fears about female Catholic activ-ism several decades after the initial pamphlets appeared. Alternatively, she served as a marker of conservative notions of enduring devotional purity and mystical wisdom, and hence a stand-in for women's imagined tender protests against modern error. To put it bluntly, Matiana and her visions remained relevant because they had come to symbolize an interwoven set of issues that would remain unresolved for several decades. Once these associations developed her origins mattered little. In addition, there was another reason for her staying power. Amid all the acrimony and violence of the Reforma, Madre Matiana began a parallel career in Mexican folklore thanks to an idiosyncratic literary form—the popular almanac.

CHAPTER 3

Of Almanacs and Magic Lanterns

IN NOVEMBER 1857 MANUEL MURGUÍA'S PRINTING ESTABLISHMENT
and bookstore, like his colleagues at the Librería Abadiano a few months
earlier, ran advertisements in the *Diario de Avisos*. In this case, they announced the availability of new almanacs, or *calendarios* as they were often
called.[1] This particular publisher had sixteen different types to offer, and in
several instances the *Diario* lists their contents. The fourth entry reads as
follows:

> CALENDARIO NIGROMÁNTICO
> *Materias que contiene—Santoral—*PROFECIAS DE MATIANA, *descripción
> sobre los sucesos que han de acontecer en la capital de México.—La re-
> camarera, artículo de costumbres, adornado con una estampa de lito-
> grafía.—Tabla periódica perpétua para hallar el día de la semana en
> cualquier mes o año.—Varias adivinanzas.—Doble sentido de una
> carta.—Y dos curiosas estampas litográficas.*[2]

Thus on the heels of the Abadiano pamphlet's publication, Madre
Matiana made her debut in the calendario-*almanaque* genre. On the surface, this bit of information simply demonstrates that the prophecies were
available for a time in two distinct formats: as a stand-alone pamphlet or
as part of an almanac. However, the seemingly innocuous coincidence of
the seer's appearance in a second kind of publication actually represents
crucial evidence for understanding her endurance and complex legacy. A
central mystery of the Matiana phenomenon is how decades later—when
few Mexicans remembered her polemical emergence in the mid-nineteenth

87

century—the prophetess still stalked the national psyche. In simplest terms, evidence suggests that Matiana's crossover into the realm of calendario literature vaulted the pamphlet seer into the pantheon of archetypal Mexican figures and secured a place for her prophetic story in the national imaginary.

Murguía's almanacs were part of a longstanding Mexican publishing tradition. Every fall during the nineteenth century the coming year's popular calendarios emerged "hot off the presses," and newspapers publicized their availability.[3] For the most part they shared the basic structure of the 1858 *Nigromántico*. First they featured the Catholic ritual calendar, or *santoral*, followed by information, stories, and images related to various topics, which depended on the targeted market niche. In the opening excerpt, Madre Matiana's prophecies—highlighted in all capital letters in the original advertisement—represent the feature attraction. After the visionary narrative, "*La recamarera*," a serialized sketch of customs and manners describing a popular social type—in this case, "The Chambermaid"—appeared with an accompanying lithograph. Finally this almanac also contained riddles, aphorisms, and a table for determining the day of the week for any given date.[4]

The revenues generated by calendario sales were very important for printers and bookshops.[5] Otherwise they would not have bothered with advertising these inexpensive publications. In some cases the publisher edited the newspaper where he placed announcements, so they probably enjoyed discounted rates. In others, bookstore and printing press owners paid to promote dozens of different calendarios, some of their own production and some printed elsewhere.[6] Prices varied, naturally; some could be purchased for as little as half a real (one-sixteenth of a peso).[7] The *Calendario franciscano* for 1858 was available at the offices of the *Diario de Avisos* (located within Vicente Segura's shop) and four other bookstores in Mexico City for the more common price of 1 real (one-eighth of a peso). By comparison a subscription to the newspaper *El Siglo Diez y Nueve* cost 20 reales per month.[8] Buying in larger quantities, naturally, made them considerably cheaper: a dozen of the *Calendario franciscano* could be had for 7 reales, 100 for 7 pesos, and 1000 for 55 pesos.[9] Some customers purchased in bulk and resold the almanacs at a profit in various locales, and ambulant peddlers hawked calendarios throughout Mexico City's neighborhoods.[10] Venders also sold almanacs during festivals at the nation's far-flung religious shrines.[11] In sum, calendarios produced in Mexico City made their way to communities far beyond the blocks surrounding the zócalo.

Clearly someone at Murguía's shop had decided that the *Nigromántico* (The Necromantic Almanac), one of the staples of the publisher's almanac line, would feature Madre Matiana, essentially by copying word for word the pamphlets sold elsewhere. Most likely the veteran printer was taking advantage of the looming symmetry between the seer's predictions of a definitive bloody conflict in October of a year ending in eight and the mounting political tensions of the Reforma period. Selling versions of Matiana's prophecies as such a year approached, be it 1858 or 1868, made basic business sense. This was probably a motivating factor for the Librería Abadiano too, and likewise for Simón Blanquel when he offered a Matiana calendario for 1867.[12] Murguía was, in general, more focused on the new market for secular printed materials than his competitors, the Abadianos. Landmark works in Mexican letters had emerged from his presses in previous years, such as the sixth edition of Latin America's first novel, Francisco de Lizardi's *El periquillo sarniento* in 1853. He also published the famous collection of picturesque fictional short sketches, called *Los mexicanos pintados por sí mismos* (1854–1855).[13] Every year Murguía unveiled an array of almanacs to target different social groups, ranging from the no-frills *Calendario económico* to the comparatively sophisticated *Calendario de Murguía*. The *Nigromántico*, as its title suggests, offered something quite different—its specialty was fantasy stories and a blithe dabbling in the occult. As previously noted, the text of the prophecies in this almanac was identical to the 1847 and 1857 pamphlets, but the context of publication was very different. Matiana had moved into the realm of spooky legend.

The calendario genre as a whole represents a fascinating and frustrating back alley of Mexican literature. On the one hand, the production of almanacs for relatively popular audiences and the diversity of material within them offer an attractive opportunity for scholars interested in expression outside the literary canon and expressly political writing. They feature fiction, devotional texts, history, treatises, fee schedules, cartoons, religious images, poetry, recipes, magic tricks, and custom and manners sketches. This hodgepodge, however, also makes them difficult to analyze. Nonetheless, close scrutiny reveals that calendarios represent a category-defying medium that sought to both form and inform a heterogeneous reading public while also simply marketing literary entertainment. The typical almanac ranged between 35 and 50 pages, but they could be as short as 10 or as long as 120 pages. In fact they functioned as hybrid platforms where the material within each booklet-like publication glides between forms, sometimes within a single feature. It is not uncommon

CALENDARIO

DE LAS PROFECIAS

DE LA MADRE MATIANA

PARA

1867.

Se vende en México, en la librería de Blanquel, editor, calle del Teatro Principal núm. 13.

Figure 6. Calendario de las profecías de la Madre Matiana, 1867. The cover nudges Mexico's legendary seer into the realm of folkloric fantasy with an illustration of a classical landscape, which holds no relation to the prophecies beyond a vague invocation of Greek divination traditions. From *Calendario de las profecías de la madre Matiana para 1867,* Imprenta A. Boix a cargo de M. Zornoza. Courtesy of the California State Library–Sutro Branch, San Francisco.

to encounter a straightforward historical account that evolves into a politically freighted morality tale. Sometimes satirical cartoons accompany essays. These, in turn, can then be followed by a paean to the Virgin Mary, a sermon-like address, and devotional imagery. Often texts and images are simply reprints of previously published material, producing a pastiche of sorts. In general production values were of secondary importance. As a result scholarly analysis generally catalogues their diversity, names prolific almanac printers, comments briefly on their picturesque qualities, and offers suppositions about reading practices.[14]

In a sense, the Matiana prophecies in the almanac genre provides the opportunity (excuse) to scrutinize this quintessentially popular arena of expression more closely. The institutional clashes and elite cultural conflicts of the era are well known, but scholars have been less successful in illuminating how the bulk of Mexicans envisioned the nation or society. The problem, of course, is that gauging historical opinion remains quite difficult. Calendarios, in contrast to many other publications of the era, represent a genre especially attuned to popular tastes. Printers crafted their merchandise to echo a spectrum of domestic prejudices and preferences. In some ways popular almanacs are remarkably varied, and as I will discuss, Matiana's prophecies only appeared within a particular subcategory of the genre. But despite contrasts and distinctions, Mexico's calendario tradition also evinces very stable patterns and structures as well, suggesting that consumers demanded an ordered representation of local diversity.

Calendarios represent a manifestation of print capitalists' efforts to produce typified Mexican literary entertainment, packaged with information dictated by variegated market demand. Of course, given the documentary gaps surrounding nineteenth-century printing, this approach requires a degree of informed speculation. There is no way to know exactly who purchased or read calendarios, how they interpreted them, or how almanacs circulated. Occasionally intellectuals of the era commented on these issues, providing us with helpful clues, but additional kinds of evidence indicate there was indeed a healthy, broad-based demand for them. Each year publishers worked to develop attractive merchandise, respond to market cues, learn from (and copy) competitors, and divine what would lure future customers. As a result, the genre provides both a reflection of popular opinion at the time and an image of society akin to discursive stone rubbing. Or better yet, in keeping with nineteenth-century metaphors, each calendario represents a "lanternslide" (the slidelike images projected by the era's "magic lanterns") of Mexican society fashioned to resonate within a particular segment of the market. In short, calendarios were commercially produced attempts to meet evolving cultural appetites and popular tastes. They offer a multifaceted image of nineteenth-century society complete with the stock social types that many Mexicans would have viewed as typical. By making the leap into the almanaque genre, Madre Matiana secured a place among these figures and symbolic status in subsequent debates about the nature of Mexican culture. This set the stage for her marquee role in satire, photography, and literature in the twentieth century. Perhaps the best argument for the significance of Matiana's appearance in calendarios is the fact that Revolutionary humorists styled their newspaper as an almanac parody named after the prophetess. Likewise, when Agustín Yáñez used her as a character in his novel he presented her as a living almanac: a human compendium of traditional knowledge and devotional arcana.

Making this case, however, requires setting the prophetess aside for a moment and peering into the realm of nineteenth-century expression and the complexities of calendario marketing.

MEXICO'S "CULTURAL PRESS"

The nineteenth century witnessed an expansion of printing and publishing in Mexico as well as a broadening array of publication genres. The colonial state and church had long been steady consumers of paper and ink, and printers depended on ecclesiastical institutions for a significant portion of their sales. As discussed in the previous chapter, much of the expansion involved newspapers and pamphlets engaged in era's heated controversies—for example, the debates surrounding liberal political reform and polemics that focused on religious tolerance. Alongside these developments, though, was an attempt to develop an arena of expression insulated from polemics and dedicated to fashioning a unified, national culture. Literary and visual-culture scholar Erica Segre labels this arena the "cultural press."[15] The calendario genre predates this development, but the mid-nineteenth-century almanacs became part of this sphere when entrepreneurs adapted this time-honored format to new endeavors. I say "part" because there were important distinctions between the materials published largely for elite and foreign audiences and those produced for the broader domestic market. Calendarios had evolved a two-part standard format: on one level, they offered the classic Hispanic-Catholic almanac material; but by the 1840s, they also included the kinds of nation-building texts and images prevalent in the so-called cultural press. Their cheaper unbound production and traditional functionality, however, left them less prone to the sanitized modern posturing that typified the elite-oriented print merchandise marketed at the same time. In general they were much more likely to include material that polite society would find backward. The reworked calendario genre, in other words, represents the ragged fringes of a movement to create national consensus and a shared Mexican identity through literature and art supposedly insulated from controversy. As a result, they offer a clearer picture of the betwixt and between realities of the time.

In many ways the cultural press represented a self-defeating project. Many of the writers, publishers, and printers involved were simultaneously playing the hardnosed game of factional politics while they waxed poetic about a picturesque Mexico and her unique and diverse populace. From approximately a century-and-a-half's remove the discursive gymnastics can seem cynical, as if the real game was securing power and marginalizing opponents, and the rest was just window dressing. Thus to the present-day reader it can seem disingenuous that a radical liberal writer known for his criticism of the Catholic Church in the newspapers was more or less simultaneously publishing nostalgic descriptions of religious festivals. However, the endurance of this endeavor from the 1830s through the 1860s, and the unpredictable nature of politics at the time, dashes such simple characterizations.

From a broad perspective, attempts to visualize unity amid glaring divergence and conflict mark Mexican art and writing during much of the nineteenth and twentieth centuries. It was not a matter of ignoring oppositions, but rather the construction of expressive practices centered on marking diversity as the wellspring of unity and the changeable foundation undergirding Mexican identities. As recent scholarship suggests, discontinuities served as the national point of origin and essentially built generative angst into Mexican expression. From a distance it seems incongruous, but it became "Mexican" to adopt this approach, and the crucible of this dynamic appears in the iconography and writings of the mid-nineteenth century.[16]

The challenge facing the architects of these strategies entailed promoting a vision of order from within endemic instability and divisive polemics. In this climate, the individuals engaged in the very conflicts that were dividing the nation also created a sphere of expression to conjure consensus. Publishing new *revistas* (magazines) and forming ostensibly open artistic and intellectual institutions (*academias*), the Mexican cultural press developed as an ostensibly neutral space. The publications they fashioned ideally strengthened shared values and discursively set the foundations of stability and order, with the help of a calculated moderation and an affected harmonious tone. All the while the market for their high-minded endeavors was skeletal at best, and most of their periodicals withered without subsidies. In other words, the writers, publishers, and printers leading this quest doggedly clung to the hope that cultural advocacy could midwife nationality, even in the face of considerable evidence to the contrary and without a viable market for their labors.[17]

The cultural press repeatedly relied on visual metaphors to make their claims, and they produced publications to broadcast these imaginings—hence the famed formative magazines such as *El Mosaico Mexicano* (1837–1842) and *El Museo Mexicano* (1843–1845).[18] In this spirit the metaphorical nation was a mosaic, a museum, a cabinet of curiosities, or a well-stocked corner store. All that was needed was careful observation and minute description of the disparate objects, peoples, and practices in a cultural space to unveil the deep harmonious core and make it palpable. Participants commonly invoked the era's new technological metaphors too; for example, one publication spoke of daguerreotyping society.[19] Much of this resides within the literary and artistic phenomena labeled *costumbrismo*, a term derived from the narrative category called the *cuadro de costumbres* (customs and manners sketch). This realm of expression is often overlooked because much of it fails to meet later standards of high art. It is profoundly derivative: despite its focus on local minutiae, it openly copied the style and content of European models.[20] At a distance the sketches also appear escapist as their production coincided with frequent political convulsions. Moreover, its encapsulation under the rubric of "customs and manners" fails to account for its complexities and its establishment of the patterns of nationalist imagining. When considered carefully costumbrista texts often reveal themselves to be hybrids of sociopolitical commentary, quasi-anthropological description, nostalgic storytelling, nationalist celebration, and cultural criticism. It is not always the most coherent admixture, but they are instrumental in understanding the era.

Perhaps because of the calendario's even more accentuated catchall nature (and the tolerance for tedium required to examine a large body of them), scholars who analyze Mexico's literary history and nation-building discourse tend to focus on the books, portfolios, and magazines of the era. Thus the famous costumbrista compilation of national types, Murguía's *Los mexicanos pintados*, has attracted much more attention than his many calendarios, although the latter may have netted him more revenue. Likewise, the stunning lithographic picture book, *México y sus alrededores* (1855), has also drawn considerable scholarly interest.[21]

It is important, though, not to draw strict boundaries between these books and calendarios. The same publishers marketed them, and calendarios frequently reprinted material from the more upmarket compilations without attribution and presumably without compensation.[22] Not coincidentally, the same establishments also produced the city's newspapers, which likewise raided the same stockpiles of content. Well-known writers appeared in all these venues and collaborated with printer-editors on specific projects.[23] In part this simply reveals the diversification strategies employed by uncertain print capitalists. Practicality (and desperation) inspired printers to raid their

Figure 7. La calle de Roldan (Roldan Street). Note the lone friar looking back at the viewer from his balcony at left. He is physically on the margins and essentially caged in his monastery. Moreover, below him the urban poor frenetically carry on everyday commerce without any regard for his presence. From J. Decaen et al., *México y sus alrededores*, 1855–1856.

finer products for down-market consumption and spruce up their cheaper fare for high-end publications. (They do not appear to have paused when it came to plundering their rivals' material either.) Of course, image quality, paper and binding, and size often had much to do with cost differences.

Still a close look at "high-end" costumbrismo provides an important foundation for understanding the "low-end" costumbrismo of the calendarios. *Los mexicanos pintados* and *México y sus alrededores* clearly targeted elite consumers. The latter was a large-format art book, and some editions include a French translation alongside the Spanish text, suggesting that publishers hoped to attract foreign readers as well. Moreover, although the original publication appeared in black and white, later expanded editions feature colored lithographs.[24] The texts and images reveal the top-down, Eurocentric representations of Mexico one would expect, even though at times they are not internally coherent. For example, in *México y sus alrededores* some writers praise the populace's devout nature, imply intense religious commitment,

Figure 8. Atrio del convento de San Francisco (The Atrium of the Convent of Saint Francis). This lithograph shows clergymen and other residents of the capital outside of the church, most likely after Mass, dwarfed by monumental colonial architecture. The artist hems the priests and churchgoers in with massive baroque facades, visually walling them off in the nation's past. The layperson who engages one of the Franciscans in the center of the image is a well-to-do woman. Thus the image emphasizes the linkage of femininity and Catholic piety with the clergy's banishment from secular spaces. From J. Decaen et al., *México y sus alrededores,* 1855–1856.

and hint at strong support for the Catholic Church. Others honor the heroes of liberal patriotism, champion state-directed reformism, and criticize priests and their "backward" practices.[25] On one level, then, this book lacked firm editorial control. But the larger portrait emerging from the text reveals a consistent, albeit bland, moderate liberalism.

Contributors certainly worried about disunity and looming political conflict in the mid-1850s, but one wonders how many consumers bothered with the essays since they are nowhere near as interesting as the dazzling illustrations. Many readers probably purchased it as a compendium of images of Mexican life and customs. The illustrations convey little doubt or tension, but as discussed further in the chapter, a gently secularized Mexico pervades these images. In a sense they offer a moderate, reformist, liberal vision of the nation. There are no public acts of religious ritual in evidence, and in general few priests or nuns appear at all. When they do they are located in their "proper" place, such as observing the populace from afar, taking part in celebrations within the Cathedral, or hanging around in the church atrium. In short, this is not so much a depiction of Mexico as it was in the 1850s, but rather a portrait of society as it should be according to the editors.

For example, in the image titled *La calle de Roldan* (*Roldan Street*), a single monk observes the bustling public market from his balcony, but he has no role in the events. Likewise, the lithograph "Interior de la Catedral de México" ("Interior of the Cathedral of Mexico") depicts the 26 April 1855 celebration of the newly declared dogma of the Immaculate Conception. It features many clergymen taking part, but in this historical event suffused with conservative political overtones they remain within the sanctuary; they are not out sermonizing in public. When they do step outside their churches, as in *El atrio del convento de San Francisco* (*The Atrium of the Convent of Saint Francis*), they do not go far. The only evidence of public religious expression is the exception that proves the rule, a depiction of the feast of the Virgin of Guadalupe taken from a hot air balloon, *La Villa de Guadalupe*. Crucially its bird's-eye representation shows vast festival crowds but no individuals, social types, or specific rituals are discernable.[26]

The social portrait offered in *Los mexicanos pintados* offers a still starker purging. Of the thirty-five "national types" described in the essays and depicted in accompanying lithographs, none are explicitly religious actors. Nor are there any military officers or common soldiers, explicitly indigenous individuals (although some images imply indigenous features), or truly elite figures. The emphasis is on modern occupations and the urban workplace. María Esther Pérez Salas opines that this was perhaps a simple attempt to avoid controversy, but the extent of the omissions suggests a much more concerted project afoot. Most of the included characters also appeared in the European texts that *Los mexicanos pintados* mimicked; in fact, only six were unique to the Mexican publication.[27] In any case the social order depicted in these pages has been "reformed," so that the most staunchly conservative figures within Mexican society are literally invisible.

Equally apparent, few women appear in this catalogue of Mexican social types, and none of them have expressly religious identities or social roles. Not a single nun or even a beata made the grade, although in a couple of instances religious belief and practice appears in the description of their lives. For example, among the possessions of the archetypal popular beauty known

Figure 9. La recamarera (The Chambermaid). The printer Manuel Murguía seems to have taken every opportunity to republish the essays and images from the famous costumbrista compilation of Mexican social types, *Los mexicanos pintados por sí mismos*, in his almanacs. This image appeared alongside the Matiana prophecies in the 1858 issue of the *Calendario nigromántico*. From Hilarión Frías y Soto et al., *Los mexicanos pintados por sí mismos*, 1854–1855. Image courtesy of the California State Library–Sutro Branch, San Francisco.

Figure 10. La partera (The Midwife). This depiction of Mexican midwifery emphasizes the "primitive" female craft of birthing. An image of San Vicente Ferrer is on the table behind the imposing woman and the tiny newborn. The artist gave considerable space to shadows in the illustration, drawing the viewer's attention to the dark, candle-lit world the subject inhabits. In short, this is a realm needing "enlightenment." It is of particular significance the way the midwife's huge shadow looms over the scene. The text accompanying the image was even more dismissive. From Hilarión Frías y Soto et al., *Los mexicanos pintados por sí mismos,* 1854–1855. Image courtesy of the California State Library–Sutro Branch, San Francisco.

as *la china* we find the material culture of Catholic devotion: Marian images and a devotional ribbon from her favorite saint.[28] The book's approach is stereotypically paternalist. The young women like the *chiera* (drink vender), the *estanquillera* (tobacco store clerk), and the *recamarera* who appeared alongside Madre Matiana in the *Calendario nigromántico* come across as fetching, vulnerable, and available girls without independent thoughts or ambitions. Their future, the accompanying texts suggested, depended on good luck in the marriage market.[29] The only lithograph where religious culture makes an appearance, albeit portrayed sarcastically, is in the essay dedicated to the *partera* (midwife).[30] This sketch and another dedicated to the *casera* (the female tenement manager) feature mature women, and both figures receive mocking treatment.[31] The image of the partera depicts a heavyset woman wearing ostentatious jewelry while she is seated in a shadowy room swaddling a newborn. Behind her San Vicente Ferrer resides upside down. Thus the artist references the folk tradition of turning a sacred image on its head and threatening to leave the image upside down unless the saint secures miraculous assistance. In this manner, the partera is the only social type branded as superstitious. The text, however, is much more smug. It laments that in the modern age older women, particularly widows, speciously proclaim expertise in childbearing. In closing the author ridicules parteras as a sham female priesthood.

In sum, the attenuated "diversity" depicted in texts like *Los mexicanos pintados* and *México y sus alrededores* conveys a watered-down version of the era's liberal reformism. Although this probably worked with foreigners, it is hard to believe that Mexicans at the time would have seen these as remotely complete portraits of society. Herein lies the danger of focusing solely on these high-end publications.

THE MAGIC LANTERN

The more market-driven calendario in many ways is a better gauge of Mexican popular identities and opinion. This is not to say that the entrepreneurs behind them, the individuals often simultaneously involved in the more elite-targeted publications as well, dropped their sociopolitical goals in these products. However, they had to be more practical as they approached the broader domestic market. The calendario publisher may have been conservative or liberal, but commercial imperatives leavened efforts to conjure the ideal nation. They needed to attract a wide array of local consumers and offer images and narratives that a diverse public would recognize and embrace, regardless of inherent contradictions. Thus print entrepreneurs produced publications that were, in most cases, simultaneously conservative and traditional as well as liberal and modern. In other words, in the calendario-almanaque universe heterodoxy *is* the picture.

During their own time, there was some debate as to the literary "value" of calendarios. Well-known intellectuals professed divergent opinions, but their consumption was generally identified as a national compulsion. For example, in 1894 Manuel Gutiérrez Nájera (1859–1895) labeled the public's annual purchase of the *Calendario de Galván* a regrettable end-of-the-year ritual throughout Mexican society.[32] He proclaimed the climate-related predictions patently absurd, and he mocked the truly precise information regarding Catholic feasts and practices. Gutiérrez Nájera even questioned the wisdom of universal suffrage in a populace that sustained this tradition and whose literary culture resided solely within the genre. Famed costumbrista writer and liberal Guillermo Prieto, in contrast, expressed unabashed affection for calendarios. In fact, on 16 December 1878 he dedicated his column in *El Siglo*, called "San Lunes de Fidel," to their history.[33]

Concurring with today's scholars, Prieto pointed to the European almanac traditions, including imported Spanish examples and Mexican imitators in the eighteenth century's Guía de forasteros. These informative publications for travelers and agriculturalists sold well, he suggests, thanks to their low cost. As a result they became standbys of renowned print entrepreneurs like Felipe Zúñiga y Ontiveros and Mariano Galván by the early nineteenth century. Originally they were rather dull, providing mostly weather, the lunar and liturgical calendars, and information about services available in Mexico City, but gradually they added new material. Galván's publications—the same ones maligned by Gutiérrez Nájera—gained distinction by including articles on history and short essays on famous buildings and stories from the nation's past; others followed suit. According to Prieto, popular almanacs of the mid-nineteenth century could be found everywhere: from the humblest kitchens, to the dressing tables of the elite, and within the nation's sacristies. A true watershed development occurred in 1836, when newly imported printing equipment allowed for more cost effective and complex publications with attractive illustrations.[34] Technological change probably had much to do with the wide variety of calendarios in archival collections. Ultimately, Prieto claims, the famed printing impresario Ignacio Cumplido entered the

calendario business and eclipsed the competition; his publications included well-written articles broaching natural history, native cultures, and
literary contributions from eminent figures like the politician and most
accomplished costumbrista writer Manuel Payno. Such was their quality,
Prieto asserted, that intellectuals safeguarded copies in their libraries. Of
course, many humbler printing establishments sold calendarios of varying
quality, some of which targeted truly modest readers. Finally, Prieto lamented the ascendency of merchant-sponsored almanacs in the 1870s.[35]
These mixed advertising with literary entertainment, usually skimping on
the latter.

Prieto proclaimed an abiding nostalgia for the pre-1870s calendarios. He
portrayed them as an enduring guilty pleasure where he could relive his baptism in the joys of reading and escape from childhood sorrows. As a result
he indulged in escapades of literary slumming amid calendario offerings. He
recalled reveling in stories about Mexico's eighteenth-century Negrito Poeta
(roughly, Blacky the Poet).[36] He also became acquainted with Madre Matiana
in the almanac named in her honor. The liberal Prieto's offhand treatment of
the seer suggests that the prophecies did not inspire in him a principled anger about alleged efforts to turn the ignorant against liberalism. To him they
seemed simply an example of the mystical storytelling long common in the
genre.

Mexican writers like Prieto and publishers like Murguía, as we have discussed, sought visual metaphors in their quest to depict the nation. This approach was not particularly original—they were simply following the long
tradition of appropriating pictorial vocabularies to enshrine the production
and sale of reading material. In Mexico, and in many other Latin American
countries, one of the more common ways to describe the costumbrista project was in terms of the "magic lantern," a precursor of both slide and movie
projectors. Emerging first in the seventeenth century and often featuring
crude, oil lamps outfitted with hot smoky chimneys to shine light through
painted slides, magic lanterns became quite popular in Europe and the
Americas. Clever lanternists created the impression of movement by sliding
images past the lens while also manipulating levers that nudged slides in different directions. Naturally skilled artisans emerged who specialized in
sketching and coloring scenes on glass. By the late nineteenth century, im-
proved technologies (limelight, and later acetylene and electric arc lamps)
allowed shows to become quite elaborate. Slide shows in some instances,
particularly in urban centers, featured hundreds of images, panoramic

TOMO I   **MEXICO, Lúnes 19 de Febrero de 1877**   NUM. 1

SEMANARIO JOCO–SERIO.

CONDICIONES	ADMINISTRACION	PUNTOS DE SUSCRICION.
Este periódico se publicará los Lúnes, á las doce del dia. El precio de suscricion, en la capital, es de cincuenta centavos adelantados, llevado á domicilio. El número suelto, doce centavos. — En los Estados, sesenta y cinco centavos, franco de porte. El número suelto, diez y ocho centavos.	Y DESPACHO GENERAL. IMPRENTA POLIGLOTA	Agencia de Publicaciones de los Sres. Delanoe Hermanos, calle del Cinco de Mayo, bajos del Hotel Gillow. Alacena número 4, Portal de Mercaderes. En el despacho de esta imprenta, calle de Santa Clara, esquina al callejon. En los Estados, casa de los Sres. Corresponsales
Editor propietario, LUCIO ABELLINI.	**Redactor en gefe, B. CICERON FLUSSAN.**	**Administrador, JUAN E. BARBERO.**

Figure 11. A jester and his magic lantern. Satirists were quite fond of this kind of image, which suggests a somewhat presumptuous self-conception. The alter ego of these particular journalists wields the magic lantern on the Earth to project the classic satirical motto: "*Ridendo corrigo mores*" (Laughing I correct customs/norms). From Rafael Bajaras, *El lloron del Icamole.*

effects, and carefully sequenced crowd-pleasing stories. In some cases projecting the slides on smoke or translucent screens further enhanced supernatural images.[37]

Journalists and costumbristas found particularly attractive the persona of the primitive, itinerant lanternist who dazzles the rabble with his slides. In fact, a satirical newspaper of the 1870s named *La Linterna* featured a devilish jester with a crude oil lantern that projected light on the globe.[38] Mexican costumbrista writer José Tomás de Cuellar titled a series of short novels *La linterna mágica.*[39] In addition, the calendario-loving Prieto likened his literary practice to the role of the roving lanternist: it was up to him to capture the images, give them discursive vivacity, and project the colors and contours of national life for others to behold.[40]

Inspired by these historical actors, one way to look at the nineteenth-century calendario phenomenon is that they function as magic lantern "slides" crafted to depict the nation, as if each calendario was "projected" through a discursive lamp. In short, we too can play the game of visualization and picture the *Calendario de la Madre Matiana* and other publications of this sort as part of a series of images forming a composite portrait of Mexican society. Following the metaphor, none of the almanacs are actually complete depictions of society and the nation, but each one captures a slice of Mexican "reality" and publishers crafted them to be consumed in this manner. Each issue is a reflection of what interested some group of Mexicans. And by extension, to buy and read calendarios was to take part in a particular kind of community conceptualization with fellow consumers. As Prieto implied in his column in *El Siglo*, it was almost a prerequisite of Mexican nationality to read them and an element of shared nostalgia to recall the calendarios of yesteryear. Their structure and the patterns of representation they contained are remarkably stable. They are, in fact, almost ritualistic in their predictability. In a very telling manner they feature the general material that everyone "needed," followed by specific texts, information, and images, which delineate distinct subgroups within the marketplace and nation. Crucially they remained open to the possibility that readers belonged to multiple groups. As mentioned before, different calendarios targeted social niches with material of interest for identifiable groups, as these groups were imagined by publishers. But in combining these materials with a formulaic presentation of general information they delivered a message: readers, despite distinct interests and ideological inclinations, were part of a larger collective—people and nation. Almost invariably, each almanac begins every year with essentially the same material—material steeped in Mexico's long and complex tradition of Catholic devotionalism. With few exceptions, every almanac frames the nation as essentially Catholic, first and foremost.

THE MAGIC OF REPETITION, STRUCTURES, AND PATTERNS

The most obvious way in which this framing is evident is the standard two-part structure of calendarios. With rare exception they begin with a handful of pages of customary information: a *notas cronológicas* section offering a timeline of key historical events; a listing of the year's movable feasts; a key for annual ecclesiastical calculations; and finally the monthly schedule of saints' days, religious holidays, fasting guidelines, and devout obligations (the santoral, as it is still known). Of course, some variation is always in evidence. The events chosen for the notas timeline may differ. For example, calendarios aimed at more devout audiences feature the sacred declaration of the Immaculate Conception, while others list events from the Wars of Independence or technological inventions. Still others do a little of both. The santoral, however, is the longest and most important text of the standard almanac material. It is typically a series of twelve charts, one for each month, ranging from 1 to 3 pages each. The days appear in a left-hand column, and the corresponding events occupy a wider right-hand column. Often lunar phases appear listed at the top of each month or alongside the appropriate day. Sometimes each month in the santoral features a small biblical illustration or *estampa* (a devotional image) related to the listed happenings. At times publishers used leftover space at the bottom of pages for sidebar information. In some calendarios, sets of *máximas* (maxims) appeared. These were typically moralistic adages, although when published outside the santoral they were sometimes simply humorous quips. As a result of these patterns there is a missal-like quality to calendarios. The santoral and other standard front matter typically averaged 30 pages. Depending on the number of images, typeface, and font size it could be longer or shorter. Less commonly, often in the calendarios produced by merchants, the santoral would appear abridged and compressed into a few skeletal tables.[41] In contrast, some expressly Catholic almanacs—such as those printed by the Abadianos, which we will discuss shortly—offered exceptionally long, narrative devotional calendars; naturally, these most likely targeted an exceptionally devout segment of the market. Some publishers inserted new patriotic anniversaries, such as 16 September, into the devotional calendar.[42] Only rarely does the santoral appear at the end. In the vast majority of calendarios all readers first encountered roughly the same 20 to 40 pages, which laid out the overarching devotional structure of the coming year. The succeeding pages featured the content that gave each calendario its unique identity.

There are both practical and symbolic reasons for this structure, although the latter were arguably unintentional. First, consumers clearly sought out the santoral and its similar, related sections. Its ubiquity and endurance suggest that the practice of purchasing it generated stable revenues for printers. Many Mexicans, apparently, felt they needed a copy of the liturgical calendar, the annual dates for important feasts, and the information that accompanied it. In other words, this material made almanacs "useful." It was also common to include additional sections of important festival dates celebrated in the various Mexican towns; and in many instances, religious feasts coincided with days off from work. Of course, this material is what gave the genre its name: it is the calendar in the calendario. The "classic" structure appears in the small (*trigésimo-segundo*, five and one half by three and a half inches) eighteenth-century predecessor, the Zúñiga y Ontiveros *Calendario manual*. This palm-sized publication featured little more than the santoral and basic information on important feasts and eclipses.[43] However, the shape of things to come peeks through in a single sonnet inserted between November and December. As the nineteenth-century dawned, calendarios became longer and offered more varied information and entertainment-oriented material. In the early nineteenth century, the Zúñiga y Ontiveros's *Calendario manual y guía de forasteros* offered a remarkable wealth of information.[44] It contained a timeline section listing each viceroy and bishop in Mexican history, the standard information on seasons and feasts, and the santoral. Most remarkable are the long tables of statistics, the names of all manner of colonial officials, and information about the state-licensed pawnshop and lottery. Perhaps most impressive are the high-quality maps of Mexico City. This content makes sense, because this particular publication served a guidebook function unlike many later calendarios. Printers still produced Guías in the mid-nineteenth century, but they became 300- to 700-page tomes, focusing almost exclusively on information. They often dropped the santoral altogether.[45]

The santoral-centered format endured in the smaller, cheaper almanacs. This conservatism probably stemmed from prevailing tastes; consumers most likely preferred this formula. Moreover, keeping the classic format made sense for printers. In the 1850s and 1860s, most publishers annually marketed several different calendarios, advertising them as a diverse selection catering to varied tastes. For example, in 1861 José María Aguilar's press advertised eight different almanacs ranging from those themed as popular, literary, and military as well as others targeting readers who preferred love stories or satire.[46] It undoubtedly cut costs and simplified production to employ the same front matter for all almanacs during a given year and print different material for remaining pages. Thus the first 32 pages of both the *Calendario de la Madre Matiana* and the *Calendario de la Perla de México* of 1867 are in fact identical.[47] Moreover, publishers envisioned consumers saving the supplemental materials and discarding the calendar-specific sections at the end of the year. In many instances, after the santoral, page numbers correspond to a larger serialized work rather than the calendario's previous pages. Individuals could collect almanac texts separated in this manner and have them bound together.[48]

On the symbolic front this structure probably facilitated the formation of a national "imagined community."[49] In Mexico, the calendario has been overlooked in this regard. As noted previously, the traditional structure assumes that every reader was *católico ante todo* (Catholic above all else) and each reader "entered" each issue through the santoral. On another level to consult these guidelines for the year's activities was to take part in a shared practice regarding the days and times set aside for the sacred. Mexicans may have had their differences, but a standard schedule of events and Catholic observances defined the rhythms of public and private life, even after the implementation of secularizing reform. Moreover, information offered alongside the santoral taught Mexicans about the devotional lives of neighbors, fellow townspeople, and the celebrations organized in other regions. Reading the regulations regarding fasting and penance and pondering the dates when particular groups of devotees or parishes put on their feasts, the public could gain an understanding of the devotional map of Mexico City. A calendario reader in the capital, for example, learned about celebrations in other cities, and what devotions preoccupied far-away fellow Mexicans. Conversely readers elsewhere consumed a picture of religious life in Mexico City, the capital and cultural model for other regions. Naturally some publishers produced calendarios specifically for provincial cities, adjusting computations accordingly.[50] The most important dates of the santoral, however, remained the same. In short, the calendario genre facilitated Mexicans' ability to imagine a national Catholic society.

Protestant almanacs published in Mexico represent an anomaly, but they are the exception that proves the rule. For example, the *Calendario protestante de los amigos cristianos para el año de 1868* retained the standard structure, while being purged of saints' days and Catholic celebrations.[51] Thus it begins with a list of provincial festivals, but the text avoids mentioning their Catholic nature. It also includes a simple calendar, tables listing the sunrise and sunset times, monthly charts of lunar phases that mimic the iconic santoral, and a list of solar and lunar eclipses. The subsequent texts venture into contentious territory: Protestant understandings of baptism and a dialogue-style explanation of how each and every "true" Christian represents one of God's "priests." Although they do not generally state their denominational affiliation, this kind of content suggests that the calendarios were part of Protestant conversion efforts. Most likely because of the underlying proselytizing goals, the editor (in this case, José Parra y Álvarez) presented this controversial information in a familiar manner. Activist Catholics viewed them in this predatory light, and in fact they denounced them as sinister weapons in the heretical assault on Catholicism.[52] Even so, the offending almanacs were relatively few. The vast majority of calendarios assumed a devout Catholic readership, tacitly conflating national culture and Roman Catholicism.

Of course this was not the only venue for the Catholic message. The Church had long told Mexicans that they were Catholics first, and religion was the primary force keeping the nation together. As discussed in the previous chapter, Catholic newspapers and pamphlets during the period following the U.S–Mexican War were quite shrill on this point. However, it was not simply tradition at work in the calendarios. Through the divergent materials and advertisements they painted a complex national picture and conveyed a sense of modernizing change in coexistence with cherished tradition. The Mexico appearing in the calendario genre is capacious. Again, the variety and enduring structural patterns evident in most almanacs suggest that numerous, relatively humble Mexicans consumed these visions of the nation and did much to shape the almanac tradition by their actions in the marketplace.

THE CALENDARIO MARKET

In the 1850s and 1860s calendario sellers hawked an impressive array of options. The previous decade's offerings were often drab, but by 1848 and 1849 publishers produced attractively illustrated calendarios. In fact, there appears to have been two distinct publishing strategies: offer a single self-titled annual or an array of almanacs crafted to accommodate niche interests. Ignacio Cumplido chose the former, and he produced the trendsetting *Calendario de Cumplido* for many years. Of course, it helped that he enjoyed a sterling reputation. Among printers in Mexico, Cumplido's products linked him to the liberal cause. In 1829 he produced *El Correo de la Federación* and subsequently *El Fenix de la Libertad*, an important newspaper dedicated to democratic ideas and liberal debates; but he is ultimately most well known as the publisher of *El Siglo*. This newspaper frequently featured the most important liberal thinkers of the era and very levelheaded editorials, when compared to other titles of the day. Cumplido also printed some of the key nation-building magazines of the cultural press: *El Museo Mexicano* (1843–1845), *La Ilustración Mexicana* (1851–1854), and *Presente Amistoso Dedicado a las Señoritas Mexicanas* (1847–1852).[53] In his calendarios he offered a mix of essays on history, civic morality, geography, regional customs, and natural science. In concert they come across as a wide-ranging curriculum. In keeping with mainstream Mexican liberalism of the era, however, they embraced religion and well-established festive rituals, although they avoided the ecclesiastical triumphalism of stridently Catholic competitors. In fact they appear at pains to demonstrate a Christian worldview alongside forays into science, literature, and history. For example the 1844 edition included short devotional texts accompanying each month of the santoral and essays exploring the greatness of God and criticizing atheism. Likewise, the 1846 edition offered the pious biography of an Iroquois beata named Catalina Tegovita.[54]

If we ponder Cumplido's calendarios as visualizations of the Mexican public there is a sense of a devout yet enlightened nation. Religion has a fundamental place, but it is not a stifling presence. Mexico embraces technological and scientific advancement, and readers learn about other countries' customs and history. The public takes part in the era's spirit of rational inquiry while sustaining Catholic culture. In sum, this is a manifestation of an accomodationist moderate liberalism. It is about gaining knowledge and learning new ways of doing things without rejecting tradition or rashly abandoning established custom.

Manuel Murguía, the publisher of the *Calendario nigromántico*, sold several different almanacs annually. He and others, like José María Aguilar, employed the "shotgun" approach. Thus Murguía's *Calendario económico* (meaning cheap) was minimalist.[55] It offered the santoral and its standard complements, blank pages for note taking, and nothing more, although the publisher sometimes included a few advertisements. From at least the 1850s until the 1870s, lean times for many Mexicans, this calendario was for sale at Murguía's shop on the Portal del Aguila de Oro. Clearly some Mexicans felt they could do without the supplemental texts but still sought out the santoral.

Of course, this was just one of Murguía's offerings during the 1850s and 1860s. His *Calendario de las niñas* offered the standard material of the *Calendario económico* coupled with a wealth of supplemental texts, which revealed what male publishers believed Mexican girls should find interesting.[56] Chaste love poetry, essays on how to love God, stories about girls in foreign countries, sheet music for polkas and schottisches, articles on the qualities of good husbands, and recipes for soap were all common features. Like many calendarios, this subgenre contained a section of maxims to live by, but in this case they were sternly patriarchal—for example, "Make your mouth the prison of your tongue."[57] Murguía also published a *Calendario de los niños* that reproduced the classic almanac structure and offered material designed especially for boys. This included illustrated cautionary tales designed to inspire hard work and diligent study habits, world history, descriptions of different religions and races, and statistics on European nations.[58] All of these distinct almanacs faced competition. The *Calendario enciclopédico de la juventud*, produced by Vicente Segura, targeted the same young male demographic.[59]

Additional almanacs trained their sights on still different niches. Murguía's *Calendario universal*, published in 1859 and 1861 essentially served as a platform for reselling excerpts of his costumbrista classic, *Los mexicanos pintados*.[60] In keeping with custom it offered the typical calendar material first and then a reprinted individual character sketch and the accompanying lithograph from its source. Murguía also included additional costumbrista stories, articles on geology, poems, humorous essays, and classical history. His self-titled *Calendario de Murguía* was similar, but it was longer and more serious, with a distinct polymath character (probably to compete with Cumplido).[61] In general all eponymous calendarios evince a flagship quality, which makes sense since they carried the publisher's name. Hence they represent the most sophisticated almanacs and generally assume a careful moderate tone. Not surprisingly they too cleave to the classic format, but in contrast to Murguía's *Calendario universal*, this almanac offered more devout texts. Thus in 1855 the *Calendario de Murguía* included a shape poem dedicated to the Holy Cross (i.e., the words on the page produce a cross), a hymn, and a poem about the Christ child. Subsequently it described the recent conflicts in Europe, issued advice on childrearing, explained how to swim, and appended a table for calculating monthly wages. Later issues also included sketches and illustrations from *Los mexicanos pintados* in addition to an array of other stories, poetry, and information on mathematics and weather prediction (i.e., how to foresee climate events in animal behavior and the stars).[62] Rounding out his offerings, Murguía also produced a *Calendario de los agricultores* that focused on farming, naturally. It too preserved the santoral-first format. Afterward readers could learn about coffee, garbanzos, and grafting, as well as enjoy an ode to country life.

To be sure, there were overtly doctrinaire offerings. Liberal-themed almanacs, however, were careful to carve out a place for religion and Catholic practices. The *Calendario de la democracia dedicado al pueblo mexicano*, produced by a onetime employee of Cumplido named Leandro Valdés, took a forcefully liberal, didactic approach but also included pious texts.[63] The 1851 edition is one of the few examples where the santoral appears at the end rather than the beginning of the publication. Instead, after merely listing the year's movable feasts, this almanac featured essays that championed public education and explained federalism. Nonetheless it also included a biographical sketch of Saint Anthony the Abbot and a rather detailed santoral. The 1852 issue returned to the santoral-first format and contained lithographs of the crucified Christ and the Virgin of Guadalupe. However, Valdés also inserted an image of Miguel Hidalgo alongside September's religious feasts as well as a liberal melodrama called *El gorro de la libertad* (*The Phrygian Cap*). Still at the end of the calendario he included a "Breve catecismo de la moral" ("Brief Moral Catechism"). This text reverently entwined Catholic Christianity and civic morality and supported the traditional mediating role of the priesthood.

Here then is a similar, but narrower, image of Mexican society. Again, the foundations of morality and social life are Catholic, but the underlying assumption is that devout readers embrace touchstone liberal initiatives like public education and federalism. It makes sense given that mounting tensions leading to outright civil war were quite palpable in the 1850s. The Leandro Valdés calendario and others like it represent an attempt to reach a wide audience and instill liberal sympathies within an acknowledged devout populace. Most liberals were themselves avowed Catholics, although critical of clerical power. The almanacs cannot be labeled antireligious by any stretch. Arguably such a stance would have doomed them in the marketplace. In fact, these publications suggest that liberals wanted to counter voices accusing them of dark anti-Christian motives.

In both Ignacio Cumplido's and Leandro Valdés's calendarios, however, culture change is a tacit assumption; hence they exemplify a gradualist posture. To the present-day readers, they seem completely uncontroversial. This was probably not the case among diehard Catholic conservatives of the time. For some the lack of forthright allegiance to Rome and deference to the clergy smacked of anti-Catholic conspiracy. The mounting polarization of the 1850s would have conditioned this reception. Furthermore, the targeting of a popular audience and the moralizing tone of these calendarios could be seen as an attempt to brainwash a populace that most political actors assumed to be devout but ignorant and gullible.

In this context the almanac market included a range of calendarios católicos that offered somewhat different lanternslides of society, but considerable overlap remained. They too barely muffled their politics.[64] Ironically, these are among the most likely to deviate from the traditional structure. For the most part, however, this involved placing additional devotional or Church-glorifying material before the santoral. For example, the *Calendario católico para el año 1851* began with an introduction that stressed the bedrock importance of religion for sustaining morality and protecting the common good in society. Perhaps for fear of alienating customers, the publisher—Manuel N. de la Vega—stressed that this particular almanac was meant for everyone, while noting that he also offered three others. (With these he covered the almanac standbys: commerce, politics, and agriculture.) Subsequently the calendario offered short essays on God and the Catholic Church and a hymn to the Sacred Heart of Jesus before giving way to the santoral. In the space left at the end of each month, the publisher inserted a text glorifying Pious IX. At this time throughout the Catholic world, the Sacred Heart devotion and praising this controversial pontiff represented clear markers of deeply conservative commitment. Dispelling all doubts, this almanac also offered a short section that briefly described French conservative Catholic thinkers, such as Joseph de Maistre and Louis Bonald, and noted that they offered several works by the former at their bookstore.

The publishing establishment of José María Andrade y Felipe Escalante (the printer that produced *La Cruz* and *La Sociedad*) offered similar almanacs, although they retained the standard structure.[65] This press's *Calendario católico para el año 1861* noted its production for the Sociedad de San Felipe de Jesús para la Propagación de los Buenos Libros, a Church-affiliated organization dedicated to combating impious publications. The almanac does not reveal exactly how the organization used the publication, but it seems logical to assume it could have been sold to raise funds and disseminate their message simultaneously.[66] A quick glance at their notas cronológicas from 1863 (during the French occupation) reveals a distinctly combative framing of piety. A timeline began at creation (7062 years before) and was punctuated by such events as Noah's flood, the Incarnation (Christ's birth), the Virgin of Guadalupe's apparition, the martyrdom of Saint Felipe de Jesús, and the canonization of Saint Vincent de Paul. This chronology culminates in Pious IX's dogmatic declaration of the Immaculate Conception nine years before the calendario's publication: a clear statement of partisanship in 1861.[67]

Perhaps the most militant offering was the almanac of the Society Saint Vincent de Paul of 1867, also published by Andrade y Escalante.[68] Its defiant tone most likely stems from the fact that liberal militias had regained control after the withdrawal of French troops in 1865, and conservative Catholics could see the tide had turned against them. In fact, this *calendario* was most likely available at precisely the same time, and perhaps in the same stores, as another almanac prepared for 1867, the *Calendario de la Madre Matiana*. After the standard front matter it presented a series of strident essays. The first explained the Catholic Church's organizational structure, labeling it the "greatest army in the world." Subsequent texts criticized religious tolerance, refuted claims that Catholicism was outdated, and attacked Protestantism. The latter specifically targeted the notion that non-Catholic Christianity was a harmless substitute for traditional belief and practice. A later article spoke directly to Mexican men, lambasting the dismissive notion that Catholicism was simply for women. This calendario then returned to Protestantism, railing against their versions of the Bible and intrinsic criticism of image-centered devotion. Finally these points were reprised in a dialogue between a priest and a credulous everyman pondering new religious options.

The publication of Catholic almanacs continued after conservatism's defeat in 1867, but the editorial tone changed. Some featured a distinct preservationist stance, as if their function was not to win over society, but rather to maintain the faith within it. The Librería Abadiano published such a calendario from the mid-1870s to the mid-1880s.[69] It deviated from the standard format, beginning with a pious chronology of world history, devout poetry, and biographies of Mexican prelates. In the 1884 edition, the santoral commenced on page 18, but it continued for a whopping 111 pages. In essence it incorporated the descriptive materials of its precursors within the religious calendar. Hence it offered a narrative for each day rather than a simple chart, with detailed explanations of religious celebrations and new militant organizations like the Apostolado de la Oración (Apostolate of Prayer). In this vein it explained the sociopolitical meanings embedded in devotion to the Sacred Heart of Jesus. In many ways this super-santoral represents a testament to a particular Mexican identity—the one trumpeted by the institutional Church and urban religious activists at the time.[70] One wonders, however, if such a long almanac was affordable outside the circle of ardent elite Catholics. On another level, only a relatively small portion of the populace embraced the time-consuming version of Catholic practice and revivalist institution building outlined in this document. Still this publication provides a vivid portrayal of this intensely pious subgroup and its conception of the nation.

Gutiérrez Nájera's sneering commentary on almanac consumption, also published in 1884, implies that most Mexicans preferred more traditional light-hearted offerings. A range of options beckoned to this audience—with standard devotional information followed by content that was designed explicitly to entertain. These publications also represent a reflection of society, albeit from a different angle. The titles of these calendarios usually made their market niche clear—for example, the *Calendario burlesco* (*The Mockery Almanac*), and the *Calendario impolítico y justiciero*.[71] Many of them, in fact, featured texts that reappropriated famous costumbrista texts in a backhanded manner. Thus the latter publication included an essay and an accompanying cartoon titled "Machine for the Making of Deputies." In the image a half-human figure with an oversized donkey-head works the crank of an elaborate modern contraption. On one end the stock costumbrista figure at the base of the working class, *el aguador* (the water bearer), obliviously rides a conveyor belt into the machine. At the opposite end a frock-coated politician emerges ready to take up his duties in the national legislature. In other words, the implication is that ignorant rubes run the nation's new institutions. Later in the same issue, a song caricatures raucous dance parties in an infamous urban neighborhood. Entitled "Un baile leperogrático" (roughly, "Dance of the Lowlifes") it describes the pulque (fermented agave sap)—besotted, melee of thieves and surging dance music. Even the famed toothsome chinas in attendance are armed to the teeth.[72]

Ironically, given her role in the realm of political pamphleteering and roots in mystical folklore, this is the subgenre of almanacs that contains Madre Matiana. Murguía also published the *Calendario profético*, which might seem like the appropriate place for the pamphlet prophetess. The 1859 issue of this almanac offers a detailed discussion of the 1846 Marian apparitions at La Salette, France, as well as the Virgin Mary's alleged prophetic pronouncements to the child visionaries involved.[73] The text relayed a message not unlike what appears in the Matiana narrative: society had angered Christ. He was poised to unleash terrible punishments barring mass repentance. However, the La Salette visions enjoyed official Vatican approval, and they earned reverent treatment from the almanac editors. Mexico's Madre Matiana did not, and hence she found herself in a different kind of almanac. Another edition of the *Calendario profético* published after 1867 went in an entirely different direction to attack conservatives, liberals, and everyone in between for their disingenuous, self-serving legacy of prophetic posturing

Figure 12. *Trajes mexicanos: un fandango (Mexican Dress: A Popular Dance Party).* This lithograph shows a selection of "social types" dancing in "typical" attire. As if plucked from *Los mexicanos pintados por sí mismos*, it features *la china* dancing with *el aguador*. She is clearly the focal point of the image with her attractive fanned-out dress and pretty face at center. All of the typical traits are on display: her skill at Mexican dances, her dainty feet, and her iconic rebozo or shawl. There is also evidence of popular devotion: the crosses and sacred images on the wall and the cross around la china's neck. In other words, religion is carefully put in its place here too—in private spaces and on the body of the popular epitome of Mexican femininity. From J. Decaen et al., *México y sus alrededores*, 1855–1856.

during the previous decades of violence and strife.[74] As mentioned previously, the *Calendario nigromántico* (the almanac that republished Matiana's prophecies in its 1858 edition) specialized in fantasy.[75] Issues commonly featured lithographs of sorcerers and included ghost stories and magic tricks.[76] They also offered articles that inhabited the gray areas between science, magic, and folklore. Thus they contain descriptions of legendary processes, such as turning base metals into silver and gold with the philosopher's stone.[77] However, like others selling this kind of material, the *Nigromántico's* writers made it abundantly clear that they were peddling myth and legend. At times they included stories debunking beliefs in magic and supernatural creatures.[78] In this context Madre Matiana represented little more than another fantastical story, albeit one of a particularly Mexican variety that spoke of the nation's difficult history. The *Nigromántico* of 1858 also included a *costumbrista* sketch from *Los mexicanos pintados*, in addition to standard fantasy fare like prophecies and riddles.

Matiana's star turn as a headlining figure of the *calendario* genre did not take place until nine years later. This time, however, the text emerged from Andrés Boix's presses under the direction of M. Zornoza.[79] As stated on the 1867 pamphlet's title page, the printer manufactured the almanac expressly for sale at Simon Blanquel's bookstore. As was his habit, Blanquel commissioned several almanacs each year from this printer and from others, and he generally specialized in sunnier fare.[80] In the fall of 1866, most likely displayed alongside the *Calendario de la Madre Matiana*, customers could thumb several Blanquel almanacs prepared for 1867, such as the *Calendario de los jóvenes*, *Calendario joco-serio*, *Calendario de los enamorados*, *Calendario de los cuentos y aparecidos*, and *Calendario del negrito poeta*.

The 1867 Matiana almanac reproduced the classic *calendario* structure, and the text of the prophecies remarkably remained the same; yet the context had shifted more still. Its historical timeline section included both ecclesiastical and patriotic dates as well, including the founding of the Mexican empire under Maximilian of Habsburg four years previous, as midwifed by Napoleon III's French armies. The *santoral* featured the standard celebrations, but it also commemorated Miguel Hidalgo's rallying cry for independence on 16 September (shared by the feasts of Saints Cornelio and Cipriano) as well as the emperor's saint day, 12 October.[81] Matiana's prophecies commenced immediately following the *santoral*, and no other supplemental texts appeared in this almanac. Blanquel probably commissioned the almanac in hopes of capitalizing on mounting trepidations among devout Catholics as liberals proved once more ascendant and another year approached that ended in the notorious number eight (the symbolic end-time according to Matiana's reckoning). But the almanac offers no mention of such fears. In fact, the images in the *calendario* suggest a distancing from her polemical origins. Instead of illustrations linked to the actual text, such as images of war or representations of Matiana's visions, the publisher inserted lithographs that blunt the text's impact. The image on the frontispiece features a classical temple against a generic, rural Mediterranean backdrop. This visual representation of Greco-Roman myth was probably meant to inspire romantic notions of Apollonian oracles. The remaining two images have nothing whatsoever to do with the prophecies. After the *santoral*, at the top of the

PROFESIAS
DE MATIANA,

Sirvienta que fué en el convento de San Gerónimo de México,
sobre los sucesos que han de acontecer en la espresada capital-
escritas por la madre María Josefa de la Pasion de Jesus, re,
ligiosa del mismo convento en cumplimi nto del decreto de 18
de Enero de 1837, dictado por el señor vicario de monjas.

Señor vicario de los conventos de religiosas,
D. Juan Manuel Irizarri.

María Josefa de la Pasion de Jesus, religiosa
del convento de Nuestro Padre San Gerónimo de
DAVID.

Figure 13. The presentation of the prophecies of Madre Matiana in 1867. This image shows the beginning of the text of the prophecies, which appeared midway through the almanac. The incongruous country scene appears above the prophecies. The printers did not even bother to find an image in vertical format to match the following text. From *Calendario de las profecías de la madre Matiana para el año 1867,* Imprenta A. Boix a cargo de M. Zornoza. Courtesy of the California State Library–Sutro Branch, San Francisco.

page that inaugurated the Matiana narrative, a generic rural manor house is pictured. Likewise, at the very end of the prophecies appears an image of two rugged islands in a calm sea backed by a cheerful sky full of birds and harmless clouds. In other words, this almanac visually unmoored Madre Matiana from her Mexican origins and set her adrift in the realm of myth and folktale borrowed from stock European images.

MATIANA, MEXICO, Y MUJERES

Looking closely at the Matiana calendarios provides a sense of how the prophetess inhabited a different realm of Mexican imagining before and after 1858. Beyond the political pamphlet she took up residence in the spooky world of the *Nigromántico*. Murguía, the almanac's publisher, likely believed she was best marketed to the audiences that wanted mystical and occult-tinged literary entertainment along with a traditional santoral. The same was probably true for the Blanquel edition in 1867. In both cases, though, it is important to note that the publishers were undoubtedly aware that some Mexicans took the prophecies seriously, and so they assumed that Matiana would sell best approaching a year that ended in eight and with invasive turmoil very much a part of everyday life. Perhaps more than any interest of theirs in the conservative political agenda, these entrepreneurs simply may have hoped to profit from the prophecies. This practical aspect of the Matiana legacy was perhaps the single most important factor in her appearance in the calendario genre. Just as Nostradamus and New Age appropriations of the Maya calendar periodically fuel publications and press coverage in the present day, the prophetess and her visions drew a paying audience at key junctures in nineteenth-century Mexico. As with so much about the Matiana phenomenon, though, much more than just the story of the prophecies is at stake.

In isolation from the larger field of almanac production, the poles of nationalist visualization appeared in expressly liberal and Catholic almanacs, although the former still portrayed Mexico as inseparable from Catholic cultural practices. Moreover, as Guillermo Prieto hinted, individual Mexicans read and often re-read multiple almanacs each year from across the spectrum of representation. On another level there were a wide range of less obviously ideological calendarios, which at first glance can seem merely trivial. Considering the enduring patterns and structures of the genre, however, deeper shared envisionings in the supplementary texts begin to emerge. The almost ubiquitous, leadoff presentation of the santoral and accompanying religious information—in addition to the frequent provision of added devotional texts and imagery—suggest an enduring and almost society-wide embrace of Catholic identity. In this sense, almanacs reveal a persistent traditional worldview and a desire to preserve a Catholic habitus, although not necessarily of the intransigent sort. The supplementary texts complicate this picture. Outside of the most militant Catholic almanacs, and in concert with the standard santoral-centered materials, the supplemental material typically offers an adulterated, defanged liberalism. Yet they avoid the blasphemies and anticlericalism of radical expression, and the texts implicitly reject the secularization of public life. Nonetheless they explore new ideas and ways of thinking while sometimes poking fun at tradition. This suggests that, on some level, most customers were comfortable with a moderate liberal vision of the nation, which entailed gradual secularization. Perhaps a better way to put it is that most Mexicans' approach to national identity was profoundly heterodox, much like the almanac genre itself. They valued Catholic traditions and wanted to share their devout sentiments, but they also sought to take part in the latest expressive fashions, to explore new ways of structuring public life, and to avail themselves of the ascendant status ascribed to that which was deemed modern, enlightened, and advanced. The commonplace nature of this admixture in the calendarios suggests that much of the populace simply did not find the contradictions troubling. In fact, perhaps they experienced this phenomenon as "Mexican."

As for Madre Matiana's fate after her calendario characterization, the evidence in following chapters shows that she essentially became the flipside of another caricature of Mexican femininity that was famously enshrined in *Los mexicanos pintados* and costumbrista paintings: la china, the intrinsically but innocently sensual figure that represented mestiza beauty and a vivacious, national spirit. Within the romantic logic of the cultural press, all "true" Mexican men desired la china with the same innate passion that they adored *la patria* (the fatherland). La Matiana and all the pious *señoronas* (matrons) she stood for, in contrast, had to be tolerated. She was, nonetheless, just as "*típica.*" In other words, the prophetess's calendario breakthrough represents a key step toward her coding as the cranky, irrational face of Mexico's popular culture. Among the secularist modernizers of the late nineteenth and early twentieth centuries Matiana came to embody sanctimony, impertinence, sexless elderly femininity, "backward" customs, and beliefs rooted in the overweening influence of Catholicism. Sampling the liberal journalistic treatment of the prophetess in the wake of her appearance in the 1858 *Nigromántico* provides some clues as to how marking the prophetess in this new way evolved from the 1860s to the eve of the Mexican Revolution.

Remarkably, there seems to have been no explicit discussion of Madre Matiana in the liberal press until a few years after 1857. Aside from advertisements and what seem like allusions to her in debates about seditious rumors and misinformation, journalists avoided the topic. (It is as if they feared pronouncing her name might jinx the ongoing battle against conservatives.) In the 1860s, however, published comments about the prophetess became relatively common and typically reveal attempts by the press to belittle traditionalist culture and conservatives. In some cases references to her merely convey metropolitan disdain for provincial customs and culture.[82] Others used Matiana to mock rivals. For example, *El Siglo* sniffed at the appearance of a wartime, clandestine, conservative paper in 1861 remarking, "they dedicate themselves to the prophetic genre like another Madre Matiana, assuring [readers] that the reform will last one week, and liberals only have 15 days to live."[83] Likewise, in 1879 *La Patria* fretted about the return of "reactionaries" to electoral politics.[84] Tartly, they opined, if this came to pass it would amount to a fulfillment of Madre Matiana's prophecies.

In a different vein some writers invoked the prophetess to condemn the very nature of Catholic custom and education. Thus in 1870 *El Libre Pensador* (*The Free Thinker*) mocked Catholicism, with its belief in miracles, ubiquitous clanging bells, and the dogma of transubstantiation, as the "noisy religion of Madre Matiana."[85] Along the same lines in 1875, *El Siglo* contributor Juan A. Mateos (a well-known liberal congressman and writer [1831–1913]) attacked *La Voz de México* for championing Catholic education, which he scorned as backward, esoteric nonsense.[86] Mateos derided priestly "erudition," sarcastically listing Madre Matiana among the Church's "sages." Catholic education, he scoffed archly, was mere "*sterculinum*" ("manure").

Other instances reveal that rival liberals used the prophetess as an epithet hurled when mocking a colleague for self-aggrandizing predictions. In a sense Matiana's deployment is a gendered insult: the prophetess signified ignorance, overheated visionary conceit, and unfounded alarmism. In other words, newspapermen accused each other of acting like superstitious beatas. Thus *El Boquiflojo* lampooned *El Monitor Republicano* in 1870 as "Mexican Anabaptists" for repeatedly predicting that various happenings or policies represented the "slippery slope" to reactionary revival.[87] These critics snickered that the prophetic foolery of old had reemerged with *El Monitor* sheltering visionaries done up in frock coats and slacks.

However, there were still publications that deployed the pamphlet prophetess in debates about changing gender norms. In this manner *El Hijo del Trabajo* (an early socialist paper) commented on the potential admittance of women as delegates to the worker's congress in 1876.[88] Apparently many male attendees believed that women would *"narcotizar"* ("dumb-down") the assembly, and blocked their inclusion. In a turn of chauvinist wit the newspaper chuckled that male workers left the door open to reconsideration: they agreed to permit female delegates "when the prophecies of Madre Matiana came true."[89] Thus *El Hijo* linked female workers to the prophetess and sexist conflations of superstition and femininity. The implication, of course, was that women could not contribute to the congress as rational individuals.

During the same year *La Metralla*, a satirical paper, produced mock prophesy in Matiana's name. Crucially, in this case we see evidence of the seer's persona being appropriated by male writers to "voice" indignation and lay claim to public opinion. On at least three occasions *La Metralla* published editorials signed "La Madre Matiana."[90] Each makes light of then-president Sebastián Lerdo de Tejada's predicament in 1876 as he faced uprisings led by Porfirio Díaz. The humor depends on a shared memory of the Matiana prophecies: just as the pamphlet visions announced liberalism's doom and a miraculous new order, so *La Metralla* sounded a sarcastic death knell for Lerdo. This passage merits quotation at some length because beyond demonstrating the seer's political deployment in the late 1870s, it anticipates the manner in which twentieth-century interpreters made use of her image, both as a stand-in for the popular mindset and the avatar of folk morality and justice. The new Matiana declared,

> Once cast into the vortex of the world, and now having returned,
> drawn by the misfortunes weighing down my unfortunate homeland,
> it is now impossible for me to return to my retirement, without first
> contributing my grain of sand to her [hoped-for] happiness . . .

> Without hatred, without bitterness, without any passion whatsoever
> against the persons causing so many ills, what my pen writes will have
> the seal of truth, daughter of impartiality, because I expect nothing
> from the present or the future.

I read in the heart of the Mexican people, the sweet [and keen] hope
that Mr. Lerdo and *his representatives*, hearing the voice of their conscience will save it from so many tears and so much bloodshed . . . How
much deception will the people take?

He [the president] will continue to fight against public opinion . . . and
he will fight to the death . . . he will gamble everything for everything,
feeding a hope, without understanding that his *up to here* is fixed.

The year 1877 will greet a new President of the Republic of Mexico.[91]

Thus this reworked satirical Matiana exhorts the president to depart of his
own accord, but she predicts that he will resist both the national will and his
own preordained fate. The implication, of course, is that Lerdo was forcing
his righteous critics to resort to violence. Subsequently, *El Siglo* attacked *La
Metralla* as alarmist cowards for playing the prophetess, but the latter kept
issuing anti-Lerdo barbs in coy, mystical metaphor.[92] Proudly, they maintained, it was the people's right to decry abuse and demand justice.[93]
Unmentioned was the fact that when these journalists ostensibly spoke for
the general populace, and conveyed their inner most desires, they did so as
Madre Matiana. In the end, these "prophecies" came true: Díaz indeed
ousted Lerdo in November of 1876.

Díaz's supporters then turned the tables and accused their own critics of
mystical pretentions. Hence in 1879, *La Libertad*, a chief pro-Díaz press out-
let at the time, skewered rivals as blustering Matianas.[94] As in previous cases,
they claimed that the infamous seer and the act of prophecy in general had
long since fallen into disrepute, and they lamented their colleagues' backslid-
ing. Along similar lines in 1880, *La Libertad* accused *La Gaceta del Lunes* of
resurrecting Madre Matiana. They equated the Mexican prophetess with
Merlin and Nostradamus and mocked their opponents as doomsayer "luna-
tics."[95] Four years later *La Libertad* maligned *El Monitor* as "the continuer of
the great work begun by Madre Matiana."[96] By the end of the century, lumping together the prophetess and all things outdated or foolish became a standard reflex. Thus in 1898, *El Contemporáneo*, a newspaper from San Luis
Potosí, published an editorial that lauded "*doctrinas modernas*" and con-
signed the useless objects and ideas of yesteryear to the metaphorical scrap
heap. Among the latter were bows and arrows, broken columns, and the
prophecies of Madre Matiana.[97]

Still the prophetess endured. In fact in 1908 the same provincial newspaper published an essay offering a typology of fanaticism in Mexico, which deployed the prophetess as the epitome of obscurantism.[98] Penned by Agustín Rivera, a priest critical of Catholic intransigence, the essay delineated two camps of fanatics: *leones* (lions, gendered male) and *zorras* (vixens; in Mexican popular parlance, loose women).[99] The former, he argued, conflated liberalism and cardinal sin and predominated among conservatives prior to 1867. In Rivera's view, as long as leones could imagine outright political victory they attacked liberalism openly with the weapons of old: "In their writings they still talk of 'heresies' and 'excommunications' . . . and they cite the 'Syllabus [of Errors]' of Pious IX, the Encyclicals of Leo XIII . . . and the Prophecies of Matiana and an additional cluster of false miracles, false prophecies, and false revelations rejected by the Catholic religion; and because of this they end up being 'counterproductive,' because their old wives' tales cause shouts of laughter among liberals and conservatives." [100]

Seeing as these tactics were not working—and with modern ideas and liberal government firmly in place—Mexico's new breed of "fanatics" opted for duplicity, earning the zorra label. Like the most devious vixens, duplicitous conservatives feigned accommodation and cultivated social bonds with liberals. Rivera argued that their strategy depended on three tiers of craven action: first, the clever manipulation of family ties; second, the revitalization of friendships forged in school; and third, the cooptation of liberals' wives and daughters. This last tactic, Rivera theorized, was particularly effective because female vanity made women vulnerable to the blandishments of prominent zorras, and most husbands tended to accommodate their wives' obsessions as mere frivolities. Once introduced in the home, Rivera warned, vixens underhandedly facilitated such things as the recent republication of the *Profecías de Matiana*, in book form and available for 1 peso and 75 cents. Zorra schemes, he warned, were working: they had kept the fanaticism embodied by the prophetess alive by exploiting the weakest members of society, women and children.

Rivera's notion of a conspiracy to upend liberalism through the brainwashing of liberals' wives and daughters is farfetched to say the least. Nonetheless the fears and paranoid speculation at work in his claims are of central importance. Rivera demonstrates that the pamphlet prophetess had become a lasting emblem of fanaticism. On a more profound level, he also reveals the linkages forged between Matiana's representation and ideas about women in general. In the process, negative discourses of devout femininity work to conjure the essential masculine modern subject (the antithesis of Madre Matiana).

And yet, Rivera's nightmare of liberal patriarchy had some basis in fact. Many women and girls had indeed embraced the cause of Catholic revival. (Rivera, though, never considered that liberalism offered little to women.) The Church indeed recovered considerable influence between 1867 and 1908. Late nineteenth-century Catholic activists celebrated devout women and their stalwart support of the Church. Modern men and nation-states, many argued, had lapsed into apostasy. Numerous voices in Mexico and other parts of the Catholic world contended that pious women could save humanity from godless liberalism through expiatory devotion and gender-appropriate activism. Women, some argued, represented Christian civilization's best hope: they safeguarded doctrinal purity, sustained ritual, and ultimately could inspire repentance among wayward men. In brief, religious activists continued to echo the gendered militancy that fueled the original Matiana prophecies. For their part, the liberal press turned the pamphlet prophetess into a reactionary shibboleth, an insult, and a vessel for their insecurities about women's roles in the modern nation. In the most fundamental sense, Matiana encapsulated hopes, fears, fantasies, and uncertainties across the ideological spectrum.

But what of the republication of the prophecies mentioned by Rivera? He omitted the name and author of this work, but only one book was published on the topic in the nineteenth century. Furthermore, by citing the book's price he made it clear that he was referring to a work published in 1889 by Mexico City's Círculo Católico (an institution at the center of Catholic activism) and available in hardback for precisely 1 peso and 75 cents. The book in question turned the short, pamphlet-length text of the prophecies into a 150-page call to arms for Catholic militants. It is to this Matiana that we now turn.

CHAPTER 4

Nuestra vidente

Mexico's Messenger of Catholic Resurgence

MARÍA CONCEPCIÓN MÉNDEZ PÉREZ GIL WAS BORN IN 1862 TO A DEVOUT landowning family in Morelia, Michoacán.[1] As a teenager in the late 1870s, she set her sights on becoming a nun, finding herself drawn to the adoration of the Blessed Sacrament. Two of her sisters were already postulants of the Dominican order (also known as the Catalinas). Concha, as she was known, followed in their footsteps, but she sensed that her spiritual destiny lay elsewhere. At first, although aware of intense yearnings, a true vocation seemed shrouded in uncertainty. Eventually, in a powerful dream she envisioned two rows of nuns within a church, all of whom were venerating the Body of Christ. Henceforth she singlemindedly sought the means to dedicate herself to the Blessed Sacrament. Her confessor and the Catalinas tried to convince her that these feelings were distractions and youthful vanities, but the steadfast girl defended her convictions. At about the same time one of her sisters, María, stumbled across encouraging portents. María had only been with the Catalinas a short time, and so she returned home when suffering from a prolonged illness. While convalescing she found an old trunk in her parents' house that contained items once belonging to the Méndez sisters' grandmother. Rummaging through the contents she found a copy of *Las profecías de la Madre Matiana*, which María commenced to read with avid interest. In this publication she discovered that the seer had foreseen the emergence of a new female religious order in Mexico devoted to the adoration of the Blessed Sacrament and the appeasement of Christ's mounting anger.

Pondering the prophecies filled her heart with the same desire to dedicate herself to Eucharistic devotion as her sister. Learning that Concha was leaving the Catalinas to seek out an order in Mexico City attuned to their calling (the Brígidas Sacramentarias), María resolved to join her.[2] Both became postulants, and later novices, of the brígidas only to become disillusioned rather quickly. Apparently economic activities and internal disputes within the convent undermined sustained devotion and contemplation. In other words, the sisters found the brígidas too worldly. These young women, however, enjoyed extraordinarily high-level contacts in Mexico City's archdiocese. First they aired their concerns with the vicar general, Próspero María Alarcón, a priest who later became archbishop and served as their primary patron. He took them to meet Archbishop Pelagio Antonio Labastida y Dávalos—apparently a distant relative of the Méndez sisters. Impressed, the prelate backed their cause. After an investigation in 1885, he removed them from the brígidas and approved their formation of a new order christened the Instituto de las Adoratrices Perpetuas Guadalupanas (Guadalupan Institute of the Perpetual Adorers; APG). A few years later, while still only twenty four, Concha—now renamed María Mercedes de la Santísima Trinidad—became the order's mother superior. A year later her sister was put in charge of training the APG's novices.[3] In short, by the late 1880s these two young women were leading a new religious order dedicated to Eucharistic devotion as outlined in the Matiana prophecies. Remarkably, sources hint that even the high clergymen backing the Adoratrices indeed had the prophetess's predictions in mind when the APG came together.

The Méndez sisters approached the Church hierarchy at the right time. In 1874 the Lerdo administration expelled one of the last female religious orders operating in Mexico, the French Sisters of Charity. Mexico's clergy keenly wanted to fill the resultant void with local religious orders for women.[4] In subsequent years many women answered the call to form new female institutions at the grassroots of Catholic revival in Mexico. For example, during this same period the Siervas del Sagrado Corazón de Jesús y los Pobres (Servants of the Sacred Heart of Jesus and the Poor) emerged in León, Guanajuato. Over the next two decades they too expanded to several cities throughout Mexico, as did the APG.[5] Both the Adoratrices and the Siervas remain active today.

Between 1885 and 1893 the APG experienced the typical early hardships described in convent histories. Internal conflicts stressed community cohesion, and priestly spiritual directors at times proved insensitive and capricious.

They also struggled to find a permanent residence and establish stable economic foundations. Nonetheless they persevered trusting in providence and cultivating patrons. They sought affiliation with an order in Rome that had a similar expiatory mission, and a few well-heeled Mexican benefactors helped with timely donations. Their most important break, though, appears to have been Alarcón's consecration as archbishop in 1892. According to the APG's published histories, on 12 December 1893, while saying Mass at the feast of the Virgin of Guadalupe, the new prelate experienced an epiphany: he envisioned the Adoratrices venerating the Blessed Sacrament at the basilica. When he broached the topic with Madre Mercedes he alluded to the Matiana visions: "Perhaps you are going to tell me that the prophecies foretelling that the Adoratrices will be at la Villa next to the Shrine of Our Holy Mother of Guadalupe are being fulfilled."[6] Alarcón then offered Madre Mercedes the old residence of the excloistered Capuchin nuns, provided that they add religious education to their duties. The sisters of the APG eagerly accepted and within a year relocated there.[7] Thus it appears that Alarcón facilitated the transfer of the APG to the Guadalupe shrine to make the Matiana visions become a reality: just as the pamphlets described, he located a new order of nuns dedicated to venerating the Blessed Sacrament at the most venerated sanctuary in Mexico. His motives cannot be fully understood, because much documentation from the Adoratrices' early years remains inaccessible. Still this anecdote suggests that the prelate and the religiosas pondered the APG's founding in this light. In any case by 1894, the new order satisfied a central provision of Matiana's prophecies, the creation of a new order of nuns dedicated to expiatory Eucharistic devotion and ensconced at the national shrine. Others noticed the parallels as well; twenty years later a reprinting of the Matiana prophecies listed the Adoratrices' presence at La Villa as proof of their accuracy.[8]

Additional evidence suggests that the Matiana prophecies were very much "in the air" among impassioned Catholic activists during the 1880s and early 1890s. In fact, as the Méndez sisters were winning over Alarcón and Labastida, archdiocesan correspondence reveals others were debating an ambitious reinterpretation of the famous visionary narrative. On 14 December 1883, a hopeful author named Dionisio A. de Jesús María engaged José Reyes Velasco, a Mexico City printer, in a discussion about his recently written manuscript on the topic.[9]

Reyes Velasco specialized in devotional pamphlets, religious institutional documents, sermons, and pastoral letters.[10] In addition, he produced polemical conservative tracts. Given the market he targeted, Reyes frequently communicated with archdiocesan censors. For example, in 1885 he sought permission to reprint a pair of pamphlets, *Las naciones enfurecidas contra Cristo y su Iglesia (The Nations Enraged Against Christ and his Church)* and *El Papa y las logias (The Pope and the [Masonic] Lodges).*[11] A couple of years later he requested a license to publish a Church-approved "moral" novel.[12]

De Jesús María and Reyes had clearly corresponded before. The former thanked the printer effusively for his enthusiastic response regarding the manuscript in question, and he promised to resubmit a revised and expanded version within a year's time. Reyes Velasco, de Jesús María anticipated, would soon sell the book by the hundreds, getting copies to chaplains, Church-atrium stalls, roving peddlers, and bookshops. Eventually, he contended, the ideas conveyed in his manuscript would spread and new editions would be in order. Alas, this testament to authorial salesmanship came to naught; de Jesús María never published this manuscript.

Despite the fact that no version of the Matiana prophecies bears his name, the young writer's unvarnished ardor provides a counterweight to the derisive commentary in the liberal press. More importantly, his testimony provides a unique glimpse of a committed, militant believer's understanding of these contested visions. He dramatically questioned Reyes Velasco as to how long it had been since Mexicans read the prophecies, and why they were no longer available. The populace, he lamented, had lost the capacity to "penetrate" the spirit of prophecy. Impious ignorance had become so common that Mexicans merely made fun of miraculous foresight and shunned such vital readings. But de Jesús María noted, citing Saint Paul, *"Prophecies are for the faithful, not the infidels"* (original emphasis). The problem, he suggested, was that the populace misunderstood Madre Matiana's predictions, and hence they did not delve into them to deepen their faith. The seer, he asserted, spoke about the imminent establishment of the Kingdom of Christ, but tragically the cursed nineteenth century marched with the Anti-Christ. Much of the flock had renounced the faith. Grave troubles were mounting as the era hurtled towards annihilation. But he asserted, "This is why the Church waits, and will not be caught by surprise amidst the inconceivable horrible burning of the iniquitous world, enemy of Christ and his Church." Meanwhile it was God's will, the impassioned author assured Reyes, that the true sons of the Church enlighten the remaining faithful lest they despair and succumb to the godless immorality of the modern world.[13]

In their zeal and devout certainty, individuals like Dionisio de Jesús María and the Méndez sisters remind us that a number of Mexicans took Matiana's prophetic warnings to heart, ignoring doubts about her origins and ridicule of her mystical narrative. Sadly few documented their feelings or resultant actions, but their role in the Matiana phenomenon was absolutely central. Without a portion of the populace who were willing to contemplate the visions seriously, it is doubtful that the prophetess's story would have endured. Admittedly, for some Matiana served as shorthand for "superstition." But beneath contemptuous attitudes toward common belief resides an unspoken admission: many Mexicans accepted miraculous visionary experience as an article of faith, and some of them saw glimmers of truth in the Matiana narrative. Mocking the prophecies hardly makes sense otherwise.

As de Jesús María revealed, the devout believer engaged with prophecy to understand hardship and steel the soul against impiety. In Europe during the same period, new miraculous apparitions and prophecy narratives affixed intense religious meaning to social experience and current events.[14] As the earnest young author suggested, finding linkages between Matiana's visions, everyday life, and history cast Mexico in the sweep of epic Christian struggle. By extension, engaging the Matiana legacy uncritically placed the faithful at a crucial juncture in the imagined, cataclysmic proceedings. Clearly such beliefs made prayer, ritual, and acts of expiation vitally important and deeply meaningful for individuals.

As with so much relating to the prophetess, the new cycle of Matiana interpretation signaled by the Adoratrices' emergence and de Jesús María's letter in the 1880s reveals the inextricable mixing of religion, politics, and gender at work. This new phase saw the addition of a reworked conservative nationalism intertwined with international Catholic militancy, making this cocktail still more powerful. Essentially what we are sampling is evidence from the militant activist base of the Church, where Madre Matiana served as a Mexican beacon of universal Catholic resurgence and a model of principled resistance, particularly among women. Now decades removed from her initial appearance in the first pamphlets, activists reassessed the visionary narrative, recasting it in much grander terms. Drinking deeply from the well of European conservative conspiracy theory, Matiana's new interpreters understood her predictions as a Mexican warning shot in a global battle. It is indeed a testament to the flexibility of the Matiana narrative that it could be made to fit within the vast international literature of Catholic militancy. It helped that so much in the text was open-ended. Another year ending with the number eight was always approaching and vague predictions of violent conflict could be projected onto social tensions in nearly any period. What is more, Matiana's apocalyptic feminism resonated with trends in the Catholic Church worldwide, while it remained poignantly meaningful to many Mexicans.

INSPIRATIONS AND ACTIONS

The 1880s indeed represented a crucial moment for Mexico's Catholic resurgence. By then conservatives had regained their footing after the collapse of Maximilian's empire in 1867. Porfirio Díaz took power in 1876 and gradually constructed a stable authoritarian regime that sought rapprochement with the Catholic Church and its supporters. Simultaneously the nation's economy benefited from more propitious conditions. Foreign markets were growing steadily and international financiers looked to developing nations for investment opportunities. The combination of political and economic stability created fertile conditions for growth within civil society, and devout Catholics took full advantage of the circumstances. The Laws of the Reform that had enflamed partisans and conditioned the initial reception of Matiana's prophecies endured, but Díaz made it clear to Church leaders (privately) that he had little interest in strict enforcement, provided the Church refrained from antigovernment activity. After decades of conflict this represented a true boon for the Church, which consequently undertook internal reform alongside institutional revitalization. For the rest of the nineteenth century and during the first decade of the twentieth century, Catholic organizations flourished and multiplied. New Church-affiliated schools, newspapers, seminaries, mutual-aid societies, devotional associations, beneficent institutions, and religious orders sprang up across Mexico. At least officially these organizations had to profess strictly religious goals, but many also hoped to halt secular liberalism's advance and establish a truly Catholic social order.[15] Much the same was happening in other Catholic nations at this time.

The APG's impressive accomplishments are a testament to this phenomenon. By 1910 several additional houses affiliated with the Adoratrices emerged and operated schools in numerous Mexican cities. They even managed to weather the Mexican Revolution, when new anticlerical legislation led to the uncloistering of the APG and the confiscation of their properties. After a period of exile, Madre Mercedes led her "daughters" back to Mexico and reestablished new houses and restarted their schools in the late 1920s. According to present-day members, during her lifetime the intrepid founder wrote about her spiritual experiences and crafted unique devotional exercises for her charges, which the Adoratrices continue to use. These writings could likely tell us a great deal about these women's understanding of their role in the Church and society during this period, but the APG will not allow outsiders to examine these documents: *"Esas cosas son muy internas"* ("Those things are very internal").[16] For nonmembers, three official biographies and a few letters in the archdiocesan archive represent the evidentiary foundations of the APG's history. They do not, unfortunately, support a close examination of the founding members' beliefs and practices, or reveal how these women understood Matiana's visions in light of their own experiences. These nuns who appear to have patterned their ministry on the expiatory themes celebrated in the prophecies must remain a suggestive echo surrounding the seer's deeper impact for the time being.

Luckily one of Madre Mercedes's contemporaries—and possibly an acquaintance—wrote at length about Matiana's significance in the 1880s. In fact, of all those who took part in shaping the Matiana legacy during the nineteenth century none did so at greater length than Luis G. Duarte y Rico (1829–1897).[17] In the 1890s when Archbishop Alarcón commented on the prophetic resonance of the APG's presence at La Villa he was most likely drawing on Duarte's recently published interpretation of the seer's visions.

Due to the marginalization experienced by traditionalist Catholics following the defeat of Maximillian and his French-backed empire, this new Matiana interpreter was something of an archconservative jack-of-all-trades during the late nineteenth century. He was born in the provincial city of Tehuacán in southern Puebla, but he was the son of a dean of the College of Law in Mexico City. His father, José Mariano Duarte, received his law degree in 1825 and became a prominent jurist.[18] His son followed in his footsteps, completing his legal studies in 1852 and serving as a judge and instructor at the National College of Law. Like so many of the men of his generation, political conflict truncated Duarte's career. According to his obituary in the Catholic newspaper, *La Voz de México*, liberalism's ascendancy in Mexico upended Duarte's promising legal and professorial vocation. Apparently he could not stomach working for the impious government and its institutions, even though many influential friends encouraged him to muzzle his criticism of liberal reform and return to the university faculty.[19] In a sense, Duarte represents the mirror opposite of puro liberals like Ignacio Ramírez (1818–1879). He remained an intransigent conservative and principled champion of ultramontane piety and politics his entire life. When liberal militias prevailed in 1867, Duarte's allegiances were a matter of public record. His name appears on a public announcement lauding the French invasion in July 1863.[20] He also secured a post in Maximilian's imperial government, even though he still maintained a private law practice.[21] He must have benefited from President Benito Juárez's conciliatory approach to imperialist collaborators, because he was not incarcerated or exiled. Regardless, he refused to make peace with the new order.[22] Some Catholics counseled accommodation with the state and sought to compartmentalize their religious and political principles. This stance was abhorrent to *intransigentes* like Duarte who cleaved to Pious IX's categorical demonization of liberalism.[23]

Diehards like Duarte had to rethink their partisan strategies and personal lives. Working to overthrow the government was no longer a real option; working for the government was repugnant. Furthermore new laws prohibited openly Catholic political organizing. Embittered but unbowed, men like Duarte looked to their counterparts in Europe for inspiration and crafted astute short- and long-term objectives. These amounted to an immediate circling of the proverbial wagons regarding religion and a farsighted institution-building crusade. The secularizing national charter and anticlerical laws were now facts of life, but this sector of the populace envisioned a future Catholic sociopolitical and cultural restoration and worked toward its realization. As the dust slowly settled in the wake of midcentury civil war, conservatives had to maintain that their endeavors were strictly private matters. Outwardly new organizations like the Sociedad Católica, the Círculo Católico, and new kinds of religious orders like the APG, claimed to focus solely on doctrine, orthodoxy, ritual, and devotion. Internally, of course, these institutions debated much broader goals. Historian Jorge Adame Goddard identified three general tendencies among this group of Mexicans: political abstentionism, academic and educational work, and collaboration in the reorganization of the Church.[24] If writing and publishing are included, this description encapsulates Duarte's post-1867 existence.

It is also important to contemplate Duarte's career in terms of the era's religious gender norms. Mexican society expected women to respond to national crisis with prayer and penance; men, however, were called to speak out and defend the Church. Intensely devout women like the Méndez sisters sought to catalyze the triumph of the Church through collective expiatory devotion and the education of children. Duarte, in contrast, fought Catholicism's enemies in print as well as through his teaching. Both before and after the liberal victory he collaborated in various conservative journalistic endeavors, such as *El*

Figure 14. Reinterpreting Madre Matiana for the late nineteenth century. From Luis G. Duarte, *Profecías de Matiana acerca del triunfo de la Iglesia*, Imprenta del "Círculo Católico," 1889.

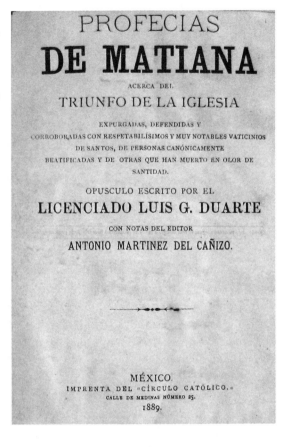

PROFECIAS
DE MATIANA
ACERCA DEL
TRIUNFO DE LA IGLESIA

EXPURGADAS, DEFENDIDAS Y
CORROBORADAS CON RESPETABILÍSIMOS Y MUY NOTABLES VATICINIOS
DE SANTOS, DE PERSONAS CANÓNICAMENTE
BEATIFICADAS Y DE OTRAS QUE HAN MUERTO EN OLOR DE
SANTIDAD.

OPUSCULO ESCRITO POR EL
LICENCIADO LUIS G. DUARTE
CON NOTAS DEL EDITOR
ANTONIO MARTINEZ DEL CAÑIZO.

MÉXICO.
IMPRENTA DEL "CÍRCULO CATÓLICO."
CALLE DE MEDINAS NÚMERO 25.
1889.

Pájaro Verde, La Voz de México, and *El Nacional.*[25] In the 1860s he worked as the secretary of a private school, and produced elementary instructional materials.[26] By the 1870s he was also publishing religious texts.[27] He also authored a dictionary in 1881, used in some public schools.[28] Given this record it is not surprising to find Duarte listed as a founding member of the Sociedad Guadalupana de Profesores (The Guadalupan Society of Teachers).[29] Mostly, though, he was known for his religious writings and his own Catholic bookstore.[30] Perhaps his most famous work was *Las Profecías de Matiana acerca del triunfo de la Iglesia* (*The Prophecies of Matiana Concerning the Triumph of the Church*), published in 1889.[31] He also produced a series of essays in the early 1890s that attacked critics of the Guadalupe apparitions.[32] In these efforts he left a trail of correspondence with ecclesiastical censors.[33] He was clearly well known and a respected member of the conservative intellectual community.

The editors of *El Tiempo* (a Catholic daily) in the 1890s referred to him as a close friend and sold copies of *Profecías* at their offices.[34] Duarte supported his Catholic journalist colleagues as well; for example, he published a series of letters in *El Cruzado* to defend Trinidad Sánchez Santos, a well-known and outspoken Catholic newspaperman.[35] He was not above infighting either. When he and his editor, Antonio Martínez del Cañizo, pursued ecclesiastical approval for *Profecías* they first lobbied for the recusal of the official Church censor, Manuel de Solé, because he and Duarte had apparently carried out a public feud in the Catholic press.[36]

Records indicate that Duarte and Martínez were in a hurry to publish the book in the fall of 1889. Although they did not mention the reason for their haste, it probably stemmed from efforts to market the book around the centennial of the French Revolution. Catholic activists the world over marked the events of 1789 as the sinister inauguration of a cursed era. Mexico's Catholic press presented the post-Revolutionary century as a time of infamy, recommending chastened contemplation rather than celebration. Moreover, they framed the centenary as the inaugural moment of a Catholic restoration crusade.[37] Mexico's Círculo Católico, the publishers of Duarte's book on Madre Matiana, had issued passionate calls to this effect throughout 1888 and 1889 in their official organ. They spoke optimistically of a global expiation movement taking shape to transform the "prevaricating and corrupt century into a century of reparation and penance."[38] Heretical error and apostasy, they maintained, had spread from France like a deadly plague. The Catholic spirit had been diminished by a perversion of customs so profound that the faithful could no longer simply avoid personal sin. As the century closed, believers had to step forward with the pope: "Let us form an immense league . . . of prayer and tears, of action and sacrifice."[39] In their view, Christ's fury was mounting and urgent collective action was imperative. As the *Círculo* stressed in another issue from December 1888, "The public sufferings we lament are punishments of national wrongdoings, because . . . Mexico has been delinquent as a nation, and as a result needs national expiation."[40] In sum, Duarte's *Profecías* represents a call to action synchronized with the centenary of the imagined global reign of error, blasphemy, and irreverence. The point was not to simply reread Matiana's prophesies—Duarte was much more ambitious. He deployed Mexico's famed visionary in order to position the nation in what he described as a long-awaited turning point in the cosmic struggle between good and evil.

Duarte and his editor, Martínez, made sure to coordinate their efforts with supporters among the clergy and the Catholic publishing community. Initially they tried to save money by publishing the book in Spain, but they found the process of ecclesiastical approval there too slow. In late September 1889, they turned to the Archdiocese of Mexico, and Martínez tried his best to flatter the provisor (the archdiocese's ecclesiastical magistrate).[41] Printing, he implied, was already underway. His blandishments apparently worked because within ten days he negotiated the recusal of Duarte's nemesis (Manuel Solé), and by 8 November his replacement, Canon Vito Cruz, issued an official endorsement—the first official validation of the prophecies by Church authorities.[42] Cruz lauded Duarte's careful analysis, noted that the text met doctrinal norms, and opined that Matiana's visions were probably divinely inspired. Best of all, he suggested, the book could potentially inspire practices to "placate the ire of God, bring on [His] mercy, and realize the triumph of the church." Three days later the provisor announced archdiocesan approval.[43] Church sanction, however, was probably guaranteed well in advance of these dates, because *El Tiempo* noted receipt of a copy of the book two weeks before Cruz issued his ruling.[44] About a month later the newspaper published a glowing front-page article praising Duarte and the book entitled "Las profecías de Matiana VINDICADAS."[45] *El Tiempo* quoted Cruz at length. Rounding out the promotion campaign, Duarte and Martínez made sure that the full text of the censor's ruling, the announcement of ecclesiastical approval, and the newspaper's endorsement appeared in *Profecía*'s front matter. In his preface, Martínez also emphasized that Catholic bookstores already stocked Duarte's opus.[46]

Duarte acknowledged that overcoming the legacy of contempt heaped upon Madre Matiana and her visions represented his greatest challenge. He admitted that parts of the original text indeed came across as foolishness and anticipated scornful reactions by both enemies of the Church and even avowed Catholics. As evident in Dionisio de Jesús María's letter and *El Tiempo*'s emphasis on "vindication," activists like Duarte felt that most Mexicans in the 1880s viewed Matiana and her prophecies as fanatical nonsense, or at best a joke. Duarte astutely addressed these issues head on. In the prologue's first paragraph he notes that many Catholics found the topic embarrassing and harmful to their cause. Some viewed Matiana's visions as superstitious stupidities inviting impious ridicule. According to Duarte, they felt that the Church's critics used the proclamations of *ilusos* (false mystics) to smear all Catholics as simpletons. Such was the vehemence of many devout skeptics, Duarte argued, that they refused to even contemplate the revelations. Others unallied with the Church, he avowed, approached Matiana amid agnostic detachment: "From the time that they [the prophecies] were published for the first time, other people read them in a bemused, festive mood, quite ready . . . to focus on what they perceived as contradictory or absurd . . . imagining themselves impartial, as they laugh at their tone of fairy-tale ridiculousness."[47] Duarte confessed that previously he too looked askance at the prophecies. More recently, however, a "young friend" convinced him that Matiana's revelations could help the Catholic cause. Perhaps this individual was none other than Dionisio de Jesús María, but Duarte provided no specifics.[48]

Given this background, *Profecías* reveals two primary, interwoven goals. The first encompasses the prophetess's public vindication by a well-connected Catholic intellectual. Thus Duarte structured the book to neutralize the legacy of disdain associated with Matiana's visions. The second entails attaching Mexico's history of instability and conflict to a reactionary European narrative of religious persecution and antimodern visionary lore that originated in the wake of the French Revolution. To accomplish these ends Duarte chose a straightforward proof-like structure. Each chapter begins with an excerpt drawn directly from the Matiana prophecies, followed by the author's analysis of its meaning in domestic and international contexts. Seemingly unaware of the 1847 Valdés y Redondas pamphlet, he claimed that the earliest Matiana publications emerged in 1857. One such printing (he did not provide precise publication information) served as his source text. Footnotes feature Martínez's commentary on Duarte's claims, occasionally pointing out similar arguments from famous Catholic figures like Pope Pious IX. These interventions function as a virtual claque backing the author's interpretation throughout the book.

Invariably Duarte's analysis employs extensive passages plucked verbatim from the second volume of French Abbot and Catholic historian Jean-Jules-Marie Curicque's *Voces proféticas* (1870).[49] This work came out of a surge of interest in miraculous apparitions and prophecy in the wake of the Paris Commune and France's defeat in the Franco-Prussian War, which roughly coincided with its initial publication. According to historian Thomas Kselman, the early 1870s featured widespread apocalyptic expectations of monarchical restoration in France. These narratives spoke of the emergence of a "great pope" destined to miraculously restore Catholicism's glory alongside a new king.[50] *Voces proféticas* was really just one of many similar texts produced at this time, but its quick translation and wide distribution made it a veritable reference work for years to come. As Duarte's *Profecías* demonstrates, Curicque's book served as a compendium of Catholic visionary narratives and seers' biographies, with every chapter bolstering the thesis that the nineteenth century represented the "time of troubles" prior to judgment day. For decades *Voces proféticas* resided in the virtual echo chamber surrounding ultramontane activism.[51]

In a nutshell, *Voces proféticas* contended that impious governments and debased customs had been provoking celestial annihilation for decades. Late nineteenth-century humanity lived on borrowed time, Curicque asserted. The Supreme Being repeatedly tried to get France's attention through natural disasters, miracles, and wars. Prophets issued multiple warnings, and yet society persisted in unparalleled decadence. Only the Virgin Mary's intersession and expiatory sacrifice by saintly individuals— mostly visionary women—had forestalled total destruction. Time and again, Curicque argued, seers embraced death to atone for collective sin and God granted temporary reprieves. But humanity was finally exhausting his merciful patience.[52]

In reality *Voces proféticas* built on an older tradition of right-wing conspiracy theory that reaches back to the late eighteenth century.[53] Writers such as the French Jesuit Augustín Barruel (1741–1820) established a lasting anti-Revolutionary narrative grounded in notions of an unfolding plot to destroy Catholic Christendom, eviscerate the established social order, and nurture hellish anarchy.[54] These theories first appeared in his controversial memoir, which Spanish and Mexican printers reproduced in translation from at least the early 1800s.[55] His architects of evil were the French philosophes, like Voltaire, and their notorious colleagues, the freemasons and the Illuminati. For Barruel the term *Jacobin* simply labeled the union of this conniving triad. Together, he alleged, they implemented a complex scheme incorporating legions of fanatical followers who had internalized the cynical ideology and seductive vocabulary of equality, liberty, reason, and rights. In addition to Barruel's writings, Mexican editions of works by other famous French conservatives from this period, such as Joseph Marie de Maistre (1753–1821) were also on offer.[56]

For many, even fellow Catholic conservatives, the abbot's theories were too farfetched. Barruel, though, sketched a primarily human plot. Some, like Maistre, asserted that divine providence allowed the French Revolution to occur because the nation had turned its back its special Catholic destiny.[57]

Still others, including Curicque, argued that dark supernatural forces were
the true intellectual authors of the transformations shaking the world.
According to historian Darrin McMahon, the apocalyptic interpretations of
profound change in France pre-dated the "Age of Revolution," and represented much more than a mere political stance as the notions flourished in
the nineteenth century. They voiced an enduring conservative worldview
sustained by shared radical beliefs, heated rhetoric, and fierce conservative
nationalism with internationalist echoes. By the time Duarte tapped into this
stream it featured an array of code words and metaphors regarding the de-
generation of society, the corruption of religion, the pernicious development
of individualism and materialism, and the "rational" attack on faith. The
Revolution, from this perspective, served as a realization of these nightmar-
ish prognostications and hence strengthened the convictions of those embracing these ideas. McMahon stresses that it eventually became an
innovative ideological culture championing a wholly new order that bore
little resemblance to the pre-Revolutionary society idealized in these
circles.[58]

Proponents ignored the diversity of Enlightenment thought while radi-
cally simplifying history to create a single, malignant threat. Detailed facts
hardly mattered, and the narrative remained simplistic, shrill, and repetitive.
Nonetheless it also proved compelling to many Catholics at the time. Words
like *philosophe, individualist, materialist,* and *freethinker* became de facto
slurs.[59] By the 1820s conservative hardliners fit liberalism into the grand conspiracy: it merely represented a rephrasing of heretical "philosophic religion"
for a new phase of the plot.[60]

In the mid-nineteenth century conservative Catholic activists in Mexico
devoured this literature, even though writers like Curicque did not include
the nation in their analyses. This, however, is precisely what Duarte set out
to do. The Mexican author wrote Madre Matiana into the pantheon of prophets sketched by Curicque, taking pains to draw connections between the
narratives surrounding European seers, the Matiana tradition, and Mexico's
unique history. In fact, such is his dependence on the French abbot's book
that long sections of *Profecías* are little more than passages lifted from *Voces
proféticas* and chained together by brief commentary.

Like Curicque, Duarte's analysis was highly reductive. Mere echoes of
similarity sufficed to impute apocalyptic congruence. The social, political,
and cultural distinctions between Mexico and Europe disappear. For example, since Matiana spoke of a great definitive conflict, Duarte mined *Voces*

proféticas for narratives predicting epic battles and proclaims celestial coordination. He did the same for other era-defining trends, such as constitutionalism. Likewise, he linked the Marianism of the Matiana prophecies to the surging Marian militancy of Europe. A conflating of the pamphlet prophetess's insights with those of her counterparts in Europe bolstered his attempt to dispel contempt for Madre Matiana in Mexico. As he repeatedly stated, since Matiana's prophecies meshed with the revelations of seers vetted by the infallible church, they too were divine visions. But the insertion of Mexico's nineteenth century into the conspiracy narratives crafted in Europe only served as one facet of Duarte's campaign. Perhaps more importantly he addressed the popular nature of the texts and the off-putting contradictions that numerous Mexican Catholics identified within the narrative.

He accomplished this by separating Madre Matiana, the eighteenth-century seer, from Madre Guerra (María Josefa de la Pasión de Jesús), the alleged nineteenth-century source of the prophetess's visions. Duarte clearly tried to reach a wide range of committed Catholics, many of whom did not embrace his ultramontane worldview. He was under no illusions that the book would convince secularist opponents. If he hoped to broaden Matiana's appeal it was paramount to disarm the negative associations linked to the prophetess, particularly the notion that she represented a tawdry outgrowth of popular superstitions. He essentially created two distinct characters to combat these assumptions. One is his Madre Matiana, a divinely inspired colonial seer whose actual words, ideas, and visions are beyond consultation. He imbued the presumptive Mexican seer with the paradigmatic character traits of the iconic simple but pure, female visionary chosen from among the lowly to convey God's message. Naturally this meant counting on the fact that many Catholics presumed the existence of such figures. No historical evidence corroborated his portrayal. In many ways his Matiana was nothing more than a saintly archetype pasted over the contested text. He then depicted Madre Guerra, the supposed author of the ecclesiastical deposition that recounted the visions, as a well-meaning but ignorant nun who unwittingly introduced inaccuracies into the prophecies. Essentially she represented another stereotypical figure. Whereas his Matiana was the model visionary channeling divine inspiration, Madre Guerra represented the narrow-minded *monjita* (little nun). It was a shrewd strategy. Any aspect that seemed parochial, superstitious, or foolish was explained away as an aberration attributable to the flawed bearer of Matiana's legacy.[61] Covering his bases, Duarte asserted that God allows this to happen to prophecies to encourage closer analysis. The archdiocesan censor, Vito Cruz, specifically praised the author's approach to Madre Guerra.[62] From this perspective, as if panning for gold, Duarte separated the nuggets of visionary wisdom from the sand and gravel accrued after two generations of oral transmission. His sieve, as it were, was Curicque's *Voces proféticas.*

Structurally, Duarte offered a crescendo-like analysis of the prophecies and Mexico's place in the world during a particularly dangerous historical juncture. Nations faced not only antireligious movements but also surreptitious attempts to dupe believers with accomodationist bastardizations like "liberal Catholicism." Sampling his rhetoric offers a taste of the intensely conspiratorial militancy he espoused. Duarte asserted that the Matiana's visions were uniquely attuned to the moment:

> a new era that we can call, "The Masonic Era," because it is the period of greatest power—almost absolute and universal—of Masonry, the clever and insidious sect that claims to eschew its real goals, works and aspirations, [as well as] all political principles and all religious ideas, so as to dedicate itself exclusively to philanthropy. Nonetheless, everywhere it propagates liberal Catholicism—detestable offspring of the rest of those [Protestant] sects, and sworn enemy of all order, of all government, of all moral principles and above all, of Catholicism—and it does so with rabid cruelty. Its tactics are like those of guerillas, of ambushes and surprises, always hiding in shadows and taking advantage of all manner of physical, moral, and intellectual obscurities in order to attack each individual according to the state of their conscience, according to the nature of their will, and manipulating all kinds of misery. These politico-religious chameleons can be at once ardent and delicate Catholics, committed Protestants, Jews, Muslims and atheists; and in politics [they can be] cesearists, fanatical partisans of monarchs, or doctrinaire republicans. And they will seize high office by any means and skullduggery, serving all governments under any system, but always in hopes of ruining all stability, and above all, in order to persecute even the glorious name of Catholic.[63]

In this manner, Duarte spent the prologue and first chapter defending the crucial importance of recent divine prophecy amid the impious minefield of modern life and stressing the imminence of celestial punishment.[64]

Subsequently he moved on to the special status of Matiana and other seers as the Virgin Mary's "ambassadresses" and their revelations of apocalyptic conflict. In doing so he linked Mexico's troubles to European militants' portrayal of the post-1789 era. In his rendering all believers were living through a desperate period during which the Mother of God defended Catholics from a blasphemous rebellion against divine order.[65] Typically his mechanism for such connections was to splice in the visions described in *Voces proféticas*, such as descriptions of a world on the brink of destruction.[66] The Virgin Mary in these passages is at wit's end, as she witnesses society's bottomless depravity and Christ seethes. Mary can only try to save the debauched world through her devotees and desperate pleas for expiation. Subsequently Duarte underscored Matiana's emphasis on *desagravio* (literally, unaggrieving) and asserted that the parallels amounted to a concordance with divine will.[67]

From collective sin and repentance, the author moved on to Matiana's discussion of expiatory practices, particularly devotion to the Blessed Sacrament. Duarte used this opportunity to link the considerably older traditions of Eucharistic piety to newer practices in vogue within militant Catholic circles. Thus he carefully tied veneration of the Host to the politically freighted worship of the Sacred Heart of Jesus, a devotion at the very core of conservative Catholic organizing in Europe and Mexico.[68] This, naturally, led him to reprint *Voces proféticas*'s reconstruction of French seer Sister Margarita María Alacoque's seventeenth-century visions (the origins of the Sacred Heart devotion).[69] This text included the dramatic imagery of the Savior's bleeding, thorn-bound heart impaled by multiple swords and lances to signify society's manifold impieties. Subsequently the Mexican author inserted the right-wing account of French history to convey to his audience the classic narrative of demonic conspiracy, the seduction of the masses, and the unleashing of modernity's calamitous reign of passions. Duarte labeled Satan *"El Señor de los Gobiernos"* ("The Lord of Governments"), and it was Satan who had been winning the struggle in Mexico and Europe since 1789.[70] The author suggested that the end of times was surely nigh, but new means of spiritual resistance—devotions like the Immaculate Conception and the Vela Perpetua—were helping the devout forestall the frightful reckoning. Duarte asserted that unity around the Sacred Heart was the surest means of victory. The goal was none other than the unanimity of all Catholic Christendom in order to prepare for the culminating battle with the beast of the apocalypse. In short, Duarte used millenarian narratives of Catholic restoration in France to visualize a parallel process in Mexico. Accompanying footnotes by Cañizo explicitly linked Mexican developments, such as domestic liberalism and North American ideological contagion, to a larger satanic plot. Lest readers miss the point, the subsequent chapter addressed Matiana's vision of Lucifer and his demons spreading the "constitutions and legal code."[71]

As in each other chapter Duarte began with a direct citation from his source, a Matiana pamphlet from 1857, including its most dramatic, and politically freighted passage: "She also viewed a gathering in hell, and the torment suffered by the demons because of peace, a copy of which reigned among Christians in her time. Lucifer was particularly anguished. They all formed a congress, and they produced the constitution and the legal code, and Lucifer ordered the demons to spread those constitutions throughout the world to pervert everyone. Then hell was emptied to make war on Christians."[72] The devil, Duarte surmised, truly feared that the new expiatory order foreseen by Madre Matiana would indeed bring devout peace and prosperity, so he sought to flank such measures with political chicanery. For the author, it was not surprising that Satan sought to blunt pious renewal, but he found the widespread participation of professed Catholics in liberal reform absolutely abhorrent: "But, what can we say about the demonic formation of the Constitution and the Code and even the progressive order [emerging] from the enunciation of the former and latter? Well those same ideas constitute the political-religious credo adopted everywhere as the tenets ordering societies. How many Catholic-liberals wear out their intellects to conciliate those supposed principles with reason, with justice, and with the truth!"[73] The next several chapters then offered a detailed picture of Mexico's history from this skeptical perspective, and hence it ventured into more original territory.[74] Duarte portrayed his nation's past as the Latin American analogue to French Catholic history. On the eve of 1810, in his telling, Mexico faced a two-pronged assault: pernicious social ideas and religious heresies encroaching from the United States, while the anarchic French ideological cancer spread to Latin America via Spanish liberalism. Mexico, framed as the Catholic bulwark of the Americas, had no choice but to assert its independence. Duarte declared sadly that Mexicans later succumbed to temptation and ideological corruption, leading to waves of conflict. He then charted the specific events Matiana allegedly foretold, such as the U.S. invasion and Mexico's Reforma. As he developed this idea, he relied on passages from *Voces proféticas* that detailed how European visionaries had warned of how impieties and anticlericalism brought on these kinds of divine punishments. Ultimately, Duarte argued that just as God allowed the Paris Commune and the Prussian invasion to chastise wayward France, he also permitted Protestant North America and the Reform-era wars to victimize Mexico.

In chapters 12 through 15 of the text, Duarte finally turned his attention to predictions of a miraculous Catholic restoration in Mexico.[75] Here he was careful to acknowledge that the Matiana pamphlet's presentation of these issues sounded fantastical, but he simply reiterated his argument that any off-putting passages resulted from Madre Guerra's deviations. Duarte focused instead on the range of visions in *Voces proféticas* that predicted a new Catholic order and linked them to Matiana's discussions of a reestablished Christian kingdom ruled alongside the Guadalupe shrine. For this author, the more farfetched aspects of Matiana's prophecies (such as the reunified Mexican-Spanish Catholic monarchy) represented mere metaphors for global Catholic unity and the new spirit of revivalism. Likewise, the prophecies' discussions of a new order of nuns served as a local manifestation of expiatory institution building taking place internationally. As he waxed optimistically, Duarte acknowledged the female-dominated dynamics of Catholic resurgence.

In fact, throughout the book Duarte privileged female visionary narratives.[76] He explained his reasons in sections of the book that addressed the Hermanas del Desagravio (the superorder of nuns dedicated to the Blessed Sacrament) and how the leaders of this collective would attain the same privileges as Christ's apostles.[77] Duarte proclaimed that the celestial recognition bestowed on women was fully merited, particularly in Mexico. The "pious sex," he recounted, had distinguished itself facing down foes with "manly vigor." According to Duarte, in Mexico women blunted the enemy assault, "exerting themselves in virtue, cultivating it [virtue] in their children, and contending, respectfully, with their fathers and husbands, in order to lead them aright, despite the depravity that surrounds them."[78] Mexican men, meanwhile, remained deaf to the Mother of God's warnings. But Matiana, Duarte proclaimed, was *"nuestra vidente"* ("our seer"). She:

> foresaw and announced the mockery of which her predictions would be a target; but still in politics her warnings can still be of value; and in regards to higher interests, this is the epoch of greatest importance, because everything tells us that the world is in a moment of crisis and supreme combat for the long-awaited triumph of the Church. If Matiana

carried out a legitimate mission, lucky Mexico because she has been expressly warned of these terrible happenings, [even though Mexico] is without political influence around the world. If Matiana, was truly inspired, lucky Mexico, because the she is indebted to the very same holy Mary, her singular protector, for those important warnings. . . . If Matiana, in sum, is a prophetess, lucky Mexico, because she will be among the first nations to gather the fruits of victory.[79]

In short, Duarte used Matiana to place Mexico at the vanguard of Catholic resurgence.

Subsequently the author unleashed several pages of florid rhetoric lauding female piety. In the process he provided us an example of the interlaced Catholic Romanticism and gendered reactionary rhetoric fueling nineteenth-century religious revival.[80] The centerpiece of his tribute to devout womanhood was the longstanding linkage of women to Eucharistic devotion as celebrated in the Hermanas del Desagravio: "Such a great God and so exhausted because of his love for us, merits the most complete and exclusive consecration from all human lineages; but already Mary has presented him, her Blessed Son, select wives, solely dedicated to contemplate and love him; souls that give themselves to him without reservation, with the sole thought of adoring him, with the singular obligation to love him, to sigh in anguish before him and to become burning lamps consuming themselves in his presence with altruistic ardor, in the most noble exercise directed exclusively to Him."[81] Women such as these throughout the Catholic world, Duarte argued, had earned special consideration. As the Mexican visionary explicitly emphasized, the women of the new order would embrace their mission, despite the fact that society had scorned them as fanatics. Heedless, the author observed, these women remained firm as powerful currents continued to drag mankind toward a richly deserved doom.

Against this chiaroscuro backdrop, Duarte implored his readers to envision the Hermanas del Desagravio's future accomplishments, glory in their model femininity, and imagine the celestial benefits they would secure for the nation: "Let us transport ourselves to this our most favored Sanctuary, in the long-awaited era of the establishment of the *adoratices*, at the very moment of installation of the first vigil. . . . There, with all the ages represented, from cheerful girlhood to weeping decrepitude, in ecstatic trance, those loving virgin wives [of Christ], who are the chosen of the Lamb without blemish, they are a magnet on Earth, attracting the blessings of heaven."[82] With dramatic flourishes such as these, Duarte took his readers inside the cloister, his imagined epicenter of Mexico's Catholic renewal, exhorting them to visualize las Adoratrices in action. He conjured their extraordinary stillness as they worshiped Christ immobilized within the Host. These nuns represented luminous beacons aflame with devout fervor: "Let us gaze upon their immobility, because they are absorbed in the immobility of Jesus Christ captive and incarnated. . . . These sublime maidens are burning with their divine love, their hearts burning brighter than [the enemies'] searing hatchets. An exhalation from her heart, a tear emerging from her eyes, reveals that they are not statues symbolizing prayer, but rather blissful mortals whose souls have climbed to the highest heavens." Alas, Duarte groaned, if only Mexico could appreciate the rapture of these love-struck religiosas. The Virgin Mary's "little candles," with Pope Leo XIII fanning the flames, would ultimately ignite the world with divine love, enflaming "the apostle, the politician, the warrior, he who rules and he who obeys." These remarkable "doves," these "mysterious messenger birds," he exalted, would herald a new era of sanctity.[83] Duarte declared that this, above all else, was Matiana's message. The nation must heed the Holy Virgin's plea, as enunciated by her Mexican seer, or provoke truly devastating punishments. The author then bolstered his exegesis with more excerpts from *Voces proféticas*. In the end, he mixed melodrama and sarcasm as he cautioned that Mexico had to take sides: the era's mounting conflict pits "the sons of Belial, the slaves of Satan, and the friends of the world" versus "the men and women who belong to the Holy Virgin."[84]

Duarte, as discussed earlier, did not invent this interpretation of history. Nor was he the first to deploy bellicose Marianism or the notion of civilization-saving female piety. For the most part, he simply recycled traditional Catholic ideas about cloistered femininity and channeled the revivalist ethos common in ultramontane circles of the time. Duarte's true contribution resides in rephrasing these ideas in the superheated Catholic rhetoric of the period and writing Mexico into the triumphalist end-of-the-world narratives originally forged in Europe. In short he inserted his country in the saga of Christian persecution outlined by the Vatican and its most ardent supporters. He did not simply equate processes in Mexico and France, but rather he carved out a unique niche for Mexican Catholics as if the nation represented a distinct theater of spiritual warfare. In a way, he fashioned an otherworldly explanation for U.S. imperialism at a time when many Mexicans found waxing North American power deeply threatening. Mexico, he argued, must defend Latin

America from the menace of Anglo-Protestant avarice and heresy, and expose the machinations of this new foe. Indeed, in *Profecías* the United States became the mythic whore of Babylon: the alluring symbol of wanton irreverence, excess, and materialism.[85] The faithful in this melodramatic rendering of history lose all the battles. Christianity's enemies seem invincible, but borrowing the time-honored reversal trope from the Book of Revelation, Duarte cast Matiana's prophecies and her Hermanas del Desagravio as the spark of a miraculous turnaround.

The immediate reaction to *Profecías* was predictable. Catholic newspapers praised the author; secular journalists expressed exasperation at the prophetess's reemergence and mocked conservatives for trafficking in superstition. Among the former, publications like Mexico City's *El Tiempo* and Puebla's *El Amigo de la Verdad* mentioned receiving copies and reminded their readers of the Church's position on the prophecies as expressed by the archdiocesan censors.[86] *El Tiempo* underscored connections between Madre Matiana's visions and recent statements by Pope Leo XIII concerning imminent divine punishments. As a result they proclaimed it their duty to second the book's call for collective expiation.[87] *El Amigo* quipped that scurrilous anti-Matiana attacks from the liberal press were proof enough of the book's merits.[88] *El Tiempo* actually sold Duarte's books from their offices, advertising its availability for almost a full decade after its publication.[89] The secular press, however, proclaimed *Profecías* recycled, antiliberal screed and questioned their colleagues' integrity. They also mocked them for wasting their time on Madre Matiana's predictions. *El Siglo Diez y Nueve* tittered about *El Tiempo*'s end-of-the-world reportage, making up their own obviously ridiculous faux-Matiana prophecy, alleging that she predicted a cheese crisis in France and foresaw the devil's appearance as a rabbit destined to drag every freemason to the depths of hell.[90] In a way Matiana's reappearance at this juncture gave secular publications an excuse to deploy the maligned popular figure anew when disparaging their conservative journalistic rivals as the Church continued to regain influence.[91] In general for these writers, she simply epitomized clumsy Catholic reassertions of fanatical banalities in order to dupe the ignorant. Some publications also deployed Matiana anew as a metaphor for overwrought alarmism.[92] The editors at *El Tiempo* were unfazed. In 1904 they featured a front-page story about a pious *indita* (young indigenous woman) who reportedly experienced a prophetic Marian apparition in October 1860, echoing earlier texts like *Voces proféticas* and Matiana's prophecies.[93] According to the author, the Virgin told the indita of the pending harsh persecution of the Church, rueful martyrdoms, and the impending political victory of Catholicism's opponents. In addition, she called for extensive acts of expiation. Ironically, the next generation of Matiana interpreters would cite this article in support of their belief in the prophetess's continuing relevance.[94]

THE EVE OF REVOLUTION

Madre Matiana's prominence gradually dimmed as the turn of the century approached, but she was not forgotten. Mexico's stability and remarkable economic growth during the 1890s bolstered those seeking conciliation between the Catholic Church and the Mexican state. The ostensible liberal Catholics vexed their doctrinaire critics (both liberal and Catholic), but they represented a large number of influential players within the regime and the Church. By the beginning of the 1900s, Catholic newspapers were no longer discussing Matiana openly, but Duarte's *Profecías* was still available. Outside both accomodationist and intransigent circles a new stream of Catholic thought had been gaining prominence since the early 1890s. Social Catholicism, with its critique of unfettered capitalism and call to social activism, became a showcase topic of the era.[95] This refreshed perspective on Catholic principles emphasized outreach and lower-class religious mobilization through greater attention to social issues. For a time it overshadowed shriller voices, although hardline conservatives never disappeared. Such was the confidence of social Catholics that some of them clamored for open, Church-affiliated political participation on the eve of the Mexican Revolution. They got their wish, but it did not last long amid the tumult that unfolded after 1910.

Given all the implications of the Matiana legacy, it is hardly shocking that as the Porfirian order wavered and then succumbed to popular insurgency, interest in the pamphlet seer picked up once again. Revolutionary mobilization brought with it a rekindled anticlericalism. In a sense this represented a reaction to the Church's revitalization, its regime-friendly reputation, and renewed social prominence. The new generation of Jacobins did not differentiate much between Christian democrats and Catholic traditionalists. Likewise, a new round of expropriations and the suppression of many religious organizations inspired fresh militancy. Both Catholic firebrands and Revolutionary sympathizers reached for the prophecies of Madre Matiana, although with very different motives.

Church activists engaging the prophecies in the early twentieth century continued very much in the tradition of their intransigente predecessors. They reveal that Duarte's interpretation still shaped this group's views more than twenty years after its initial publication. One place where this appears is in the state of Oaxaca. There an examination of the Matiana legacy by a prominent local priest named Luis G. Santaella (1835–1911) enjoyed de facto archdiocesan endorsement, appearing serialized in ecclesiastical province's official organ—the *Boletín Oficial y Revista Ecclesiástica de Antequera*—and also in a separate 38-page pamphlet.[96] The archdiocese's printing press (La Voz de la Verdad) published the *Boletín*, Santaella's disquisition on the prophecies, and the region's Catholic newspaper.[97] In many ways Santaella's life paralleled Duarte's. Born to a prominent conservative family, he studied law only to find his career halted because he refused to swear allegiance to the Constitution of 1857. He, however, opted to become a priest, gaining renown as an educator, preacher, and writer.[98] Father Luis and his sister, María, were provincial church stalwarts. Miss Santaella worked energetically as an officer of Oaxaca's Sociedad Católica de Señoras (Catholic Women's Society) and published devout poetry.[99] For a time Father Luis served as archdiocesan secretary in the late 1880s and early 1890s. He was the top official overseeing his prelate's efforts in 1901 to instill rigor in the Oaxacan clergy through periodic priestly conferences and examinations.[100] He also occupied a number of prestigious posts but repeatedly returned to his parish ministry.[101] Alongside his pastoral duties he published on the Virgin Mary's campaign against modern error, served as a columnist for the *Boletín*, and delivered fiery sermons at special events.[102] In sum, Santaella was very much a well-known regional figure of the era's militant Catholic ferment.

Santaella cites Duarte's *Profecías* as the definitive interpretation of the Mexican prophesies, and he copies its structure. As in Duarte's model, Matiana appears as the Mexican representative in a chorus of visionary voices warning of treachery emanating from France. In keeping with the well-worn patterns of conservative conspiracy theory, the periods of persecution and punishment blur together. The litany of state-directed anticlericalism and secularization merges with war, natural disaster, and social conflict. In brief, this 1910 Matiana text offers the same story of persecution, with assurances that the punishment phase is only beginning. Ironically this ever-useful framing remained a linear narrative—impious persecution leads to divine punishment followed by glorious religious triumph—but the authorial present (be it 1857, 1889, or 1910) was always the time of ungodly tyranny and incipient castigation. The devout reader, as it were, was always trapped with little recourse beyond expiatory piety. The goal of these texts, as de Jesús María insinuated and Duarte detailed at length, was to inspire such devotional activities and exhort believers not to lose heart, because the Church's triumph was imminent.

Santaella does not address the Revolution directly, but anxieties linked to the crisis at the top of the Porfirian order in 1910 haunt his reassertion of Matiana's importance. In keeping with conservative Catholic engagements of the Mexican seer reaching back to the early 1880s, he stresses the faithful's duty to contemplate the maligned seer's visions seriously. In addition, Santaella reiterates Duarte's thesis that Mexico's troubles emanate from heretical North American schemes. In contrast, however, he predicts that the United States teeters on the verge of civil war given its decadent social order and mounting racial tensions. He goes so far as to assert that this looming conflict will cause U.S. economic interests to abandon Mexico precisely as Matiana predicted. Santaella finally suggests that all evidence points to the definitive conflict and triumph of the Church set to occur in 1918, or at the latest 1928, in keeping with the prophetess's predictions concerning October of a year that ends in the number eight.[103]

Santaella's interpretation is, for the most part, nothing more than an updating of Duarte's *Profecías*, but within a few years widespread social violence indeed rekindled the pamphlet prophetess's fame. As before, the uncertainties of war and social unrest combined with the trepidations sparked by anticlerical agitation to make the visions freshly relevant. As if part of a strange reenactment, a new, more fiercely secularizing constitution promulgated in 1917 (the eve of yet another year ending in the number eight) stoked seeming synergies between the prophecies, political happenings, and cultural conflicts as the Constitution of 1857 had sixty years earlier. The question of fervently devout Catholic women's roles in the nation (both real and symbolic) also remained a salient unresolved quandary. Nonetheless, the very different set of conditions shaped by social rebellion, Revolutionary state building, and rapid modernization made the next phase of Matiana's "career" very different.

PART II

Fitting *Fanáticas*

CHAPTER 5

Eso no tiene madre

Satire and Seer in Revolutionary Mexico

BY 1917 THE MOST DECISIVE BATTLES OF THE MEXICAN REVOLUTION
had been decided, and a particular faction, the Constitutionalists, had
emerged victorious. A stable government eventually emerged from this frac-
tious group over the next two decades, but Mexicans were in no way certain
of this at the time. Quite to the contrary, violent rivalries among the victors,
regional uprisings, and myriad armed bands throughout the nation remained facts of life. Moreover, the suffering caused by years of insurgency
remained acute. In this context, on 1 July 1917 a new satirical newspaper hit
the stands in Mexico City. It promised a bold take on politics and society,
although not in a straightforward manner. Its motto revealed a madcap mission: "A prophetic, truth-telling newspaper; it will block the sun with a finger,
bark at the moon, and serenade the morning star."[1] This statement of endeavors appears on the masthead of each issue, but Mexicans at the time would
have presumed irreverent parody from a mere glance at the new periodical's
name, *La Madre Matiana*. The newspaper's founder, Pedro Hagelstein y
Trejo (under the pseudonym Ángel Prieto Heds), essentially took the legendary clairvoyant as his paper's comedic alter ego. Of course the prophecies of
Madre Matiana had been provoking Mexicans for decades, but the Mexican
Revolution vaulted them to a whole new level of prominence. In the years
leading up to this newspaper's emergence, various publications revisited the
Matiana legacy. For example, a 1914 broadside recycled an apocalyptic litho-
graph from the 1890s by famed graphic artist José Guadalupe Posada to illustrate its commentary on the prophecies' Revolutionary significance. Titled
"The End of the World is Near: The Prophecies are Fulfilled," and originally

sold for 3 cents, the broadside muses that recent unrest was perhaps a prelude to the bloody denouement predicted by Matiana.[2] Moreover, two new versions of the prophecies recounted the original visionary story and charted their supposed fulfillment amid Mexico's insurgency and World War I.[3] Their titles—*Profecías completas de Madre Matiana* (1914) and *Las verdaderas profecías de Matiana* (1917)—reveal that a new phase of mystical awareness and embellishment was in full swing. For the first time the prophecies required qualifiers: ostensibly "complete" and "true" editions imply efforts to codify a diversity of predictions.

Skeptical voices chimed in too, and their interventions underscore further the surge of interest in the prophetess at this time. For example, the newspaper *Ecos* claimed that the U.S. military occupation of Veracruz in the spring of 1914 sparked virtual Matiana mania. Lamenting that the seer was "achieving indubitable celebrity among the popular masses," this publication pronounced the prophecies to be superstitious nonsense.[4] *Ecos* claimed that few cared about the visions prior to recent upheavals. Market stalls at Mexico City's Plaza del Volador allegedly offered Matiana pamphlets for a pittance, and vendors even surreptitiously slipped free copies into purchased books.[5] Greedy printers, the paper complained, were simply taking advantage of credulous Mexicans, especially women, amid heightened uncertainties. A few months later the official organ of the Methodist Church in Mexico also broached the topic, although with greater sensitivity. It theorized that poverty and hunger caused by war, combined with the impending winter, bolstered widespread belief in the prophecies.[6] Mexicans were indeed facing previously unknown levels of hardship. Alongside Revolutionary violence, extreme food shortages and epidemics battered the populace between 1915 and 1918.[7]

Matiana's renewed fame would spill into the next decade as well. Several publications invoked her memory in 1920, some extensively. *El Informador* in Guadalajara labeled Matiana as the epitome of stubborn superstitious absurdities.[8] The city of Monterrey's *El Porvenir* mentioned the prophecies' strangeness—as well as discomfiting accuracy—in an article about natural disasters, fires, and active volcanoes. Throughout the republic, they claimed, people feared impending calamity.[9] In May 1920 this same periodical even published an open request for a copy of the prophecies, suggesting that perhaps demand outstripped the supply at this juncture.[10] In at least one instance, Madre Matiana appeared as a symbol of female insanity: residents of Monterrey nicknamed a deranged homeless woman after the prophetess in

1927.[11] In addition, a large number of rural Catholics in Oaxaca embraced a young indigenous girl's apparitionist claims in 1928 due to the convergences between her alleged visions, earthquakes, church-state violence, and the prophecies.[12]

Timing is everything, as the saying goes, and the adage is particularly apt in regards to prophecy and satire. As described in the previous chapter, in 1910 Luis Santaella identified October 1918 as the likely climactic moment of conflict and miraculous intercession predicted by Madre Matiana. From a certain ideological perspective the combination of foreign invasion, civil war, renewed anticlericalism, and widespread misery ratified such claims. Even outside of conservative Catholic circles, it is clear that revolution catalyzed a fresh attentiveness to the legendary prophecies. Pedro Hagelstein and his close collaborators at La Madre (Félix C. Vera and Francisco Sánchez Marín) obviously recognized the seer's topical potential and marketing value when founding the newspaper.[13] Moreover, the transformation of Mexican discourse in subsequent decades reveals that his ploy marks the beginning of a distinct era in the Matiana phenomenon. Prior to 1910, both promoters and critics focused on the predictive value of the prophetic narrative and its call for a collective expiation. Beginning in 1917, the seer's backstory and even her prophecies steadily lost importance, while the Madre Matiana persona, construed as a quintessentially Mexican popular figure, gained preeminence. This shift is so pronounced that the remaining chapters of this book analyze twentieth-century contributions to the Matiana legacy as acts of appropriation rather than straightforward reinterpretations. In other words, journalists at the satirical La Madre Matiana in 1917, photographer Lola Álvarez Bravo in 1935, and novelist Agustín Yáñez in 1962, all commandeered the legendary visionary to "voice" their respective claims about the nature of Mexican culture and society.

The seeds of this development were already in evidence during the nineteenth century. In the wake of Matiana's calendario cameos, satirists as early as 1876 produced editorials as the prophetess as if she expressed "public opinion" (see chapter 3).[14] Likewise, another famous Mexican writer and public figure, Manuel Payno, put the seer to work in literature before Yáñez, albeit only briefly. In his artful parody of nineteenth-century society, Los bandidos de Río Frío (1889), the author set his impish epic in motion through the scandalous actions of an indigenous curandera named Matiana, a character specializing in superstitious quackery.[15] Thus Payno introduced Mexico's "backward" customs and social types by referencing the pamphlet

Figure 15. Matiana's resurgence meets José Guadalupe Posada's "Fin del Mundo." 1914. Image courtesy of the Jean Charlot Collection, University of Hawaii Manoa Library.

prophetess. In both of these instances, however, these precursors deployed their Matianas in a relatively superficial manner.

In contrast, the twentieth-century cases featured here reveal distinct actors who essentially played the part of the prophetic *fanática* (female fanatic) as a means of constructing the nation, debating gender norms, and analyzing popular culture. The individuals in question seized upon Madre Matiana because of her reputation in some circles as the quintessence of popular fanaticism and female irrationality. Their endeavors represent reformist performances and exercises in nationalist memory making. Each in their own way attempted to "fit" the symbolic fanática in the modern nation and use her to explore and establish the boundaries of national identity. Naturally, this was not without contradictions.

The evidence actually reveals a generative paradox at work, akin to those present in the era's emergent Indian-centered nationalism (*indigenismo*) and enduring debates about law and order that coalesced around notions of banditry. As with these phenomena, Madre Matiana represents an inspirational dilemma for those seeking to incorporate groups and social types deemed adverse to the modern nation. Scholars have shown how both "the Indian" and "the bandit" became topics of obsessive concern and recurrent contradictory representation.[16] At times they appear as irredeemable obstacles to advancement and unity, but in other instances they symbolize the primitive origins of the imagined national spirit. Twentieth-century Mexican nationalists in particular seized on the idea that the indigenous represented the characteristic *mexicano*, but at the same time they sought to westernize and modernize Mexico's native peoples, standardize their representation, and assimilate them within a homogenous, mixed-race nationalism.[17] A similar but seldom examined process took place in regard to an archetypal female figure: the intensely and publically pious Catholic woman. This social type bedeviled Mexico's nation-builders. On one level, gender norms, Church-centered identity, and miraculous thinking made her incompatible with modern notions of rationality. On another, the fanática could encapsulate the essence of popular culture and bring to it the elemental legitimacy often imputed to female figures. The nationalist imaginary, therefore, had to integrate devout women in some fashion. This is what took place as the actors featured in part II of this book engaged the Matiana legacy. By appropriating the *profetisa* (prophetess) they endeavor to control, transform, and assimilate the representation of pious womanhood. In the process they also attempt to capture the primordial authenticity typically attached to religion, folk practices, and femininity. This dynamic is important in and of itself, but these cases also contextualize the seer's remarkable staying power. Madre Matiana came to personify interwoven cultural issues that remained unsettled throughout the Revolutionary process. Mexicans struggled to accommodate popular religiosity and devout femininity within their notions of modern national identity, and this made the figure of the fanatical female seer useful in a variety of ways. Hence dissecting a nearly forgotten satirical newspaper offers important insights into Mexico's cultural history and a framework for analyzing subsequent contributions to the Matiana phenomenon.

ARMANDO DESMADRE

The relative weakness of national identities in Mexico during the nineteenth and early twentieth centuries set the stage for La Madre (as the editorial staff nicknamed their publication). Generations of erstwhile nation builders struggled to find a recipe for consensus and a broad sense of national community. Festering uncertainties, in turn, fueled satirical expression in all its modalities. In many ways the obvious contradictions in social norms, professed ideals, government policies, and popular practices invited ridicule. Despite the emphasis on mockery, however, satire usually flourishes amid campaigns to effect social change, but it only rarely qualifies as truly revolutionary dissent. Since at least classical times the genre has functioned as a predominantly reformist form of expression.[18] In essence, it resides among the tools readily deployed in efforts to "improve" society and often serves groups seeking to define themselves.[19] Thus it is hardly surprising to find satire deeply embedded in the insecure nationalisms of Latin America.[20]

Given the Revolutionary context in which it developed, it is somewhat surprising that La Madre did not emerge sooner. Conservatives like Duarte and Santaella had kept Matiana's memory alive between the 1880s and 1910 and gave her a stern reactionary stamp. Subsequently the flurry of Matiana material that accompanied Revolutionary violence in the mid-1910s catapulted the visionary into the national consciousness anew. Some of it contained additional prophecies related to recent events and reaffirmed the conspiracy theories of Catholics like Duarte. Finally, the promulgation of a new, more anticlerical constitution only five months before La Madre's inaugural issue bolstered the seer's relevance still further.[21] The decision to launch the newspaper with 1918 only months away gave it a potent, mischievous timeliness. Hagelstein and his staff seized the moment, exploiting both the general anxiety of the era and the deeper legacies of reverence and contempt surrounding Madre Matiana.

Certainly much of the newspaper's offbeat approach to social criticism stems from Hagelstein (1877–1932).[22] According to the trade unionists and leftist newspapermen who gathered in 1935 to honor his legacy, La Madre's owner-editor was a lion of the Mexican radical press. For them he represented a principled intellectual dedicated to the ouster of President Porfirio Díaz and a stalwart of the Revolutionary cause.[23] Although accurate in some respects, tracking Hagelstein's life in the newspapers where he sparred with rivals offers a more interesting and complicated portrait. Moreover, the fragments of his biography therein provide tantalizing clues as to what inspired the man eventually nicknamed Padre Matías (a masculinization of Madre Matiana).[24]

Although originally from Guanajuato, in the mid-1890s Hagelstein became a fixture of Mexico City's cultural ferment while still quite young. The future satirist studied law, but he abandoned this field before receiving his degree. As befits stereotypes common at the time, he embraced the student pastimes of urban carousing and journalism, and then abandoned more "respectable" pursuits.[25] Years later an angry critic quipped that Hagelstein's reputation was primarily established in "those places that out of respect for the public we refrain from naming."[26] Simultaneously he was also deeply involved in the city's theater scene and organized many veladas (musical-literary soirees). His sister, Dorotea, was a popular contralto and young Pedro acted and sang too, although he did not match his sister's acclaim.[27] A front-page photograph from 1901 in El Tiempo Ilustrado reveals Hagelstein as a dashing member of Mexico City's Club Dramático, a theater company.[28] During the same year he performed poetry readings at veladas—in at least one such instance, he earned top billing.[29] Clearly the man who would one day play the satirical fanática in La Madre loved the performative arts. He also tried his hand in the business side of theater: In 1901 and 1902, Hagelstein was the chief administrator of the Compañía de Opera Mexicana, a group that performed in the capital and toured throughout Mexico.[30]

Remarkably, alongside these endeavors, the ambitious Mr. Hagelstein made his mark in the press—as a reporter, editor, administrator, and media entrepreneur. In 1896, when only nineteen, Hagelstein led a student newspaper called El Estudiante; he faced defamation charges within months of its founding.[31] At about the same time he also ran an innovative illustrated newspaper called *México Artístico*.[32] Over the next few years, Mr. Hagelstein took on a wide array of tasks for numerous papers. He contributed articles and reviews, completed editorial tasks, and periodically launched his own publications with various partners. For a time he even tried to establish an independent news agency called the Agencia Internacional de Informaciones Hagelstein y Bonilla.[33] Ultimately, in the first years of the 1900s, he cemented his reputation working as a reporter for *El País*, a prestigious progressive Catholic daily.[34] Indeed, although seemingly out of step with *La Madre*'s later anticlericalism, during his youth he enjoyed close ties to the Church-affiliated press. On at least one occasion Hagelstein published a florid description of religious ceremonies in *La Voz de México*, a conservative Catholic publication.[35] He even administered this confessional daily for a brief period in 1904.[36]

Mexican journalism demanded diverse skills, flexibility, and a tolerance (or predilection) for instability and conflict. For his part, Hagelstein clearly knew how to patch together a livelihood. He also seems to have relished confrontation even though his politics remained rather moderate. Early on he cultivated a reputation for trenchant theater reviews, and he vociferously defended his honor when an aggrieved dramaturge insulted him. As he matured, though, he revealed a penchant for brawling. For example, in 1911, Hagelstein and another colleague confronted a congressman after said representative directed vulgar gestures toward them in the press gallery during a legislative session. Scandalous fisticuffs ensued in full public view outside congress.[37] A year later a different congressman left Hagelstein bruised and bloodied when a barroom argument escalated into a physical confrontation.[38]

Such anecdotes, although informative, can lead to an exaggeration of his rebelliousness. The same is true of the posthumous praises bestowed by friends in the mid 1930s: a time when being *revolucionario* conferred considerable cache. However, social excess and a willingness to violently defend one's honor were part and parcel of the era's journalistic culture.[39] In this light, from early on Hagelstein had been playing the role of the passionate young artist and newspaperman, and doing so to great effect.

Looking closely, he was really a member of the establishment and a veritable celebrity. In fact, when he turned twenty-one newspapers covered the festivities, praising his charms and noting the attendance of "the most distinguished [members] of our literary bohemia."[40] Hagelstein bolstered his reputation further by excelling as an organizer of patriotic festivities, charity events, and associations, such as the Agrupación Mexicana de Periodistas (Association of

Mexican Journalists).[41] Not surprisingly society pages in the early 1900s tracked his presence at public galas where he rubbed elbows with President Porfirio Díaz, important officials, and foreign dignitaries.[42] In short, the future boss of *La Madre* was a socialite: *El Popular* gave his "elegant" marriage front-page coverage in 1902, and *The Mexican Herald* gushed about his wife's bejeweled attire at a ball in 1903.[43] He even appeared among the participants at the Círculo Porfirista's (a pro-Díaz organization) banquet.[44]

The still-young Hagelstein's trajectory, however, shifted as the Porfirian order showed signs of weakness and factions began to maneuver for advantage on the eve of the Revolution. In 1904 he and some associates founded a polemical newspaper called *Los Sucesos*. Among these collaborators were Felix C. Vera and Francisco Sánchez Marín, who would also help him found *La Madre* in 1917. Decades later his admirers identified this endeavor as the watershed moment when Hagelstien joined the opposition.[45] His critics at the time and even his onetime collaborator and brother, Luis C. Hagelstein, claimed that *Los Sucesos* was merely a mouthpiece for General Bernard Reyes and his followers (known as *reyistas*), a formidable, relatively popular faction with ties to the army.[46] Initially this group lobbied Díaz to anoint Reyes, a longstanding important ally, as his successor, but after the aging president marginalized his old comrade some reyistas supported the regime's over-throw.[47] Whatever his commitment to Reyes, after 1904 Hagelstein's association with bitter partisanship overshadowed his previous socialite and mainstream-reporter reputation. As might be expected, these proved rocky years for him and many other journalists. The government suppressed *Los Sucesos* on numerous occasions and jailed Hagelstein at least eighteen different times.[48] In one widely debated instance, he served a seven-month defamation sentence for criticizing a public official.[49]

Nonetheless, as *La Madre* would show in later years, Hagelstein's specialty was more cutting rhetoric and caricature than actual radicalism. In this regard his early experiences as an actor and devotee of the theater quite likely informed his approach to social criticism. There is some evidence that he had long been drawn to the idea of role-playing and impersonation. One of his earliest ventures from 1897 was an illustrated weekly that featured color lithographs and political cartoons named *Frégoli*, after the world-famous quick-change artist and master of mimicry and impersonations, Leopoldo Frégoli.[50] The Italian performer toured widely in the Americas, and dazzled Mexico City in December 1896 where he performed multiple roles in various comedies (allegedly fifteen to twenty in one instance) and carried out dramatic role changes. For example, theatergoers showered him with applause when he, playing a schoolgirl, sang in a beautiful soprano and then instantaneously switched into a tuxedo and showed off a manly baritone.[51]

This master of impersonation was all the rage in Mexico City when the teenaged Hagelstein was pursuing his own drama career. His journalistic homage to Frégoli did not last long, but it hints that the germ of *La Madre*'s carnivalesque, satirical cross-dressing may have been planted in this period. Whatever the origin of his inspirations, by 1911 *Los Sucesos* was falling apart and Hagelstein and his collaborators, at one point, abruptly fled the newspaper's offices.[52] Indeed, many publications collapsed in the turbulent years of Revolutionary warfare. In all probability the adaptable Padre Matías returned to freelancing. When he launched *La Madre* in 1917, however, he deployed a new stage name of sorts (Ángel Prieto Heds), perhaps to distance himself from previous conflicts.

At first glance, *La Madre* appears to offer a straightforward send-up of "superstition" and the Catholic Church. A mannish, piously attired Matiana appears on the masthead skewering priests with an outsized phallic sword (see Figure 17). Sections parody the santoral and the writing style of devotional texts and calendarios. The 9 September 1917 issue, however, reveals a more complex approach to popular religiosity and pious femininity. In this case a front-page article titled "*Lo que tiene y no tiene madre*" ("What Has and Does Not Have a Mother") pivots on a vernacular phrase. *La Madre*, as it were, used this essay to indulge in "her" favorite trick, tapping the rich, Mexican usage of *madre* and its permutations. There are few words in popular Mexican usage with similar, coarse complexity and offensive potential. A book on Mexicanisms published in Spain during the 1890s stressed Mexican's hypersensitivity to the term.[53] Never, it argued, should one inquire after "*tu/su madre*" ("your mother") in Mexico; ask instead, it suggested, for "*su mama*" ("your mom"). Simply saying *madre* carried potent insulting connotations.

The key to *madre* and its many derivations since at least the eighteenth century is the insinuation of extremes, usually bad and sometimes good.[54] According to one slang dictionary, *madre* is among the foremost "major Mexicanisms" on a par with the equally generative *chingar*, which is loosely translated as "fuck" but also means to rape, violate, or ruin. To be the *chingón* is to be the perpetrator of the act of violation or domination (and by extension to be powerful or great), and to be the *chingado/a* is to be the subjugated victim/loser.[55] In a similar vein *madre*'s meanings are complex. Alone it often means worthless or useless, like "*pos [sic] me importa madre*" (roughly, I don't give a damn).[56] In related usage, "¡*La madre!*" conveys abrupt rejection of excuses or opposing arguments.[57] Likewise, to be "*hasta la madre*" is to be absolutely fed up.[58] During the Revolutionary era it also described exceptional brutality: "*dar en la madre*" meant to mortally wound or strike decisively.[59] Hence Mexicans also use *madrazo* (a harsh blow) and "*partir la madre*" (annihilate or destroy).[60] Like many colloquial terms, though, in some contexts negative connotations are inverted. Thus "*a toda madre*" (loosely, all pure mother) denotes excellence.[61]

A partner of *madre* in Mexican argot is *desmadre*. Here too, the issue is the signification of excess and the outer limits. A combination of the prefix *des-*, connoting negation or inversion, and *madre*, it usually implies chaos, confusion, and anarchic behavior.[62] But it too bears violent connotations. According to a dictionary of expressions used during the Mexican Revolution, *desmadrar* originally referred to the act of separating calves from cows, but came to mean to gravely wound. Likewise, a *desmadrado* is the victim of brutal assault.[63] In the reflexive form, *desmadrarse*, it means to gravely wound one's self.[64] In this manner it can also mean to break or ruin. Thus *desmadre* can refer to disorderly happenings, extreme violence, and outrageous behavior. The phrase "*esto va de desmadre total*" indicates an event getting completely out of hand.[65] As a result, the common phrase "*armar desmadre*" means to cause trouble or foment disorder and a *desmadrozo/a* is a troublemaker. This was the role *La Madre* archly embraced.

Making the most of *madre*, *desmadre*, and related sayings served as standard *La Madre* practice. In fact featured columns were entitled "*Madradas*" and "*Desmadres*." This practice was not simply about generating laughs. To categorize events or actions in terms of "what has or does not have a mother" amounts to a marking of the limits of social acceptance. Their weapon, in this case, is the vulgar expression of extreme contempt, "*no tiene madre*," set up in a series of paired stanzas. To be branded as such represents an offensive means of imputing a complete lack of scruples or shame.[66] It also denotes the most debased existence possible and abject aberrance.[67] In this text *La Madre* mentions policies or happenings considered positive and quips, "*Eso si tiene madre.*" Subsequently, the text describes a related deed or event deemed galling and declares, "*Eso no tiene madre.*" Of course, part of the joke is, who better to make these determinations than *La Madre*, the appropriated prophetess? The writers deploy the expression to mock individuals and institutions, but the seriousness beneath their jests is palpable. For example, *La Madre* praises the Revolutionary state's anticlerical reforms, underscoring assumptions about priests' reputations as sexual predators and exploiters of the masses. Then "she" condemns Church efforts to block the government's new laws by claiming rights enshrined in the Constitution of 1917, after the ecclesiastical hierarchy had refused to abide the recently revised national charter. In subsequent dyads La Madre targets hypocritical judges and shady provincial politicians.

Thus the reader "witnesses" these journalists enacting a role, so to say. In fact the newspaper's commentary entailed simultaneous performances: playing the legendary seer, affecting the castigating diatribes and illogical certainty associated with devout women, communicating in the everyday witticisms of common Mexicans, and staging desmadre. La Madre's Matiana is a demented, impertinent, and yet uncannily insightful "battle-axe" who knows no fear.[68] As a seer she also has mysterious powers of discernment, and she uses these talents to expose fraud and corruption. But she also talks nonsense. Even while induling in parody, La Madre was producing a satirical nation-building rhetoric. The appropriation of a legendary popular visionary and proceeding to use her to determine "lo que no tiene madre" represents a demarcation of values. In the process the editors implied that Matiana was quintessentially Mexican and that Mexicans remained deeply superstitious. Of course, this is satire, and hence La Madre relished contradictions.[69] They portrayed their namesake as a clownish zealot, and this provided them license to scoff in all directions. The Matiana character, as drawn in La Madre, embodies the miracle-obsessed quirks, the charming ridiculousness, and the caustic wit of el pueblo (the people). All the while, even though La Madre made fun of the national "self" it was paradoxically also taking part in its construction. True to the satirical genre, the newspaper assumes a public, moralizing stance, speaking for the populace as it targets folly and corruption. Although these journalists conjure desmadre, they seek social advancement and hope to win "hearts and minds." Their derision, however, remains open ended without offering solutions. La Madre, like most satirical ventures, is called to reveal not resolve.[70] Crucially, in 1917 "she" does so in a recognizably Mexican female voice. Over time, though, Hagelstein and his staff would switch to crass masculine-voiced sarcasm as Revolutionary nationalism evolved.

POSITIONING AND PLAYING THE PROPHETESS

There are a number of studies that examine Mexican women and gender in the Porfirian and the Revolutionary periods. They address the reframing of patriarchy, female agency in institutions, feminism, women in the work-place, and the gender dynamics of marriage and daily life.[71] Works analyzing literature and art also help contextualize the Matiana phenomenon.[72] For the most part, though, Mexican historical scholarship underutilizes satire. At times it serves as a mere gauge of political resistance and rivalry. For exam-ple, humorous prose, verse, and caricature function for some historians as evidence of principled opposition to authoritarianism before the Mexican Revolution.[73] *La Madre*'s ridicule, though, goes well beyond the politics of humiliation and defiance. "She," and a number of her forbearers, probed the shifting boundaries of Mexican identity. The core of their wit resides in em-blematic characters that violate and mark the bounds of propriety. Often simple jester-like transgressions inspire laughter. At other times the object of ridicule appears on the other side of social acceptance, while satirists make their popular, rule-bending alter-ego the defender of shared values. In the present case, *La Madre* implies that the fanatical mystic is more sensible—and more Mexican—than their satirical victims. On another level, both Matiana and the backward populace she represents function as the butt of jokes and the protagonists of *La Madre*'s reformist nationalism.

Madre Matiana had become a multivalent metaphorical figure before the twentieth century, and preceeding engagements of fanaticism, piety, and femininity created the opening for *La Madre*'s appropriation of the Matiana persona in the late 1910s. But the seer also represented a real challenge for these journalists. Sensitive to the culture around them, *La Madre* could not leave the ideas, practices, and "irrationality" embodied by the Madre Matiana figure out of their representations of the nation. To manage this tension they engineered a clever reversal: they portrayed the (in)famous visionary as an offbeat popular avenger.

In the context of the times this was a novel strategy. Crafting an elite mas-culine honor was a central part of the construction of Mexico's public sphere during the preceding decades. Only men deemed *de honra* (of known educa-tion, liberal principals, status, and manly valor) could speak for el pueblo.[74] *La Madre*'s gambit represents a premeditated contravention: it deploys a rag-ing female religious voice—the antithesis of modern masculine decorum—in staking its claim to public opinion. Simultaneously, it depicts desmadre to expose the untoward in Mexican society. Women's actual voices were absent, but this newspaper intertwined *lo femenino*, *lo fanático*, and *lo mexicano*.

A pair of theoretical approaches bolsters this interpretation. Scholars have long focused on the historical processes that shape nationalism.[75] Nira

Yuval-Davis's examination of representations of women in nationalist identity narratives is instructive.[76] Female figures are crucial in depictions of the nation, where they commonly appear as symbolic embodiments of all that marks off the collective identity. In this sense, "women serve as reproducers, not only of the labor force and/or of the future subjects of the state, but also as the reproducers, biologically and ideologically, of the national collective and its boundaries."[77] Much of the nationalist magic materializes in the treatment of widely recognized social identities. In reality such identities are little more than longstanding storylines and character types that outline alleged similarities and distinctions between the self, various groups, and outsiders. These often have their roots in myth, history, and descriptions of custom. As with the ideas surrounding the nation itself, identity narratives do not require airtight definition so much as frequent expression. In this manner they gain the aura of normativity, although they require continual re-adaptation.[78] Once lodged in the collective imagination identity narratives can channel emotions, convey understandings of history, bolster visions of the future, and shape notions of social organization. In essence, as Yuval-Davis has shown enduring identity narratives represent struts in the framework of meaning. They are also crucial to arguments for change; hence, they often appear in "diagnostic" discourses that examine alleged national problems.[79] Competing social projects often employ distinct identity narratives. Again, the gendered positioning of characters in these narratives shapes their logic. Female figures often carry the "burden of representation": they embody the people, morality, customs, and land. Figures like Madre Matiana are carefully placed in relation to other, frequently masculine, representations. Often they function as "symbolic border guards" of "us" versus "them," and legitimate versus illegitimate.[80]

Another theoretical approach entails examining the appropriations of Madre Matiana as acts of impersonation. In this sense, *La Madre*'s satire is akin to what cultural historian Jill Lane reveals in Cuba's long history of blackface theater.[81] In a sense, just as Cuban writers and actors parodied their black countrymen, Pedro Hagelstein and his staff indulged in a kind of cross-dressing as they pretended to be a devout popular prophetess. The parallel resides in Cuban engagements of African-imbued culture and Mexican approaches to Catholic religiosity. For Cuban nationalists blackness remained an intractable problem, because they viewed everything African as backward, irrational, and thus incompatible with modern nationhood. At the same time, they were desperately searching for popular practices that they could label uniquely Cuban, and much of what they found was obviously shaped by the legacy of slavery and the cultural transformation wrought by the importation of Africans to the island. Their Mexican counterparts also grappled with race, but a more stubborn obstacle proved to be popular religious culture. Regarding Catholicism, however, scholars of Mexican history emphasize the intent among reformers to banish religion from the public sphere.[82] Strong devout identities, particularly among women, aggravated secular nation builders (such as nineteenth-century liberals and twentieth-century revolutionaries), but the assimilation functions of satirical impersonation have yet to receive scholarly attention in the Mexican context.

Blackface theater in nineteenth-century Cuba featured stock satirical characters, which allowed nonblack social actors to stereotype popular culture and control its representation while constructing "national" modes of expression.[83] Plays ridicule supposedly typical figures, but they represent them as inimitably Cuban. Lane's analysis centers on these staged acts of imitation, which she claims reveal the making and faking of a new Cuban identity. She argues that performing stereotyped blackness created a setting where Cubans could invent, share, and practice the behaviors associated with a new mestizo nationalism. Playing the maligned religious "other" in Mexico reveals a similar effort to contain Catholic piety and practice, and simultaneously construct legitimate national behaviors, beliefs, and customs. Stereotyping and mocking female fanaticism through impersonation also amounts to an attempt to assimilate the assumptions of authenticity attached to devout femininity, while gaining control of the popular and its representation.

RIDENDO CORRIGO MORES

Pedro Hagelstein's Madre Matiana did not descend from the ether as *La Madre* joked. In fact, a look back at this newspaper's irreverent predecessors is essential in order to place it in the proper context. Mexico's satirical tradition goes back to colonial-era broadsides and flourished during the nineteenth century.[84] Particularly after 1850, newspapers solely dedicated to satire were common.[85] They belong to a legacy of reformism grounded in notions that top-down cultural transformation represented a crucial step toward prosperous nationhood. It is for this reason that the sustained dedication to biting social commentary emerged from liberal and Revolutionary journalism. This raison d'être appears artfully characterized on the masthead of *La*

Linterna (see Figure 11, chapter 3).[86] It features a smirking jester who shines a bright light on a dark globe. In doing so, he illuminates the paper's motto scrawled across the Earth's horizon: *Ridendo corrigo mores* (Laughing I set customs right). It is a rather presumptuous claim, but it has its origins in the broader satirical tradition. Variations of this slogan appear in French newspapers and other Latin American publications. Further emphasizing the enlightenment-through-mockery mission, the weekly labeled itself "*jocoserio*" (*jocoso* and *serio*, simultaneously playful or funny as well as serious).[87] On a more practical level, a sales strategy was also in play. In Mexico serious commentary was common but often pedantic. Satire offered an escape, but it entailed a balancing act. At times the serio smothered the jocoso in many publications, engendering clumsy ridicule of popular custom.

As discussed in previous chapters, nineteenth-century male writers also assumed the female voice for divergent purposes. Liberal publications mockingly conjured fanatical women in their criticisms of the Catholic Church and proclerical politics. In contrast, conservative satirists turned the wholesome Catholic woman or girl into the personification of Mexican practicality, contrasting her commonsense traditionalism with liberal radicalism.[88]

In a related phenomenon, satirical publications often presented themselves as characters drawn from popular culture. Sometimes they personified their periodicals as logo-like figures, like *La Linterna*'s jester. At other times a specific persona anchored the editorial voice. In this sense, articles and caricatures featured the emblematic figure as if publications were documenting his or her misadventures. Usually the satirists chose figures with unsavory traits associated with the lower social orders; in other words, they drew on the Spanish picaresque tradition.[89] In some cases, though, they are fantastical imps instead of social types.[90] The key was marking these characters as violators of propriety and exploiting the comedic potential of their crass behaviors among social betters. In doing so satirists established their claim to public opinion.[91] Pedro Hagelstein and his staff also embraced another dimension of the picaresque tradition, the lampooning of piety.[92]

Several journalistic forbearers probably inspired *La Madre*. In the 1870s a newspaper called *Juan Diego* also played the part of the people's seer.[93] Other publications chose sinister namesakes; for example, *Mefistófeles* exploited notions of the devil's unsettling prescience, and *La Madre Celestina* assumed the character of the infamous procuress of Golden Age literature.[94] However, *La Casera*, a more lighthearted endeavor, offers a particularly useful illustration of male journalists' impersonations of female figures. The editors chose

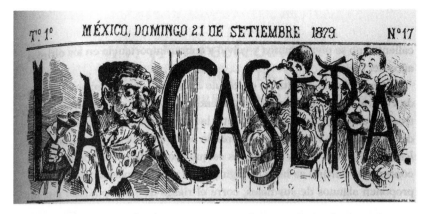

Figure 16. Eavesdropping for the nation. From *La Casera*, 21 September 1879. Courtesy of the Sterling Memorial Library, Yale University.

a widely recognized social type, the elderly female *vecindad* (tenement) manager featured in the era's costumbrista literature.[95] A combination of the downwardly mobile busybody and nagging rent collector, this character was ubiquitous in Mexican urban life. On the masthead she is a bug-eyed snoop straining to hear through a wall. Opposite her, caricatured *políticos* recoil in shock as she tolls a bell: *La Casera* has discovered their misdeeds and sounds the alarm. Thus, as befitted this figure, the newspaper promised to expose the untoward happenings in the vecindad-nation. In some cartoons the scold also batters public figures with a broom—a class and gender appropriate weapon. The writers also lay claim to the archetypal casera tricks: gossip, subterfuge, and impertinence. In other words, they deployed stereotypes of womanly guile.[96]

Another late nineteenth-century precedent for Pedro Hagelstein's Madre Matiana appeared in *El Padre Cobos*, a newspaper renowned for its derisive opposition to the Díaz regime. In this case, the publication's namesake and another broom-wielding matron, doña Caralampia Mondongo, defend society together. Padre Cobos appears as the good-hearted, progressive pastor reminiscent of Miguel Hidalgo who tends to his "flock" (i.e., the Mexican nation). He represents society's moral compass and protects democratic ideals. At times he paternally tries to coax better behavior from public figures. His low-key ministrations, though, set the stage for indignant sermons when provoked. At these times he rallies the populace to defend the nation.[97] His female counterpart, however, is more relevant to Matiana's legacy. With her cumbersome name, a combination of a feminized obscure male saint's name and a street-food favorite (tripe soup), doña Caralampia Mondongo represents a truly popular female figure. Her first name alludes to outmoded naming traditions—that is, selecting odd names from the santoral.[98] Her surname is both a dish of Afro-Latin origin and also served as a denigrating epithet of the era to describe lower-class adornments and those who wear them.[99] Characterized as a liberal version of the honest mexicana, she appears as the image of popular domesticity and feminine umbrage. She is a sturdy señora reluctantly drawn away from home by troubling public happenings, and once perturbed she is an energetic punisher. As with other female satirical figures, her political task is an extension of her domestic duties; she cleans up the public sphere. A key thread linking these figures is the stereotyping of female discernment: doña Caralampia intuits and attacks, whereas *La Casera* pries and spies. *La Madre Matiana*, naturally, divines and divulges. It is important to note these celebrated female satirical figures are not thinkers. As feminist scholars point out, as in many portrayals of women, these characters do not possess the "civilizing evaluative gaze" reserved for men. Instead they depend on instincts, wiles, and miraculous foresight.[100]

THE REVELATIONS OF *LA MADRE*

Alongside Hagelstein's newspaper, Mexicans could purchase new editions of the prophecies that had been published elsewhere. Quite likely they served as sources of additional predictions, while at the same time unwittingly providing fodder for the satirists at *La Madre*. Probably the most important was the anonymous 1914 pamphlet, *Profecías completas*, which cost a meager 10 cents at the time. At first the author cites the two Matiana almanacs, the *Calendario nigromántico para 1858* and the *Calendario de la Madre Matiana para 1867* (see chapter 3), as his sources, and offers a straightforward recounting of the prophecies from that era. It is in a long postscript devoted to historical and contemporary commentary where changes appear and the tone gradually sharpens. *Profecías completas* presents a simple history of Matiana's role in Mexico, claiming that older individuals recalled hearing prophecies as children and experiencing their fulfillment as they aged. The unknown author lists examples, such as the foundation of the "*Sacramentarias* of the Villa de Guadalupe" (a reference to the Adoratrices Perpetuas Guadalupanas; see chapter 4), and the occupation of Veracruz in 1914 by the U.S. military. Subsequently *Profecías completas* becomes quite shrill, embracing the apocalyptic portrayal of North American machinations prevalent among archconservative predecessors like Duarte: "They have informed and been the black soul of our politics; the Mephistopheles of our governments."[101] The author complains that the United States, with its freemasonry and Protestantism, destroyed Mexico's convents, ignited the War of the Reform, and more recently armed the Zapatistas (a specious claim even for the time). He thus blames North America for Revolutionary atrocities, particularly the widespread rape of innocent young women. As his rhetorical ire peaks, the anonymous author is essentially screaming: "They foment the Revolution of today! They are the martyers! Them . . . !"[102] And yet he reminds readers that the scheming heretics to the north remain mere instruments of Mexico's richly deserved divine punishment.

Aside from updating the anti-American, Catholic nationalism of the nineteenth century, these passages actually offered little that Mexicans had not heard before. Additional predictions and novel constructions of the seer's persona appear elsewhere. For example, the 1914 pamphlet claims that Madre Matiana foretold of acute national suffering amid a succession of three presidents named Francisco. This prophecy does not appear in the original nineteenth-century texts. During the Revolution, though, this specific prediction was widely repeated. Apparently the fact that Francisco León de la Barra (May 1911–November 1911), Francisco Madero (November 1911–February 1913), and Francisco Carvajal (July 1914–August 1914) occupied the presidency struck some as an ominous coincidence. The precipitous rise and fall of Madero, in particular, appears to have stirred sharp interest in the prophecies. Writing in the mid-1940s, Carlos M. de Herédia, a skeptical Jesuit, claimed that Madre Matiana was a topic of considerable concern during "the time of Madero."[103] Indeed, his star-crossed fate more or less read like a prophetic cautionary fable: he was the dissident voice from the periphery that deposed the dictator (Porfirio Díaz) and secured the presidency alongside peasant revolutionaries, only to be unseated and brutally murdered within a few years.

Perhaps the most innovative aspect of *Profecías completas*, though, was its sentimental portrayal of Madre Matiana, which had no apparent precedent. The author holds forth at length about an exceptional, tenderhearted visionary who overcame her low station in life in order to warn fellow souls of a terrible destiny. This newly imagined Matiana transcends the disparaging treatment of her ecclesiastical superiors and the abuse she suffers at the hands of inquisitors. Pure and retiring, she weathers spiritual torment and alienation because those around her could not understand her visions or her personal struggle. The author beseeches readers to "see" the nation's seer as a preternaturally knowing, melancholy resident of San Jeronimo's cloisters. Like Duarte in the late 1880s, the author works from the old template of idealized female piety. His embellished Matiana lifts her face to the heavens, her hands clenched with prayerful intensity, and peers into the future ablaze with divine love. How horrible, the author moans, for her to see "us" amid so much bloodshed and desolation. How it must have pained Matiana to contemplate the widows and orphans, and how she—the poor convent servant— must have chastised her own flesh as a result. Reminding readers of the Revolutionary turmoil of the moment, the author asserts that it truly was Mexico's duty to embrace the seer's expiatory crusade. He also opens the door to all manner of future additions, cautioning that much was probably omitted from the source texts due to secretiveness of convent culture and inquisitorial investigations. Ultimately, the pamphlet speculates that Matiana made additional important predictions and demands an official archival investigation to recover the prophecies in their entirety.

In 1917 yet another anonymous writer explicitly strove to update Duarte's marriage of the Mexican visionary and European mystical lore. The work's full title makes this abundantly clear: *Las verdaderas profecías de Matiana: comparadas y coordinadas con otras profecías semejantes de este y del antiguo continente acerca del triunfo final de la Iglesia y del Fin del Mundo* (*The True Prophecies of Matiana: Compared and Coordinated with Similar Prophecies from this [World] and the Old World Concerning the Final Triumph of the Church and the End of the World*).[104] The author of *Verdaderas profecías* claimed that previous editions of Matiana's prophecies were no longer available and couched his offering as a much-needed reassessment given world war in Europe, revolution in Mexico, and new Church-sanctioned prophecies.[105] In the end, *Verdaderas profecías* represents little more than a rehash of Duarte's demonic conspiracy thesis. Nonetheless the apocalyptic histrionics, blinkered paranoia, and maudlin portrayal of female piety evident in both the "complete" and "true" versions of the prophecies probably had much to do with Pedro Hagelstein's irreverent approach to the seer.

When *La Madre* uncorked its own derisive mysticism midway through 1917, the newspaper touched off a celebration among opponents of then president Venustiano Carranza (1859–1920). One of the voices of the Mexican exile community, Texas-based *La Revista Mexicana*, praised it as a bold send up of the Revolutionary government: "Just the name of this newspaper represents a threat to the bearded president."[106] In fact, although actual circulation statistics remain a mystery, thanks to this exile publication's extensive coverage of *La Madre* we have an idea of what the first issues contained.[107]

Founded in 1915, *La Revista Mexicana* focused on interpreting Mexican news and reporting on the lives of Mexicans in the United States. It also presented itself as a standard bearer of anti-Carranza opinion. Like many factional newspapers, it set up shop near the border, and until 1920 *La Revista Mexicana* served as a key critic of the emergent Revolutionary state.[108] Beginning in 1916, the writers invoked the prophecies in a manner that illuminates why the pamphlet prophetess became the namesake of a newspaper. In a long article titled "La situación mexicana," published on 16 April 1916, they set out to characterize the various Revolutionary factions. None of the leaders received favorable treatment, but Carranza drew the brunt of their ire.[109] The newspaper sardonically postulated that his permanence in Veracruz in 1916 when his rivals, Pancho Villa and Emiliano Zapata, controlled Mexico City was due to his superstitious fears about Matiana's predictions. *La Revista Mexicana* then proceeded to provide a haphazard "biography" of the seer and maintained that many of Matiana's predictions had already come true, citing the story of the three presidents named Francisco. The newspaper avoided the more outlandish aspects of the visionary narrative, such as the celestial restoration of Catholic monarchy. It placed emphasis on a still unfulfilled prediction, and purportedly quoted directly from the prophecies: "Mexico will also have a president with a great beard, and he will be dragged through the streets of Mexico. Afterwards, peace will be reestablished."[110] Carranza was well known for his bushy goatee. As with the three Franciscos, predictions regarding a bearded president did not appear in nineteenth-century versions of the Matiana narrative. In fact, given the outpouring of critical commentary regarding *"el president barbudo"* in *La Revista Mexicana*, it seems quite likely a "revelation" concocted by this particular newspaper. Several editorials invoked visions of the populace dragging Carranza through the streets. Over time it served as an all-purpose expression of contempt for the regime. The newspaper taunted Carranza with quips stating that Matiana was closing in on him, and issued joke warnings that perhaps he should shave.[111] *La Revista Mexicana* called to the prophetess directly, "Madre Matiana . . . the time is approaching for the fulfillment of your prophecy."[112] In sum, this exile newspaper cast the seer as the popular voice of anti-Revolutionary anger.[113] They even published separate "open letters" to Carranza and the seer. The former demanded that the "so-called president" abandon the presidency or face Madre Matiana.[114] The latter begged Matiana to make her prophecies come true and rid Mexico of Carranza and the insurgent hordes.[115] *La Revista* also republished an "interview" with Matiana from another newspaper, *El Pueblo*, where she appeared as a ghastly crone raging about corruption and the looming destruction of the nation:

¡Qué ma' va este mundo!...	What a mess the world is!...
¡Qué mal van las cosas de México,	What a mess of things in Mexico,
hijo!...	son!...
¡Raza de caimanes con pies de	Race of caimans with elephant feet,[116]
elefante,	
raza que en la Cámara llaman	race in Congress called smoke-
trashumante,	passers [roving],[117]
porque a semejanza de los	because just like "autos" they belch
"autos" echa	
bocanadas de humo por	mouthfuls of smoke from their
la retaguardia!	backsides!
¡Ten a todas horas prendida la mecha	Keep the wick lit at all hours
y a cada momento consérvate	and at every moment stay
en guardia!...	on guard!...
Por tantas mentiras, por tantos	Because of all the lies, all the
embustes	scams
y desbarajustes...	and bungling...
... yo, que soy la Madre Matiana,	...I, who am Madre Matiana, I
te juro	swear
que antes del infierno sale	that Quasimodo will get out of hell
Cuasimodo	before
Y antes en lo obscuro	and in darkness
ha de ver un ciego	a blind man will see, before
que escapes al hierro y escapes	you escape the pan and escape
al fuego...	the fire...
¡Población maldita, cuna	Damned nation, crade of rotgut[118]
del tlachique	
madre del colonche	mother of homebrew[119]
y abuela del ponche;	and grandmother of punch;

ya vendrán los tiempos en que se te achique	times are coming when it'll shrink on you[120]
ese orgul'o [sic] necio, orgullo que ahora	that stubborn pride, pride that now
te da ciertos aires de conquistadora . . .	gives you certain conquering aires . . .
¡Conmuévete y llora	Tremble and weep
porque el cumplimiento de mis profecías	because the fulfillment of my prophecies
se acerca a medida que pasan los días! . . .	approaches as the days pass! . . . [121]

Many characteristics of Matiana's appropriation by critics of the emergent Revolutionary government and society are visible in this passage. The re-worked prophetess vents about the deplorable state of the nation, rampant disorder, and the inept and profoundly corrupt nature of the new political class. The text critically characterizes Mexican popular custom as a culture of drunkenness. Ironically, neither this excerpt from *El Pueblo* nor *La Revista Mexicana*'s other commentary addressed the original visionary predictions. Clearly it was not really Matiana's reputed foresight that interested journalists; it was the expressive potential within a popular female character marked as deranged yet prophetic and authentic. The Matiana character was essentially irresistible, because she was both a fixture of Mexican popular culture and could "see through," as it were, the new order.[122] Notably *La Revista Mexicana* made no mention of Matiana's historical linkage to church-state polemics in previous generations. Truly the San Antonio weekly evinced only a shallow interest in the original prophetic narrative. In the end the provenance hardly mattered—Matiana made good copy.

La Madre, then, seized on enduring concerns attached to Matiana's prophecies and new fears kindled by the Revolution. It is nearly impossible to determine the paper's circulation, but in addition to Mexico City it reached at least the northern state of Sonora and the port city Veracruz.[123] *El Demócrata* of Veracruz claimed in 1924 that *La Madre* was the bestselling paper among the poor at the time.[124] Most likely, *La Madre* found her way around Mexico on the rail lines. The newspaper's inaugural issue included a manifesto, which appeared in verse form:

Pues que la "Madre Matiana"	Well the "Madre Matiana"

Muy ducha y clarividente	So gifted and clairvoyant
Ha de "zurrar la badana"	Is destined to "dress down"
A todo bicho viviente.	Every louse that lives.
Al político inmoral	The immoral politician
Y al cacique abusador	And the abusive strongman
Ha de ponerles bozal	She will muzzle them both
Aunque les cause dolor.	Despite the pain they'll suffer.
Al patrón insolentado	And the arrogant boss
Que al proletariado veja	That mistreats the proletariat
Lo ha de poner enjaulado	She'll put him in a cage
Como león tras de la reja.	Like a lion behind bars.
Para que la cuña apriete	For the wedge to hold
Del mismo palo sera.	it shall be of the same tree.[125]
Y a todos los de bonete	Thus all those of the bonnet
	[the clergy][126]
"La Madre" flagerá.	"La Madre" will lash.
Su espíritu está cansada	Her spirit it is tired
De ver tanta atrocidad	Of seeing so much atrocity
Y por lo tanto ha bajado	And hence she has descended
Del éter a la Ciudad	From the ether to the City
Su principal objetivo	Her principle objective
Será vigilar con celo,	Will be to watch with zeal,
Que el poder Ejectuvio	That the Executive branch
Cumpla del pueblo anhelo . . .	Complies with the peoples' needs . . .
Vallarta, Ocampo y Arteaga	Vallarta, Ocampo, and Arteaga
Aunque muertos, vivos son,	Although dead, continue living,
Exigen que no se haga	They demand that there not be
De su obra una omisión . . .	Of their life's work any omission . . .
La buena "Madre" ha mirado	The good "Mother" has seen
Desde su obscura morada,	From her dark abode,
Que en México se han burlado	That in Mexico they have mocked/
	cheated

De la ley inmaculada . . .	The law immaculate . . .
"La Madre" no callará	"La Madre" will not be silent
Las ofensas y atropellos	The offenses and abuses
Y todo lo contará	All of them she'll expose
En prosa o en "romances bellos"	In prose or in "beautiful odes"[127]

Naturally, as these verses show, the editors played up the all-seeing capabilities attributed to the prophetess. But they also added a zealous patriotic fervor for the rule of law to the mix. The Matiana of old, the newspaper claimed, had miraculously returned to the city to keep an eye on the government and make sure it served the people. Rhymes list her targets and proclaim her ready to confront whoever needs humbling: politicians, petty strongmen, etc. *La Madre* also promised to turn Matiana against her alleged original creators—the Catholic clergy—with the clever use of the popular proverb recommending the "wedge" (i.e., remedy or fix) be hewn of the same wood as the obstacle or problem. With this statement the editorial staff revealed themselves to be firmly within the rationalist camp that criticized the seer as a clerical invention designed to manipulate popular ignorance. Corruption and incompetence, as additional stanzas attest, were their Matiana's primary targets. She would champion progress and law and expose chicanery and malfeasance. Moreover, in a deliberate flourish *La Madre* also pledged to defend the constitutional legacy of nineteenth-century liberal reformers: Ignacio Vallarta (1830–1893), Melchor Ocampo (1814–1861), and José María Arteaga (1827–1865). For most Mexicans living in 1917, the irony of an "alliance" between the legendary reactionary prophetess and figures like Ocampo and Arteaga would have been obvious. Both men died in the battle against conservatism and French imperialism in the 1860s and had become celebrated martyrs of the liberal cause.

This staged paradox helped establish the newspaper's critical stance; they were uniting the powers of folk visionary legend and notions of national principles against corruption and incompetence in Revolutionary society. In the hands of these journalists Madre Matiana would be an intrepid and energetic voice protecting the public interest. In the penultimate stanza of their inaugural manifesto they boasted:

"La Madre" en la sepultura	"La Madre" in the tomb
No tuvo temor ni espanto	Was not scared or spooked

| *Así que una celda obscura* | And hence a dark cell |
| *No le causará quebranto.* | Will not cause her anguish.[128] |

Matiana had come back from the dead, these satirists joked, and if she had not been frightened by the gloom of the sepulcher, the threat of earthly prison (i.e., censorship and persecution) could hardly deter her, or rather Pedro Hagelstein, the newspaper's owner and editor.

This new Matiana, in many ways, represented a fringe social figure echoing the classic *pícaro/a* (ne'er-do-well or rogue) of Spanish literature and satirical precursors, but she was also grounded in an irreverent take on baroque female piety. Her visionary legend and in-between character provided Hagelstein and his staff with a wide range of options, and they made the most of them. On one level she was the pamphlet prophetess: a figure of humble origins with a remarkable ability to predict the nation's future, pinpoint society's failings, and dictate the means to set Mexico aright. They coyly presented her visions as both patently silly and uncannily accurate. In this way *La Madre* teased the reader, implying that deep down Mexicans feared that Matiana indeed glimpsed a calamitous destiny for the nation. However, just as important as the seer persona, these journalists often rendered Matiana as an archetypal beata or, more disparagingly, as a beatona: a popular female social type routinely vilified by liberal writers in previous decades.[129] Often this figure appeared as a spinster who cultivates an ultra-pious image, aggressively backs the clergy, and spews superstitious hokum and condemnations. In this manner she represented a sanctimonious idiot savant and a gendering of popular Catholicism taken to its extreme. This Matiana was, for all intents and purposes, the village fanática. Another characterization in play was the spinster busybody, the *metiche* in Mexican parlance (like the casera).[130] In concert these traits gave the journalists at *La Madre* license to craft deliberately convoluted muckraking in popular slang.

The final facet of this satirical project was Matiana's representation as popular punisher—a madre on the rampage, as graphically depicted on the masthead (see Figure 17). In the hands of Hagelstein and his staff she became the stout, common Mexican woman who exposed charlatans and deviants. Although not particularly original, this persona was of obvious utility. Thus Matiana, the *vengadora* (avengeress), dominates the newspaper's early issues and reveals how the writers saw themselves. In the newspaper's first era (1917) she appeared as a brawny *marimacha* (man-woman) in penitential sackcloth, attacking clergymen.[131] In addition to the impaling of one priest on her saber,

Figure 17. La Madre Matiana's masthead in 1917. From *La Madre Matiana*, 9 September 1917. Courtesy of the University of Texas Library, Nettie Lee Benson Latin America Collection.

and the suggestive apparent penetration of another, anthropomorphized bats (perhaps political vampires) and other miscreants flee her wrath. The snake of deception slithers through the frame. In the newspaper's second era (1923) she appears much tamer (see Figure 18). This Matiana was in many ways a throwback to the colonial-era servant of the first pamphlets. She comes across as an ungainly old maid, dressed in a beata's habit, performing her cleaning chores. Unlike the Matiana of 1917, she carried the gender-appropriate broom (like doña Caralampia Mondongo); no longer was she the sword-wielding attacker. Instead, in the redesigned masthead she keeps her head down and sweeps away a string of politicos in front of the Chamber of Deputies. She is decidedly less aggressive and masculine. Nonetheless Matiana—and by extension *La Madre*—were tidying up Mexico at the symbolic threshold of the republic.

In this manner the multifaceted visionary character established the rhetorical range of the newspaper. The spirit of *La Madre*, as constructed by the editors, was particularly biting during its inaugural era. The paper's freewheeling style in 1917 was probably a reflection of the simmering tensions between the city's rapidly growing working class, employers, and the Carranza administration.[132] The new government had forcefully repressed a general strike in 1916, and the relationship between urban workers and the state was antagonistic. Hagelstein and his staff attacked a range of public figures and groups from a vague pro-working-class perspective. They avoided, however, a focused attack on Carranza or direct criticism of the

Figure 18. *La Madre Matiana*'s masthead in 1923. From *La Madre Matiana*, 24 May 1923. Image courtesy of the Biblioteca de la Universidad de Sonora.

new constitution.[133] If we heed *La Revista Mexicana*'s analysis, *La Madre*'s mere existence encapsulated a critique of the president. Occasionally, though, they directly targeted him. For example, Carranza appeared in a cartoon as the doomed libertine Don Juan Tenorio from the Mozart opera, arrogantly ignoring the populations' complaints, taking whatever he desired, and threatening critics with violence.[134] The newspaper also mocked the United States's global pretentions and sneered at its melting-pot society.[135] In addition, regional politics attracted *La Madre*'s indignation. The most effective satire emerged from texts crafted to mimic the calendarios, where the prophecies had appeared in the past, and efforts to make the most of the exaggerated language and turn-back-the-clock nature of the prophecies. A rich intertextual playfulness took shape as *La Madre* lampooned popular devotional culture. Thus the newspaper produced a spoof santoral throughout its existence, featuring absurdly named saints—like San Eleuterio Chueco (Saint Eleutherious Crooked) and San Chocho (Saint Dodderer).[136] Typically these faux saints served as the patron saints of maligned individuals and groups, or simply allowed the journalists to issue barbs of various kinds. In this vein, there were announcements for mock feasts, such as that of "San Porfirio Díaz, tyrant of Mexico, emulated by locals and foreigners," and the "Exaltation of the Holy Cross, a cross long borne by the population." Another section titled "Máximas y sentencias" ("Maxims and Sentences") played simultaneously on notions of the beata as sanctimonious scold and the almanac tradition of printing aphorisms. *La Madre*'s dictums typically twisted customary sayings into off-color puns or quick jabs at shortcomings, such as laziness and lawlessness.[137]

By *La Madre*'s second era of publication (as seen in issues from 1923), Pedro Hagelstein and his staff had altered the newspaper's tone. In many ways the changes to the newspaper's masthead fit the evolving Mexican political climate. It is possible that Carranza shuttered the original publication, or the newspaper may have become insolvent at some point. By 1923 relations between urban workers and the state had begun to solidify in more stable, paternalist structures.[138] In the second coming of *La Madre*, the editorial staff focused on more measured muckraking. The writers were more openly conservative, although they maintained their posture as defenders of the Revolution. The paper still contained the parodied santoral and sections titled with variations of *madre*, and these largely functioned in the same fashion. But the calendario spoof lost prominence. In 1923 an advice column with what seems like fictitious correspondence allowed writers to mock Americanized slang and youth culture. President Álvaro Obregón (1880–1928) appeared caricatured with some frequency, but the representations were relatively tame. For example, one cartoon depicted Obregón as an oafish "cop on the beat" monitoring North American ambitions armed with part of the Mexican Constitution (Article 27, which restricted foreign landholding) dangling precariously from a hook replacing the arm he lost in the Revolution.[139] In sum, the second era of *La Madre* was distinctly cautious. It gives the impression that the editors were trying to avoid irritating the government—perhaps treading lightly amid tensions surrounding the looming presidential transition. Indeed disgruntled Revolutionary generals led by Adolfo de la Huerta rose up in December 1923 after Obregón's selection of Plutarco Elías Calles as his successor. *La Madre* at this time maintained a generic pro-industrialization stance and even muted its previous anticlericalism. In addition, the editorial staff clearly found modernizing urban culture disconcerting. Customs were changing around *La Madre* without much regard for "her" satirical guidance.

In terms of political commentary, the revived newspaper often focused on provincial corruption, but it held only veiled criticism of the federal government. *La Madre* insinuated that the Obregón administration allowed abuses, but the editors were clearly playing it safe. Most Mexican's remained deeply cynical about politics. They assumed that regional bosses manipulated voting and pocketed resources, and their suppositions were mostly accurate. President Carranza tried to control provincial politics but frequently failed.[140] Obregón's deal making brought more federal influence in local affairs, but this scarcely meant a new era of transparency.[141] In the articles that criticized events outside the capital city, *La Madre* opted to spotlight local politicians in embarrassing and compromising situations. Thus sections appear with titles like "La república encuerada" ("The Naked

Republic") and "Puebla en camisón" ("Puebla in a Nightshirt"). Sometimes they featured letters from readers asking for help in the face of corrupt or lax local functionaries. Such was the case in "Tampico en calzones" ("Tampico in Underwear") on 28 June 1923, where a group of self-described poor women complained about their callous municipal president and his prying and destructive sanitary brigades. *La Madre* subsequently tried to shame the offending politico into embracing his duty to serve the unfortunate. Still, it hardly counted as hard-hitting journalism.[142]

The social commentary of this era, however, was notably conservative and more direct. At various points the newspaper targeted peasant agitation for land (the central grievance of the Revolution in many regions). For example, one "*Desmadres*" column labels *agraristas* (land-reform activists) as bandits dragging the nation toward barbarism due to their contempt for property rights. The newspaper warns President Obregón that *agrarismo* would ultimately cause him serious headaches if he allowed it to develop unchecked.[143]

In regard to gender norms, the editors were much more forward. They lashed out against the emergent feminist movement and young men of suspicious sexual orientation. For example, *La Madre* published a misogynist critique of the First Congress of the Pan-American League of Feminists.[144] They mocked it as a "modern women's pageant," a mere handful of ugly women whining about marriage, childrearing, and inequality.[145] For these journalists the gathering revealed a misappropriation of Revolutionary ideals and preposterous gender rebellion. They labeled the attendees *rojas* (reds) and insinuated that unnamed forces lurked behind the conference. In no way, the newspaper argued, could "*feministas*" speak for Mexican women. Echoing Catholic traditionalism, they asserted that the nation's "true" women were innately devout, focused on their children, and self-effacing. They would never take part in such an unseemly event.

La Madre also resorted to the hackneyed ignorant female trope. In this case, a reporter parodied his maid—whom he called his "gata" (literally, female cat, and often a derisive nickname for maids[146])—and mocked her enthusiasm for the feminist conference and the request for higher rates of women's pay. Describing her as pock-faced, dark-complected, and "skinnier than a leg on an anemic spider," the author skewered her prattle on social equality, quoting her idiomatic malapropisms in what one could call satirical maid-speak:

No lo digo por su mercé, questá muy aparte, sino por los que joroban a una y quieren tener lopresión encima diuna, y son abusadores de los pobres prolitariados y queren quiuna siamuele y nomás ellos chupan la sangre de los pobres, que semos iguales y parejos con esos patrones. . . . Hay está su escoba, su trapo de sacudir y su montón de ropa sucia. Ya no soy desas que se matan todo el día tabajando por tortillas duras. ¡Viva lamor libre y la nivelación de los secsos [sic].

I'm not saying this about your grace, cuz you'r real different, but only about those who are screwing us and want to have doppresion on a gal, and are the abusers of the poor proliterarians and wanna a girl t' wreck herself and just so they can suck the poor's blood, tho we're equal and as good as them bosses. . . . So here's your broom, your dust rag and your pile of dirty clothes. I'm not one-a-dose that kill themselves all day working for stale tortillas anymore. Long live free love and the leveling of the seckes.[147]

Ultimately, as evident in this rendering of popular female speech tinged with racist contempt, the author belittles his "gata's" attempts to deploy concepts she could not even pronounce. He also slighted the Ciceronas (female presumptive orators) at the conference she sought to emulate.

The policing of Mexican masculinity was also an acute concern of *La Madre*. Articles mocked the exaggerated mannerisms and leisure activities of the capital city's youth.[148] On 28 June 1923, the paper also published a poem characterizing *"el fifí,"* the urban dandy of implied homosexuality, as a repellent "social calamity":

Existe un ente	There exists a figure
sin semejante	without compare
por lo chocante	for being annoying
Es el fifí.	It is the fifí.
Cierto que viste cual damisela	You must have seen this damsel
media calada, fina chinela,	fancy stockings, fine slippers,
pulidido talle de colibrí;	polished hummingbird waisted;
se pinta y riza, se unge y perfuma,	applies makeup and curls, annoints and perfumes

se contonea con gracia suma . . .
. . . Y ¿es un hombre? . . .
  Dicen que sí.
Frente al espejo pasa las horas,

tiene desmayos, cual las señoras
y vuelve de ellos con pachulí
discute y charla sobre modistas,
depiladores, manicuristas . . .
. . . Y ¿es ese un hombre?
  Dicen que sí. . . .

No en la oficina o en el bufete
sino en los cines, el cabaret,
y en otros dignos centros así,
gasta su vida nuestro pedante
zángano entero, cursi, tunante,
¡Por fin! ¿es hombre? . . . ¡Es el fifí!

Mas a derechas
si es masculino
o es feminino
nunca entendí:

Se que es un ente
sin semejante
por repugnante:
¡¡Eso es Fifí!![149]

Sashays with consumate grace
. . . And is it a man? . . . That's what
  they say.
In front of the mirror passing the
  hours,
fainting spells, just like the ladies
and comes to with some pachouli
argues and chatters about stylists
depilatories, manicurists . . .
And is he a man? . . .
  That's what they say.

Not at the office or at the practice
but at the theater, the cabaret,
and in other such dignified places,
our prig squanders his life
a complete leech, pretentious, scamp,
So! Is he a man? . . . He is the fifí!

Hence in truth
if he is male
or female
I never could tell:

I know that he is a figure
without compare
in terms of repugnance:
Such is the Fifí!!

Sarcastic interventions such as this offer a glimpse of the insecurities present for the staff of *La Madre* (and within patriarchal society more broadly) and reveal that the appropriated prophetess was in very different territory. She was now monitoring gendered social identity, fashion, and personal appearance. The verses also show the paper taking part in the construction of the homophobic, working-class masculinity that emerged during the early twentieth century. Here *La Madre* essentially joined in the mounting criticism of bourgeois masculinity at the time, which entailed a nationalist juxtaposition of the sturdy Mexican male laborer-citizen and pampered men of the urban upper class.[150] The latter, as the poem indicates, were savaged as aberrant, effeminate parasites.

La Madre may have been more politically cautious in 1923, but the newspaper distinguished itself in other ways. In essence the newspaper opted for a different kind of desmadre, and it gained a special kind of notoriety as a result.[151] According to Carlos Monsiváis, La Madre in the 1920s serves as an early exemplar of a particular form of Mexican identity performance: the collective celebration of crass, sexually suggestive commentary. He argues that the newspaper delighted in using popular albures (vulgar puns) as headlines, and the texts helped cement the notion that vulgarity, and a fondness for lewd humor, was quintessentially Mexican.[152] Frequently headlines allude to sex organs, sodomy, and ejaculation. For example: "¡¡Con esa lengua que tienen hacen sabio a mi pelón . . . !!" ("With that tongue [blather] that they have they make my baldy [penis] seem genius!").[153] Of course, by making lengua the subject and mi pelón the direct object, the insinuation of fellatio is clear.[154] Indeed the level of graphic vulgarity is quite surprising for the era. Additional bawdy headlines include: "No me aprietes los limones porque te llenas de jugo" ("Don't squeeze my lemons or you will be covered in juice"); and "No me cierren las petacas que faltan dos talegas" (literally, "Don't close the suitcases on me because two sacks still are not in"; but figuratively, Don't close those big buttocks on me because my balls are still coming).[155]

Aside from their attention-getting impropriety, much of the rhetoric employed by the newspaper featured allusions to crops and livestock, and thus reveals a deliberate nod to rural society, the origin of most Mexicans at the time. This represented a new strategy for the newspaper. Instead of sticking with the stereotyped fanatical female impersonation, they increasingly assumed a working-class, masculine voice drenched with ribald scorn and bravado.

The editorial shift in La Madre between 1917 and 1923 may have been inevitable. In the earlier issues the newspaper closely parodied the Matiana narrative tradition and the calendario genre. Thus much of the satirical humor emerged from playing the prophetess and twisting devotional literature's conventions. It was quite astute, given the up-tick in Matiana's fame from 1914 to 1918, and it probably attracted readers. In later issues the newspaper still shows remnants of this approach, but it focused much less on the seer's characterization. Pedro Hagelstein and his staff had moved beyond the character that originally gave them a unique journalistic personality. They had established their own identity as La Madre, which no longer depended on parodies of the pamphlet prophetess. Instead they switched from the beata's rants to a common man's sarcasm and vulgar commentary. Most likely the Matiana character lost its allure as the plausibility of imagined prophetic fulfillments faded. The anti-Carranza associations linked to Matiana in earlier years were no longer relevant and the sense of Revolutionary-era gloom had dissipated as well. The change made sense for other reasons too. The newspaper's target audience appears to have been the city's growing population of rural-origin, male laborers. This group also served as a target of official nationalism; it was probably good for business and politics to speak in their voice. Not surprisingly, *La Madre* reproduced the prejudices and social conservatism of this part of the population and the emergent state. In essence, it appears that Hagelstein and his staff were trying to ride the wave of evolving Mexican nationalism. During uncertainty and widespread suffering they chose a female visionary alter-ego who evoked mystical tradition, miraculous thinking, and popular irrationality, and thus aptly presided over real-life desmadre. In contrast, amid the consolidation of the new state's power and national economic recovery, a foul-mouthed masculine voice better fit the hyper-male Revolutionary nationalism taking root in the 1920s.

At some point after 1923 *La Madre* ceased publication. According to Hagelstein's friend and colleague Ricardo Arizti, the veteran journalist had sustained the newspaper thanks to the support of Emilio Portes Gil (1890–1978), an important politician, government minister, and, for a time, interim president of Mexico (1928–1930). This bit of information suggests that *La Madre*, like *Los Sucesos* two decades earlier, had ties to a faction within the government. This quite likely explains the newspaper's cautious political stance in 1923. *La Madre* had proven to be Hagelstein's most successful venture. In addition, Arizti claimed, it was the realm where he most fully unleashed his personality. Nonetheless, at some point the brash satirical prophetess succumbed to a "boycott." Arizti did not provide more detail, but *La Madre* may have been a target of Portes Gil's rivals: perhaps Luis Morones (1890–1964), the famously corrupt union boss of the Regional Confederation of Mexican Laborers (CROM).[156] In any case, Hagelstein, el Padre Matías, died proud and poor in 1932.

LA MADRE Y LA NACIÓN

In most examinations of nationalism, scholars focus on elite efforts to fashion cultural hegemony. Typically the printed word and rhetorical endeavors to define the nation serve as evidence; hence historians are sensitive to language, ideas, norms, and practices discursively linked to the nation and those marked for marginalization. In short, scholarship follows intellectuals of the past in their search for the essence of the nation.[157] As Craig Calhoun points out, the "success" of various quests for national foundations is not nearly as important as the practice of talking and writing about search and discovery. Myth and invented tradition gain traction through reiteration and repeated adaptation. Over time the revisitings and almost ritualized description of "discovered" origins proves central to peoples' framing of their worldview in nationalist terms. Hagelstein as well as his predecessors took part in this process, but they did so from a tentative stance. In other words, since satire usually criticizes without offering solutions it is well-suited to the indecisive nation building common in post-colonial settings.

For scholars like Calhoun, a tipping point is when nationalist identities gain clear precedence over other categorical identities (for example, religion and class). These issues are particularly important in Latin America because nation builders largely failed to reach this watershed until the 1930s. It was not, however, for lack of trying. But identities rooted in pre-Columbian and colonial history (such as unique indigenous cultures, racial hierarchies, religious orders, and occupational or class distinctions linked to ethnicity) proved difficult to surmount. In Mexico this challenge is evident in the endeavors launched by liberal and Revolutionary nationalists. As in other societies, these movements spoke of freeing the populace from the "oppression" and "obscurantism" of older corporate ties, identities, ideas, languages, and customs. Most of all Mexico's secular nationalists bemoaned fanaticism and the strong affinities between the populace (particularly women) and the clergy. In part, this stemmed from the formidable challenge offered by the conservative Catholic nationalism voiced by the likes of Luis G. Duarte.

In many ways it was the inability of any group to assert a clear cultural hegemony for the century following Mexican Independence that created auspicious conditions for publications like *La Madre*. Nationalist insecurities inspired enduring conflicts over the values of the nation. They also sparked experimentation in the discursive arena. The appropriated prophetess and other characters in the satirical press give us glimpses into the process. Particularly in the context of the joco-serio tradition, Mexicans deployed social types at the margins of liberal and Revolutionary discourse. The characters themselves are borderline figures, and the mirth they inspire masks boundary-finding and frontier-marking agendas. In the late 1910s Madre

Matiana represented the fringe figure par excellence: she spanned reality and legend, the fanatical and insightful, and the mysteriously sacred and derisively profane. Moreover, she bridged colony and nation (the criticized and idealized past and the imagined but illusive future). As such, she represented an excellent vehicle for satirical explorations of the national.

Much of the scholarship on nationalism centers on how states work to manufacture feelings of belonging and fuse these sentiments to the prevailing social order. Processes of national identity formation, though, are often too chaotic for easy manipulation and control. William Beezley draws our attention to the importance of unscripted popular diversions in Mexico. He argues that a mix of almanacs, children's games, local festivals, and popular theater in the nineteenth century gradually shaped a flexible national consciousness. He asserts that this hodgepodge of entertainments proved more successful than elite efforts to create a homogenous, Eurocentric Mexican identity. This largely market-driven process celebrated the nation's cultural and social diversity instead.[158] In Beezley's variegated sources, and in the present book's close examination of the calendario-almanaque genre, a heterodox liberalism is in evidence. In general, popular diversions evince moderate republican notions of citizenship and a gradual porous secularization, while revealing that most Mexicans continued to cherish Catholic practices and beliefs. This suggests that a broad cross-section of the Mexican populace bought into, literally and figuratively, a rather elastic nationalism. They were omnivorous in their consumption of national narratives and their participation in emerging cultural practices.

Popular theater and other pastimes also underscore a crucial additional issue: sharing jokes and making fun of society's acknowledged shortcomings represent experiences that strengthen collective identification. It is akin to the dynamics of nineteenth-century social dance.[159] The experience of moving together to specific rhythms, the development of a communal vocabulary of steps, and the internalization of melodies and lyrics can produce a powerful sense of belonging. It follows that the shared pleasures of political humor and a familiarity with a set of satirical characters can also create bonds of affinity. Derision, like dance and misery, loves company.

The role of gendered representation and satirical impersonation in nationalist expression, as outlined by Nira Yuval-Davis and Jill Lane, gives these observations added weight. Although not stated explicitly, efforts by nation builders and social reformers to spur change through ridicule frequently depend on the manipulation of gendered social types. They play on established metaphors, stories, and characters that remained anchored in the discourse of nationalist contestation. The *La Madre* case highlights the use of stereotyped notions of femininity and religious fanaticism, but precursor publications used other female figures. Humor and political critique hinged on the delineating and transgressing of norms and boundaries symbolically embodied by female characters. In the most straightforward representations, there were allegorical feminine personifications of the nation, constitutions, and the "people." Typically "she" passively suffers due to a public figure's misdeeds.[160] More complex representations of the nation appeared in conservative satire, where devout women's idealized propriety and incarnation of innate Mexicaness serves as the foil of radical liberalism's embrace of foreign ideas. Doña Caralampia Mondongo shares some of these characteristics, but like *La Casera*'s namesake she is the people's champion, drawn from the gallery of recognized popular types. Crucially, both of them are borderline figures in terms of class, and the satirical act of political humiliation stems from receiving a tongue-lashing, or a beating, from a broom-wielding matron. *La Madre* deployed a multifaceted figure: all at once she was the deranged prophetess, the fanatical beatona, and the visionary nemesis of corruption.

The reformist strategy in Madre Matiana's satirical impersonation depended on Mexicans recognizing themselves in the prophetess, while understanding that she epitomized "backwardness." In a sense, like the satirical figures of Cuban blackface theater, she was an anti-colonial representation. Her illogical beliefs and actions rooted in the past were the target of ridicule. By making a hash of Catholic traditionalism, mysticism, and contemporary politics she marked *beatería* as outmoded in the modern nation. In this sense Matiana was a negative representation; she stood for what Mexicans were supposed to leave behind. Nonetheless, the audience was to identify with her. She may have been wrongheaded, but at a deep level she represented a just, raw, popular indignation. Despite blinding superstition, she "saw" for the people, and a quarrelsome impertinence led her to speak for them too.

The contradictions in *La Madre*'s satirical project appear cloaked in contempt, but they are inescapable. Mexico's secular nationalism placed pious women outside the bounds of citizenship and rational public debate, but they endured regardless, periodically barging into the public sphere during flare-ups in church-state conflict. Matiana and her beatería are thus akin to banditry's repeated recurrence in Latin American discourse: she represented the antithesis of modern nationhood while also symbolizing the primordial. *La*

Madre's jests played on feminized religious identities and how they fit, or fail to fit, in the modern national imaginary. These identities represented obstacles to unity, colonial traditions, and irrational mindsets, which were slowing progress. In fact much of *La Madre*'s humor, particularly in 1917, emerged from the dramatized desmadre that resulted from the positioning of female fanaticism relative to Mexico's liberal, nationalist norms. In the process, however, the newspaper declared prophetic longing, miraculous thinking, and santoral-centered customs as quintessentially Mexican. *La Madre* belittled these aspects of popular culture, but it did so in a manner that acknowledged their prevalence and authenticity. Faced with this realization, these journalists attempted to quarantine Mexico's "backwardness" within Madre Matiana's satirical persona—a character that they ostensibly controlled. New impersonators, however, were waiting in the wings.

CHAPTER 6

Picturing the Prophetess

Lola Álvarez Bravo's Madre Matiana

ALTHOUGH PEDRO HAGELSTEIN'S NEWSPAPER CEASED PUBLICATION in the 1920s, decades later Mexicans still remembered its vulgar, performative style. Famed critic Carlos Monsiváis's recollections of *La Madre*'s excesses make this exceedingly clear.[1] In fact, some of the caricatures that once graced its pages were selected for a 1947 retrospective exhibit on Mexican cartooning.[2] More importantly the issues attached to the seer's persona—Catholic social identity, popular religious culture, and the conflation of fanaticism and femininity—remained very much in play in Mexico after the publication's demise.

In fact, until the 1940s intense conflict and debate continued about Catholicism's place in Mexican society. Revolutionary centralization, draconian anticlerical legislation, and government attempts to secularize popular culture fueled lasting unrest.[3] Urban Catholic activists organized marches and boycotts, and as tensions led to the Cristero Revolt (1926–1929), anti-Revolutionary peasants, mostly in western central Mexico, battled government forces crying "Long Live Christ the King!"[4] These movements never actually threatened the Revolutionary government's hold on power, but they greatly limited state control in some areas. Simultaneously, as an act of protest against anticlerical laws, the Church hierarchy withheld the sacraments and ceased performing religious services. State officials confiscated Church property anew, prominent clergymen fled the nation, and progovernment forces infamously murdered a number of priests. It was during this time that Madre Mercedes led her religious order, the Adoratrices Perpetuas Guadalupanas, into exile in San Antonio, Texas (as noted in chapter 4).

Hoping to defuse tensions in 1929, President Plutarco Elías Calles agreed to restrain his anticlericalism and allow Mexican bishops to return from exile if the hierarchy would call off the uprising. Outright warfare ceased, but many combatants felt betrayed by the "arrangements," and tensions remained high. Sporadic violence flared again in the mid-1930s, as bands of rural *cristeros* again rose up in response to a wave of secularizing educational reforms and campaigns to extinguish popular practices deemed superstitious by President Lázaro Cárdenas's administration.[5] Rebels targeted public-school teachers involved in these endeavors, killing many of them. In the end, both camps branded their opponents murders and exalted their respective martyrs.

Denunciations of the clergy and Catholicism were also a common theme within Mexico's radical nationalist art movement, which was enjoying the peak of its celebrity in the late 1920s and 1930s. Diego Rivera frequently included mordant portrayals of corrupt, libidinous priests and indulged in antireligious commentary in his murals. In the mid-1930s perhaps the most famous graphic artist of the era, Leopoldo Méndez, produced a series of lithographs commemorating the fallen schoolteachers titled *En nombre de Cristo* (*In the Name of Christ*).[6] Some of these images depict fanatical assailants flaunting the cross as they slaughter the unarmed messengers of Enlightenment. Catholic firebrands, for their part, regularly portrayed President Calles as a brutal modern Caesar—a persecutor of the faith and tyrannical martyrer. In general, it was not a time of subtleties or nuances.

In 1935, Lola Álvarez Bravo (1907–1993) was a peripheral figure in Mexico's art scene when she took the enigmatic photograph described in the introduction to this book. In it an unfashionably dressed mannequin is surrounded by men in modern workday attire, which the artist entitled *La Madre Matiana*. The image truly emphasizes a "fish-out-of-water" situation, an exceptionally prudish female figure "trapped" in a masculine public space. What could the photographer have intended by naming this image after the infamous pamphlet prophetess?

After Matiana's moment in the sun as a newspaper namesake and satirical figurehead, the polemical visionary began a gradual drift toward oblivion. The production of new editions of the prophecies, as far as we know, ceased in 1917.[7] The Matiana prophecies were still in play, but by the 1920s urban Catholic activists and Church-affiliated publications abandoned her. Ironically, after the efforts of Luis G. Duarte and those carrying on his legacy, like Luis Santaella in Oaxaca, it is as if she had again become an

Figure 19. *La Madre Matiana,* ca. 1935. Photograph by Lola Álvarez Bravo. © 1995 Center for Creative Photography at the University of Arizona.

embarrassment. Outside urban areas, though, evidence suggests that some Catholics still took the prophecies quite seriously. In fact, it was one such case, an apparition movement that took shape in 1928, that first drew the prophetess to my attention. Due to a dearth of documentation on popular religious thinking or the manner in which common Mexicans deployed prophesy narratives, it remains perhaps the only instance where local invocations of the Matiana prophecies can be examined in a concrete historical moment.[8] Therefore, it merits a brief summary in order to better understand Álvarez Bravo's entrée into the league of Matiana reinterpreters.

The events began simply enough: sometime in the spring or summer of 1928 a young indigenous girl known as Nicha began claiming that she could communicate with the Virgin Mary in a small cave above her Oaxacan village of San Francisco Ixpantepec. Her visions coincided with the height of religion-imbued unrest nationally, and considerable violence of this sort was also occurring in the region surrounding her pueblo. Oaxaca had also experienced an intense and destructive earthquake in early August of that year, followed by a spate of intense rains and flooding. These natural events compounded local conflicts and economic hardship rooted in approximately fifteen years of festering Revolutionary violence that preceded the events of 1928. Some Catholics feared that the new spurt of government anticlericalism and rumored schisms within the local priesthood truly threatened their individual salvation. In other words, some Oaxacans experienced the 1920s as a disconcerting "time of troubles." Nicha claimed that the Virgin warned her of looming cataclysmic divine punishment unless the faithful focused their energies on collective supplication and atonement. (Remember that the Matiana prophecies spoke of anti-religious persecution, great bloodshed, and Catholic triumph in an October of a year ending in the number eight.)

By the fall of 1928, hundreds of pilgrims were streaming toward Ixpantepec's *gruta* (grotto), and soon additional visionaries in nearby towns also came forward. At first it appears that the local priest, Father Ausencio Canseco, and committed Catholics from the nearby parish seat believed that truly divine portents were unfolding in their midst. Soon a local movement of sorts emerged to secure Church approval of the visions. However, it was not long before acrimony split the faithful, as doubts surfaced regarding the nature of Nicha's claims. Activity at the grotto probably peaked as 1928 came to a close. In 1932 the apparition movement was clearly waning; by 1934 it had collapsed.

There is not enough space in the current study for a full recounting of this complex incident, which reveals the interplay of indigenous and Hispanic visionary cultures while bringing the gender dynamics of Catholic practice into sharp relief.[9] What remains relevant to Madre Matiana's broader legacy is how notions of the feminine, mystical, and fanatical came to the fore in a specific community. Essentially, three voices "tell the story" of Nicha and her visions from divergent perspectives, and the respective historical actors were all committed Catholics and close collaborators before the conflicts of the 1920s drove them apart. Perhaps the most important was an elderly, devout Church benefactress and stalwart parochial school principal named Matilde Narváez. She had been the right-hand woman, so to say, of Father Canseco for decades and raced to the site when news of Marian miracles reached her. However, when the padre's opinion of Nicha turned critical, Narváez became the seer's advisor and the burgeoning movement's epistolary champion. She wrote to archdiocesan officials to emphasize the pious, rustic orthodoxy of events at the grotto, and she vouched for Nicha's saintly character. She even remained convinced of the divine character of the visions, even after the movement collapsed. Nicha returned to anonymous indigenous girlhood, and Narváez became an indigent pariah. It is also quite possible that she coached Nicha's visions. For example, a number of the girl's proclamations—in Narváez's telling—emphasized the importance of expiatory devotion to the Blessed Sacrament (seemingly echoing the Matiana tradition). Such was this woman's importance that Canseco labeled her the primary force behind activities at the grotto and the chief propagator of dangerous religious errors.

The priest, for his part, argued that extraordinary visions were indeed occurring at Ixpantepec, but he claimed they were the work of the devil. His report to his superiors stressed absurd contradictions in the visionary testimonies he collected and underscored preposterous and unorthodox pronouncements issued by Nicha. In fact, Canseco's writings reveal a dismissal of all the women involved, whereas he offered a careful analysis of the mystical marvels reported by men. Narváez in his rendering comes across as a pious busybody and misguided fool. Nicha and her mother appear as unreliable, ignorant Indians. In short, Canseco reproduced the classic, gendered delegitimizing discourses. He essentially framed Nicha as a modern-day ilusa and Narvárez as a deluded beata. Some locals took this still further, suggesting that the latter's obsession with the visions inaugurated a decent into madness.

Neither Narváez nor Canseco mentioned Madre Matiana, but the padre's one-time trusted assistant, a man named Hilario Cortés, placed the pamphlet prophetess at the center of visionary fervor. Cortés produced his reconstruction of the apparition movement decades after its disintegration when he fancied himself the region's chronicler. In his view, there was nothing sacred or diabolical about the affair. He dismissed it all as a tawdry scam hatched by bumbling miscreants hoping to swindle the ignorant amid profound social unease. In fact, he asserted that Nicha's initial claims encountered only disbelief, and this prompted her to issue predictions of looming divine retribution. According to Cortés, it was the synergy of her threats, the powerful earthquakes of 1928, and popular understandings of Matiana's prophecies that sparked the brief surge of visionary zeal. "*El vulgo*" ("the rabble"), he lamented, even hailed Nicha as a seer of national import.

Despite his dismissive attitude toward popular beliefs, Cortés's testimony hints at a plausible explanation for Matilde Narváez's actions. She was by no means a mere ignorant beata. She had been a respected local religious figure and trusted ally of Canseco's for years. (In all likelihood Cortés had been her pupil.) In this context becoming the spokeswoman of the apparition movement represented a breach of gender norms and Catholic principals of authority. Socially her choice carried considerable risk, and she was undoubtedly cognizant of this fact. Cortés never mentioned her by name, but his invocation of the Matiana prophecies' influence among Nicha's supporters hints at her reasons for breaking with her pastor, asserting an independent interpretation of the visions, and publically championing the apparitions. (Narváez may have actually read Duarte, but almost certainly encountered Santaella's Duarte "update" in Oaxacan pamphlets or the archdiocese's official bulletin.) Her decision makes more sense in light of the apocalyptic feminism embedded in the Matiana tradition. She quite likely viewed the indigenous girl's visions as evidence that Matiana's moment of truth was indeed nigh: widespread suffering, natural disasters, and violent unrest combined with craven attacks on the faith called devout women, such as herself, to step out in front of tepid churchmen and lead an expiatory crusade. Alas, the miraculous triumph of the Church never materialized, and Narváez lived in shame for another decade.

Of course, the linkage of Matiana and motivations cannot be proven conclusively. But if nothing else, the prophecies' importance to those embracing Nicha's visions demonstrates that Matiana retained a place in the popular imaginary into the early 1930s. As Cortés's testimony proves, the famed prophetess would remain a symbol of backwardness. In a sense he followed in the footsteps of rationalist critics and satirists of previous years.

Matiana's fame was clearly waning by the 1930s, but for a few artists and intellectuals she still served a crucial purpose. The fact that she symbolized traditionalist pious femininity, unwavering commitment to the Catholic Church, beatería, and fanaticism made her attractive to those engaging questions of modernity, popular custom, and social change. One of these was Lola Álvarez Bravo. In all likelihood she was very familiar with the newspaper named after the seer (and quite possibly additional Matiana publications) from her youth in Mexico City. Many viewers of her art in the mid-twentieth century would have also recalled the pamphlets, broadsides, satirical journalism, and various engagements of the Matiana tradition. There is hardly any written documentation produced by Álvarez Bravo that sheds light on her motives for any of her photographs. At best she gave titles to the published works and sometimes labeled her unpublished negatives in suggestive ways. She claimed that the titles, although sometimes incomprehensible to viewers, reminded her of what she was thinking when she took the photographs.[10] Still her Matiana image has weight in light of the prophetess's broader legacy. Moreover, we can analyze this particular photograph alongside other images in which the artist explores both popular piety and gender. Doing so reveals a different realm of satirical practice than the irreverent journalism of the late 1910s and early 1920s. Lola Álvarez Bravo offers a subtler critique of Catholicism and devout social identity, although she essentially seconded the masculinist dismissal of pious femininity. However, her approach is much more nuanced. Her photos reveal genuine sympathy alongside a deft exposure of the farcical, contrived, ironic, and futile. More specifically in her contribution to the Matiana phenomenon, this artist—thanks to photographic sleight of hand—forces the nation's prophetess and maligned symbol of irrational religiosity to "sit" for an unflattering portrait.

THE WOMAN BEHIND THE CAMERA

Álvarez Bravo was the wife of celebrated Mexican photographer Manuel Álvarez Bravo from 1925 until 1934, and she learned her craft debating art, taking pictures, and working in the dark room with him.[11] This relationship also placed her in the thick of the Mexican avant-garde art world. Prior to their separation the couple's home served as a bohemian hangout and gallery space where the already famous and the up-and-coming congregated and discussed each other's work. Not surprisingly, she became an active member of the famed Liga de Escritores y Artistas Revolucionarios (League of Revolutionary Artists and Writers) in the 1930s. This was a particularly heady time for the organization. They attained a national and international prominence previously unimaginable for Mexican intellectuals. Many felt that radical art could forge a new national consciousness and help shape Revolutionary transformation. For Álvarez Bravo it was also where she built a lasting network of friends and colleagues. For much of the 1930s she and trailblazing artist María Izquierdo shared a downtown apartment. As a result she counted many painters, poets, and writers as close personal friends for the rest of her life.[12] In fact, she gained considerable recognition as a portraitist of Mexico's radical intellectual community thanks, in large part, to these relationships. Her first truly independent work, however, emerged when she was a photographer for a government-affiliated education magazine, *El Maestro Rural*, in the mid-1930s.[13] All told there could hardly have been a more secular or intensely nationalist milieu in which to develop as an artist. Despite this, Álvarez Bravo's art reveals a sensitive, understated touch. It is free of the strident anticlericalism and attention-getting blasphemies of the famous muralists.

By entering the legacy of Matiana representation and appropriation, the artist was in many ways bringing together two of her abiding interests. On one hand, both her published pictures and unpublished negatives reveal repeated explorations of popular culture and its public performative dimensions. Thus she took many photographs of indigenous festivals, processions, religious acts, gatherings, and events like funerals. On the other hand, her representation of Madre Matiana is but one of several works where she scrutinizes the relationship between humanity and human simulacra—in other words, between real humans and the humanoid figures/characters "we" create and infuse with meaning. In fact, Álvarez Bravo's habitually juxtaposed effigies, masks, statues, and mannequins with the common people who manufacture them and put them to use. Such moments and settings afforded the opportunity to explore a variety of issues with a peculiar sense of humor. This is particularly true of explicitly religious settings. In fact, the longstanding and varied Mexican tradition of image-centered devotion provided endless opportunities for this sharp-eyed artist.

Like many of her colleagues inspired by the radical nationalism in vogue at the time, Álvarez Bravo patrolled Mexico's streets and trekked to its villages to depict the lives of workers and native peoples. First she travelled with her husband, but subsequently she went alone on personal assignments for *El Maestro Rural* and numerous illustrated magazines. She also photographed folk art for the English-language publication *Mexican Folkways* and accepted numerous commissions from government agencies. Luckily for the struggling, newly single photographer, many of her artist friends worked in state ministries and helped her secure commissions. Piecing together assignments she gradually established a lasting artistic reputation. Finally in 1941, Álvarez Bravo secured her own government post as the chief photographer for the Instituto Nacional De Bellas Artes y Literatura (INBA). She remained there for the next thirty years. Among her obligations for the INBA was photographing folk dances in Mexican villages for the national dance troupe.[14] Thus she was very much a part of the international infatuation with Mexico's folk customs characteristic of the era following the Revolution.[15] In essence she joined the legions of anthropologists, folklorists, enthusiasts, and teachers traipsing off to pueblos to document "authentic" practices. It bears mentioning that for the Mexican government—the patron of many of these travelers (including Álvarez Bravo)—the root goal of these sojourns was to reshape popular custom and fashion a shared secular nationalism from local "traditions."[16]

The intrepid photographer, however, was interested in more than popular festivals and dances. As her works attest, she also sought out cramped workshops. In both cases she was clearly drawn to the tension between lived, sweaty realities and sometimes off-key actions and images in public and private settings. Her photographs draw attention to the overlooked, unsettling, and ironic captured in commonplace settings. Álvarez Bravo sought to make viewers take note of tensions, oddities, and absurdities to which they were inured. In doing so she produced images that span the gamut from the gentle underscoring of the unique, quirky, and paradoxical to outright mockery.

The rich variety of Mexican Catholic imagery and pageantry offered Álvarez Bravo ample opportunities to treat religious modes of representation. However, she showed scant interest in the nation's famous religious images and their shrines. Unheralded life-sized santos in various states of repair or those appearing in awkward or comical poses attracted her attention. Her photographs of these statues do not capture devotees praying, performing penance, or making offerings before sacred figures. Instead they reveal that the artist preferred to approach santos during the long hours of devotional "downtime." Not only did she eschew actual image-centered piety, but also she avoided images that attracted frequent devotee visits altogether. Thus her photographs lack the masses of mementos, *milagros* (representations of body parts that allegedly received miraculous cures), and scrawled testimonials that crowd shrine images, or similar items often placed alongside or pinned to santos in village churches. Occasionally, she reveals a bouquet of flowers, a lonely image or token testifying to a miracle received, or a single burning candle alongside her subject. But the evidence of minimal devotion actually accentuates the forlorn quality of her photographs. It is as if she found the pathos of lonely devotion and the evidence of fervent desperation particularly inspiring. Álvarez Bravo also captures the mundane ironies stirred by Catholic images in storage. In the process she created numerous images that are simultaneously poignant and comical, which display bedraggled santo solitude as the sacred statues "watch over" otherwise abandoned ritual space, or preside over unconsecrated storerooms, hallways, and workshops.

The artist, sadly, failed to explain her artistic goals in detail beyond vague statements about chronicling Mexican reality, but these comments shed some light on her production of the Matiana image. She portrayed herself as a mere witness conveying the truths—often hidden or ignored—of her times, and capturing on film Mexican customs and traditions as they disappeared: "If something useful results from my photography, it will be in the sense that it is a chronicle of my country, of my time, of my people, of how Mexico has been changing."[17] In talking about her work she spoke in terms of a restless searching and looking, rescue and retention, serendipity and discovery. Her images, she claimed, were primarily a combination of *"el hallazgo y la búsqueda"* ("the unexpected discovery and the search"): "There is an element of continual searching that one does with the eye, to see the things that are generally ignored, those of which no notice is taken, but in the moment in when you are attuned, you discover them."[18] She claimed to set out with her camera not really knowing what she would encounter, and she declared that sometimes the emotional impact of what she saw drove her to take certain pictures. In some instances when inspired by the setting, light, and activities taking place around her, Álvarez Bravo would set up in an advantageous location, frame a specific backdrop, focus on a particular area, and then hope for a good composition to take shape in the chosen space. She joked that some images were largely the product of good luck.[19] Her fundamental goal, particularly in terms of popular culture, remained preservation, or so she said: "This is what I have always wanted: to rescue and detain the remainders of what is left from an era, of a city, of a group of people, which are changing completely. This is where my great interest in the popular comes from."[20] This sentiment, however, veils her own reformist nationalist stance. Álvarez Bravo also admitted that she hoped to draw attention to the plight of common Mexicans and native peoples. Part of this entailed spotlighting popular belief and "superstition."

Perhaps her statements represent little more than retrospective boilerplate and an understandable restatement of clichés embedded in modern photography at the time. However, there is a fundamental sincerity in her photography; it seems she truly believed she really was "finding" Mexican culture in situ and saving slices of it for posterity. There is a testamental quality to many of them. Carlos Monsiváis appreciated this aspect of her work. He gave her credit for surpassing numerous obstacles, particularly the machismo of the Mexican art world and the tradition of political grandstanding among artists, and he praised her unwavering dedication to her craft and mission. He argued that she simply kept walking, traveling, looking, and frankly photographing Mexicans. Others had indulged in fashionable radicalisms, eventually becoming anachronisms in their own lifetimes.[21]

Álvarez Bravo's actual images reveal a subtle wit and irreverence, while they also telegraph considerable sympathy for the Mexican poor's desperate circumstances and attendant longing for divine assistance. In her approach to Catholic statuary a more instrumental artistic praxis is in evidence. In her writings she spoke of seeking out the uniquely playful, understated Mexican sense of humor, although in these images the artist does much to create rather than simply capture the comical.[22] These photographs underscore the man-made nature of santos, with incongruous ironic expressions and disheveled appearances; any notion that they hold sacred power suffers in these images. A key weapon in her arsenal was a two-part process of decontextualization. First, she had a preference for subjects that showed little or infrequent devotion, or moments when no pious activities were taking place. Thus her work breaks the linkage between sacred simulacra and devout human agency. Although rarely considered by most viewers when observing images of saints, Álvarez Bravo evidently understood that human actions, not the simple existence of the carved image, create the aura of sacrality. Second, the very act of photographic representation essentially separates sacred statuary from the surrounding sights, sounds, and smells common in Catholic devotional spaces. The photographed santos are no longer part of an assemblage of images in a particular place, which typically appear arrayed in a quasi-narrative fashion. Likewise, the photograph also extracts them from a series and legacy of imagery and ornamentation that serves as a visual history of local piety, hope, and concern. Gone is the enveloping smell of wax, soot, and hints of incense. Furthermore, the viewer does not encounter believers praying in the pews, does not perceive murmured supplications in distant corners of the sanctuary, nor overhear group prayers, such as the Rosary, taking place nearby. All of these sensory experiences are commonplace in Mexico's ritual spaces today. In fact, it is rare to find churches truly empty. The same was undoubtedly true when Álvarez Bravo took her photographs. Thus, once decontextualized, almost all statues representing Christ, the Virgin Mary, or the saints are absurd on some level. The stagey postures, the hokey approximations of mystical rapture, and the overwrought anguish frozen in perpetuity can seem transparently ridiculous. In addition, when they also exhibit tarnished halos, threadbare finery, matted hair, stylized gore, and chipped paint, santos can appear pathetic. To put it another way, the images testify to clumsy human attempts to conjure the sacred and fabricate settings conducive to emotive fervor.

Moreover, the artist's photographs capture the santos' confinement behind altars, in cramped niches, and within glass cases and thus suggest thoughtless, empty convention. In short, the artist's choices of time, space, subject, and setting reveal a critique of Mexican popular religious practice: a critique that also comes through in the photograph titled *La Madre Matiana*. But the published image named after the legendary prophetess features still greater complexity: a clever multifaceted satirical statement rests beyond the debunking of popular beliefs. For the most part, though, it is invisible to viewers today because they remain ignorant of the wider Matiana phenomenon. All at once this photograph combines the artist's deconstruction of popular piety, her examination of human simulacra vis-à-vis flesh-and-blood humanity, an ingenious subversion of the conventions of portraiture, and the artist's commentary on the gender dynamics of "fanaticism" in Mexico.

To appreciate the full scope of Álvarez Bravo's work in this regard the present chapter offers a discussion of her unpublished images before progressing to the analysis of her published works. This is done knowing that negatives cannot be evaluated in the same way as an artist's publically available photographs. They represent images deemed unfit for use by the photographer or an editor. Perhaps they did not accomplish a particular artistic, commercial, or illustrative goal. Some of these images may have simply failed to interest one of her many patrons. Alternatively they also failed to impress Álvarez Bravo enough to merit more attention. Nonetheless they provide insights into the artist's approach to popular culture and photographic representation. It is particularly useful to link the themes and patterns revealed in her negatives with works that Álvarez Bravo cropped and printed with exceptional care.

LOLA'S "SANATORIO"

Sifting through the artist's archive of published images turns up a remarkable quantity that feature statues, effigies, and masks—all common in Mexican culture. Álvarez Bravo clearly pursued the expressive complexities intertwined with simulacra and disguise. She also seemed to enjoy a kind of inside joke that was embedded in the act of self-consciously representing "representations." At the milder pole of artistic commentary, for example, are depictions of workers making wooden horses to serve as carousel mounts and theatrical props.[23] These images depend on a straightforward irony: fake chargers appear to snort and gallop while around them artisans toil to produce these effects, and in some cases put them in motion.[24] At least one of these pictures, "Saliendo a la ópera," eventually emerged in publication.[25] In other instances Álvarez Bravo targeted unintended absurdities. She produces this effect by offering glimpses of the jumbled storage or carefree placement of folk simulacra before or after "use." This dynamic is evident in her images of the traditional Judas effigies produced for Holy Week celebrations on the Saturday before Easter. These outsized figures were destined for a ritualized collective venting of devout anger at the betrayer of Christ, but they also had long offered the masses a potent opportunity for satirical dissent.[26] Other artists before her, most notably Diego Rivera, were also drawn to Judas burnings and their reputation as episodes of ludic celebration and mordant popular expression. The famous muralist depicted crowds reveling in festive chaos as Judas effigies representing politicians, capitalists, and priests bobbed above them prior to their destruction and disgorgement of coins, sweets, and sausages.[27] Although she also published images of a Judas burning that featured teeming throngs, Álvarez Bravo's negatives reveal quieter moments outside of the festive spotlight.[28] They capture Judas effigies being made and stored hastily along walls in the workplace.[29] In one negative a humble individual reads a book while relaxing between the legs of a gigantic cartoon-like figure, while other Judases "pose" stiffly all around him. Alternatively negatives and at least one published photograph reveal individuals carrying Judas figures in the street, juxtaposing the tiny human porter and the outsized caricature of humanity.[30] In one unpublished image all that is visible are the diminutive legs and feet of the person transporting the towering star of the day's celebrations. These pictures summon a distinct whimsical irony because they capture real humans in the company of extravagant dummies, which loom over mundane activities. Most likely Álvarez Bravo also meant to underscore the contradiction between behind-the-scenes labor and the festive excess associated with Judas burnings. Thus an individual accomplishes the intellectual task of reading beneath a huge man-made symbol of human greed; in another instance, the epitome of betrayal is unceremoniously lugged down a public thoroughfare. In both cases, the trick is capturing the humdrum moment, which the viewer knows is only a prelude to the explosion of anarchic scorn.

Similar tensions are in play in Álvarez Bravo's depictions of the Mexican Catholic statuary, but the context is very different. Judas figures and their fiery annihilation were freighted with the satirical before the artist so much as raised her camera. Santos, as they are generically called in Mexico, are not supposed to be funny. From an orthodox perspective they represent holy intercessors and focus the faithful on exemplary figures and pivotal moments in the mythic life stories of sacred characters. For many Catholics, the images themselves are suffused with divine power, and some are quite famous due to longstanding miraculous reputations. "Visiting" such an image, devotees believe, can secure divine assistance or an outright miracle. Numerous shrines in Mexico are chock full of mementos attesting to the mysterious powers of particular images. They can be small or life size, and sometimes they are lavishly painted, gilded, and dressed. Some, rendered as martyrs, can be quite gruesome. In addition, images of Christ and the Virgin Mary sometimes wear the accoutrements of royalty, such as ornamented cloaks, fine mantles, and bejeweled crowns.[31] Furthermore, for the devout, the manipulation of these images is frequently a central facet of their devotion; for example, followers dress the santos distinctly for specific occasions and parade them through the streets during scheduled celebrations or in moments of collective crises. However, as in most Catholic countries, Mexican churches and private spaces are also full of ordinary, rather humble images. Santos that lack enduring devotions or widely acknowledged fame often appear neglected. In reality there are many more seemingly forgotten images than those fussed over and showered with renown.

Two distinct images of Christ stored in the same envelope (which Álvarez Bravo marked simply "Santos") also merit attention. The first photograph features an image inspired by a moment in the traditional Passion narrative, when Christ received a brutal whipping. The Passion of Christ has long been a popular subgenre of religious images in Mexico. Numerous communities maintain enduring devotions dedicated to their respective images of "Cristo de la Columna" ("Christ of the Column") like the one photographed by Álvarez Bravo. In this instance the artist depicts a spare, sunny space occupied by a gruesome, poorly carved statue of the tortured Savior. Humbled on his knees, and bound to the column, Christ suffers alone. The long-haired Redeemer wears nothing but a frilly velvet and lace skirt and fixes his gaze on the ground. His expression reveals little or no emotion, unless its blankness is taken to suggest resignation. Blood smears cover the statue's arms and legs, but most alarming is Christ's lacerated back. The kneeling body appears to have been whipped with such ferocity that several of his ribs are visible through the gore. Álvarez Bravo made sure to place what are essentially gaping, bloody openings in Christ's torso in the middle of her composition, and she thus draws attention to the grotesque dimensions of Catholic religiosity. In the picture a small painted *ex-voto* leans against the column and a

Figure 20. untitled, n.d. [Image of Christ tied to a column]. Photograph by Lola Álvarez Bravo (posthumous reproduction from an original negative). © 1995 Center for Creative Photography at the University of Arizona.

bouquet of fresh flowers rests beneath Christ. They alone attest to devotion. Candelabras and mostly artificial flowers arrayed symmetrically around the image frame the tableau of suffering, but none of the candles are lit and the votive candleholders in front of the altar remain empty. As a whole the photograph speaks of sterility. The bright light entering the room from an unseen window at left, the complete absence of places to kneel, the clean grid-patterned floor, and a surprising lack of devotional clutter suggest a staged and forgotten scene of sadistic torment and maudlin sentiment. Missing is any presence of the sublime or profound.

A second photograph from this set of negatives features a curiously posed, seated Christ perched well above the height of most individuals in a glass display case.[32] To the left a single burning candle is visible, and in front of the case are two small floral offerings. The flowers to the left occupy a small vase. Those to the right reside in a bottle and appear wilted. Again the artist includes evidence of continued, albeit limited devotion to this image. Surrounding the glass enclosure are the details of external decorations, wallpaper patterns, and the texture of the stone basin below the encased *cristo* in sharp focus. The glass, however—due to grime and glare—is partially opaque, making it so that the viewer contemplates the seated figure as if through a slightly hazy film. This magnifies the melancholy quality exuded by the unusual expression and posture of the image. Christ does not appear on a throne; instead he hunkers with his knees jutting towards his chest. His legs show signs of bleeding sores, but it hardly approaches the grotesque extremes of the previous image. His wounds, short cape, rustic crown (perhaps of thorns, but it is difficult to tell), simple white loincloth, and the stylized lily scepter in the statue's left hand allude to the scorn Christ suffered before the Crucifixion.

This Cristo's expression, however, can be read in various ways, none of them appropriate for devotional purposes. Álvarez Bravo took the photograph from the side, so that the image seems to look away from the viewer. He does not gaze up toward the heavens nor grimace in agony, as commonly seen in more typical images. Instead the image leans his head on his right hand and perches with an elbow on his right knee, staring into the distance. His countenance conveys disappointment, frustration, and simple boredom. In short, what the artist captures is a Christ rendered with a remarkably mundane, ambivalent, human expression. What probably drew Álvarez's Bravo's attention was the evocative combination of this blasé presence and the sacred figure's encasement in a glass box affixed to the wall. This Christ does not exude power or pathos. He just seems trapped, like he has been restrained and waiting for a very long time. As a whole the photograph makes Catholic image-centered piety seem farcical, or at best dull. The allegedly sacred representation of the Christian God comes across as merely despondent. Is it a commentary on the fickleness of devotee attentions or a portrayal of popular religiosity as bordering on absurd? It is arguably both.

Álvarez Bravo explored the photographic possibilities offered by Catholic devotional imagery in a different manner at a santo-making workshop, as evident in yet another set of negatives. In this case five

Figure 21. untitled, n.d. [Image of Christ in a glass cabinet]. Photograph by Lola Álvarez Bravo (posthumous reproduction from an original negative). © 1995 Center for Creative Photography at the University of Arizona.

snapshots reveal the artist focused on the human act of production behind the existence of saintly simulacra. As with her interest in Judas figures, the artist telegraphs an avid interest in the moments outside of the cultural events for which the statues were ostensibly carved. In fact, a pun she employed in titling these negatives attests to her satirical approach to this subject: *"Reportaje: santeros, muñecas, 'sanatorio.'"* ("Reportage: saint-makers, dolls, 'sanitarium'"). The matter-of-fact term "reportage" suggests that she may have taken these pictures while on assignment. It also implies that she saw these photographs as documentary evidence regarding popular cultural practices. Indeed, this is how she described her approach to photography in general.[33] Her subtitle, though, suggests a more instrumental approach. There she employs *muñecas* (dolls), a label no devotee would assign to a saint's likeness. Secondly she placed *"sanatorio"* in quotations marks, and thus indulged in a private joke redolent with sarcasm. Literally the term denotes a hospital, a setting where healing takes place (*sanar* meaning "to heal" and *-torio* being a common locative suffix).[34] In this case, Álvarez Bravo plays with the word *san* meaning *saint* and archly deploys *sanatorio* as if it meant place where saint making occurs, in the way *laboratorio* signifies a place where lab work happens. Of course, she simultaneously invokes the accepted definition—and thus summons notions of illness and healing—and acknowledges her anthropomorphic word play by putting the term in quotation marks. Thus her jest marks the space represented in the photographs as a species of doll factory and hospital where saints are fabricated or fixed.

In some ways the images in this set of negatives contrast sharply with the gruesome Christ at the column photograph. First, these spaces are absolutely overflowing with human clutter. Raw chunks of wood, planks, unfinished *santos*, frames, crumpled papers, and castoff columns fill every nook and corner. The chaotic mounds allow the photographer to take comical snapshots. For example (see fig. 22), a tiny Saint Michael (the archangel, and, according to Catholic lore, field marshal of the celestial armies) raises his sword as if attacking a heap of saint-making detritus.[35] Meanwhile towering over the bellicose mini-*santo* and the workshop debris a life-size Virgin Mary holds her hands together prayerfully and stares blankly into the distance while an unnerving androgynous saint peers down upon the entire scene from a precarious corner roost. On the other hand, these images also stress the ironic place of image-centered devotion in Mexican culture.

Figure 22. untitled, n.d. [Santos in storage]. Photograph by Lola Álvarez Bravo (post-humous reproduction from an original negative). © 1995 Center for Creative Photography at the University of Arizona.

Figure 23. untitled, n.d. [Santo-making workshop]. Photograph by Lola Álvarez Bravo (posthumous reproduction from an original negative). © 1995 Center for Creative Photography at the University of Arizona.

In all the other negatives in this series, Álvarez Bravo juxtaposes the human workers, engrossed in their respective labors, and the human simulacra in various states surrounding them. Again, she keys on the reigning disorder and the routine human manufacture of the presumably sacred. In the third negative in the series, two men focus on minute tasks while oblivious to the amassed junk and the biblical statues in their midst. The mess engulfs their endeavors and threatens to bury them while they labor on, seemingly unconcerned. In this image a small Mary and Joseph stare intently at the floor, while a large headless and handless saint (probably Saint Francis) and an intact, but equally unpainted, muscular Christ loom over the workers. In essence, the photographer has captured "saint making." As for the latter image, workers sculpted him for another staging of the Savior's scourging with the requisite downcast gaze and ready-to-bind crossed wrists. In a way he awaits the column leaning against another unpainted santo in the center of the photograph.

For the most part it is clear why Álvarez Bravo chose not to publish these images. The cramped, overstuffed spaces and the harshly lit workshops do not make for pleasing compositions. They do, however, document the photographer's enduring interest in religious imagery and her approach to this aspect of Mexican popular culture. As with her depictions of the Judas figures, the proximity of human laborers and the human effigies allows her to explore certain issues in depth. In both cases she contrasts the focused, intense work of the real humans and the stiff, often incongruous or ironic stances and expressions of the statues. Additionally, as the sanatorio negatives suggest Álvarez Bravo mischievously emphasizes the less-than-holy production of the sacred. As a result she demystifies the santos. Unpainted, divorced from ritual contexts, and unceremoniously stored, they are foolish at best. Their expressions and seemingly nonsensical or comical poses in these settings mock the attributions of special power or mystical relevance to what are simply wooden mannequins. Some of the same themes reappear in her published photographs, but the more polished images reveal a better-realized critique of popular religious culture. In all likelihood this had much to do with the artist's decision to print and circulate these pictures.

WOMEN, MEN, AND MASKS

In a number of works Álvarez Bravo actually depicts human actors in religious settings. In these very different kinds of photographs her treatment of actual popular religious events and devout human actors also features a marked attention to gender. For the most part, only women appear in unequivocally pious postures. In this regard the artist, perhaps unwittingly, reproduced widely shared assumptions concerning female indigenous piety, in addition to anticlerical stereotypes concerning religious women. Her images generally show devout, poor, indigenous women in self-effacing postures and anonymous groups. Examples of this approach to femininity and religiosity appear in a pair of photographs composed in 1946 and taken in a Zapotec village in Oaxaca.[36] *El Ruego* (*The Plea*) centers on a densely packed group of women and girls kneeling in a church doorway. The impression is that a completely full Mass is taking place and creating an overflow of devout femininity. However, their fervor is such that they willingly suffer on their knees. In this image and others, Álvarez Bravo chooses to render pious, indigenous women in beautiful obscurity. Their faces are completely hidden. Often, as in *El Ruego*, she took the pictures from behind her subjects, although in some photographs women appear in shadowy

Figure 24. El ruego,
1946. Photograph by
Lola Álvarez Bravo.
© 1995 Center for
Creative Photography
at the University of
Arizona.

profile. In almost all cases, rebozos (shawls) conceal individual identities
and expressions. In fact, the most salient iconographic element of these
photographs is the shawl-covered female head and body: shorthand for
indigenous peasant femininity—and by extension elemental Mexican
womanhood—in Mexican art.[37]

In images like this one the artist portrays collective devout femininity
as an unthinking conformist mass. One of Álvarez Bravo's most famous
images is *Entierro en Yalalag (Burial in Yalalag)*; it depicts a funeral procession as it passed her camera. The foreground features about twenty-five
women in iconic, white Sierra Zapotec dresses ambling alongside a coffin,
while a handful of men form a line at the top of the picture that hems in
the women below. Most of the image is taken up with these women's bodies, although all but six of them are completely shielded by their garments
and rebozos. Only one of these figures reveals any personal features. The
others are too distant and their faces are underexposed. For the most part,
the women all stare at the rough ground around their feet. The downcast

postures and the obscuring of hair and visage convey humility and anonymity. In other words, both of these images suggest a dampened popular female spirit and a limited capacity for independent thought.[38] The shawl-draped heads and bodies may as well be interchangeable. Álvarez Bravo's devout indigenous women kneel, huddle, and plod en masse; they form a sincere but solemn herd. Viewed alongside the photographer's striking portraits of her fellow female artists, like Frida Kahlo and María Izquierdo the effect is even more pronounced. The celebrity images represent the other pole of Mexican womanhood—they are modern, unique, freethinking individuals.[39]

In a sense these pictures of devotion play to long-standing assumptions of an essential Mexican femininity, particularly the notion that the nation's women—especially native women—are innately devout paragons of selfless abnegation. The images of devout, indigenous women inspire pity. The dirty bare feet in *El Ruego* speak of poverty and a life of crushing hardships. These women and girls have few adornments and the solace they seek in religion

Figure 25. Entierro en Yalalag, 1946. Photograph by Lola Álvarez Bravo. © 1995 Center for Creative Photography at the University of Arizona.

Figure 26. Frida Kahlo, ca. 1944. Photograph by Lola Álvarez Bravo. © 1995 Center for Creative Photography at the University of Arizona.

must be secured on unforgiving cold stone. In this regard the image echoes the predicament of their proceeding sisters making their way amid the specter of death over uneven dirt and rock.

In contrast, popular masculine figures appear very differently in Álvarez Bravo's photographs; they do not occur in similar poses of pious suffering. Instead, in a manner akin to the satirical journalism at *La Madre Matiana* in 1923, men enact another Mexican role: that of masculine buffoonery and even profane mockery. These images expose religious custom as man-made farce, much like the sanatorio negatives. As in her representations of devout women, she preferred to hide her subjects' faces, but in a very different manner. Men at religious festivals often appear in costumes or wearing masks. Merely playing parts, they hide their personal identities. In their incognito role-play Álvarez Bravo also suggests a deeper lurking irreverence. She accomplishes this through two mechanisms. First, she juxtaposes human faces and man-made masks. Then she emphasizes male expressions of vulgarity in ritual settings. Fittingly, in some instances, she also draws attention to the comical expressions apparent on the ceremonial masks.[40]

The simple presence of masks activates time-honored iconographic assumptions in western art. To masquerade often conveys a hiding of the self and the inaccessibility of the soul. Masks freeze dissimulating expressions and communicate an attempt to hide from others and time.[41] Unlike an individual's face, a mask cannot respond or change; it does not record a moment. Its obfuscating rigidity suggests a never-ending and somewhat imperviously irreverent stance before all happenings, regardless of their import. For example, in *San Isidro Labrador* (n.d.), the artificiality of the mask on the male figure and its smirking expression clashes with the pious countenance of the male saint on the banner spanning much of the photograph. Unlike the mask he looks reverently to the heavens.[42] Álvarez Bravo composed the shot to bring the mustachioed mask and the saint's bearded likeness nearly face to face to thus force comparison. The impact in this particular case is one of off-key silliness amid an ostensibly devout procession. The mask of dissimulation hides the man's face and suggests a deeper ambivalence regarding his relationship to the devotional practices unfolding around him. Meanwhile the saint's face gazes heavenward in unconditional pious rapture. Complicating the message is the photograph's presentation as documentary evidence of folk customs. Both the masked man's participation and his irreverent bearing become artifacts attesting to national "tradition," essentially making masculine impiety a Mexican trait.

Álvarez Bravo goes much further in *La Manda*, an image she created in 1946. The title refers to the practice, understood among believers as a grave obligation, of fulfilling solemn vows made to a sacred figure, such as a shrine image.[43] However, this picture features a barefoot masked man in the iconic white shirt and homespun pants of the indigenous peasantry; his stance is remarkably irreverent. The combination of the hat, the frowning goateed visage covering the man's face, and the rustic hobbyhorse he straddles suggest that this figure was attired as a ranchero (read non-Indian) for a customary performance. In all likelihood Álvarez Bravo took this picture at a festival that featured the kinds of theatrical ritual events performed in some indigenous communities. What gives the photograph a satirical edge is its pointed whimsical vulgarity. Besides being a theatrical prop, the carved horse is also an outsized phallus. Moreover, the man in the photograph grips his "steed" in a manner that suggests masturbation, and his masked face appears to contemplate mournfully his wooden member. The figure's pants are even stained. In

Figure 27. San Isidro Labrador, n.d. Photograph by Lola Álvarez Bravo. © 1995 Center for Creative Photography at the University of Arizona.

concert this image conveys a comic futility and an intrusive masculine profanation of a supposedly sacred event. The artist's choice of title adds another level of irreverence. To "*cumplir la manda*" (roughly, keep the promise), as it is expressed, often includes a public performance of pious devotion and devout commitment, such as a pilgrimage, penitential acts, or both. The combination of the subject's vulgar stance and the artists label derisively parody an integral dynamic of popular Catholic practice.

A less jarring—but in some ways more effective—presentation of belief and devotion that conjures notions of masculine irreverence is Álvarez Bravo's *La Última Cena, (Pocos los escogidos)* (*The Last Supper, [Few are Chosen]*). Although the artist never explained the circumstances surrounding its production, this photograph, taken in 1935 like *La Madre Matiana*, in many ways brings together the artist's previously discussed approach to santos with the more overtly satirical criticism of religious custom seen in *La manda*. This picture also broaches the topic of sacred effigies and communication, or the

Figure 28. La manda, 1946. Photograph by Lola Álvarez Bravo. © 1995 Center for Creative Photography at the University of Arizona.

Figure 29. *La Última Cena (Pocos los escogidos)*, ca. 1935. Photograph by Lola Álvarez Bravo. © 1995 Center for Creative Photography at the University of Arizona.

lack of communication, as it were. *La Última Cena* features an image of Christ and six statues of saints seated around a long altar in what appears to be a sacristy or storage space. In reality, then, this is only half of the Last Supper party: six apostles are missing. The saints sit in groups of three at opposite ends of the table. Five of them are bearded. A sixth beardless figure is probably Saint John, commonly depicted clean-shaven to emphasize his youth.

In a fashion, Álvarez Bravo winks at orthodox religious roles while poking fun of tradition in this odd version of the iconic Last Supper. Female figures may appear in collective pious anonymity, virtuous anguish, or devout ecstasy, but debate and discussion is the province of the "fathers" of the Church. Here six sainted apostles gather on benches as if attending a meeting called by the Savior. The Christ figure gestures with his right hand, as if speaking to the others from an imposing throne-like chair in the center of an altar. However, Álvarez Bravo underscores the figures' artificiality. Although gesticulating, Christ's mouth is tightly closed. Ironically the image captures a conference of biblical men in which no information can be exchanged. All those in attendance are clearly wooden replicas.[44] Each saint—the "chosen," as it were—looks to the Jesus figure who apparently holds forth, but the light flooding the room highlights the fabricated metal halos stuck to their heads. It is not known where Álvarez Bravo found this scene. She might have discovered this "meeting," but it is also possible that she posed the figures. In the foreground a table designed specifically for votive candles sits empty, and a fragment of an ornate column sits to one side. Álvarez Bravo photographed a "gathering" of holy figures in an unconsecrated space where there is scant evidence of devotional activity. The picture emphasizes the human act of staging. These santos are frauds and have no wisdom to impart. Catholicism and its sacred effigies offer nothing transcendent. In fact, they are mute. The "men" congregated here are even less "real" than the masked figures in other photographs. Mexico's image-centered religiosity, Álvarez Bravo insinuates, is a charade. In this image it is literally a dialogue of the blind, deaf, and dumb.

A PORTRAIT OF LA MADRE MATIANA

The concert of photographs discussed thus far provides the crucial context for Álvarez Bravo's *La Madre Matiana*. Looking at them together reveals a deft, simultaneous engagement of artistic conventions rooted in Christian iconography of the Renaissance, elements of avant-garde surrealism, and prevailing assumptions about photography, particularly in regard to the representation of the human figure and face. In many ways the impact of her work depends on the balancing act she gamely sustains. At the outset, she both depends on and undermines the qualities of truth and transparency that most people ascribe to photographs. Because of their mechanical production and their ability to seemingly freeze time, photographic images are often understood as snapshots of reality fixed in a flat, usually rectangular, vista for our close examination. Subsequently we consume them as simple glimpses of the past.[45] Furthermore, viewers, and sometimes artists too, impose a distinct ethics onto the image. We often assume that the photographer and the presence of the camera are neutral and do not influence the behaviors of those captured on film. Documentary photographers like Álvarez Bravo worked within these norms, for the most part. These photographs are to be read, at least initially, as "real" captured moments that reveal deep truths about Mexican society and culture. Of course, artists often manipulate these assumptions.

The next level of Álvarez Bravo's work on devotional art and popular customs emerges in the way she experiments in the overlapping gray areas between norms of representation that pertain to human features: portraiture, type imagery, and imaginary or mythic figures.[46] In many ways she succeeds in getting distinct representational norms up and working in a single image. First, as an accomplished portraitist herself, she understood the fundamentals of the genre. A portrait is supposed to capture the subject's distinctive character and offer a glimpse of the inner self through the skillful depiction of the visible exterior, posture, gaze, accessories, and iconographically charged setting. These elements work in concert to let the viewer imagine that he or she perceives the distilled nature of the person in question. This is certainly the case in Álvarez Bravo's portraits of her famous friends. In type imagery, the goal is not to convey a sense of a fundamental personal essence, but rather to render the subject as somehow epitomizing a larger group. This approach was very common in Latin American photography, particularly the collectible *tarjeta de visita* (carte de visite) genre fashionable during the nineteenth century and postcards and photojournalism of the twentieth century.[47] Type imagery also informs many indigenista images and scholarly depictions of folk culture, like those of Álvarez Bravo, although she establishes a distinct tone in her images despite deploying some of this genre's conventions. Finally there are imaginary, mythic figures, such as those in religious painting and sculpture. Their primary visual function, however, is to downplay individuality and group typologies in order to convey allegedly universal values; they remind viewers of exceptional behaviors and exemplary stories through facial expressions, iconographic elements, and symbolic postures.

What is remarkable about Álvarez Bravo's photography is how close examination reveals her putting these dynamics in play while also subverting them. It might be tempting to chalk this up to a reliance on surrealist convention: the irrational juxtaposition of seemingly realistic images. This, however, robs the photographer of one of her unique gifts: a genuine sensitivity to gender, popular Catholic practice, and the settings of devotion. On the most basic level she often approaches her task as a portraitist. In part these images function in concert as fragments of a larger composite portrait, so to say, of Mexican popular culture. However, in the more literal aspects of individual shots she tweaks representational conventions and viewer expectations rooted in traditional portraiture. For example, she approaches images of Catholic saints originally produced as idealized, imaginary figures and photographs them as if they were individuals sitting for a portrait. It is a deceptively simple, clever trick; the artist knowingly goes along with tradition. If devotees treat specific santos as special, powerful, living individuals that require their attention and the currying of favor, why not shoot them as such? The impact is disconcerting at first, but it serves the artist's subtle, satirical project. The statues cannot meet the standards of portraiture, and expectations of deep revealing insights into individual character are dashed on first glance. The photographed image cannot be viewed as a complex knowable person. As a result the viewer instinctively marks them as contrivances. The tendency is to see the photographed santo as a crude effigy rather than sacred representation. On another level since these are lifeless statues—and Álvarez Bravo makes sure this is readily apparent—these images scramble assumptions surrounding photographs as moments liberated from the hurtling realities of life. No longer can they be considered as freeze-frames snatched from the march of time. Sacred statuary cannot move or respond to events, and yet Álvarez Bravo places them in the visual amber of photographic representation, a medium suffused with these suppositions. Devotional images are produced, even mass-produced, with different modes of display and visual consumption in mind. By capturing them through photography, the artist jerks them into a different realm of visual meaning. As mere effigies they cannot be more than superficial references to human qualities and intense experiences; and hence their portrait-like representation makes them laughable. Could there be a more devastating critique of image-centered devotion? In the final assessment it is at least as effective as the state-sponsored campaigns involving saint burnings and calculated profanations of the Revolutionary era.[48] Álvarez Bravo's satirical treatment of devotional images, however, never reached a truly wide audience. In addition, there is no guarantee that their demystifying message would be read by much of the populace. More than likely devout Mexicans—by all accounts avid consumers of religious imagery, then as now—would simply refuse or reject the artist's photographs of santos as unattractive because they violate convention. Thus she is essentially preaching to the secularist choir in these photographs.

Many of the elements examined in Álvarez Bravo's other photographs are simultaneously at work in *La Madre Matiana*. First, the mannequin serves as a pseudo-santo, a "sacred" figure of reactionary politics and conservative propaganda that appears much like a traditional santo. This allows the artist to employ the effigy to mark traditional devout identities as ludicrous and hollow; in other words, out of step with modern Mexico.[49] Naming the photograph after the legendary prophetess amounts to an appropriation similar to the irreverent journalists' Matiana masquerade in previous decades, and invoking an infamous popular figure leads Álvarez Bravo to employ an approach that diverges from her other captured images of female piety. She clearly engages the conventions of portraiture: the photograph is a snapshot of the legendary Madre Matiana, the epitome of backwardness and fanaticism that has been gendered female. The joke emerges from the artist's conjuring of the impossible, a portrait of the pamphlet prophetess "in action." In contrast to the real living women depicted elsewhere, the gaze is fully upon the female face of piety, but it is fake like those of the santos. In short, it is an ironic portrait: this figure is but an effigy of beatería—a female social identity grounded in cultural practices, beliefs, and ideologies as sterile and shallow as the mannequin Matiana.

Crucially Álvarez Bravo quarantines her subject in plain public view and positions her ersatz femininity against Mexican masculinity. The avatar of fanaticism appears as a prudish outcast in a throng of modern men. The accentuation of Matiana's isolation is especially evident in comparison between the published image and an unpublished variant. In the alternate picture, Álvarez Bravo composed the shot from a lower point of view, perhaps crouching and in vertical perspective. Only the centered Matiana and three men behind her are visible, while distant tree branches and the slivers of sky form the background. This picture also emphasizes the staring youth, but the published image's eye-level point of view brings the hats and heads of numerous male figures into focus behind Matiana. Instead of a "natural" backdrop employed in the variant, the artist chose to frame her Madre Matiana amid a veritable wall of modern masculine humanity. In so doing, Álvarez Bravo emphasizes Madre Matiana's out-of-place presence in a secular, male-dominated public space. For the most part, these men surrounding her function as popular "types" juxtaposed against the mannequin's sham individuality. The male figures evoke evolving Revolutionary modernity, which was taking over Mexico's public spaces; they are representatives of the larger changes within the nation. The sea of hats behind them implies the presence of the nearby masses they represent. The array of observable clothing, hats, features, and skin tones hint at the cross-class, mestizo unity trumpeted by nationalists of the radical left during the 1930s era of popular front politics. Together these surrounding types speak of "movement," in both the political and cultural sense.

The mannequin's old-fashioned, excessively modest attire heightens her seclusion still more. As with other images, it is unclear if the artist came upon this scene or staged the shot. Looking at both the published image and the variant, it is hard to believe there was not some level of collusion between the photographer and the four principal masculine individuals in the

Figure 30. untitled, n.d. [Variant of "La Madre Matiana," ca. 1935]. Photograph by Lola Álvarez Bravo (posthumous reproduction from an original negative). © 1995 Center for Creative Photography at the University of Arizona.

photograph. The Matiana figure may, in actuality, be simply a fortune-telling figure like those that occasionally appear at popular festivals even today.[50] For a few coins a customer can choose a piece of paper from the cup in the mannequin's hand with a vague message about his or her destiny. This may explain why one of the men in the photograph appears to be demanding payment from the young man intent on the objects in Matiana's hands. Likewise, the man to the far left in the published image is perhaps reading a previously purchased prediction. Nonetheless even if she simply stumbled upon this scene, by titling the image "La Madre Matiana" the artist activates the pious associations, social anxieties regarding women and Catholicism, frustrations concerning public female support of the Church and conservative ideology, and, of course, the legacy of derision linked to the visionary in Mexican culture. The artist essentially traps a representation of prudish, vacuous female piety and obstinate sanctimony in the public sphere to dramatize its absurdity in the modernizing nation. In other words, if the men represent action, change, and collective movement, Madre Matiana, caught between them, mindlessly stands for rigidity and stagnation.

Aside from the masculine "types" engulfing this Matiana, however, the pivotal figure in this photograph is the youth staring at the camera. Unlike the mannequin, his likeness fulfills portraiture's time-honored criteria and hence can be "read" by the viewer in keeping with the genre's standards. In fact, the photograph is framed in such a manner as to highlight the contrast between his unique lively visage and piercing gaze and the cold emotionless countenance of the artist's Matiana. He is not a child but rather an individual on the cusp of manhood. His relative youth makes him a representative of Mexico's future, and as such he bears witness to the photographed moment. His serious presence and knowing gaze suggest he understands the artist's actions. The photographer's hand in these effects is even more obvious if we glance at the unpublished variant. There the boy appears younger, almost baby-faced, and curious as he looks down at the photographer. In the published image, though, his deadpan sincerity and cap sets the tone and renders him emblematic. It is impossible to know for certain the artist's intentions, but perhaps he represents a worker-to-be, the idealized agent and imagined beneficiary of Mexico's Revolutionary renovation at the time. Crucially as representative of the new generation he evinces no interest in the pseudo-santo figure. The three other men surrounding her engage the mannequin in some fashion; the glaring youth alone ignores her altogether. He appears cognizant of her ultimately irrelevant, albeit irksome, presence in modern society. He looks past her. Moreover, he communicates this awareness through the camera to the viewer.

Thus although accomplished by different means, Álvarez Bravo's commentary on religion and devout identity in *La Madre Matiana* (1935) is also one of containment through performative mockery. She renders the nation's prophetess, and the feminized traditionalism she stands for, ridiculous. Like the santos of *La Última Cena*, her Madre Matiana is a drab fake with nothing to say. Her painted lips are sealed shut. She is but a lingering reminder of outmoded ideas and customs. She cannot move with (or against) the masses surrounding her; nor can she adapt to change or evolve with the times. Like a carved santo she is a ghost of Mexico's stubborn past. As with the newspapermen who previously appropriated her persona, the implication is that through satirical representation viewers would recognize and reject the irrational folly the pamphlet prophetess represented. However, the humor only works because Matiana retained palpable symbolic power at the time. In essence, Álvarez Bravo neutralizes certain facets of Mexican popular culture by producing a "portrait" of Madre Matiana stranded and publically exposed as empty and powerless. Nonetheless well beyond 1935, Catholicism, female church activism, and a wide array of behaviors and beliefs associated with the prophetess remained strong. The Revolutionary process proved unable to tame these aspects of popular culture and also failed to replace the prevailing assumptions conflating devout Catholic identity and Mexican femininity.

CHAPTER 7

A Disjointed Modernity

Madre Matiana and the Writings of Agustín Yáñez

FOR THE RESIDENTS OF TIERRA SANTA, THE 1920S OFFERED A GRIND-ing, miserable existence, sealed off from the nation's quickening transformation. No priests, soldiers, or schoolteachers set foot in the blighted region, although rumors of distant upheavals and dramatic change flitted between residents. It was as if both the Catholic Church and the vaunted Revolution had sidestepped this corner of Mexico. Tierra Santa merely languished, a backwater of abject poverty and ignorance.

Madre Matiana, with her raptorlike intensity and the battered vigor of a contorted mesquite, embodied what remained of hope. Her complexion was grave, dark, and clean: it had been cured by the relentless sun and wind and polished like a washing stone, with the exception of two deep channels leading down from her eyes, as if carved by centuries of tears. No one, though, had ever seen her cry. Her face was indeed striking but Matiana's hands served as the most awe-inspiring reminder of her unique status. Skeletal and yet powerful, they allegedly bore burdens from the other world to the Earth and vice versa. For her peasant neighbors these abilities conferred a fearsome destiny, which paradoxically both consumed and sustained the preternatural go-between. The eldest residents maintained that she had not changed since their childhood.

Despite trepidations, locals sought her out. They knew that she would travel to the seat of calamity regardless of the hour and without a thought to recompense. Matiana was always available for those seeking consolation, cures, and miraculous assistance. Likewise, her home housed a trove of healing herbs and sacred images, and her prodigious memory safeguarded local lore. For all intents and purposes she was a living almanac and devotional encyclopedia, remembering the significance of each day and leading efforts to beseech God and the saints. Tierra Santa even expected Madre Matiana to ward off epidemics, coax rain from the clouds, and outfox the devil.

For these reasons alone the old woman seemed indispensable. But the residents of Tierra Santa also thought that she investigated and punished every illicit act. Death, they believed, served as the medium of redress—death or the incapacitation of humans, animals, lands, crops, and tools.

For Matiana the pressing expectations and desperate hopes represented a tremendous burden. She was, quite simply, exhausted. Her neighbors may have imagined her as a mystical marvel, but she knew her limits and remembered her actual age. The trusted curandera sensed that she was incapable of shielding her community from looming changes—changes that she intuited, but could not fully grasp. As she puzzled over the first appearance of an airplane, Matiana recalled stories of her birth and its coincidence with the U.S. invasion and annexation of Mexican territory (1846–1848). She also recalled the *pastorelas* (folk ritual theater) of her youth, in which she played both the Virgin Mary and "Temptation." Modulating her movements and demeanor with innate skill, Matiana plumbed human nature: as she witnessed her ability to incite men's lustful delusions that she realized that she could "read" others. People, she deduced, were largely transparent: gaze, action, speech, or silence telegraphed hope, desire, scheme, and sin. She understood this was her true gift, but it seemed wholly inadequate for the tumult closing in on Tierra Santa.

Such was the characterization of Madre Matiana and rural Mexicans (the residents of Tierra Santa) in Agustín Yáñez's 1962 novel *Las tierras flacas*.[1] In it resides perhaps the most complex Matiana over one hundred years after the first prophetic pamphlets appeared in Mexico City. A character in a tragic allegorical saga, she simultaneously serves as traditional Mexico's conscience, memory, soul, avatar of justice, and collective spirit. In this author's hands, though, she is not a real prophetess. In reality, she is little more than an acutely attentive witness to the nation's difficult past and an astute observer of humanity. This, Madre Matiana realized, was the sum total of her visionary grace. Nonetheless, it was with particular angst that she sensed a drastic transformation bearing down on her rustic homeland for which she had no antidote or incantation.

In Yáñez's novel it seems like the impossible has occurred; the pamphlet prophetess, the erstwhile mouthpiece of reactionary mobilization, the quintessentially Mexican beata, and the satirical caricature of popular fanaticism finally speaks for herself. Matiana, for the first time, appears to be a "real" person. But this work of fiction merely represents the most ambitious, carefully crafted appropriation of the prophetess. Yáñez, a famous author, academic, politician, and functionary, placed his version of the legendary Madre Matiana at the center of twentieth-century culture change. The author never received much attention for this work, but in it he resurrects the prophetess and turns her into a fully developed principal character endowed with extraordinary importance. Perhaps even more remarkable, a male author invents the thoughts, motivations, and life experiences of this durable symbol of popular piety, Catholic feminity, and cultural authenticity. The work depicts Madre Matiana's interactions with a cast of equally symbolic characters as she ponders her fictional community's vulnerability to new outside forces. Ultimately the reader realizes that a tragedy is in the offing. The emblematic protagonist cannot contain or redirect the whirlwind of modernization closing in on Tierra Santa.

No one before Yáñez had attempted such a sustained reinterpretation of Madre Matiana and the cultural dynamics she had come to represent. At its core the text is a post-Revolutionary lament—a veritable where-have-we-gone-wrong novel—where Yáñez conjures an impoverished rural community that represents a primordial Mexico caught in the throes of externally imposed transformation. Implicitly he asks if the new order failed to address this part, the most authentic part, of the nation's deepest needs. Madre Matiana stands in for the bedrock of beliefs and practices that had sustained the nation's suffering masses since time immemorial, but which seem incapable of doing so amid a dawning modern reality. The repurposed pamphlet seer represents the tired soul of Mexico's heartland battered by history and oppression and yet tentatively approaching Revolutionary change. From the very beginning it is clear that a melodramatic clash looms. Ultimately Madre Matiana suffers a violent and brutal assault, yet bitterly clings to life. She emerges diminished but emblematic in a new unsettling way. Yáñez recasts her as a manifestation of Mexico's disjointed modernity—a state the nation can only escape when Tierra Santa transcends everything the curandera-seer represents. From the post-Revolutionary present of Agustín Yáñez in the early 1960s, that development appears nowhere in sight. Mexico remains encumbered by an ill-fitting mix of modern advancements and irrational traditions.

At first glance it seems odd that this exceptionally well-connected author would insert the pamphlet prophetess into simmering debates about the nature of post-Revolutionary Mexico in the 1960s. Mexicans had not forgotten Matiana completely, but she no longer inspired careful consideration. All that seemed left was the dismissive interpretation of her legacy. This is perhaps best appreciated in an undated broadside—most likely from the 1930s—entitled "La doctrina de la Madre Matiana."[2] In this publication's visual representation she no longer exudes strength or invokes the pamphlet-almanac story of colonial piety. Gone are the echoes of a nation-saving, nation-cleaning mission, or foresight of any kind, as had been present in the early 1920s. Instead she appears as a one-eyed—or ineptly winking—fortuneteller, sporting gypsy-like hoop earrings and unseemly facial stubble. Moreover, her lower lip sags distastefully and her partially visible torso suggests obesity. The mock catechism beneath her "portrait" does not reference upheaval, change, or mysticism. It simply renders as dogma the unrelenting victimization of common Mexicans at the hands of a corrupt political order. Although the target is official venality, the broadside implicitly criticizes "superstition" by couching the denunciation as a catechistic recitation—an essentially passive act—and imploring absurdly named saints.

Despite Matiana's cultural diminishment, Lola Álvarez Bravo's photographic exploration of the Matiana legacy still remained topical in the mid-1930s because tensions between the Revolutionary government and the Church remained combustible. Afterward the legendary seer progressively devolved into a mere flippant gesture to a previous generation's manias.[3] Official Church publications distanced themselves, ignoring her completely or classifying her as little more than prophetic folklore typical of difficult times in the past.[4] In broader social arenas she appears as the name gracing a cantina or a catchphrase—such as, "*Ni lo dijo la madre Matiana*" ("Not even Madre Matiana said so")—to describe baffling occurrences.[5] In other instances she appears in expressions of exasperation, such as "*Si quiere explicaciones, que se las pida a la madre Matiana* " ("If you want answers, ask Madre Matiana").[6] In a few cases she still appeared as a whimsical reference to misguided political forecasting, as she had in the nineteenth century.[7] In this spirit one reporter even joked about indulging in "*matianismo*

Figure 31. La doctrina de la madre Matiana, n.d. Courtesy of the University of California, Berkeley, Bancroft Library.

económico" as he proffered his own financial predictions in the mid-1940s.[8] Others looking back on the Revolutionary struggle deployed Matiana as a metaphor for the widespread superstitions fanned by the era's turmoil.[9] These kinds of allusions overlap somewhat with essays that conjure Madre Matiana in order to mock apocalyptic thinking in general.[10] Predictably, such commentary included statements associating the prophecies with superstitious elderly women.[11] In the 1950s and 1960s the newspaper *La Crítica* followed in the footsteps of its satirical forbearers, featuring a periodic column called "The New Prophecies of Madre Matiana" dedicated to sarcastic political critique.[12] But it did not engage the prophecies' original content or the historical seer's persona in any meaningful way. Offhand jokes about Matiana even crop up in articles broaching worries of nuclear war in the early 1960s. One reporter mischievously likened Nikita Khrushchev to the Mexican prophetess due to his blustering predictions of capitalism's demise.[13]

AN AUTHOR AND FUNCTIONARY

Agustín Yáñez was born in Guadalajara, the capital city of Jalisco, in 1904.[14] His parents were from Yahualica, a small, rural town, approximately fifty miles to the northeast, in a region called Los Altos. To this day it maintains a reputation as one of the most traditional and fervently Catholic corners of Mexico. Yáñez visited Yahualica frequently and spent numerous long stays there as a youth, and he later used the region as the backdrop for much of his fiction.[15] He grew up in a deeply religious household. His father, a one-time follower of Francisco Madero (Mexico's moderate democratic Revolutionary), was an avid reader of Guadalajara's conservative Catholic newspaper, *El Regional*, and his mother spoke at length of her hometown's customs.[16] As a youth he attended the seminary in Guadalajara, and he briefly contemplated joining the priesthood before focusing on law. He also joined the Catholic Association of Mexican Youth (Asociación Católica de la Juventud Mexicana; ACJM), an important node of religious militancy and anti-Revolutionary organizing throughout the late 1910s and 1920s. During those years the ACJM, and likeminded organizations, served as the institutional framework for urban protests and passive resistance. In some instances they also provided logistical support for armed counter-revolutionaries during the Cristero Revolt (1926–1929). Few educated urban youths like Yáñez actually took up arms, but many sympathized with the peasants who fought the new government.[17]

In sum, the future author came of age immersed in conservative religious and political circles. Moreover, Yáñez's writing career began in Catholic journalism and Church-approved religious fiction. Nonetheless in the late 1920s and early 1930s he made a series of choices that distanced him from his youthful commitments and allowed him to scale the ranks of post-Revolutionary officialdom. Political scientist Roderic Ai Camp labels Yáñez an important figure in a pivotal generation of Mexican intellectuals who became state functionaries: men born between 1900 and 1920 who were too young to fight in the Revolution but shaped cultural policy between 1940 and 1970, a period crucial to the evolution of the Mexican state and its relations with society.[18] Yáñez, however, seems relatively unique in that he brought together early Catholic activism, international literary fame, and national political prominence.

Alongside his forays into devotional literature, Yáñez completed his education in law and gradually became part of wider intellectual circles while editing a literary magazine from 1929 to 1930.[19] He only practiced law briefly, but gained recognition for oratory and writing. At more or less the same time, he also worked for the famed intellectual José Vasconcelos's ill-fated presidential campaign. Finally in 1931, Yáñez moved to Mexico City and entered the staunchly secularist milieu of Revolutionary-era public education.[20] Initially he secured a teaching post at the National Preparatory School (the veritable finishing school of the secular elite) while he studied philosophy at the national university.[21] Eventually he took a job in the ministry of education, a hotbed of efforts to secularize Mexican culture, and rose through the ranks as a favorite of the young Marxist minister, Narciso Bassols.[22] When Bassols's star faded alongside the reforms he championed, Yáñez followed him to the ministry of the treasury. There his career briefly stagnated when his provocative mentor was dispatched to a diplomatic post. But through a renewed focus on writing and editorial work, Yáñez found his way back to the ladder of national prominence. His ticket to fame and influence, ultimately, was the astounding success of his first novel *Al filo del agua* (*The Edge of the Storm*), which was published in 1947.[23]

As his celebrity grew in the early 1950s, he attracted the attention of President Adolfo Ruiz Cortines (in office, 1952–1958). For the next two decades he circulated at the very highest levels of Mexican politics. First, he became a speechwriter for Ruiz Cortines, who in turn appointed him governor of Jalisco in 1953, an office he held until 1959. Afterward he served subsequent presidents in various capacities. Most notably, Yáñez served President Gustavo Díaz Ordaz as minister of education from 1964 to 1970, working at the heart of the regime throughout its violent crackdown on student protests in the late 1960s. Perhaps most damning, unlike other prominent intellectuals of the era he chose to remain silent and support the president through the repressive actions of 1968. According to Camp, Yáñez managed to stay largely aloof without being a part of an identifiable faction or building a personal following. Remarkably, in the rough realm of Mexican politics he maintained a reputation for honesty and competence.[24]

Literary scholars often underscore Yáñez's commitment to reformist realism. In 1960, just two years before publishing *Las tierras flacas* he opined that the Mexican novel's core characteristics included an engagement of the nation's central problems, true-to-life narratives, a distinctly Mexican vocabulary, the construction of a *retrato crítico* (critical portrait) of society, and a prophetic sensibility.[25] Although other marquee Mexican writers in the 1950s, like Juan Rulfo and Carlos Fuentes, were breaking away from this unambiguously reformist, nationalist stance, Yáñez remained committed to this approach throughout his career. From his early short stories to his more mature novels he constructs national "reality," pointing out problems and alluding to what could, should, or would take place in Mexican society. Yáñez, in other words, retained obsolete notions of literature's role as a nation-building vehicle long after most Mexican writers jettisoned such ideas.[26] However, it is precisely the throwback nature of his writing and his costumbrista-like interest in the minute details of popular culture that make his work valuable today. A telling irony resides in the fact that this approach connects him to the nineteenth-century literary world from which Madre Matiana emerged.

Most of Yáñez's work grapples with the impact of modernity in "traditional" settings in some form or fashion. Some emblematic issues remained central to the writer for decades. For example, he repeatedly focuses his critical gaze on caciquismo (brutal rural patronage systems), a stance common in the mid-twentieth century, and very much in keeping with the national government's generic portrayal of endemic problems throughout the countryside at the time.[27] In a nutshell, this somewhat disingenuous proposition holds that local greed and authoritarianism impedes the progressive modernization championed by the one-party state.[28] Much the same can be said for his abiding critique of fanaticism. The gendering of these problems leaps off the page: the masculine face of backwardness is the brutish cacique, and the feminine face of obscurantism appears in his *"mujeres enlutadas"* (black-clad women in mourning) and Madre Matiana. Typically he suggests that enlightened state intervention represents the appropriate solution to these enduring problems, largely oblivious to the antidemocratic, corrupt legacy of such strategies in Mexico. Likewise, Yáñez ignores the cacique-infested foundations of the Revolutionary government itself (both in urban and rural contexts).[29]

Despite what present-day readers might term his statist developmentalism and unabashed sexism, Yáñez does explore issues with genuine sincerity. Again his approach echoes liberal reformers of the nineteenth century, who also envisioned literature as a unique vehicle of social change and relied on minute description and parable-like narration in hopes of achieving their ends. The author, like his predecessors, viewed the novel as the appropriate arena for didactic examinations of social ills and the framing of solutions. His novels also have much in common with the criollista novels of the early twentieth century and their search for modern authenticity within ostensibly "primitive" popular culture.[30] In his case he repeatedly wrote stories set in the Mexican Revolution, either its outbreak in 1910 or the belated extension of Revolutionary change and state-led development in subsequent decades. Frequently he begins on the eve of change, with disquiet bubbling to the surface and storm clouds approaching. Yáñez persistently draws a line in time between a traditional past and a Revolution-mediated modern destiny. Implicitly Mexico must make the leap to a fully rational modern existence; the dramatic tension often stems from the notion that parts of Mexico (or the minds of some Mexicans) resist transformation. The challenge then resides in this fundamental dissonance.

In large part because of Yáñez's stylistic and thematic traditionalism, later works like Las tierras seldom attract analysis. Overwhelmingly, when scholars approach Yáñez they focus solely on Al filo and its acknowledged pivotal place in the Mexican canon.[31] His approach to literature "worked" in the late 1940s, but it sounded off key a decade later. Reviews written at the time of Las tierras's publication remained polite, but the writers hid behind plot description and avoided deeper engagement.[32] After the author's death, though, renowned cultural figures harshly judged the novels written after Al filo. Neither Octavio Paz nor Carlos Monsiváis—the two titans of Mexican literary criticism—ascribed any importance to them whatsoever.[33] In contrast, present-day Guadalajara-based scholars (the author's regionalist paisanos, as it were) often depict him as a uniquely adept chronicler of the region's past.[34] Praise and criticism notwithstanding, his writings conflate tradition, popular religion, and femininity in a manner that colors the way we understand Revolutionary Reformism. In this regard novels like Al filo and Las tierras represent constructions of history, culture, and gender that inform period efforts to reshape popular culture.[35] In truth, passages of Al filo brim with beautifully crafted depictions of rural life and customs. At the time of publication few authors focused so carefully on the centrality of Catholicism in Mexican life, the hushed but steady rhythms of parish life, and the intimate experience of devotional practice. Yáñez also lavished attention upon widely recognizable religious social types that other writers ignored. Despite the rationalist critique embedded in his well-known work, a marked compassion and often sincere affection surrounds his representation of devout characters. The sensitivity he demonstrates for devotional culture and deeply religious social environments undoubtedly stems from intimate personal experience. His youthful writings, moreover, suggest that he too was once an intensely devout, committed Catholic. In fact, examining these texts provides crucial context for the later novels.

CATHOLIC FICTION

Although rarely examined, Yáñez began his writing career by producing sentimental devout fiction with a distinct reactionary political message, precisely as the church-state conflict roiled Jalisco. One of his earliest works, a collection of three short stories published in 1925, is particularly useful for plotting the trajectory of his subsequent career and placing his appropriation of Madre Matiana in perspective. Dedicated to the Sacred Heart of Jesus and called *Llama de amor viva* (*Flame of Living Love*), the collection was originally written in 1923 and offered effusive narratives of exemplary Eucharistic piety. Yáñez was only nineteen at the time.[36] He also authored another story collection in 1925 thematically organized around Christian charity.[37] The narratives collected in *Llama* are quite literally "love stories," centered on the Blessed Sacrament (the devotion anchoring the Matiana prophecies) and published with the archbishop's imprimatur. As he would many times during the rest of his career, Yáñez seized upon the region surrounding Yahualica for an iconic rural backdrop suffused with nationalist sentiment. In *Al filo* and *Las tierras* he emphasizes hidebound austerity and fanaticism, but his youthful writings offer virtually the opposite: a fervent Catholic counternationalism amid the Mexican Revolution grounded in a simple, pure collective piety and a unifying and all-enveloping culture of belief. Moreover, in these early works the author renders female piety in a distinctly eroticized register, which echoes the profoundly sensual nature of mystical expression intertwined with the legends of sainted visionaries.

The first story, "¡Es el Amor!" is set in the village of Acasico, where an exploited circus dancer (i.e., an unloved, precociously worldly, miserable young woman) passing through town experiences a miraculous vision while the idealized pastor of Yahualica says Mass for the peasant faithful. Just as he consecrates the Host, the dancer sees a cheerful boy scampering down from the altar to give her his precious flaming heart. She is subsequently overcome with chaste passion for the beautiful blond man, who she envisions descending from the heavens to inhabit the Eucharist. Afterward, filled with divine love, she impassively withstands physical and verbal abuse from the circus boss until the righteous priest and community leaders free her. The story then turns to her new blissful, exceptionally pious life and its interruption by degenerate revolutionaries terrorizing the peaceful region. At the climax of the story the ex-circus performer, now rechristened Luz (light), heroically outwits marauding rebels bent on defiling the Blessed Sacrament—and by implication the female protagonist. Hearing of the rebel's approach she sprints ahead:

> Behold that woman running along the picturesque path that leads from [the town of] Mexticacán to the Sanctuary. Nothing distracts her, an intense urgency prevents it. The elms and willows along the way seem to incite her to run. The woodpeckers and the mockingbirds cry out: Run! Run!
>
> Don't you recognize her? . . . It is Luz, the acrobat martyr, the rejuvenated flower, the woman in love . . .
>
> To receive Jesus, to please him, to live for Him, to *desagraviarlo* [placate him]: this was her total existence. Luz had offered herself as a Eucharistic victim. She relished the delights of her Lover, and her soul, tender and caring, once sad and orphaned, dallied in the fervent dialogues of an impassioned woman that has given herself completely to the arms of her first love and offers up all her youth and her thoughts as a gift to her Lover. Divine Passion![38]

Just before the ungodly radicals can reach the village church, Yáñez's romantic heroine bolts the sanctuary's formidable locks. Hearing the exasperated gunshots and savage battering of the wooden doors behind her, Luz turns, approaches the altar, and prayerfully consumes the threatened Host. When the brutes finally break in, all they can do is murder her as she shouts defiantly, "*¡Jesús mío, soy tu víctima! ¡Mi patria!*" ("My Jesus, I am your victim! My Fatherland!"). In closing, Yáñez depicts a heavenly procession where the blond manly Christ and the beautiful Luz are united in mystical eternal matrimony.[39]

The other two stories in the collection take the theme of Eucharistic devotion in different directions, but they both maintain the author's emphasis on the foundational nature of feminine piety. The second, entitled "La estrella nueva" ("The New Star"), narrates a terminally ill girl's last days set within a romanticized parish life. Yáñez juxtaposes bucolic splendor with the

protagonist's tragic demise as he details her innocent passion to receive her
First Communion. Ultimately she expires in a state of spiritual bliss after consuming the Host.[40] The last story, "La cruzada infantil" ("The Children's
Crusade") is, in reality, more of a sermon. It begins with a statement of the
author's enthusiasm for the Mexican Eucharistic Congress of 1923—arguably
the initial inspiration for the book—and then expounds on the social import
of devotion to the Blessed Sacrament. Then Yáñez opts for a first-person retelling of a trip to a Jalisco village where he encounters a moving tableau: a young
ranchera mother and proud father coach their three-year-old daughter
through a flawless, baby-talk recitation of Eucharistic teachings and passages
from Ripalda, the traditional catechism: "*Oh Saglado Banquete en que Clisto
es nuestlo alimento . . . Yo cleo, Jesús mío, que estáis plesente en el Santísimo
Saclamento del altal*" ("Oh Sacwed Banquet in which Chwist is ouwr food . . . I
bewieve, my Jesus, that you are pwesent in the Holy Sacwament of the
Altaw").[41] This dulcet performance, in turn, transitions to a disquisition on
the patriotic importance of women's role in transmitting Catholic doctrine to
their children:

> Napoleon lacked Christian mothers in order to consolidate the empire;
> our country also lacks modest mothers, fervent mothers, who instead
> of busying themselves with vain things and material delusions, begin
> to shape, patiently, the hearts of their children. There are not enough
> true mothers that nurture the spirit in their little ones, so that, by pre-
> serving the lily of divine chastity, there Jesus of the Eucharist will
> come to reside. It is saddening, the sophisms and pretexts that some
> mothers offer in order not to take their children to the angelic banquet.
> How are children to take part in the combat of life, without the nour-
> ishment of the bread of the strong?[42]

In short, the obvious implication is that diligent yet humble Christian
motherhood produces devout communities and strong pious nations. Yáñez
eventually predicts Mexico's spiritual and social renewal thanks to the revived Eucharistic fervor stoked by the congress of 1923.[43]

Given Yáñez's later critical appraisal of the clergy and popular Catholicism,
it is somewhat shocking to read *Llama* today. Thematically and stylistically
it is very much within the tradition of Catholic expression in the early twentieth century. Ideologically, although he does not veer into apocalyptic extrapolations, Yáñez approaches the intransigent conservatism of Luis G.

Duarte and his nineteenth-century interpretation of Matiana's prophecies. These stories unfold within the era's militant Catholic understandings of the Sacred Heart of Jesus and Blessed Sacrament as intertwined devotions grounding the Church's battle against modern error. Likewise, the author echoes the triumphalist sociopolitical overtones ascribed to these practices, which were envisioned as the fountainhead of a restored Christian order. At a deeper level, his rendering of popular piety reproduces the Church hierarchy's most ardent visions of reformed lay orthodoxy: an orderly, deferential, sacrament-centered religiosity controlled by the clergy and responsive to Rome. In many ways, then, this book represents a distillation of the era's conservative Catholic imaginary. Of course Yáñez was not even twenty when he wrote these stories. He had yet to experience much beyond Guadalajara's Catholic schools and activist networks. Nonetheless given the pious conservatism expressed in *Llama*, it is understandable that he was not eager to acknowledge these writings later. Their current rarity, apparently, stems from efforts to destroy evidence of this phase of his literary career.[44] Clearly Yáñez changed during the two decades that separate his devout short stories and his greatest literary achievement, *Al filo*. Nonetheless echoes of these early works endured.

THE STORM'S EDGE

Al filo returns to the Revolution of 1910 and features the author's vision of a typical Mexican community and its experience of the nation's allegedly definitive cultural conflict. In this work Yáñez is particularly interested in the deep tensions he imagines on the very eve of the legendary upheaval. Like much of his writing, the motor of his archetypal characters' struggles is the clash of tradition and modernity and the abrupt transition from one all-encompassing reality to another. From the epigraph that graces the first chapter, it is clear that Yáñez presumes to capture the nation's essence "before the tempest," although it is readily apparent that famously conservative, predominantly mestizo, rural Jalisco—particularly Yahualica—serves as his microcosm for all of Mexico.[45] *Al filo*'s characters are, for the most part, unambiguously marked: they either desire emancipating change or seek to maintain Mexico's archaic social norms. They all, nonetheless, sense on some level the stifling "climate" before the metaphorical storm. Enlightenment lurks in the world beyond the village and the agents of obscurantism maneuver to hold it back amid ominous portents and murmured confessions.

Liberating ideas, irreverent equalities, and new customs seep into town via newspapers, songsters, and migrants. Meanwhile priests and a clutch of fanatically devout women labor to silence those who long for a freer existence. Desperate individual yearnings, though, also threaten the pueblo's (i.e. nation's) pious seclusion. In brief, Yáñez renders pre-Revolutionary Mexico as a bleak Catholic dystopia. The novel's crescendo of conflict subsequently leads the reader to a satisfying triumph of freedom. Painful as the experience is for many characters, the story ends with the previously repressed fictional community poised to reap the fruits of progress.

As noted earlier there is a tendency among present-day commenters to view *Al filo* as a straightforward snapshot of life in rural Jalisco before 1910. Read alongside archival documentation, the novel represents a more interesting project than simple narrative portraiture. Yáñez does not so much reconstruct the past, but rather he crafts an edifying montage. As a result the novel is historically informed and appropriates pre-Revolutionary history in complicated ways.[46] Of particular interest is the author's shifting portrayal of religious practice and the clergy. His earliest writings, as we have seen, reproduce the Church hierarchy's fantasy of submissive lay fervor. Thus in *Llama* religion represents a pure and simple social good and Catholicism represents the organic foundation of authentic nationhood. In *Al filo* the Church is primarily a reactionary force suppressing personal and collective advancement. Ultimately its repressive methods undermine individuals' mental and emotional health, causing them to act out in aberrant spasms of deviance and violence.[47] In short, the author conjures a collective Freudian psychodrama. Ironically, in both *Llama* and *Al filo* the laity is still largely obedient and fervently pious, but in the latter work this appears as a product of overweening clerical power. In a curious fashion, though, Yáñez's portrait of Mexican Catholicism sometimes clashes with documentable historical trends within the Church; at other times it echoes them. First, his supposition that the austere Catholic culture of Los Altos (the region within Jalisco Yáñez knew best) was somehow representative of the entire nation is preposterous, but his depiction of the Church's impressive strength in Jalisco rings true in other ways. Quite simply, in very few other regions in Mexico could the Church staff parishes as fully maintain such a variety of large lay institutions and exert as much influence as in Jalisco's villages and towns.[48] What is remarkable in the archival record is the broadly upbeat, even giddy, assessment of modern orthodoxy and lay fervor among parish priests in Jalisco before, during, and after the Mexican

Revolution.[49] This was certainly not the case in the entire nation. For example, in Oaxaca, a heavily indigenous state to the south, most curates described considerable frustration in their efforts to get common Catholics to embrace priest-centered, sacramental religiosity.[50] Thus while their counterparts in southern Mexico condemned popular superstition and intractability, priests who ministered near Yahualica heaped praise upon the flock. The divergent tenor of parish ministries between these regions is quite striking. In other words, although the level of priestly influence and the orthodox nature of popular religiosity were by no means homogenous across Mexico, there was certainly much more evidence in Jalisco of the Church's success in both realms. This does not mean, though, that Yáñez's portrait of a browbeaten laity in *Al filo* mirrors the historical reality of Los Altos. However, his image of rural Catholicism draws on the relatively close congruence between everyday lay practice and the clergy's notions of proper religiosity. Most likely, his personal experiences served as inspiration. Therefore we must be mindful that what he often portrays as the nature of rural Catholicism broadly is probably modeled after the church's most ardent, relatively well-off supporters from cities and larger towns. These were the sectors particularly attracted to the new Catholic associations that appear in *Al filo*—like the Asociación de las Hijas de María (the Association of the Daughters of Mary) or the Apostolado de la Oración (the Apostolate of Prayer). Likewise, these groups were the ones taking part in the intense spiritual retreats (the *encierro*, or "lock in") showcased in the novel to dramatize the clergy's intrusive authority prior to 1910. Historical evidence reveals the enduring importance of these institutions and practices after the Revolution as well.[51]

When it comes to the clergy, Yáñez supplies an array of priests to represent clerical types rather than historical figures or individuals. In doing so he creates a nuanced panorama of the early twentieth-century Church in the broader sense, rather than a true portrait of historical parish life. There is the goodhearted curate, Father Martínez, who oversees the parish. A product of the mid-nineteenth century, he invokes the strict but empathetic traditionalist of a previous era. He truly wants what is best for his flock, but he is hobbled by blinkered thinking. The mounting general malaise he confronts in the confessional alarms him, but he persists in believing that his parish can be isolated from change.

Working beneath the pastor are additional archetypal modern priests, the most important of which are a pair of contrasting figures that represent

historical constituencies within the Church. Father Reyes—a newly ordained, enlightened priest—carries on an innovative popular ministry
thanks to Martínez's encouragement. Essentially, he represents the "good"
clergy. A charismatic reformer and organizer, he provides a flexible voice
in terms of doctrine. His is a constructive, positive faith attuned to engaging the changing world and reaching out to the congregation in new ways.
Reyes thus resides in the progressive wing of the early twentieth-century
Church, a group Yáñez undoubtedly knew well from his youth. Guadalajara, in fact, served as a nerve center of new Catholic thought and experimentation in Mexico during the author's upbringing.[52] Balancing out the
clerical spectrum, Father Islas, is a sickly, intransigent martinet wielding
excessive sway over the community's most devout women. He cultivates
the aura of a living saint among his followers, and he champions a negative
piety centered on fear, abnegation, penance, and feverishly repressed sexuality. As Yáñez emphasizes, Islas holds power that is ideological rather than
physical:

> A cursory glance cannot discern the power of this ecclesiastic, who
> presents a deplorable first impression, like a sick person suffering from
> chronic neuralgia that may pass out at any moment. His eyelids and
> lips tremble, a quaking that increases before and after breaking into
> speech: a laborious operation in which the contracting space between
> his eyebrows, a bugling vein in the center of forehead, the nostrils of
> his very delicate nose, and the quavering pavilions of his ears take part.
> When he becomes silent his jaws shift around internally. [He displays]
> the physiognomy and manners of artists, maniacs, lacking cordiality.
> His voice whines weakly; and yet his female devotees have found in
> him supernatural charms.[53]

Islas, naturally, sneers at Reyes's "modern" methods. Instead he foments a
cult of virginity and stokes his disciples' mystical fantasies. His rival, in turn,
accurately gauges Islas's oppressively fanatical influence and cautiously
works to mitigate his power in the parish. Ultimately, the story reveals that
the would-be mystical saint actually harbors secret carnal obsessions that no
amount of self-mortification can temper.

Thus *Al filo* is not an indictment of Catholicism and the clergy in its total-
ity. Father Martínez's myopic traditional conservatism attracts the author's
critical eye, but Yáñez saves his fire for Father Islas and the women under his

spell. In fact, the author's depiction of the realm of Mexican religiosity represented by Islas oozes sarcasm as he details the obsessions of the "wise and virtuous Padre" and the tragically reactionary, superstitious existence of his followers. (Yáñez himself marked off the above descriptive phrase in quotation marks).[54]

Al filo is particularly censorious of the repressive internal dynamics and harsh conformism within the Hijas de María, a devotional organization brought to the pueblo by Father Islas and filled with his most obsessive female followers. As the reactionary padre lectures an aspirant, "The Association is a carriage that carries souls directly to heaven; however, at the cost of a harsh life full of mortifications, of renunciations; she who arrives out of frivolous curiosity, vainglory or any other mundane reason, is completely disgraced through the worst humiliations, and it would be better for her had she never aspired to the glorious title of Daughter of Mary."[55]

Those that do join the Hijas de María, the author reveals, shun the "natural" sentiments that lead young women to marriage and motherhood; instead they commit themselves to compulsive self-examination, perpetual virginity, and mindless penitential excess. Keeping them in line is an at-once laudatory and cautionary folklore of past members: for example, a founding member named Teofila Parga's fervent commitment and exemplary abnegation led to alleged miraculous capabilities such as prophecy—and a saintly death reputedly enveloping the town with the scent of lilies. In contrast, the ill-fated Maclovia Pérez left the association to get married and subsequently faced abject poverty, degrading madness, and ultimately a squalid death in her own filth.[56]

Such are the conservative social pressures in Yáñez's allegorical community that the Hijas de María actually set the tone for the entire town:

> Many religious organizations guide the pious activities of old and young, men and women. But ... the Daughters of Mary ... define the character of the pueblo, imposing a rigid discipline, a very rigid discipline, in terms of dress, walk, speech, thought and feeling among the young ladies drawn to this species of convent life, which makes the town a monastery. It is much frowned upon that a young girl reach the age of fifteen without belonging to the Association of the black outfit, the blue cord, and the silver medal; of the black high-necked outfit, long sleeves, and skirt down to the ankle; to the Association where the various members watch over one another with zealous rivalry, and

from which expulsion constitutes a grave, scandalous stain, which resonates in all reaches of life.[57]

According to Carlos Monsiváis, in this passage and others, a central feature of
the author's approach to Mexican women in the novel is their subjugation. For
Yáñez, "Women are the property of fathers, brothers and husbands; they are
the well of ignorance that protects the purity of the faith, they are the torrent
of resentment, which when it overflows, always dumps first on other women."[58]

Yáñez also offers something of a parable in the side story of a young man
whose spiritual apprenticeship to Father Islas leads to flamboyant mystical
delusions. Eventually this cautionary figure descends into lunacy and sexual
deviance. Throughout *Al filo*, in fact, the author sows doubts about the masculinity of those engaged in this sort of Catholicism (particularly Islas). The
clear implication is that while it may be objectionable for women to embrace
irrational beliefs and practices, it is entirely aberrant for Mexican men to do
so. Ultimately as Islas's ability to inspire fearful obedience weakens, he suffers a massive public seizure while celebrating Mass. The spectacle of him
foaming at the mouth and swelling up grotesquely in church definitively
breaks the hold of his brand of spirituality. Symbolically, Yáñez unmasks
intransigent Catholicism as intellectually and morally bankrupt.

Another important facet of *Al filo* is its examination of the key role Yáñez
ascribes to rumors, portents, and prophecies in Mexican popular culture, a
tendency that carried over to *Las tierras* as well.[59] There are interesting parallels again at work between the novel and what appears in historical evidence.
First off, at pivotal junctures in the narrative an elderly oracle-like character
named Lucas Macías appears, interpreting happenings and voicing predictions. As revolution approaches he proclaims that the Anti-Christ is clearly
afoot and the world's end is imminent. Moreover, when news of political
upheaval and Francisco Madero's efforts to unseat President Porfirio Díaz
come to light in 1910, Macías announces that unnamed prophecies had foretold these developments. Immediately Macías's statements—quite possibly
an allusion to the Matiana prophecies—enter the whirlwind of fear, news,
and gossip swirling about town. Yáñez also incorporates historical occurrences to stress the widespread anxieties sparked by Halley's comet in April
1910. Here the author appears to draw on period commentary from
Guadalajara's newspapers and broadsides on catastrophic prophecies linked
to Biela's Comet in 1899 as well as the later Halley.[60] Many Mexicans shared
these fears, as evidenced in the satirical engravings of awestruck crowds

Figure 32. The Whole World Will Be Burned to a Crisp, 1899, by José Guadalupe Posada. The text relates a European prediction for November 1899. The same illustration appeared in a 1910 broadside announcing Halley as "The Comet of the Centenary of Independence." In keeping with stereotypes about pious femininity, the woman in the center appears in a tremulous prayerful pose. From Julian Rothenstein, ed., *Posada*, 68.

GRAN COMETA Y QUEMAZON,

QUE MUY PRONTO SE VA A VER:

EL MUNDO SE VA A VOLVER TODITITO CHICHARRON.

¡El mundo se va á acabar! Nos vamos á tostar irremisiblemente! ¡Qué á tostar! Ya quisiéramos! ¡A volvernos ceniza!
Un gran astrónomo de Europa lo ha predicho últimamente; ya no para Noviembre del año de

1899, sino para el mes de Octubre próximo. Esta catástrofe horrorosísima la va á anunciar el cometa gigantesco que aparecerá en estos días; este astro malévolo será el que chocará con la tierra, haciendo mil averías, por

beneath streaking comets, earthquakes, volcanic eruptions, and flaming meteors. Perhaps the most arresting of these is a broadside that featured a print by Manuel Manilla and a short text that mocked the 1899 predictions.[61] Famed engraver José Guadalupe Posada produced many similar images, which first graced handbills for Biela and reappeared in 1910 when similar anxieties accompanied Halley.[62] Commentary on Madre Matiana and Posada's dramatic "Fin del Mundo" ("End of the World") appeared together in 1914 (see figure 15).

In a way Yáñez's novels simply incorporate longstanding assumptions about the prevalence of superstition as evidenced in these images. He also emphasizes these supposed omens in order to bolster his presentation of the Revolution as the true watershed of Mexican history. The Earth and the heavens, so to say, announce its arrival. The author surely learned from his elders, and he probably consulted the era's newspapers closely. Additionally he must have recalled a good deal from his own youth in the provincial city of

Guadalajara, where it just so happens that questions of natural disasters, ce-lestial portents, political rumor, and collective expiation were actually hotly debated issues.

In particular, as an eight-year-old in 1912, the author experienced the marked disruptions of life in Guadalajara from multiple earthquakes and resultant disputes concerning divine punishment, seismic forecasting, and popular prophecy. Yáñez essentially cites these disputes in *Al filo* when he names two priests involved in these controversies, José María Arreola and Severo Díaz, as he describes the fictional townspeople agonizing over Revolutionary upheaval and Halley's Comet. The real-life polemics these clerics took part in, however, centered on over one hundred earthquakes that unhinged Guadalajara between May and August 1912.[63] Most of them were small, but reporters described absolute panic during the most intense quakes. These moments brought crowds—and allegedly women in particu-lar—into the streets and plazas to beseech the Almighty on bended knee. In short, historical documents describe events similar to those depicted by Manilla and Posada. Few casualties resulted, but reporters noted consider-able architectural damage and thousands of residents camping in Guadalajara's parks for weeks amid angry demands for mass expiatory ac-tion. Many locals simply fled the city, as coolheaded merchants advertised camping equipment and dubious quake-sensing gadgets.[64] This memorable summer brought many of the cultural tensions Yáñez explored in his writ-ing to the fore. It bears emphasizing that the tempest of rumors, expiatory fervor, prophecy, panic, and recrimination took shape in the state capital. In other words, the "backwardness" that this author symbolically walled off in rural Mexico was, in fact, very much in evidence in the city where he grew up. What is indeed remarkable in the press coverage of this era is how the jumble of Revolutionary rumor, natural disasters, panicked piety, and acrimonious debate jockey for space on the printed page. In this regard, Yáñez's portrait of early twentieth-century life outside the centers of insur-gent mobilization may indeed capture how many Mexicans experienced the period.

The frenzy began 7 May 1912 and both the Catholic press represented by *El Regional*, and its secular rival, *La Gaceta de Guadalajara*, covered the events closely. Within days they were at odds over the appropriate collective response.[65] The first intense temblor occurred at approximately 6:33 a.m., sparking stunned, bleary-eyed households to spill out into the streets. Soon four even stronger afternoon quakes truly put the city on edge. Theaters shuttered their doors, workers abandoned shops and factories, and church-goers fled groaning temples. Rumors abounded of widespread death and destruction in neighborhoods as well as nearby towns, although journalists reported only a single fatality. Worried citizens converged on newspaper offices desperate for news. Stories circulated of noxious vapors escaping from nearby canyons and ongoing strange subterranean noises. Many residents recalled church bells clanging cacophonously as towers wobbled.[66]

The papers that week, and for much of the summer in fact, were crammed with additional apocalyptic news. On 8 August alongside the earthquake coverage, *La Gaceta* discussed riots in Mexico City sparked by news that a statue of the Virgin Mary in a neighborhood church had begun to move, raising the Christ child in her arms and rolling her eyes heavenward. When scores of believers converged on the church and police attempted to block access to the sanctuary a riot broke out in which officers killed two men.[67] On many days newspaper reports detailed battles in northern Mexico, which overshadowed accompanying seismic coverage.[68] Distraught, Guadalajara's devout residents began organizing processions. On 10 May, five hundred of them took to the streets at midnight, and many observers kneeled prayerfully as they passed.[69] On 14 May the Catholic daily *El Regional*'s editorial page claimed that God was clearly punishing Guadalajara for impious government and collective irreverence. Now, the paper declared, mass acts of desagravio were in order: the city had to atone for collective wrongs, blasphemies, and indifference.[70] Secular voices trying to dampen mounting anxiety stressed scientific explanations, the centrality of building design and construction, and the unpredictable nature of seismic events.[71] Government officials, for their part, refused to allow public processions. On 21 May Church leaders began three days of expiatory rituals structured to comply with legal restrictions, but many Catholics remained unsatisfied with this accommodation. They remained convinced that only large-scale, collective repentance would appease a justifiably angry God.[72]

Amid the rising tensions an array of opinions emerged. Secular journalists complained about numerous wild theories and catastrophic predictions. Broadsides hawked in poor neighborhoods reported (falsely) that the Ceboruco volcano in neighboring Nayarit had obliterated entire towns. Various astronomical explanations also circulated, and others spoke of destabilizing subterranean gasses, underground volcanoes, and weather-related causes.[73] Meanwhile business leaders cautioned that profound economic troubles loomed, as panic brought commerce to a standstill. The government called on the Mexican Institute of Geology, whose team arrived in Guadalajara on 16 May.[74] On several occasions they issued reports rejecting claims of imminent calamity, but it did little to calm the populace.

Soon popular earthquake prophets were having their day. A barrio dweller named Agapito Centeno gained notoriety for issuing earthquake predictions based on observed cloud formations. *La Gaceta* pronounced him a fraud but adopted him as a source of levity amid the prevailing angst.[75] In addition, the parish priest of Tlaquepaque, Vicente Michel, investigated a self-proclaimed prophet, who sought to coordinate acts of atonement with him. Apparently the presumptive seer caused quite a stir before judicial authorities arrested him.[76] News of these events travelled far, and a José Guadalupe Posada broadside reimagined his pronouncements, exaggerating the resulting panic.[77]

On several occasions from May through August of 1912, Guadalajara's residents thought that the rash of seismic activity had ebbed only to have it begin anew. And each new spurt of seismic activity ratcheted up tensions between the devout and secularists. After an intense quake on 25 May, frustrated Catholics besieged authorities demanding permission to organize processions. Rejected, they converged upon the city's shrine to the Virgin of Guadalupe, extracted the sacred image from the sanctuary, and defiantly marched down the street behind the national patroness. Two policemen blocked their path but stood aside after a fierce scolding from angry female marchers. But finally a squadron of gendarmes and mounted police broke up the procession and arrested a few fervent scofflaws.[78] By this time anonymous satirists had begun to mock pious hysteria in various broadsides, which Catholics added to their list of grievances.[79]

Early on the two priest-scientists mentioned by Yáñez in *Al filo* had emerged as frequently consulted specialists. However, Father Arreola achieved the most fame—followed by infamy—when he publicized very specific earthquake predictions. This phase of Guadalajara's earthquake panic, the last as it turns out, began after a strong quake on 19 July at 6:30 a.m. disgorged crowds of women in various states of undress into the streets, where they allegedly commenced praying intensely. Later that day Arreola issued his forecasts. Most troubling was his prediction of a truly ruinous earthquake for 6 August, which sparked an almost immediate revival of intense fears, angering civil authorities.[80] Clearly detecting the volatile state of public opinion, *La Gaceta* published Arreola's full prognostications on both the 22nd and 23rd.[81] A tense fortnight ensued during which detractors increasingly questioned Arreola's predictions. Mexico's Institute of

Geography, for example, issued a detailed critique of his methods.[82] One local businessman offered a 1,000-peso wager against the forecasts.[83] The Catholic newspaper, in turn, backed Arreola with renewed calls for organized expiation.[84] According to the secular newspaper, *La Gaceta*, a fresh batch of alarming broadsides further fueled popular unease, and all over town *las comadres* (older women) swapped scenarios of imminent destruction.[85] Makeshift attempts to bolster structures materialized throughout the city and few people slept indoors. All of the city's parks and plazas were full of temporary shelters.[86] *La Gaceta* reminded readers of how Halley's Comet had inspired false prophecies of 1910. Still Guadalajara remained apprehensive. Some residents managed to salt their anxiety with humor, attaching signs to improvised earthquake hovels like: "*Villa Sísmica*," "*El peor temblor*," "*Villa del Borregaje*," and "*Sal si puedes*" ("Seismic Village," "The Worst Temblor," "Rumor Town," and "Get Out if You Can"). Despite these jests, *La Gaceta* declared that irrational fears had become pervasive, stoked by outrageous rumors too numerous to list.[87]

Tensions, understandably, peaked as the predicted day of seismic reckoning neared. On the first of August residents took up positions in parks and plazas in anticipation of a strong 6 a.m. earthquake; it never occurred. Sensing a definitive shift, *La Gaceta* attacked *El Regional*, the "uneducated" classes, and those clamoring for processions. The paper also uncorked a newly dismissive attitude toward Arreola. No longer was he a scientist or geologist, as they referred to him previously; now he became a crackpot *loco de sotana* (lunatic in priest's attire). In a sense, these journalists began feminizing Arreola, lumping him together with *las comadres*. Still all of Guadalajara was on pins and needles the night of 5 August, although encampments enjoyed food tents, games, and lively music until about midnight. *La Gaceta* labeled the general panic "*Areolitis*." The priest, they complained, was just like the self-styled earthquake predictor and popular clown Agapito Centeno; the padre was merely concocting "*borregages*" ("outlandish rumors"), although Arreola had the "clerical" press to help broadcast his quake "dogma." Finally, 11 a.m. on 6 August arrived, and nothing happened. Guadalajara had become a national laughingstock, *La Gaceta* lamented.[88]

THE HOLY LAND

Memories of prophetic apprehensions at the dawn of the twentieth century and the unusual summer of 1912 remained vivid for Jalisco residents of

Yáñez's generation, and clearly they made a lasting impression on the author as well. One of his contemporaries, the local chronicler Zenaido Michel, a native of Chilquilistán, Jalisco, expressly linked unease related to comets, earthquakes, and end-of-the-world fears to local understandings of Madre Matiana's prophecies: "From the beginning of the month of November 1900 . . . the 'warnings' began to circulate that the end of the century would coincide with the end of the world. These beliefs had their basis in versions propagated by uneducated people, arguing that they had heard the prophecies of knowledgeable people, like la Madre Matiana and others, claiming that at the moment when the century came to a close a catastrophe would unfold during which fire would rain from the skies and on land a massive earthquake would ensue from which no living being would emerge."[89] Michel went on to specify that the terror generated by these predictions "produced among the inhabitants of the region an uncontrolled psychosis," which inspired huge numbers to attend the Virgin of Guadalupe's feast on the eve of 1900. In a similar fashion, journalists looking back on Guadalajara's revolutionary history from the 1960s recalled how the synergy of astral phenomena, wartime rumors, and the earthquakes of 1912 inspired many residents to consult the prophetess's predictions of national calamity.[90] Ironically, at more or less the same time these writers reminisced about Jalisco and Madre Matiana, Yáñez redeployed the pamphlet prophetess in *Las tierras flacas*.

As previously discussed, *Al filo del agua* and its artful presentation of regional traditionalism cemented Yáñez's reputation in Mexican letters. He never matched its elegance or popularity. While Yáñez ran the state of Jalisco for most of the 1950s Mexico's literary culture shifted. The nature of this swing is evident in the way *Al filo* ends as a new age of modern freedom symbolically dawns, while Carlos Fuentes's *Death of Artemio Cruz* (1962) encapsulates the era in the putrid body of his mortally ill and morally repellent protagonist.[91] Yáñez's upbeat interpretation of the Revolution had become quite dated. Pronounced cynicism and disenchantment characterized the era; thus a very different climate greeted the new novel. The author's effort to catch up with stylistic developments is painfully apparent: italicized flashbacks and interior monologues appear periodically, the point of view shifts abruptly, and misgivings suffuse the novel. Nonetheless, Yáñez maintained his stately tone, his folkloric treatment of popular culture, and his preference for iconic social "types." Lamentably he also filled the novel with rustic sayings plucked from Jalisco's vernacular. As a result *Las tierras* languishes in affectation. The author's enduring obsession with devout femininity, however, makes it worthy of our attention.

As we have seen, the gendering of piety and fanaticism represents a central facet of *Llama* and *Al filo*, but it is even more prevalent in *Las tierras*. In long passages Yáñez portrays Mexico and its national struggles through his fictionalized Madre Matiana's thoughts and feelings. Tacitly admitting that the Revolution was not a straightforward watershed moment, he sets the story in the turbulent 1920s. Still Yáñez remained committed to a bifurcated conception of history that pitted tradition against modernity. Throughout the narrative Madre Matiana remains the pivotal character. Her principles set the standard of popular integrity; her acquiescence to Revolutionary change represents the Mexican people's rejection of the old regime; and finally, her mutilation symbolizes the nation's transformational suffering. The legendary Matiana essentially serves as the author's muse, but he takes considerable artistic license. First he turns the figure of the urban convent seer of colonial tradition into a rural spiritual specialist beyond the reach of the institutional Church. He then combines her with the iconic (somewhat generic) folk figure of the peasant female healer, the curandera in Mexican parlance. As in many nationalist traditions—and as in *Llamas* and *Al filo*—Yáñez fuses custom, belief, and collective worldview with essentialized femininity. Mexico's difficult past and telluric problems scar Matiana's mind and body. In the new age men wield ideas, technology, and the means of change; and they fight each other over the nation. The curandera-seer bears witness and internalizes and embodies history. In the end, though, her main function is that of a symbolic victim. Her blood stains the threshold between past and present, and her anguished bitterness defines Mexico's troubled modernity.

In truth symbolic female characters that embody traditions and social pathologies are a ubiquitous presence in Yáñez's writing. In *Al filo* he identified Catholicism's oppressive hold on women as the fundamental cause of explosive social tensions in 1910. It is their pent-up desires and misdirected instincts that spark action as the nation's blunted natural energies mount behind a dam of Catholic repression. His eve-of-revolution story describes a society pushed to the brink of cataclysm primarily by suffocating fanaticism and priestly control of women's minds and bodies—the emblematic battleground of national identity. For Yáñez, it appears, the true modern society emerges only when women are won over and changed. *Al filo* also sketches the old regime's stifling of Mexican masculinity: an oppressive quasi-theocratic system in which priests cow the nation's men and exercise extraordinary control over wives and daughters. It is when female characters, driven to deviance or mental instability, act out that they unleash masculine rebellion. As in *Las tierras*, the definitive struggle takes shape as a symbolic act of male violence is perpetrated on a female character. In the earlier novel the long marginalized dissidents rise up and defeat the agents of obscurantism. Thus during *Al filo*, he lays out his argument for Revolutionary modernity: Catholic fanaticism kept Mexico in a backward state and drove the populace to destructive revolt, but a dawning new order allows men and women a fresh start "after the storm." The fratricidal violence is, by implication, attributed to centuries of psychological and emotional repression.

Las tierras offers a less optimistic view of Mexico's destiny, but it too is an exercise in memory making regarding the Mexican Revolution. Published fifteen years later, Yáñez essentially writes from within the state, providing an angst-ridden reformer's perspective. This novel represents an internal critique about Mexico's brusque modernization. The author has not given up on the promise of Revolutionary modernity, but he laments the failures that still hamper the nation's advancement. It would seem that the purifying tempest of *Al filo* missed the author's new allegorical locale. Like many towns in Mexico, Tierra Santa experiences "revolution from without."[92] The nation's heroic insurgency took place elsewhere, so that only embellished truths and outlandish hearsay reach the remote, barren plain. Each village in the region bears the name of a symbolic biblical town (e.g. Bethany, Jerusalem, Damascus, etc.). Despite change elsewhere, the cacique and his offspring exploit the region mercilessly and block change. The community lives addled by oppression, fanaticism, and ignorance. The author's version of Madre Matiana, the cantankerous heart of the people, serves as the vigilant liaison between a desperate populace and providence. As in many nationalist narratives, the emblematic representative of the past is present as the future dawns, although she must give way as the new order takes shape.

In these works, Yáñez gestures to actual problems Mexico faced in the wake of the Revolution. Many regions, like the imagined Tierra Santa, looked on the new government with suspicion.[93] How could they be sure new leaders would not be worse than the previous tyrants? As his characters wonder, once revolutionaries entered their villages, would they ever leave? What did the oft-celebrated concept of "progress" mean in concrete terms? And finally, what kind of future awaited them in an ostensibly irreligious modern social order? The novel's engagement with these concerns represents the most insightful facet of *Las tierras*, despite the fact that the author does so through stereotypical characterizations. Much of the story, though, comes across via melodrama.

Yáñez introduces the reader to the troubled national past through Rómulo, an indecisive, struggling peasant who represents the rural everyman.[94] Deep down he knows that society is corrupt, unjust, and backward, but he feels powerless. He recalls his dead grandfather, an honorable progressive leader of the region who eschewed superstition and passed on a deep love of the land. He also taught Rómulo the value of prudence, equality, and the rule of law. Clearly this ancestral memory represents Mexico's legacy of nineteenth-century liberalism. Nonetheless, Rómulo cannot live up to his grandfather's teachings. He lacks the strength of will and courage amid a revitalization of ignorance, superstition, and fear. Tierra Santa has fallen prey to brutal cacique rule on one hand and fanaticism on the other. As a result, Rómulo appears emasculated—without drive, courage, or authority—and on the verge of ruin. The local strongman, Don Epifanio, threatens to take his land after years of unsuccessful scheming to make Rómulo's daughter, Téofila, a member of his collection of concubines; he was only thwarted by her untimely death. Moreover, Rómulo's wife, Merced, a symbol of popular female frustration, excoriates her husband for his inaction and desperately seeks magical means of vengeance against the hated cacique.[95]

The reader only encounters Teófila's life through characters' recollections, and yet she provides the omnipresent dead-daughter backstory that fuels the narrative and strikes a crucial symbolic figure. Teófila represents both the principal values and the unrealized potential of the young nation. She symbolizes a lost opportunity to fuse the deeply authentic with the progressive and modern. Young, beautiful, and intelligent, she excelled in the stereotypically feminine realm of religion while also acquiring new faculties; she had embraced the socially useful modern woman's vocation of teaching. As Rómulo's tortured memories reveal, she knew Catholic prayers exceptionally well and gained admiration for her flawless recitations of the catechism. When she was old enough, Teófila left the region to study and become a schoolteacher; she returned to Tierra Santa as a skilled operator of a new sewing machine, purchased with great sacrifice by her parents. They desperately hoped that Teófila's newfound talents would revive the family's fortunes. In a remarkable passage, Yáñez describes Teófila's sewing through the lustful observations of Don Epifanio: she presents an awe-inspiring synergy of a blossoming young woman's feminine form and a modern technological marvel.[96] To her parents' dismay the cacique's infatuation resulted in relentless pressures and galling insinuations. They resist, particularly Merced, but with their land and livelihood hanging in the balance a debt-for-daughter arrangement seemed inevitable. Teófila, however, died of a mysterious affliction before the hated tyrant could sully her purity. Her memory plagues the characters, but her sewing machine plays a crucial role in the novel's denouement.

Thus Yáñez lodges a family tragedy at the center of his allegorical Holy Land. Essentially borrowing the storyline of official, post-Revolutionary nationalism, he alludes to the potential of Mexico's era of Independence and the abortive ascendency of nineteenth-century liberalism. He then sets up the advent of Porfirian authoritarianism and the stubborn resurgence of fanatical Catholicism as forces that were holding Mexico back. Yáñez's villain, Don Epifanio, even contemplates fabricating a miraculous Catholic apparition and pilgrimage devotion in order to exploit his credulous neighbors still further. Simultaneously the author "documents" latent, unsullied liberal principles and a glimmer of modernity's unrealized promise. As Rómulo faces mounting debts and the prospect of losing his land, he learns of mysterious outsiders seeking local partners willing to join an ambitious irrigation project. He fretfully mulls his options and recalls the ideals of his grandfather. In fact, it is through his bitter memories that the reader first encounters Madre Matiana and the depths of fanatical thinking that dominate the populace.

In Tierra Santa, masculine domestic norms have been subverted. Women control meaning and cultural practice, while men like Rómulo shamefully wallow on the margins. This has come about because a dysfunctional cacique patriarchy and pervasive ignorance reins. In essence, premodern authoritarianism and religious obscurantism hold peasant manhood hostage.

Yáñez dramatizes feminized fanaticism's chokehold on Tierra Santa through Rómulo's memories of Teófila's difficult birth.[97] As news spread that Merced had gone into labor, a flood of women descended on his ranch. Each brought bizarre local medicines, fetid poultices, bath concoctions, myriad candles, and miraculous images. Madre Matiana served as the unquestioned mistress of bizarre practices, transforming Rómulo's rustic home into a dark and gloomy space of female sovereignty and suffocating superstition. The women filled the room with billowing chili smoke to induce fits of coughing and thus stronger contractions. The hapless Rómulo fretfully recalled:

> The body of the poor Merced, and the room, was full of medals, images, scapulars, cords, little bags with relics from the saints inside, bones and hairs of ferocious animals, or magic herbs that they made her smell from time to time. The cord of San Blas was around her neck, and a ribbon, the measure of Santo Domingo of Silos's crook, was around her stomach. Occasionally Matiana made her kiss an image of San Ramón Nonato,[98] which she always carries on such occasions even when they progress easily . . . the good people had hauled everything holy or miraculous they had in their homes . . . many holy candles, every single one at the ranch, were burning in the room; in that light the women looked like a circle of witches.[99]

Anxiously Rómulo protested as Matiana kneaded Merced's belly as if it were maize dough, causing howls of agony. But the fierce midwife summarily banished him from the premises in a hail of humiliating insults and returned to her brutal labors. Finally Matiana and her assistants hoisted Merced from a beam and forced the infant's birth by pulling on a belt cinched around her abdomen. Rómulo, the man of the house, bitterly recalled dithering outside while listening to his wife's anguished screams.

In several succeeding passages Yáñez writes from Matiana's point of view, and he presents the mounting evidence of inevitable violent change and the embattled visionary's apprehensions. Ultimately Matiana's personal reflections reconstruct rural society's progress toward a breaking point and expose the healer-seer's limitations.[100] The initial setting for these revelations is a frightening apparition: an airplane—a harbinger of encroaching modernity—flies over Tierra Santa, terrifying the residents who are convinced that Satan has taken on a new dangerous guise. Naturally, they race to alert their aged paladin and priestess. As she interrogates her neighbors, the healer-seer slips into periods of trance-like remembrance (rendered in italics by the author). She attests to her intimate knowledge of the region's tragic history (the Teófila saga, and Epifanio's life of bottomless depravity) and her private trepidations and increasing fatigue:

> *I cannot reveal all the things I know and have seen, with my eighty-some*

*years weighing on me ... It is like the Devil knowing more because he's
old than because he is the Devil. ...*

*People, deep down: What complete hell! ... My eyes bring me suffer-
ing, they wear me out, when even against my will they scour, search, and
scrutinize the innermost nature of others ... Year in and year out, day
in day out, land, people, and defenseless animals are brought unarmed
before the mysteries of illnesses, violent storms, usury, all types of injustices, and all manner of evil ... There are not enough hands to fight all
these battles, or for that matter, to ward off Satan and the other malignant spirits constantly circling the plain, always gaining strength, pursuing souls ...*

*Some say I'm a witch, and there have always been those trying to
bring me down, to incite the innocent farmers against me: I've never
feared anyone, not even the Devil. But I'm tired now of walking alone,
accompanied only by my soul, on the pathways and trails at all hours of
the day and night; I'm tired of assisting those at death's door and standing vigilant over the dead; and I'm tired of standing up to the arrogant
[oppressors] ...*

*I live poorly. I ask no one for help, regardless of my struggles. I feel the
pain of others and forget my own. I do not brag about my successes or
suffer my failures. I oblige no one to call on me. However, it is just not in
me to forgive injustices. The punishments stemming from my judgments
come from above, which means that they are just, and even I can't stop
them, although many times I have wanted to. Vengeance of the witch,
say those feeling the pain. Our Lord knows this is not true. The people
know too.*[101]

As her interior monologues reveal, Yáñez refashioned Matiana into a different kind of popular avenger—one very distinct from the type deployed by his
satirical predecessors. She remains ignorant and superstitious, but her heart
beats for Mexico's humble poor. She represents the sum total of the comfort-
ing rituals, dogged solidarities, and moral principles that sustain them.
Nonetheless, as her musings show, the troubles of Tierra Santa—be they of
natural, supernatural, or human origin—are exhausting her and her arcane
knowledge. She is proud of her efforts to protect the lowly but feels over-
whelmed. The new threats to her community, she acknowledges, were mul-
tiplying and of a completely different order. In a huff she conveys her deep
misgivings to her neighbors, and thus publically points out sweeping

transformations on the horizon: "Satan in person or as an airplane, it is all the same: it must be another of his forms. Or worse, it is the Devil inside men, making them fly around in the air."[102]

In a sense Madre Matiana—the pamphlet prophetess anchored in Mexico's collective memory of baroque mystical piety—serves as the bellwether of collective destiny. In keeping with longstanding patterns of gendered storytelling, she can perceive but not inaugurate the coming Revolution; that is a man's job. As the subplots begin to converge, Yáñez further bolsters Matiana's symbolic connection to the Mexican nation. Again, the medium of literary revelation is her "memory;" and in this instance, he simultaneously "nationalizes" and "folklorizes" Matiana by revealing her youthful participation in the Tierra Santa's pastorelas. The aging healer-visionary and popular avenger, however, offers something none of the male characters can provide—a personal, intimately embodied connection to the nineteenth-century struggles of nationhood as well as traditional customs:

> *I almost never think of when I was a girl; I myself find it hard to believe that I ever was one.* . . . *When I didn't know anything about the dead, evils, cures, struggles, jealousies, threats, calamities, or schemes of the Devil—I don't think I even knew he existed. Here, it has always been the same, on the Plain* [i.e., Tierra Santa] . . . *Always* [I lived] *without venturing beyond the Plain, here I remained locked in. Not even in the time of the French* [i.e. the 1860s]. *I was still a child. They said I was born the year the Americans finally stole a great deal of land from us* . . . *Steal me? The French, make off with me? That is what my family feared* . . . *but what I remember most is the commotion I caused taking part in the Christmas performances.*[103]

The young Matiana, experienced a remarkable sense of empowerment as audiences, particularly men, responded to her instinctive embodiment of different characters. First she was a simple shepherdess, but later she became the embodiment of "Temptation," Eve, and the Virgin Mary—and the cardinal virtues and inveterate vices ascribed to each archetypal female figure:

> *In fact, I felt as if I truly was the actual Virgin* . . . *and hence it required little effort to appear full of grace, purity, and humility, because emerging from deep in my soul at that moment were the virtues, gestures, and the appropriate tone of voice. The same thing happened with Gila* [the

*shepherdess] and Temptation. No one taught me the movements and
other expressions that occurred to me; they welled up from deep springs,
flowing from my nerves and veins, thrilling me. As the Virgin, I felt I
would sacrifice myself in order to defend the Baby Jesus in my arms . . .
But the public, especially the men, liked to see me as Temptation. They
swore they had never seen anything like it.*[104]

Matiana was too young to understand the simultaneously disdainful and
desirous utterances her portrayal of the licentious allegorical character inspired, "tart, minx, tramp, slut . . ." In fact, although she sensed their meaning she was afraid to ask, but she mostly longed to know why "as they spoke
them they seemed to name something bad that was also pleasurable, desirable." Thus Matiana realized she was enveloped in the murky yet intoxicating
realm of prohibitions and passions. As she recalled:

*Of one thing I had no doubts: whatever was going on, I was the cause of
the thoughts, sufferings, and appetites reflected in the eyes, the open
mouths, and the constant agitation of lips, hands, and entire bodies . . . I
can't deny that I liked the feeling of causing all the feigned revulsion and
contortions. God forgive me, but the words they spoke harried me like
biting mosquitos; or better yet, like moths stubbornly flying around and
around a flame, whether it burns them or not. That is how I became a
seer, reading their intentions in their expressions; guessing the meaning
of their words. Soon they started saying: she is a witch, and started calling me Madre Matiana.*[105]

In crafting Matiana's memories and backstory, Yáñez essentially roots his central character at the allegorical frontier of the nation's past, present, and future.
Ironically, or perhaps deliberately, Yáñez's synchronization of the prophetess's
"birth" with the U.S.–Mexican War, and his presentation of her life experience
as a metaphor for the nation's fraught evolution between the 1840s and the
1920s, uncannily resonates with the actual history of the Matiana phenomenon. (It is indeed possible that he researched the history of the prophecies.)
However, the author goes further than making her a mere metaphor for the
nation. In charting her youthful theatrical exploits and elderly apprehensions
he makes Matiana the veritable embodiment of standard tropes of female representation and a stand-in for the national spirit. On the cusp of womanhood,
she (the daughter of national humiliation and foreign defilement) signifies the

unknowing personification of fertile yet vulnerable possibilities, primordial desires, and male delusions of possession. In her old age she represents faith, justice, history, superstition, and the very soul of the Mexican people. Essentially, Yáñez cast her as the epitome of both poles of Mexican popular femininity, as represented in the nation's costumbrista tradition: in her youth she was la china; and over time she became la beata.

Not surprisingly, Yáñez deploys a symbolic male figure to ignite revolution in Tierra Santa. For this task he plucks his change agent from the stock pile of biblical archetypes: Miguel Archangel (the commander of God's armies), a disinherited, bastard son of the feared cacique—Don Epifanio—returns to Tierra Santa calling himself Jacobo (the patriarch who forges the Chosen People's covenant with God).[106] Exile and experience beyond Tierra Santa had transformed him, and he returns determined to liberate his homeland. In other words, Miguel comes to drag the backward community into the light of modernity. Bringing the Christmas narrative symbolism full circle, he announces himself at Tierra Santa's pastorela performance, an event cynically exploited by his father. Jacobo and his men stage the epic battle between Satan and Saint Michael, and much of the populace witnesses a new kind of spectacle. Yáñez entwines the action scenes of Catholic folklore with allusions to the looming battle between Mexico's old and new order. Jacobo dramatically defeats evil and awes the crowd with lighting effects; but at the end of the show he reveals that they have simply witnessed the marvels of electricity.[107] Thus modernity announces itself at the heart of traditional ritual, and the cacique's spell is broken. On another level, Jacobo—the emissary of modernity—unveils his powers in this deeply traditional and authentically Mexican cultural performance, albeit with a Revolutionary twist.

The remaining chapters slowly build to the violent climax. Merced seeks exemplary punishment of the hated cacique. Rómulo and other men join the Revolutionary cause. Madre Matiana, crucially, supports Jacobo; thus the symbolic soul of popular culture gives her blessing to the new order. However, there is no place for her in the new Mexico. In the battle that ensues, the cacique's goons gouge out her eyes, leaving the onetime seer's eyeballs dangling from gaping bloody sockets while she wails in agony.[108] Jacobo ultimately triumphs and the cacique and his minions perish, but the community's visionary guardian is left sightless and bitter. No longer can she see and speak for Tierra Santa, and no one takes her place.

Las tierras is a narrative of the disruptive coming of modernity to traditional Mexico; however, Yáñez closes the novel on a somber, cautionary note.

Victory achieved, the new leaders lose interest in the uneducated people of Tierra Santa. Madre Matiana, and the traditions she symbolizes, have been neutralized. Disfigured but not dead, she disappears into the symbolic darkness of her home—a space that previously served as the community's herbarium, pharmacy, and devotional storehouse. In short, Matiana, and all she stands for, is banished from the public sphere. Electricity arrives, but no concerted effort is made to implant truly emancipating ideas or practices. Moreover, in the wake of violent change, a popular devotion emerges surrounding Teófila's sewing machine. Locals allege that it works miracles by association with the saintly dead girl, and they inaugurate a veritable pilgrimage tradition to the laborsaving appliance (a contraption emblematic of modern femininity). Fanaticism, as it were, endures in new guises. The Mexican Revolution, Yáñez implies, failed in perhaps the most fundamental sense: the agents of modernity, lacking patience and sensitivity, missed the opportunity to transform popular culture. Old ways endure and mix with the new in discomfiting fashion: Madre Matiana still haunts the nation.

Conclusion

Mexico's Matianas

HOW OFTEN IN NARRATIVE TRADITION HAVE EMBLEMATIC WOMEN borne the figurative assaults of social change or embraced the ultimate sacrifice for humanity? Likewise, how often have Latin America's writers and artists encapsulated the struggles of el pueblo in female suffering? Thus, although gruesome and in a way disheartening, Madre Matiana's violent battering and metaphorically freighted blinding offers a fitting end to this investigation of the seer's role in Mexican history. Stepping back from Yáñez's allegorical angst during the 1960s and pondering *Las tierras flacas*'s place in the wider Matiana phenomenon, it appears that staging the silencing of the seer was precisely what the author intended. As long as the legendary female figure personifying popular Catholic custom and irrationality retained both vision and voice, Mexico remained the prisoner of tradition. The maiming is also appropriate for another reason: Yáñez, by all appearances, was the last opinion-maker to engage the prophetess's history with care. Like few others, he seems to have researched the pamphlet prophetess's history and mulled her shifting role in popular culture. As *Las tierras* ends he quarantines her in the past, although he allows that her influence lingers on.

In doing this, Yáñez paradoxically brought Matiana back into the discussion of Mexico's "national problems." She apparently remained of interest to him years later, because on 11 November 1976 he gave a lecture in Guadalajara titled "La Madre Matiana y la comunidad" ("Madre Matiana and the Community") at a conference organized by the Mexican Institute of Social Security (IMSS).[1] Presumably it addressed aspects of the novel and the character's symbolic importance in Mexican culture, but no record of his presentation endures. In reality, Yáñez's literary depiction of Madre Matiana's downfall only commented on a fait accompli: she was already banished to a metaphorical scrap heap as far as most Mexicans were concerned.

If you inquire about Madre Matiana today in Mexico, few recall any knowledge of the once-polemical visionary figure; most proclaim complete ignorance. A handful offer hazy memories of stories told by grandparents or assert that she is just a spooky figure akin to the boogeyman in North American folklore, or the *el coco* in many Spanish-speaking countries. Every so often over the last few decades a journalist dabbling in historical curiosities references the prophetess, or employs her in a quip on some happening deemed inexplicable. Usually they offer only hasty snippets of the Matiana visions and equivocal stabs at her origins, if they bother at all.[2] In perhaps the most surprising example, one writer invoked the prophetess in reference to the mysterious increase in home-run hitting at the beginning of the 2006 professional baseball season.[3] Occasionally, however, an inquisitive reporter digs deeper and provides a somewhat accurate sketch of her history. Such was the case of Armando Fuentes Aguirre, a reporter at Guadalajara's *El Informador*, who did not mention his sources but attributed Matiana's initial emergence to broadsides published in 1856. He also credited her subsequent fame to conservative agitation against liberal reforms enshrined in the Constitution of 1857 and later Catholic efforts to revive her prophecies amid twentieth-century church-state tensions.[4]

Remarkably the prophetess retains a toehold in the realm of humor, holding a position that remains vaguely reminiscent of her starring satirical role in previous generations. For example, an enterprising Querétaro artist named Erik de Luna makes creative use of her spooky reputation. He sells postcards and his own version of Lotería (Bingo) featuring *calavera* (skeleton) cartoons commemorating the mordant nicknames—naturally, all female—that Mexicans employ for death. Hence alongside "La Chupona" ("The Sucking One"), "La Dientona" ("The Toothy One"), and "La Descarnada" ("The Fleshless One"), he includes La Madre Matiana.[5] De Luna was not the first to deploy her as a stand-in for death; at some point in the mid-twentieth century she began appearing in this fashion.[6] The image he offers is a calavera headshot with a sparse toothy grin and a traditional indigenous head wrap restraining a full head of hair lined with gray. He also endows her with drooping cheekbones evocative of an old crone's saggy features. Dangling from nonexistent ears, skull pendants accentuate a gallows-humor take on Matiana's modest social origins: she represents a popular avatar of death—mortality as an indigenous *viejita* (little old lady).

Figure 33. The prophetess in present-day Mexico, "La Madre Matiana," Erik de Luna, postcard, 2005. Madre Matiana appears as an elderly indigenous woman against a backdrop of ancient Mesoamerican geometric motifs. She is a mere minor pop-culture figure, and her connection to historical controversies and politics has been largely forgotten. Courtesy of Erik de Luna.

Beyond the association of the prophetess with humble social groups and elderly femininity, the artist evokes no knowledge of the visionary's complex past or preceding appropriations of her persona. His choice to make her indigenous and enshrine her in the calavera tradition, nonetheless, suggests that Matiana's indelible *mexicanidad* endures even if most Mexicans remain ignorant of her past incarnations.

As stated at the outset, it is not possible to uncover the full "truth" about Madre Matiana. The working assumption throughout this study has been that the prophecies and prophetess herself represent politically motivated apocrypha devised to influence the contentious disputes that marked Mexico's early national history. Given the absence of evidence regarding the seer before 1847, and the fact that the prophecies' tone is more in tune with mid-nineteenth-century conflicts than colonial mysticism, it is most likely that the Matiana phenomenon began as a bit of mystical fiction of instrumental inspiration. This should not, however, diminish her importance even though the writing of Mexico's history has long been marked by a tendency to elide, or at least greatly underestimate, the importance of popular religious belief and practice. Under no circumstances should she be caricatured as a mere example of the clergy's manipulation of the populacho (riffraff) and reflexively dismissed. Moreover, her origins became irrelevant once the visionary narrative and Matiana's persona secured a niche in the Mexican consciousness. Once a significant cross-section of the population ascribed social significance to her "revelations" and conferred meaning on her as a symbol of female piety or fanaticism, Madre Matiana became quite real in a manner her initial creators probably never imagined. This is particularly true considering the issues projected on her: cultural and political legitimacy, Catholicism's role in the nation, popular custom as the wellspring of Mexican identity and the cause of intractable backwardness, the feminization of devout identities, and debates about women's role in the public sphere. There was certainly nothing fictitious about the importance of these topics in Mexico's first 150 years of independent existence. Moreover, I contend, Matiana's endurance and cycles of reinterpretation stem from the festering nature of these matters long after the context of her fabrication became irrelevant. As long as Mexicans struggled to accommodate devout femininity and popular religiosity within their notions of a modern nation and society, Matiana mattered.

The impetus for this study, therefore, emerged from an initial interest in historical polemics and expressive conventions related to religion and gender. Over time it gained momentum because Madre Matiana leads to important, yet often overlooked, corners of history; for example, nineteenth-century almanac marketing, as well as the complexities of satirical expression. Two overlapping dynamics stand out about the prophecies and their visionary protagonist—the evolving history of interpretation and acts of outright appropriation. For the sake of clarity, this study emphasized the former during the nineteenth century and the latter in the twentieth century. When looking over the entire Matiana phenomenon, however, they should be considered together. Another way to think of this is that all reinterpretation involves a degree of appropriation, and appropriation, in the most obvious sense, represents a particular form of reinterpretation.

Beginning with the very first pamphlets, the invention of Madre Matiana represents an act of appropriation and rhetorical impersonation. Although it cannot be absolutely determined, there was most likely a man, or group of men, who felt that their pamphlet would have the greatest impact if voiced in a humble, female, pious register. In concocting the visionary narrative they reached into the narrative traditions and historical memory of colonial female mysticism in order to create a composite seer, which they then discursively inhabited and used to address the mounting polemics of the day. They selected long-standing, specific hagiographic tropes and practices that activated notions of feminine affinities for the state of collective morality and religious ideals about the ordering of human society. Of particular import was the central role ascribed to fervent Eucharistic devotion. The Blessed Sacrament's connection to notions of social solidarity, exceptional female piety, Church infallibility, and divinely ordained political order gave the prophecy narrative its grounding in Catholic teachings and religious gender norms. Most likely Madre Matiana's creators hoped to influence popular groups, and they were probably also targeting devout women.

Moreover, it is also important to stress that in analyzing Matiana's many incarnations we are sampling different streams of nationalist expression. In each instance the prophetess and the narratives attached to her carry the nation-building ideals and historical assumptions of distinct groups. It is important to remain attentive to how women commonly serve as symbolic markers and embody the purported values or spirit of the nation in each case. As Nira Yuval-Davis points out, female characters in nationalist texts are for the most part carefully "positioned." All of the cases examined in this study function as identity narratives, which outline the boundaries of what is "Mexican," who belongs to the collective, and what beliefs and social norms are "authentic." Madre Matiana repeatedly serves as the emblematic sentinel patrolling these limits. Ironically, in this light sternly reactionary, apocalyptic inflations of the prophecies and irreverent satirical appropriations of the seer use her in fundamentally the same way. Matiana identifies enemies, frauds, fools, apostates, and traitors.

Appropriating the popular female mystical voice in this context makes sense. Matiana's creators were not trying to win an intellectual debate (that was taking place in other forums); they were issuing a pious, emotional call to arms. Given what we know about the history of prophetic movements, this mode of expression was grounded in a tradition of narrative strategies of sociopolitical critique. At a very basic level, using a female figure to proclaim that liberalism threatened to dissolve the foundations of Christian order gave this argument greater power. Most likely Matiana's inventers hoped their pamphlet would have an immediate impact. When they spoke of a climactic bloody conflict and the reestablishment of Catholic order and pious harmony in a year ending in the number eight, they probably hoped to witness a conservative restoration in 1848. However, as far as the historical record tells, the Valdés y Redondas edition had little impact. Madre Matiana simply did not capture Mexicans' attention in her first decade. As with so much regarding the visionary's legacy, it probably had to do with timing and a lack of promotion. Some important players, though, evidently did notice her.

Fellow printers, like Luis Abadiano y Valdés, just a few doors away, and Manuel Murguía, the consummate almanac peddler, clearly mulled over the Matiana narrative during that ten-year span. At some point these entrepreneurs arrived at a similar conclusion: the latter half of 1857 represented an auspicious moment for reprinting and publicizing the prophecies. As detailed here at some length, the reason for this development was probably the mounting polarization occasioned by radical liberal ascendency in 1854 and 1855, and the drafting of a new federal constitution in 1857. Perhaps more important, however, was the frantic conservative printing campaign that sought to convince Mexicans to reject these developments. This multifaceted publication blitz, I have argued, became increasingly shrill and apocalyptic following the liberal charter's promulgation in February 1857 and its constitutionalization of recent laws that threatened the Catholic Church's sociocultural influence and economic foundations. Particularly galling for conservatives was what they viewed as a sinister marginalization of religion in public life. As the middle ground evaporated that summer and fall, newspapers spoke openly of looming civil war, and Madre Matiana once again enunciated her call for repentance and a repudiation of liberalism and its totemic manifestations (constitutions and legal codes). This time the populace apparently took note. The dual manner of her reappearance likely had much to do with her impact at this crucial juncture. In short, her appearance in both pamphlet and almanac formats secured Matiana's niche in the national psyche for the next century.

Perhaps the Abadiano pamphlet of 1857 should not be considered a reinterpretation. The press merely copied the Valdés y Redondas publication. However, their energetic marketing of the prophecies for a handful of months leading up to a brutal war surely had much to do with Matiana's wider impact. It is impossible to determine this printer's intentions with certainty, but documentation from the Librería Abadiano indicates that they manned a node of the conservative Catholic intellectual community and publically championed conservative causes. In addition, they depended on a traditional model of Church-centered print commerce. In other words, their ideological and economic interests meshed with Madre Matiana's condemnation of liberal reform.

For at least a handful of months in late 1857, Mexicans could purchase either the Abadiano pamphlet or Murguía's Matiana almanac. The latter's inclusion of the prophecies in his *Calendario nigromántico* expanded the seer's reach even further, but by virtue of its distinct presentation it certainly qualifies as an act of reinterpretation, even though he too essentially reprinted the original text. Murguía, though, decided that Madre Matiana belonged in the almanac subgenre of ghost stories, alchemy, and occult-themed storytelling.

Matiana's appearance in this venue may seem innocuous, but it arguably had significant consequences. As a cheap, market-sensitive stepchild of Mexico's "cultural press," the almanac genre represented a crucial space where writers and editors conjured a fragmented portrayal of Mexican cultural identity for popular consumption that was akin to popular magic lantern slideshows of the era. They also celebrated a cast of imagined national types and responded annually to perceived consumer demand. In this context, Madre Matiana stood with la recamarera, la coqueta, la casera, and other costumbrista figures, and thus entered the pantheon of stock Mexican characters. In part this can be explained by her ability to fill a void in the era's gallery of social types. She fit the role of the elderly devout woman of fervent faith and zealous allegiance to the Catholic Church: the beata. Individually each almanac functioned like a magic lanternslide, capturing an imagined slice of Mexican life. Thus she and her fantastical story represent a visualization of the most intensely devout segment of society, a group caricatured as elderly, fanatical, and female. As noted, although equally "Mexican," Madre Matiana fit in the larger panorama of nineteenth-century almanac representation as the antithesis of la china—the young, mestiza object of masculine national desire.

It is important to keep in mind that amid the extraordinary polarization of 1857 the *Profecías de la Madre Matiana* could be consumed from divergent interpretive positions. On one level, archconservative readers and those given to mystical prophecy could approach them at face value—as actual colonial premonitions of nineteenth-century events and divine portents that described the eventual triumph of Catholicism against modern error. This seems to be more in tune with the stand-alone political pamphlet produced by the Librería Abadiano. On another level, Mexicans could enjoy them as down-market fiction or as a costumbrista sketch. This flexibility probably has much to do with why Madre Matiana endured. Interestingly, in the decade following 1857 the seer appeared in another pamphlet (1861) very much like the previous printings, and ultimately as the titular figure of an almanac named in her honor (1867). Of course, the tensions and enmities of 1857 were very much alive after ten years of bloodshed and destruction. As another year ending in the number eight approached, the prophetess once more became particularly marketable. The eponymous calendario, like its predecessor, tacitly presented Matiana as legend rather than divine prophet. Arguably, appearing ensconced in these distinct platforms made her palatable to those who read them out of devout concern, and those, like Guillermo Prieto, who read them for "fun."

The decade from 1857 to 1867 was thus the formative juncture for Madre Matiana's eccentric legacy. As evident in liberal journalistic sources, from the 1860s until the Mexican Revolution she functioned as a deprecatory trope. Editorialists used her to critique "alarmism," as a slight when maligning rival political analyses, and as a gendered slur attached to ideas, actions, and groups deemed "reactionary." Simultaneously she also served as a metaphor for backwardness and irrationality. Critics of the Church referred to Catholicism as the "noisy religion of Madre Matiana," while others made offhand comments invoking the prophetess when dismissing outmoded ideas and customs. In the 1880s, the most uncompromising segment of the "politically Catholic" populace adopted the prophetess as a standard bearer of the new spirit of religious militancy. The women of the Adoratrices Perpetuas Guadalupanas successfully established a new religious order, seemingly centered on Matiana's expiatory prescriptions. Dionisio de Jesús María's promises to publish an expanded version of the mystical narrative for the new generation give a glimpse of the kinds of individuals engaged in this process. Alongside them, influential clergymen were similarly interested in the pamphlet prophetess as a symbolically Mexican figure to issue the clarion call of Catholic resurgence.

However, the most complete portrait of the seer's revalorization in these circles resides in Luis G. Duarte's 1889 book, a publication sanctioned by important Church-affiliated institutions like the Círculo Católico, the archdiocesan curia of Mexico City, and the Catholic press. This author's intervention represents a forceful appropriation of the original narrative and a recasting of its protagonist as the local voice of the Church's international struggle. By grafting the Matiana visions to right-wing conspiracy theory and apocalyptic Marianism from Catholic Europe, Duarte changed the tenor of the seer's message and reinterpreted Mexico's nineteenth-century travails. Although echoes of reactionary constructions of history emanating from France were present in the original pamphlets, Duarte's *Profecías* emphasized these connections at a much more explicit, detailed level. Previously the narrative underscored how local actions angered God and how the nation could regain divine favor. Duarte offers a much grander explanation for the nation's troubles. He argues that Mexico represented the American theater of the global struggle between divine order and demonic heresy. In this light, all of the nation's nagging problems and difficult post-Independence history represented "proof" of the nation's victimization at the hands of a satanic scheme to foment Protestant North American avarice and French ideological contagion.

Duarte also reshaped the Matiana persona. No longer was she merely a figment of an imagined baroque femininity and mythic pious utopia. *Profecías* presented her as one of a select cadre of visionary messengers speaking out against impiety across Catholic Christendom. Matiana became part of an illustrious sisterhood: she had been selected by the Virgin Mary from among all Mexican women to help combat the devil's treachery and halt his New World Jacobins. Moreover, surveying trends throughout the Catholic world, Duarte seized the opportunity to hold forth on the singular importance of devout women as the expiatory foot soldiers of Catholic revitalization. Thus, in a sense, Matiana now bore a two-fold significance in Mexico's conservative Catholic nationalism: she represented the nation in the pantheon of Marian shield bearers, reaching back to the most famous sainted visionaries, like Catherine of Siena; and simultaneously, she was the exemplar of humble and vigorously devout Mexican womanhood. In other words, she served as the screen upon which Duarte projected a patriarchal pious militancy on the nation's devout female populace.

It also bears noting that this ambitious author aimed his interpretation of the Matiana story at a different audience. In the past, print entrepreneurs crafted pamphlets and almanacs for a general audience. Duarte, in contrast, labored to offset the association of the prophecies and the seer with popular superstitions and to make Matiana and her message more attractive to middle- and upper-class Catholics—the sector of society who read Catholic newspapers and purchased polemical conservative books. He accomplished this feat by redrawing Matiana as if she was interchangeable with her sainted European counterparts, while ascribing all that sounded farfetched or superstitious in the original pamphlets to the ignorance of Madre Guerra, the humble nun and alleged informant who recounted the seer's life and visions. Duarte's interpretation proved durable and influential. Copies of his book were still being advertised nearly twenty years after its publication, and a pair of pamphlets—published in 1910 and 1917 respectively—offered little more than an update of his central thesis.

Social revolution in the early twentieth century, however, catalyzed a distinctly different phase in the Matiana phenomenon. First, it led to a sharp spike in interest for the prophetess's visions of national calamity. Real fears that the expanding conflict represented the definitive bloody upheaval emerged in new and old versions of the prophecies. Such was the impact of Matiana's renewed fame that some observers associated her visions specifically with the Revolutionary period. Looking back in the 1940s, Jesuit scholar Carlos M. de Heredia claimed that many people debated the predictions during the time of Francisco Madero (roughly 1910–1913).[7] Newspapers and broadsides at the time linked the popular clamor surrounding the prophecies to the U.S. occupation of Veracruz in 1914. Likewise, Agustín Yáñez's literary exploration of the nation's difficult Revolutionary transformation evolves as an allegory of the nation's agonizing exit from an era dominated by Madre Matiana.

As underscored in the beginning of part II, the new phase of interpretation ushered in by the Mexican Revolution featured an increasing emphasis on the seer's persona as well as the aspects of popular culture she ostensibly embodied, and a gradual waning of interest in the original narrative and the actual prophecies. In the three cases detailed here—the satirical newspaper called *La Madre Matiana*, the photographs of Lola Álvarez Bravo, and Agustín Yáñez's *Las tierras flacas*—I stressed the symbolic positioning of the Matiana figure as well as the dynamics of appropriation employed by the actors involved.

In *La Madre*, humor and satirical reformism depend on the mischievous placement of the pamphlet prophetess relative to various satirical targets. At times the newspaper's namesake embodies lo mexicano. In other instances comedic critique emerges from staged contradictions: the fanatical Matiana makes more sense and is more concerned for the nation's well-being than the individuals charged with public authority. Moreover, these irreverent journalists used their emblematic namesake to delineate and transgress borders. Thus the seer's beata-like rants and fanatical nonsense shatter the proprieties of language and logic, but simultaneously spotlight corruption and lies. Perhaps most importantly, this Matiana violates political gender norms: she is a rash *fanática* holding forth in the public sphere. In a sense the satirical premise of the entire journalistic endeavor resides in the effort to police evolving modern mores with a female zealot plucked from the past.

These complexities of female religiosity are also present in the other cases. In Lola Álvarez Bravo's photograph named after the seer, the compositional placement of devout femininity makes the image work. Again, the trick depends on satirical paradox. The Matiana mannequin is the central figure, and she serves as the image's titular protagonist; yet the picture conveys her irrelevance. The pious sanctimony and backward fanaticism she represents is absurd in modern public settings. Likewise, in *Las tierras flacas*, Madre Matiana serves as the central symbolic character and guiding plot device. Her backstory defines the watershed moments of Mexico's troubled history, and Yáñez repeatedly employs her to "guard" various symbolic realms. Furthermore, it is the climactic violation of her body (the symbolic blinding of the seer) that signals the point of no return—the unraveling of tradition and the transition to Revolutionary modernity in Mexico.

In discussing these acts of appropriation I underscored their similarity to other instances where Latin Americans indulged in the satirical impersonation of maligned social groups and popular cultural practices. As in these cases, while "playing the prophetess" they were also simultaneously fabricating "authentic" identities and norms of national expression. Regarding the newspapermen at *La Madre*, in the stereotyping and performance of la *fanática* we can perceive an effort to make Mexicans see themselves and the nation in the legendary prophetess. By extension, of course, these journalists sought to identify themselves as the authentic voice of the people through the appropriated visionary. In deploying her in a derisive comedic project they sought to cultivate solidarity through collective laughter at the national "self" and "our" customs. At a deeper level, this newspaper carried out a didactic project designed to teach new norms and maintain others in the theatrical space of journalistic farce. In many ways Álvarez Bravo did much the same through her photographic images. Both she and journalists at *La Madre* provided repeated reminders of the constructed nature of their endeavors. The reporters and cartoonists were clearly irreverent men, not female mystics. Likewise, in Álvarez Bravo's *La Madre Matiana* the glaring youth in the photograph reminds viewers that an act of staged representation is in process.

Finally, each of these cases attempts to assimilate the authenticity that associations linked to devout femininity via impersonation. It is part of a broader discursive maneuver to commandeer the popular so as to control the high ground of nationalist representation and thus effect change. This comes through most clearly in Agustín Yáñez's novel. He imbues the nation's visionary with deep historical significance and social power. Then he proceeds to think and speak for her; and perhaps more importantly he writes her memories, or rather, the nation's memories. All the while the novel plots Madre Matiana's demise, even though Yáñez laments the failure to truly replace her. Ironically, even blind and figuratively banished the seer still holds the key to the nation's shortcomings. Looking back over the seer's wider legacy reveals that the author perhaps felt he had to approach her existence in this manner. As with the other Matiana interpreters and impersonators, Yáñez fit the emblematic fanática into the nation—albeit uncomfortably— before dispatching her. Still the cultural traditions she represented could never be wholly expunged from the national psyche. If they could, the symbolic structure that sustains his insights about the nature of Mexican history and culture would disintegrate. In reality Madre Matiana made *his* visions possible.

Appendix

THE PROPHECIES OF MATIANA,

A Servant from the Convent of San Gerónimo of Mexico,

Concerning the Events that Will Come to Pass in Said Capital

Written by the Mother María Josefa de la Pasión de Jesús, Nun of

aforementioned Convent, in compliance with the Decree of 18 January 1837,

Pronounced by the Vicar of Nuns[*]

Mr. Vicar of the Convents of Nuns, don Juan Manuel Irisarri,

María Josefa de la Pasión de Jesús, religiosa of the convent of Our Father San Gerónimo of this capital of Mexico, and under your lordship's supervision, I promptly and gladly obey your express order of January of the current year 1837, directing that I write a full account of the revelations that Señora Matiana del Espíritu Santo had at this convent, which were communicated to me by her two confidants, doña Francisca Montes de Oca and Señora Paula Ramírez.

They may seem the stories of crones and the illusions of demented women, or dreams; but be that as it may, I must attempt with the greatest effort to fulfill the destiny that God Our Lord has brought me to this holy house through his ultimate Divine Providence and great mercy. Our Lord Jesus Christ and his Most Holy Mother always choose weak, low instruments and humble souls for their great works, and hence it should not come as a surprise that what I am about to declare was previously in the hands of servants and now emerges from a nun, the most undignified and worst one inhabiting the Earth.

---

[*] *Las Profecías de Matiana*, 1861, UCBL. The following represents my translation of the Matiana prophecies from this pamphlet. I have tried to retain its original style as best as possible. In the original text some information appeared in footnotes. In order to provide greater clarity, I have placed them within the text in brackets. My own editorial insertions are footnoted at the bottoms of the pages.

The Chronicle of Señora Matiana del Espíritu Santo

The venerable Mother Sebastiana Maya, religiosa of the convent of San Juan de la Penitencia of this city, brought in to her convent a young girl of only a few years to be her companion. They called her Matiana, and she came from Tepotzotlán. Mother Sebastiana had a brother, a priest of the order of San Diego of Mexico, who was called Father Miguel Maya, and she entrusted him with the spiritual instruction and direction of Matiana. She proved the perfect disciple of these two teachers, because they say that when she left San Juan she already performed miracles, and while she was there too.

Due to the death of Madre Sebastiana, Matiana left San Juan and entered the convent of the Incarnation, and while she was there, it is said, the Holy Virgin Mary ordered her to come to San Gerónimo. Immediately she obeyed and came, and entered as did all the servants. Mother Catarina de San Ignacio Villajare—the one that was demented, and due to her illness ate more than was normal—took her on. Matiana sought to avoid incurring any costs for her patroness, and selflessly used her own food and salary to cover the costs of Madre Catarina. She had nothing more than the clothes she wore. She subsisted on stale bread, which she received as alms from other servants.

Here in the convent there had been founded a sodality whose memory had almost been extinguished. Matiana revived and expanded it, even outside of the cloister. Its members exerted themselves in acts of charity, especially with sick and dying women. Matiana also stressed humility to such an extent that nuns and laywomen swept the convent and the waste drains. Even the prioress complied with everything Matiana said. Such was her obedience that the ladies of her time were greatly impressed and treated her with great respect. She told them their futures, they attested.

There was no shortage of the shadowy murmurs and derision that servants of God always suffer: regardless, Matiana never lost her spirit for igniting flames of divine love in all the people that knew her. I believe that her doctrines bore fruit for several residents of this holy house, because she worked as best she could with nuns and laywomen. She excelled in humility, silence, avoiding speech with those nearby, and spending nights in prayer. She made two women, both beyond their thirties, her companions and confidants, and she taught them and led them along her path. One was doña Francisca Montes de Oca; the other, named Maria Paula, was of Indian nobility. She held spiritual meetings with two saintly priests, Father Miguel Maya and Father Joaquin

Rojas, both dieguinos.* The honorable Matiana, however, was the most blessed, and she began to enjoy the great grandeurs of God Our Lord, who manifests his glories in all times, as shall be seen in what follows.

While Matiana was cloistered, the Holy Virgin told her in one of her moments of rapture: "I have brought you here to be my ambassadress with the nuns. Tell them that I have chosen this convent so that from here will emerge the third foundation of the Placation of the Sacramental Christ,† which will take shape in my Sanctuary of Guadalupe because it is the place destined for the appeasement of the Blessed Sacrament. They will not believe; they will scoff. They will call it the foundation of lies, fables, dreams, illusions, and much laughter; but if the nuns do not accept it, I will go bestow this grace on those who least deserve it." That is how Our Lady expressed it, with these exact words.

It was also told to Matiana that the kingdom in the time of the upcoming foundation would suffer extreme poverty; and Our Lady said that when they dig the foundations of the new convent a well or a spring of oil will be found miraculously emerging so that this oil can be the source of the wax that will burn continually at the altar and vigils. The convent that will be established in the Sanctuary of Guadalupe for the nuns of the Desagravio will first be inhabited by the Capuchin religiosas. They will go there to sanctify the locale, prior to the arrival of the nuns of the Desagravio. She told Matiana of the great benefits and good fortune that will come to the kingdom and the city with the establishment of this, our order, and that it will be the last foundation in the world before the Day of Judgment. Furthermore, this new and ultimate order of the Blessed Sacrament would provide more saints for the Church than all the previous orders from their beginnings until the end, including the order of Our Father Saint Francis who has produced so many.

Our Lady made great promises concerning the persons that took part in the third foundation. The founding nuns, among God's many great women, would enjoy a privilege only granted to the Holy Apostles.

She also told Matiana that through the sacred book of the new order's constitutions other orders would experience renewal, regaining their primitive fervor. Tepid clergymen would be converted. Sinners, almost all of them, would turn back on their ways and beg for mercy because now the time of

---

* The Barefoot, or Discalced Franciscans.

† Desagravio de Jesús Sacramentado.

pardon has arrived for all; because this is the means to placate Divine Justice and soothe our angry Lord.

Matiana saw the founders in the mind of God; she saw the constitutions.[*] She saw their vestments of white and ivory and understood their significance, but since she loved the order of San Diego, she asked Our Lord if the nuns' habit could be the same color as the dieguino fathers. To this she did not receive a response because it should be the same as it was originally decreed, except for the color of the cape. That had not been declared.

Matiana also viewed a gathering in hell, and the torment suffered by the demons because of peace, a copy of which reigned among Christians in her time. Lucifer was particularly anguished. They all formed a congress, and they produced the constitution and the legal code, and Lucifer ordered the demons to spread those constitutions throughout the world to pervert everyone. Then hell was emptied to make war on Christians, and they even possessed the animals; they attacked the good ones and not the bad ones. Thus Matiana saw and announced the great tragedy of the insurrection, the persecution of Spaniards, their expatriation and all. She omitted the imprisoning of the pope and the events in Spain, France, and Rome so as not to make her recounting overlong. But Matiana saw it all: the revolution in America taking place when the archbishop was named Francisco Javier, as was the viceroy; the second independence established by Iturbide, and that he would enter convents, his coronation, and that nothing would come of his efforts because he did not remain loyal to the King of Spain. If he had upheld the commission which he had claimed for himself, he would be a duke or a great nobleman of the first order in the city. Matiana's confidants assured me that among other things, the king would come here whether or not men want him, because God wants it so. [Footnote in original: Matiana said that there would be withering, sustained gunfire in the streets and that they would be littered with dead bodies. She foresaw the destruction of farms, the sacking and the digging out of things from underground. She saw many excommunicated individuals, and also that in the palace no one died. Then when music sounds in the streets all the shooting would stop: they would not shoot another bullet. And then we will say, now the time has come for the foundation. The white flag would fall on the tower. And then a boy would announce at all the convents that no one would again shoot a single bullet.]

---

[*] In this case *constituciones* (constitutions) refers to the new order's official bylaws.

Matiana saw the attack of 1828 just as it happened.[*] She perceived the arrival of Anglo-Americans to the kingdom; she saw their sects, including their maxims and regalia, and that they would be the killers of martyrs, and how we would owe great quantities of money to them. Matiana foretold of the martyrdoms in the capital and the exit of nuns from all the convents. [Footnote in original: Even if it was midnight the nuns were forced out.] She even saw how the capuchinas would be in such poverty and need that they would beg at the gates of senators for leftovers from their meals.

Matiana, however, also foresaw the return of Spaniards to the kingdom, and that they would be received with applause, and those that had managed to stay and suffer would be recognized as stalwarts of the city. She also witnessed the coming of the King of Spain, and how without being forcibly expelled or collecting on their debts the Anglo-Americans will retreat to their homeland. The king will have a new palace next to Our Lady of Guadalupe and contiguous with the new convent of the religiosas. It will take place in the following manner. The Americans[†] would go to Europe to bring the king. The Spaniards would resist and make war; and it would be Spain's last war. This would take place to prevent the coming of the king. They will want to be independent, it if is allowed. He will come and Spain will accept the will of God. They will let him come, and then the two kingdoms will be reunited as before; however, in the past he governed the Indies from Spain, and in the future he will live in the Indies, while governing Spain. Matiana saw that this capital city by supreme order would bring together all the religiosas, making sure that none remained in the streets, and would lead them back to their convents where they would find everything they had left in their cells. Even just a piece of straw stuck on the door when they left would still be found in the same place, because not even the wind would move and God would do many miraculous favors for the religiosas. Matiana also declared that the nuns of Mexico would not do what had been done in Puebla.

In the same manner the ex-cloistered men would be returned to their convents. I believe that the pope will order this; and that his return will be marked by the singing of matins in his convents during the nativity of Our Lord Jesus Christ, and churchmen will be very happy. Our Lord will grant them every aid so that they can happily carry out his holy will. All of this will be followed by consolations and blessings from heaven, peace, union,

---

[*] Probably the text here refers to the 1828 Parian Riot in Mexico City.

[†] *Americanos in the original text refers to Mexicans, distinguishing them from Spaniards.*

and wealth. Suppressed orders, such as the Jesuits, *juaninos*, *hipólitos*, and *belemitas*, will be founded anew, and all will be in order.

Our Matiana told her companions about everything that is written here, and she directed them to make sure they did not miss the special celebration that she observed in honor of the Holy Spirit on the second day of the feast of Pentecost, even if they lacked alms and a proper Mass, because this was the only light that remained for the foundation. They fulfilled her wishes.

Matiana made doña Francisca her official representative and delegated to her that if, knowing of her visions, any of the nuns asked to be included in the foundation of the new order, then she should select three of them. But she stressed that they had to request this of their own free will; no one should be pressured. And if none of them asked to be considered among the three then she should organize a drawing to select from those who signed up for the foundation. If there are three individuals who request the slots, then there should not be a drawing, and only those three should be considered. If all of them wish to join the Desagravio and weep for their inclusion, then two of the positions should be chosen by drawing to console them. More than this will not be approved; but if need be, five shall come from San Gerónimo. In the same manner, Matiana said that the nun that takes charge of the foundation should be informed and instructed in all these things that were manifested to Matiana. The Holy Father in Rome shall send the constitutions to establish this new institution here, and by the hand of Santiago happiness will come to the kingdom, city, and community. [Footnote in original: It is understandable if you honorable sir[*] seek information about how the constitutions arrived from Rome. Mr. Archedereta told us from the beginning that the Holy Father wrote him directing him to bring about the foundation, and that His Holiness sent him the constitutions that were brought by Mr. don Diego de Agreda.] To the religiosa leading the new order shall be declared the great benefits and promises she will enjoy and how she will have the good fortune to attain privileges only granted to the Apostles. This I believe is for the three founding women; it is a privilege granted by the Holy Virgin. Said religiosa will suffer greatly, without securing temporal consolation, and without gaining spiritual consolation. They will judge her simple, ilusa, insane, a liar, and a fanatic; they will mock her, but she will have to speak out, and she will struggle greatly to get them to believe her, since there will not be any documentation, and later Our Lord will make it all clear. This nun will

---

* Here the text addresses the Vicar of Nuns Juan Manuel Irissari directly.

write to the Holy Father and inform him of the will of Our Lady in these events, and the Holy Father will send the necessary licenses without declining anything that is requested. When the response comes from Rome they will move the capuchinas from Our Lady of Guadalupe and transfer them to the capuchinas of Mexico City, while they find a new convent for them. They will never again have to leave there. Our Lady will do great favors for her capuchinas, she will console them and give them the strength to leave their convent, which will be left clean and without any marks: only the nave and the altars of the Church shall remain. And then the clothes of the three founders will be made with great haste, and the day they are to leave for the Sanctuary the prelate will come early in the morning. The three of them will renew their profession at the hands of the prelate and make a solemn vow to remain observant of the new and holy institution with all possible perfection. He will dress them in their habit, scapular, and waist cord; without veil though because they will already be professed. And since they are professed to this rule and they will bring about the foundation they will not pass through a novitiate. After the professions have finished, they will continue to hold elections, the same as the usual triennium, with a mass of the Holy Spirit, with the Blessed Sacrament on display. All the nuns will vote to choose their prioress from one of the three professed to the new institution, and once elected they will place an imperial crown on their prioress and lead her to the seat of the mother prioress. The will sing a "Te Deum," and all the *gerónimas* will render obedience to her as will her own two nuns. Once this has finished, they will lead the founders in procession wearing capes and bearing candles to the gates, where they will see them out of the cloister. They will leave at the hour of the Tercia,[*] which coincides with the time the Holy Spirit descended. They will be taken to the Sanctuary in a carriage. [Footnote in original: With them they will take to the Sanctuary the ashes of the religiosa that died, that would be Mother María Josefa de San Felipe, as well as those of Matiana and doña Francisca Montes de Oca, to bury them in the new convent.] At the moment when they arrive at the convent they will discover the Blessed Sacrament and they will commence with the vigil in the tribune of the large church, because that is where the placation will take place. That same day two professed nuns from the convent of San Juan de la Penitencia will also be brought to the foundation; they will take the habit and profess at the same time, because they will not have to pass through a

---

[*] Mid-morning prayers.

novitiate since the foundation will be approved in both convents from the beginning. In the same manner the prelate will go about taking professed religiosas from every convent in the capital, with the exception of the Indian convents, including those from La Concepción to the most recently founded, from the shod to the discalced.[*] All of them will have to pass through their novitiate in their respective communities; they will organize a drawing of all the religiosas, and whoever has the good fortune will be the one taken. They will bring one Capuchin nun from the Guadalupe Sanctuary and another from Mexico City in this drawing. Thus all the founders together in their convent will discover the spring of oil, and it shall spill copiously across the floor; thus symbolizing the spreading charity in the hearts of Christians. The number of the nuns will always be forty-six, because this is the number of stars on Our Lady of Guadalupe's cloak. The charter will direct that there be servants of Mary who will serve the nuns, and the mother superior will decree their number. But here they will be twelve, and instead of calling them servants of Mary they will give them the names of the Holy Apostles. Due to the poverty of the city neither the aspirants nor the religiosas will have dowries, nor shall they receive funds from rents. Instead they will be maintained by Divine Providence, the religiosas as well as *las Apóstoles*,[†] chaplains, sacristans, and lay financial stewards who will serve as the convent's agents. The foundation will take place in the month of October in a year eight. [Footnote in original: The new order will spread such that all the sanctuaries of Our Lady will house nuns of the Blessed Sacrament.] The founders will bring all the furnishings that they use in their cells with them, due to the privilege of great poverty; but there is a law stating that the religiosas coming from other houses cannot bring so much as a printed image. In the same manner they will bring from San Gerónimo a crown and palm of silver for the nuns, and the Holy Child, with which they will profess. They will also bring all of the utensils of the sacristy, chalice, patens, and the rest. Anything of silver they will return, and they will do the same with everything else once they have provided themselves with all the needed items; however, they will not return the crown and the palm.

Matiana also said that from the Sanctuary of Guadalupe two additional foundations will emerge, one to los Ángeles and the other to Toluca, and they

---

* The Conceptionist convent was the oldest in Mexico City, so this means from the oldest to the newest order in the city. The "from shod to discalced" comment refers to the different rules of various orders. In this context it means from most relaxed to most strict.

† The "servants of Mary" who assist the nuns.

will establish other convents of the Desagravio in Santa Cruz. [Footnote in original: there will not be difficulties or surprises at the bringing together of so many religiosas of different rules and statutes that it is said will go form the new order of the Desagravio. And because some people will not understand, Señora Paula told me this story. A very powerful man that has a great many country homes, orchards, and gardens builds another home in a more pleasant, mild, and fertile climate. He directs that they plant him a great orchard and from his other gardens and orchards they bring the best fruit trees with roots and flowers intact, and they plant them in the new garden, because he wants fruits throughout the year. This story symbolizes how each nun will come from a different convent only at the initial foundation; later, if others want to join, the new institution will not receive them.] The link that will join the different houses of the new order is the wax that will be used in the continual vigil; it will come from the oil. The government will issue an order stating that all the churches where the Blessed Sacrament is deposited must have lamps burning. They will calculate what this costs in olive oil and then they will use this money to order candles measuring two-and-a-quarter varas[*] be made with the pounds of wax corresponding to their customs, until they reach the year's expenditures. The same should be done with the pound-weight candles that shall continually burn on the altar night and day: even though it should be deposited, the wax should always burn. An honorable gentleman shall be named steward for each house, and he should be faithful to his commission. Said gentleman shall deliver to each church the quantity of oil corresponding to what is spent each year, and he shall receive wax in exchange and not transacted money and he will scrupulously render accounts. None of those who are charged with the lamps, be they priests or pastors, will give less than what they purchase of the other oil; because if it is not this way the obligation with which they have been charged at the beginning will fade in importance. There shall be no selling of the oil from the spring, and if someone considers its sale it will evaporate from the vessel in which they carry it. Once the steward has the wax he will take it to the Sanctuary to give it to the nuns, who will have a special room for storing only wax. The soap with which the linens of the sacristy are washed will be that which comes from the mountain, so that it will not be the common kind.

Informed of all that happened to Señora Matiana, Father Miguel Maya, since he was her spiritual director, went personally to see the Illustrious

---

[*] Approximately two meters.

Señor Haro,[*] and commended his daughter Matiana completely to him, so
that he could test her spirit. And said archbishop took under his charge the
three that I have mentioned: Matiana, doña Francisca, and Paula. He relieved
the confessors of the three and sent them all to the Reverend Father León, a
Dominican priest, and on other occasions to Father Marín, of the convent of
San Camilo. Both of them were Inquisition examiners and they assured me
that they treated them very harshly, and yet Matiana appeared to be very
happy with all that was happening to her. The Illustrious Señor Haro sometimes went to the grille to see Señora Matiana, and so she could go to the
grille they lent her a skirt and shall. At the grille they talked of all the things
that I have written; and what Señora Matiana shared with His Excellency
about the extreme poverty that America[†] would experience in this period,
and because the foundation of the Appeasement had to take place, the prelate
was left perplexed. He asked her if she wanted lamps for the Blessed
Sacrament. And then she told him that when they when they dig the foundations for the convent of the Sanctuary they will find the well of oil and it will
be for the lamps of the Blessed Sacrament, and the soap from the mountains
will be for washing the linens of the sacristy, etc. . . . His Excellency wanted
to test Señora Matiana, and so one day at two in the afternoon he decided
that he would go to the grille without telling her. When he climbed into his
carriage he told the coachman: "To San Gerónimo." When he met Matiana
she recounted for His Excellency the hour when he decided to come, and
what he had told the coachman. The archbishop was awestruck.

At about that time Matiana was coming to the end of her life, at thirty
years old or so. She had revealed in that holy convent so many portents that
were known in her time and also various ladies have told me that one day
while she was writing the archbishop they called for her as a ruse in order to
see what she was writing. She stopped writing and went to see what was
wanted of her, but when they went to look at her letter they found it blank
even though she had already written a half page or so. In front of everyone
when she returned she began to write where she left off, and thus the nosy
ones were foiled. The malady that finally brought her death was a cilice that
dug so deeply into her waist that it was necessary to destroy it in order to
take it out. After examining her wound the doctor directed her to prepare for

---

* A reference to the eighteenth-century Archbishop of Mexico Alonso Núñez de Haro y
Peralta.

† Again, *América refers to Mexico in the text.*

death and take the Holy Sacraments. They informed the archbishop and he ordered that Reverend Father Maya be allowed to enter the convent in order to confess her, but only as long as she was ill. The women that cared for her believe that Matiana had sworn a vow of obedience to her spiritual director, and hence she did not take medicines and food unless she could write Reverend Father Maya and receive his reply. As a result they witnessed the following happening: Matiana said she wanted to eat chayote and *tejocote.*[*] They asked the nurses at the time if they could give this to her; they said yes. They then wrote the father to ask for his approval, and presuming his agreement, they told Matiana that he said she could eat whatever she liked, and right there they cleaned and pitted the tejocote and they told her to go ahead and eat. She obeyed and ate it. A short while later the priest's reply arrived saying that she could have one half of a quarter of the chayote, but under no circumstances should she eat tejocote. As soon as Matiana heard this she sat down quickly and spit it out in its entirety as if she had never chewed it.

Some days later she died, but before expiring she kissed the feet of Father Maya and told those in attendance, "This soul is like a diamond." She is buried in the stair of the young girls at the entrance of low choir in the middle of the side altar. Señora Paula is buried in the same place too. After the death of Matiana, the Most Illustrious Señor Haro came and told the women that they were to forget about Matiana's things and never speak of her again, in part because of the great sadness they felt, but also because of all the extraordinary things. He ordered that they no longer discuss Matiana, and that they cover up everything, so that in the future all would glow with an even greater splendor. She had a very simple soul; she dreamed of cradling the Christ child as he slept in her arms. But she did not live long enough for proof of what had come to her . . . and thus the flame that had burned in the hearts of nuns and laypersons began to dim. [Footnote in original: I have finished with Matiana in providing the most prompt declaration that I could, with the best possible examination of my memory—*Laus Deo.*]

---

[*] Respectively *Sechium edule,* related to melons and cucumbers and squash; and Mexican hawthorn (*Crataegus pubescens*), a crab apple–like fruit.

Notes

INTRODUCTION

1. The classic parlor game whereby a message is whispered from one person to the next in a group of players and the last person announces it to the entire group. Typically the original statement is much changed by the end.

2. Agustín Yáñez, *Las tierras flacas* (Mexico City: Editorial Joaquín Mortiz, 1962). For an English translation see Agustín Yáñez, *The Lean Lands*, trans. Ethel Brinton (Austin: University of Texas Press, 1968). Much of the portrait of Madre Matiana's "past" appears in the original Spanish edition, 80–95 and 180–85.

3. Lola Álvarez Bravo, *La Madre Matiana*, 1935, CCP. This image is frequently reproduced in books about the artist's work: for example, see Olivier Debroise, *Lola Álvarez Bravo: In Her Own Light* (Tucson: Center for Creative Photography, University of Arizona, 1994), plate 7; and Elizabeth Ferrer, *Lola Álvarez Bravo* (New York: Aperture Foundation, 2005), plate 18.

4. For the earliest extent issue, see *La Madre Matiana*, 9 September 1917, UTBC.

5. Luis G. Duarte, *Profecías de Matiana acera del triunfo de la iglesia: expurgadas, defendidas y corrobadas con respetabilísimos y muy notables vaticinios de santos, de personas canónicamente beatificadas y de otras que han muerto en olor de santidad*, ed. Antonio Martínez del Cañizo (Mexico City: Imprenta del Círculo Católico, 1889).

6. Edward Wright-Rios, *Revolutions in Mexican Catholicism: Reform and Revelation in Oaxaca, 1887–1934* (Durham, NC: Duke University Press, 2009).

7. Maria Josefa de la Pasión de Jesus, *Profecías de Matiana, sirvienta que fue en el convent de San Gerónimo de México, sobre los sucesos que han de acontecer en esta capital* (Mexico City: Valdés y Redondas, 1847), UTAL.

8. Maria Josefa de la Pasión de Jesús, *Profecías de Matiana, sirvienta que fue en el convent de San Gerónimo de México, sobre los sucesos que han de acontecer en esta capital* (Mexico City: Imprenta Abadiano, 1857), YSML. For advertisements, see *Diario de Avisos*, 10 July, 15 July, 6 August, and 3 September 1857.

9. de la Pasión de Jesús, *Profecías de Matiana*, 1847. Unless otherwise noted all translations are mine, and in each case I have worked more to convey meaning and feeling in English rather than provide a literal translation.

10. Ibid.

11. Ibid.

12. Ibid.

13. Ibid.

14. *Calendario nigromántico para el año 1858* (Mexico City: Imprenta de Manuel Murguía).

15. María Josefa de la Pasión de Jesús, *Profecías de la madre Matiana sirvienta que fue en el convent de San Gerónimo de México, sobre los sucesos que han de acontecer en al [sic] espresada capital* (Mexico City: Imprenta de la calle del Cuadrante de Santa Catarina, 1861).

16. Nancy Leys Stepan, "Race and Gender: The Role of Analogy in Science," in *Anatomy of Racism*, ed. David Theo Goldberg (Minneapolis: University of Minnesota Press, 1990), 38–57.

17. See Josefina Muriel, *Conventos de monjas en la Nueva España* (Mexico City: Universidad Nacional Autónoma de México Instituto de Investigaciones Históricas, 1994), 296–300; and José Velasco Toro, "Matiana, mística del imaginario y 'voz de ultratumba,'" *Ulúa* 10 (2007): 39–71. The latter, however, carefully describes several Matiana texts.

18. The catalog reference is as follows: AGN, GD14, Bienes Nacionales, 1824–1847, vol. 200, exp. 27. It states "Documentos de convento de San Jerónimo: oficios, cartas y un expediente sobre revelaciones de la Madre Matiana."

19. In cases of female mysticism the kind of documents often produced in the 1700s included spiritual diaries, autobiographical compositions elicited by spiritual directors, confessor-written hagiographies, and inquisitorial reports. On these topics, see the introductory essays in Asunción Lavrin and Rosalva Loreto López, eds., *Monjas y beatas: la escritura femenina en la espiritualidad barroca novohispana, siglos XVII y XVIII* (Mexico City: Universidad de las Américas-Puebla; Archivo General de la Nación, 2002); and Lavrin and Loreto López, eds., *Diálogos espirituales: manuscritos femeninos hispanoamericanos, siglos XVI–XIX* (Puebla: Instituto de Ciencias Sociales y Humanidades de la Benemérita Universidad Autónoma de Puebla and Universidad de las Américas-Puebla, 2006).

20. Roberto González Echevarría, *Myth and Archive: Toward A Theory of Latin American Narrative* (Cambridge: Cambridge University Press, 1990).

21. See Harry Sieber, *Language and Society in La Vida de Lazarillo de Tormes* (Baltimore, MD: Johns Hopkins University Press, 1978), xi–xii.

22. See Anthony R. Pagden, "Translator's Introduction," in *Hernán Cortés: Letters from Mexico*, ed. Anthony R. Pagden (New York: Grossman, 1971), xxxix–lxvii.

23. On the issue of *letrado* expression, see Angel Rama, *The Lettered City* (Durham, NC: Duke University Press, 1996).

24. Antonio Rubial García, *La santidad contovertida: hagiografía y conciencia criolla alrededor de los Venerables no canonizados de Nueva España* (Mexico City: Universidad Nacional Autónoma de México and Fondo de Cultura Económica, 1999), 11–16.

25. Lucas Alamán, *Historia de Méjico desde los primeros movimientos que prepararon su independencia en el año 1808, hasta la época presente* (Mexico City: Imprenta de José María de Lara, 1849–1852).

26. Michael P. Costeloe, "Federalism to Centralism in Mexico: The Conservative Case for Change, 1834–1835," *The Americas* 42, no. 2 (1988): 173–85; and Jaime E. Rodríguez, *Down from Colonialism: Mexico's Nineteenth-Century Crisis* (Los Angeles: Chicano Studies Research Center Publications, University of California, 1983).

CHAPTER 1

1. On the Jesuit expulsion from the Americas, see Magnus Mörner, ed., *The Expulsion of the Jesuits from Latin America* (New York: Knopf, 1965). For a concise summary of the issues surrounding the expulsion see David A. Brading, *Church and State in Bourbon Mexico: The Dioecese of Michoacán, 1749–1810* (Cambridge: Cambridge University Press, 1994), 3–19.

2. AGN, GD 61, Inq. 1768, exp. 11, fs. 152–73. This quotation appears on 154: *"por los que al presente persiguen mis amados hijos de mi Compañía."*

3. Fred Hageneder, *The Meaning of Trees: Botany, History, Healing, Lore* (San Francisco, CA: Chronicle Books, 2005), 150. According to Hageneder, the terebinth (*Pistacia terebinthus*) appears in the Old Testament on numerous occasions, but it has often been mistranslated as "oak." Apparently it was in a sacred grove of terebinths that Abraham received his calling from God (Gen. 18:1).

4. AGN, GD 61 Inq. 1768, exp. 11, fs. 152–73. The implication, naturally, is that her official declaration is the pamphlet's original source.

5. The Mexican prophecies pertaining to the Jesuit expulsion can be found in the files generated by the Inquisition's efforts to extirpate these mystical narratives that criticized the Bourbon regime; see AGN, GD 61 Inq. 1768, vol. 1522, exp. 1 and 2. For a discussion of these cases and others, see Felipe Castro Gutiérrez, "Profecías y libelos subversivos contra el reinado de Carlos III," *Estudios de Historia Novohispana* 11 (1991): 85–96.

6. This story seems to have really captured the popular imagination, because it appeared in numerous different depositions from different cities. The actual father of the disabled boy from Puebla also gave his testimony; see "Expediente y averiguación de la profecía sobre el regreso de los Regulares de la Compañía atribuida a un niño hijo de D. Miguel de León del comercio de esta ciudad," AGN, GD 61 Inq. 1768,

vol. 1522, exp. 2: 71–79. Don Miguel stood by the temporary cure of his son and his claims about the Jesuit's return to their houses, but did not claim to understand its deeper meaning.

7. Deposition of Don Joseph Miguel Escalona y Matamoros, AGN, GD 61 Inq. 1768, vol. 1522, exp. 2: 100–102. Another account featured a missionary's deathbed prophecy much to the same effect, although with less poetic flourish.

8. Deposition of R. P. Fr. Joaquín del Castillo, AGN, GD 61 Inq. 1768, vol. 1522, exp. 2: 98. Castillo described the deathbed prophecy and the savage horse miracle, but he maintained that he never gave these stories any credence.

9. In addition to the avenging painting of the Jesuit founder, Saint Ignatius Loyola, other testimony from Veracruz also mentioned the crippled boy from Puebla. A vision attributed to a Guatemalan nun sounds very similar to the Spanish Capuchin's prophecy; see AGN, GD 61 Inq. 1768, vol. 1522, exp. 2: 44–48.

10. Deposition of Diego Joseph de Retana, AGN, GD 61 Inq. 1768, vol. 1522, exp. 2: 103v. Retana's testimony is the source of this elaborate retelling; the visionary in his version was a schoolgirl. There were still more versions of this prophesy that cited different female seers; see Castro Gutiérrez, "Profecías y libelos." See also, Deposition of Rafael Curiel, AGN, GD 61 Inq. 1768, vol. 1522, exp. 2: 102. In Curiel's testimony a venerable nun replaces the schoolgirl in the story. He also spoke of the crippled boy and the discovered Jesuit prophetic writings.

11. Testimony amassed by investigators suggests even more antiexpulsion visions were in circulation. Several informants testified to hearing such a variety of prophecies that they could not remember them all. Some may have simply been trying to obscure the trail of prophetic critique, but the common expression of these sentiments is clear. Individuals spoke of hearing them from servants and acquaintances, or they just overheard the tales randomly in the street and at the workplace. One witness, commenting on the story of the crippled boy, argued that the family's attempts to publicize the miracle stemmed from a well-meaning enthusiasm. They were honorable people, he maintained, who were moved by concern for their son and affection for the Jesuits of Puebla. Inquisitors apparently agreed. They halted the family's efforts to secure church approval of the miracle and silenced their publicity campaign, but they did not punish the boy or his parents. See Deposition of Felis Lince, AGN, GD 61 Inq. 1768, vol. 1522, exp. 2: 103; Deposition of Don Joseph Miguel Escalona y Matamoros, AGN, GD 61 Inq. 1768, vol. 1522, exp. 2: 100–102; and Castro Gutierrez, "Profecías y libelos."

12. José Antonio Gerrer Benimeli, "Los jesuitas y los motines en la España del siglo XVIII," in *Coloquio internacional Carlos III y su siglo: actas* (Madrid: Universidad Complutense, 1990), vol. 1: 453–84.

13. Castro Gutiérrez, "Profecías y libelos," 87–88.

14. See Stuart B. Schwartz, *All Can be Saved: Religious Tolerance and Salvation in the Iberian Atlantic World* (New Haven, CT: Yale University Press, 2009).

15. Don Pedro Rodrígues Campomanes, R. P. General de San Francisco de Asís, *A todos los religiosos y prelados y súbitos*, 14 November 1767, BN, Archivo Franciscano, MS, 118/ 1575.3.

16. Fray Manuel de Náxera, Comisario General de estas provincias de Nueva-España, 20 July 1768, BN, Archivo Franciscano, MS, 118/ 1575.3.

17. For an interesting comparison, see Charles F. Walker's discussion of polemical convent prophecies in eighteenth-century Lima, *Shaky Colonialism: The 1746 Earthquake-Tsunami in Lima, Peru, and its Long Aftermath* (Durham, NC: Duke University Press, 2008), 21–51.

18. Fray Manuel de Náxera, Comisario General de estas provincias de Nueva-España, 20 July, 1768, BN, Archivo Franciscano, MS, 118/ 1575.3.

19. Ibid. Ironically he cited the Jesuit-authored *Artificios de los hereges* written in the seventeenth century.

20. Ibid.

21. Antonio Rubial García, *La santidad*, 1–16.

22. Caroline Walker Bynum, " . . . And Woman his Humanity: Female Imagery in Religious Writing of the Later Middle Ages," in *Gender and History*, eds. Caroline Walker Bynum, Steven Harell, and Paula Richman (Boston: Beacon Press, 1986), 257–88.

23. For a detailed discussion of these issues see, Laura A. Lewis, *Hall of Mirrors: Power, Witchcraft, and Caste in Colonial Mexico* (Durham, NC: Duke University Press, 2003).

24. Heinrich Kramer and Jakob Sprenger, *Malleus Maleficarum*, as cited in Lewis, *Hall of Mirrors*, 116.

25. Bynum, " . . . And Woman his Humanity."

26. *El camino verdadero. Coloquio entre el dulcísimo Jesús y la alma su esposa, deseosa de agradarle y servile y ansiosa por amarle y gozarle en su divina unión* (Mexico City: Imprenta de Luis Abadiano y Valdés, 1851).

27. Ibid., 200–206.

28. On this issue, see Alison Weber, *Teresa de Ávila and the Rhetoric of Femininity* (Princeton, NJ: Princeton University Press, 1990), 18–19. The famous passage from Paul is 1 Cor. 14: 34–37.

29. Jean Franco, *Plotting Women: Gender and Representation in Mexico* (New York: Columbia University Press, 1989), 3–55.

30. Asunción Lavrin, "Unlike Sor Juana? The Model Nun in the Religious Literature of Colonial Mexico" in *Feminist Perspectives on Sor Juana Inés de la Cruz*, ed. Stephanie Merrim (Detroit, MI: Wayne State University Press, 1991), 61–85.

31. Franco, *Plotting Women*, 3–55.

32. Bynum, " . . . And Woman His Humanity."

33. William A. Christian, *Visionaries: The Spanish Republic and the Reign of Christ* (Berkeley: University of California Press, 1996), 1–12 and 394–402.

34. Frank Graziano, *Wounds of Love: The Mystical Marriage of Saint Rose of Lima*

(Oxford: Oxford University Press, 2004), 29. As Graziano notes, in Catholic teaching we find expression of this issue in the concepts of *imitanda* (that which merits imitation) and *admiranda* (that which inspires admiration) as applied to saints.

35. Rubial García, *La santidad*, 198–200.

36. Bynum, *Holy Feast and Holy Fast: The Religious Significance of Food to Medieval Women* (Berkeley: University of California Press, 1987), 13–30 and 73–112.

37. Ibid. For an interesting exploration of food asceticism and women's identities see Rebecca J. Lester, "Embodied Voices: Women's Food Asceticism and the Negotiation of Identity," *Ethos* 23, no. 2 (1995): 187–222.

38. See Linda Ann Curcio-Nagy, *The Great Festivals of Colonial Mexico City: Performing Power and Identity* (Albuquerque: University of New Mexico Press, 2004).

39. See Margaret Chowning, "The Catholic Church and the Ladies of the Vela Perpetua: Gender and Devotional Change in Nineteenth-Century Mexico," *Past and Present* 221, no. 1 (November 2013): 197–237.

40. Bynum, *Holy Feast and Holy Fast*, 232–33.

41. Ibid., 137–39.

42. Ibid., 251.

43. See Weber, *Teresa de Avila*; Carole Slade, *Saint Teresa of Avila: Author of a Heroic Life* (Berkeley: University of California Press, 1995); and Gillian T.W. Ahlgren, *Teresa de Avila and the Politics of Sanctity* (Ithaca, NY: Cornell University Press, 1996).

44. For example the Librería Abadiano's holdings currently at the California State University's Sutro Library (SL) contain several Mexican examples, including, *Día quinze: exercicio en honra de la admirable virgen, seráfica doctora, y madre Santa Teresa de Jesús* (Mexico City: Imprenta Nueva Madrileña de los herederos del Lic. D. Joseph de Jauregui, 1783); José Manuel de Jesús, *Sermón de la seráfica madre y doctora Santa Teresa de Jesús: predicado en el día de octubre de 1820 en la iglesia del Convento de Carmelitas Descalzas de esta ciudad de México* (Mexico City: Imprenta de Alejandro Valdés, 1820); *Himnos para dar gracias por la mañana y noche: y letrilla de Santa Teresa de Jesús* (Mexico City: Imprenta de las Escalerillas á cargo de Agustín Guiol, 1831); and Francisco Nepuen, *Método facil, que se propone á los que practican los ejercicios espirituales, para que puedan formar santos propositos, en orden al nuevo arreglo de vidas* (Mexico City: Imprenta de Luis Abadiano, 1840). See also Rosalva Loreto López, *Una empresa divina: las hijas de Santa Teresa de Jesús en América* (Puebla: Universidad de las Américas, 2004).

45. Weber, *Teresa de Avila*.

46. Ahlgren, *Teresa de Avila*, 171.

47. Slade, *Saint Teresa*.

48. Kristine Ibsen, *Women's Spiritual Autobiography in Colonial Spanish America* (Gainesville: University of Florida Press, 1999).

49. For a helpful periodization of colonial piety, see Rubial García, *La santidad*, 51–76.

50. For a more extensive treatment of Saint Rose, see Graziano, *Wounds of Love*.

51. See David A. Brading, *The First America: The Spanish Monarchy Creole Patriots and the Liberal State, 1492–1867* (New York: Cambridge University Press, 1991).

52. Ibid.

53. Rubial García, *La santidad*, 1–6 and 30–51.

54. Carlos Sigüenza y Góngora, *Parayso occidental: plantado y cultivado por la liberal benéfica mano de los muy catholicos y poderosos reyes de España, nuestros señores, en su magnifico Real Convento de Jesus María de Mexico* (Mexico City: Universidad Autónoma de México and Condumex, 1995). This book is a facsimile of the first edition published in 1694. For a detailed analysis of this text, see Kathleen Ross, *The Baroque Narrative of Carlos Sigüenza y Góngora: A New World Paradise* (Cambridge: Cambridge University Press, 1993).

55. For the broader context of Sigüenza y Góngora's writing, see Kathleen Ross, "Historians of the Conquest and Colonization of the New World: 1550–1620;" and David H. Bost, "Historians of the Colonial Period: 1620–1700," in *The Cambridge History of Latin American Literature*, eds. Roberto González Echevarría and Enrique Pupo-Walker (Cambridge: Cambridge University Press, 1996), vol. 1, 101–42 and 143–90, respectively.

56. Sigüenza y Góngora, *Parayso occidental*, 148. For more on this passage, see Asunción Lavrin, "El más allá en el imaginario de las religiosas novohispanas," in *Muerte y vida en el más allá*, eds. Gisela Von Wobeser and Enriqueta Vila Vilar (Mexico City: Universidad Autónoma de México, 2009), 181–201. The translation is mine. I have taken the liberty to insert modern punctuation for the sake of clarity.

57. For recent scholarship on these issues, see Lavrin and Loreto López, *Monjas y beatas*; Lavrin and Loreto López, *Diálogos espirituales*; Ellen Gunnarsdóttir, *Mexican Karismata: The Baroque Vocation of Francisca de los Angeles, 1674–1744* (Lincoln: University of Nebraska Press, 2004); and Nora E. Jaffary, *False Mystics: Deviant Orthodoxy in Colonial Mexico* (Lincoln: University of Nebraska Press, 2004).

58. For published versions of these writings see Lavrin and Lorreto, eds., *Monjas y beatas*; and Lavrin and Lorreto eds., *Diálogos espirituales*. For a unique Peruvian example from the perspective of a one-time female slave, see Ursula de Jesús and Nancy E. Van Deusen, *The Souls of Purgatory: The Spiritual Diary of a Seventeenth-Century Afro-Peruvian Mystic, Ursula de Jesús* (Albuquerque: University of New Mexico Press, 2004).

59. Jaffary, *False Mystics*, 1–18.

60. See Pamel Voekel, *Alone Before God: The Religious Origins of Modernity* (Durham, NC: Duke University Press, 2002); Rubial García, *La santidad*, 84–87; and Brian Larkin, *The Very Nature of God: Baroque Catholicism and Religious Reform in Bourbon Mexico City* (Albuquerque: University of New Mexico Press, 2010).

61. Jaffary, "María Josefa de la Peña y la defense de la legitimidad mística," in *Diálogos*, eds. Lavrin and Loreto López, 120–33.

62. Ibid.

63. Ibid. In this case, it was one of de la Peña's confessors who arguably tried to escape inquisitorial sanction for supporting her. Jaffrey stresses that in reality de la Peña was adapting Saint Teresa's teachings to her own time and the modes of practice in Mexico.

64. "El tratado spiritual de María Josefa de la Peña," transcribed and edited by Nora E. Jaffary, in *Diálogos*, eds. Lavrin and Loreto López, 134.

65. Ibid., 140.

66. Ibid., 142.

67. Ibid., 142. Another Mexican mystic, María Ignacia del Niño Jesús, described similar conversations with Christ regarding liberating souls from Purgatory in 1802. See "María Ignacia del Niño Jesús, cartas," in *Diálogos*, eds. Lavrin and Loreto López, 376–83: in particular, see the letter penned 31 January 1802 to Sor María's confessor, Fray Manuel Sancho del Valle, 377–78.

68. Ibid., 143.

69. Gunnarsdóttir, *Mexican Karismata*, 67–74.

70. Jaffary, *False Mystics*, 14.

71. Asunción Lavrin, "María Marcela Soria: una capuchina queretana," in *Diálogos*, eds. Lavrin and Loreto López, 77. Within the same collection, see also, Elia Armancanqui-Tipacti, "La propia escritura y la re-escritura de un transcriptor de 'Vida de la Madre María Manuela de la Ascensión Ripa," 228–42. At issue in the latter case is a reworking of a mystical nun's 1799–1824 writings in 1889.

72. de la Pasión de Jesús, *Profecías de Matiana* (1861), 1.

73. Ibid., 8.

74. Ibid., 13.

75. For a synthesis of ideals regarding convents, see Margaret Chowning, *Rebellious Nuns: The Troubled History of a Mexican Convent, 1752–1863* (Oxford: Oxford University Press, 2005), 63–66.

76. Rubial García, *La santidad*, 40.

77. For the case of a famous beata in Querétaro, see Gunnarsdóttir, *Mexican Karismata*.

78. For analysis of a colonial cartoon lampooning a colonial beata, see Jaffary, *False Mystics*, 165–69.

79. "El Chuchumbe," AGN, GD 61, Inq. 1776, Vol. 1052, exp. 20, fs. 292–95. I owe this quotation to literary scholar Elena Deanda. For more on this song, see Elena Deanda, "El Chuchumbe te he de soplar: sobre obscenidad, censura y memoria oral en el primer 'son de la tierra' novohispano," *Mester* 36 (2007): 53–71.

80. This alcoholic beverage is made from fermented sugarcane juice.

81. Antonio García Cubas, *El libro de mis recuerdos* (Mexico City: Secretaría de Educación Pública, 1946), 30.

82. See Chowning, "The Catholic Church and the Ladies of the Vela Perpetua," 197–98.

83. For example, see "Milagros de la Reforma. Zoología: La beata." BPJ, miscellanea 376, no. 5. This text without author or date (the tone and the title suggest perhaps a late 1850s or 1860s publication date) is a mock scientific treatise on Mexico's "fauna." The beata is classified as the female of the same pernicious "species" as the friar.

84. Bynum, *Holy Feast*, 23.

85. On the colonial period see Lewis, *Hall of Mirrors*.

86. Ibid.

87. See Richard L. Kagan, *Lucrecia's Dreams: Politics and Prophecy in Sixteenth-Century Spain* (Berkeley: University of California Press, 1990), 86–113.

88. Ibid., 114–33. Her downfall stemmed, in part, from her break with visionary mores. Lucrecia did not stick to accepted feminine devotional themes or champion the establishment of a shrine or new religious order. Instead of avoiding overtly political topics, like most mystical women, she waded into court intrigue. In addition, as a laywoman she lacked the devout reputation and institutional protections afforded nuns.

89. Ibid., 86.

90. The collective, public nature of historical visionary movements is consistently underscored by scholarship. For examples of modernizing Catholic cultural environments, see Thomas Kselman, *Miracles and Prophecies in Nineteenth-Century France* (New Brunswick, NJ: Rutgers University Press, 1983); William A. Christian, *Moving Crucifixes in Modern Spain* (Princeton, NJ: Princeton University Press, 1992); Christian, *Visionaries*; David Blackbourn, *Marpingen: Apparitions of the Virgin Mary in Bismarckian Germany* (New York: Alfred A. Knopf, 1994); Paolo Apolito, *Apparitions of the Madonna at Oliveto Citra: Local Visions and Cosmic Drama* (State College: Pennsylvania State University Press, 1998); Ralph Della Cava, *Miracle at Joaseiro* (New York: Columbia University Press, 1970); and Wright-Rios, *Revolutions in Mexican Catholicism*.

91. Kselman, *Miracles*, 60–83.

CHAPTER 2

1. *Calendario nigromántico para el año 1858*. The text of the prophecies from this almanac can also be consulted at the BN, Fondo Lafragua, but it has been separated from the rest of the almanac and bound with other documents in RLAF 348 LAF; *Calendario de la Madre Matiana para el año 1867* (Mexico City: Imprenta A. Boix a cargo de M. Zornoza) SL, Mexican Pamphlet Collection.

2. Eric Van Young, *The Other Rebellion: Popular Violence, Ideology and the Mexican Struggle for Independence, 1810–1821* (Stanford, CA: Stanford University Press, 2001).

3. See Donald F. Stevens, *Origins of Instability in Early Republican Mexico* (Durham, NC: Duke University Press, 1991); Michael P. Costeloe, *The Central Republic in Mexico, 1835–1846* (Cambridge: Cambridge University Press, 1993), 1–30; and Will Fowler, *Mexico in the Age of Proposals, 1821–1853* (Westport, CT: Greenwood Press, 1998).

4. This outline of scholarly interpretations of Mexican instability draws on Brian Connaughton's synopsis; see "A Most Delicate Balance: Representative Government, Public Opinion, and Priests in Mexico, 1821–1834, *Mexican Studies/ Estudios mexicanos* 17, no. 1 (2001): 41–69.

5. Antonio Annino has made this argument in a number of publications; see, for example, "Soberanías en lucha," in *De los imperios a las naciones*, eds. François Javier Guerra et al. (Zaragoza: Ibercaja, 1994), 229–53. For Annino's analysis in English, see "The Two-Faced Janus: The Pueblos and the Origins of Mexican Liberalism," in *Cycles of Conflict, Centuries of Change: Crisis, Reform, and Revolution in Mexico*, eds. Servín et al. (Durham, NC: Duke University Press, 2007), 60–90.

6. Fernando Escalante Gonzalbo, *Ciudadanos imaginarios: memorial de los afanes y desventuras de la virtud, y apología del vicio triunfante en la República Mexicana—tratado de moral pública* (Mexico City: El Colegio de México, 1992).

7. For a probing discussion of these issues and others see François Javier Guerra, *Modernidad e indepenencias: ensayos sobre las revoluciones hispánicas* (Madrid: Editorial Mapfre, 1992). For a short English-language synthesis of his interpretation see, François Javier Guerra, "Mexico from Independence to Revolution: The Mutations of Liberalism," in *Cycles of Conflict* eds. Servín et al., 129–52.

8. Donald F. Stevens, *Origins of Instability*, 107–18.

9. Connaughton, "A Most Delicate Balance," 41–69.

10. For a discussion of sedition, rumor, and gossip amidst insurgency see Van Young, *The Other Rebellion*, chapter 14, especially 328–34.

11. See Francisco Javier Santamaría and Joaqúin García Icazbalceta, *Diccionario de mejicanismos* (Mexico City: Editorial Porrúa, 1959), 147–48. See also José Martínez Pérez, *Dichos, dicharachos y refranes mexicanos: colección moderna con interpretación* (Mexico City: Editores Mexicanos Unidos, 1977).

12. "Profecías, descubrimientos, y opinions opuestas," *El Boquiflojo*, 17 March 1870. Looking back on his youth during the Mexican Revolutionary era in Jalisco, Enrique Francisco Camarena stressed how in rural areas far from the struggle many borregos flitted about town. Some of them, he noted, proved wildly false and others true. Regardless, he opined, they mixed with the prophecies of Madre Matiana and unsettled the locals. See "Hace cincuenta años," *El Informador*, 4 April 1965.

13. Will Fowler, "Dreams of Stability: Mexican Political Thought during the 'Forgotten Years.' An Analysis of the Beliefs of the Creole Intelligentsia (1821–1853)," *Bulletin of Latin American Research* 14, no. 3 (1996): 287–312. Fowler

stresses that our tendency to talk in terms of "chaos" and a simple two-part struggle is due to an overdependence on José María Luis Mora's and Lucas Alamán's writings. In his view, both of these actors oversimplified the situation to bolster their own ideological positions; see 305–6.

14. Josefina Zoraida Vázquez, "Los años olividados," *Mexican Studies/Estudios Mexicanos* 5, no. 2 (1989): 313–26.

15. Erika Pani, "'Las fuerzas oscuras.' El problema del conservadurismo en la historia de México," in *Conservadurismo y derechas en la historia de México*, vol. 1, ed. Erika Pani (Mexico City: Fondo de Cultura Económica, 2009), 11–42.

16. Catherine Andrews, "Sobre conservadurismo e ideas conservadoras en la primera república federal (1824–1835)," in Pani, *Conservadurismo y derechas*, vol. 1, 86–88.

17. See Costeloe, *The Central Republic.*

18. For studies of local movements that challenged the state, see Peter F. Guardino, *Peasants, Politics, and the Formation of Mexico's National State: Guerrero, 1800–1857* (Stanford, CA: Stanford University Press, 1996); and Guy P. C. Thomson and David G. LaFrance, *Patriotism, Politics, and Popular Liberalism in Nineteenth-Century Mexico: Juan Francisco Lucas and the Puebla Sierra* (Wilmington, DE: Scholarly Resources, 1999). For a broader perspective see John Tutino, *From Insurrection to Revolution in Mexico: Social Bases of Agrarian Violence, 1750–1940* (Princeton, NJ: Princeton University Press, 1986); and Leticia Reina, *Las rebeliones campesinas en México, 1819–1906* (Mexico City: Siglo XXI Editores, 1980). On less frequently analyzed conservative-leaning popular movements see Jean Meyer, *Esperando a Lozada* (Zamora: Colegio de Michoacán, 1984); Guy P. C. Thomson, "La contrarreforma en Puebla, 1854–1886," in *El conservadurismo mexicano*, eds. Fowler and Morales Moreno, 239–64; and Zachary Brittsan, "In Faith or Fear: Fighting with Lozada" (PhD diss., University of California, San Diego, 2010).

19. Erika Pani, *Para mexicanizar el Segundo Imperio: el imaginario político de los imperialistas* (Mexico City: Colegio de México, 2004), 184–87.

20. See Fowler, *Mexico in the Age of Proposals,* 5.

21. See Voekel, *Alone Before God*; and Connaughton, *Dimensiones de la identidad patriótica.*

22. Will Fowler, *The Liberal Origins of Mexican Conservatism* (Glasgow, UK: Institute of Latin American Studies, 1997). See also Pani, *Para mexicanizar,* 23–188.

23. Will Fowler and Humberto Morales Moreno, "Introducción," in *El conservadurismo mexicano en el siglo XIX*, eds. Fowler and Morales Moreno (Puebla, Mexico: Benemérita Universidad Autónoma de Puebla, 1999), 11–36. See also Cecilia Noriega and Erika Pani, "Las propuestas 'conservadoras' en la década de 1840," in *Conservadurismo y derechas*, vol. 1, ed. Pani, 175–213.

24. Erika Pani, "Dreaming of a Mexican Empire: The Political Projects of the 'Imperialistas,'" *The Hispanic American Historical Review* 82, no. 1 (2002): 3–9.

For a more in-depth examination of the Maximilian empire see Pani, *Para mexicanizar el Segundo Imperio.*

25. Will Fowler, "Valentín Gómez Farías: Perceptions of Radicalism in Independent Mexico, 1821–1847," *Bulletin of Latin American Research* 15, no. 1 (1996): 39–62.

26. Will Fowler, "El pensamiento político de los moderados, 1838–1850," in *Construcción de la legitimidad política en México en el siglo XIX*, eds. Connaughton et. al. (Zamora, Michoacán: El Colegio de Michoacán, 1999), 275–302.

27. See Jaime E. Rodriguez, "Introduction," in *The Divine Charter: Constitutionalism and Liberalism in Nineteenth-Century Mexico*, ed. Jaime E. Rodriguez (Lanham, MD: Rowman and Littlefield Publishers, 2005), 1–34.

28. For a concise summary of the evolution of Catholic thinking on liberalism, see Brian Connaughton, "The Enemy Within: Catholicism and Liberalism in Independent Mexico, 1821–1860," in *The Divine Charter*, ed. Jaime E. Rodriguez, 183–204.

29. Period commentary conveys these associations. For example, a writer critical of the famed printer Ignacio Cumplido's claims to be the best printer in México quipped that if it were not for some of the truly masterful artists in his employ, he would simply be another scuffling resident of Las Escalerillas. See "Remitidos," *Diario de la República Mexicana*, 18 January 1847, as cited in Javier Rodríguez Piña, "Rafael de Rafael y Vilá: el conservadurismo como empresa," in *Constructores de un cambio cultural*, ed. Laura Suárez de la Torre (Mexico City: Instituto de Investigaciones Dr. José Luis Mora, 2003), 318–19. See also Lilia Guiot de la Garza, "El portal de los agustinos: un corredor cultural en la ciudad de México," in *Empresa y cultura en tinta y en papel*, eds. Laura Súarez de la Torre and Ángel Castro (Mexico City: Instituto de Investigaciones Dr. José Luis Mora, 2001), 233–44.

30. I owe this observation to Kenneth Ward, the curator of Latin American books at the John Carter Brown Library. A WorldCat search reveals a handful of Valdés y Redondas publications from 1847 and 1848.

31. See *Diario de Avisos*, 10 July, 15 July, 6 August, and 3 September 1857.

32. Valdés was the son of a printer and renowned editor of the *Gaceta de México*, Manuel Antonio Valdés y Munguía. The elder Valdés had worked for the Jesuit press at the Colegio de San Ildefonso prior to the order's expulsion, and he later joined the staff of Felipe de Zúñiga y Ontiveros. For more information on these printers, see W. Michael Mathes, "Origins of the Sutro Library and the Mexican Collection," in *Latin American History and Culture: Series 4, The Mexican Rare Monograph Collection, 1548–1861* (Woodbridge, CT: Primary Source Microfilm, 2003), v–xiii; available in pdf at *microformguides.gale.com/Data/Download/3265000A.pdf*. See also Lilia Guilot de la Garza, "El competido mundo de la lectura: librerías y gabinetes de lectura en la ciudad de México, 1821–1855," in *Constructores*, ed. Suárez de la Torre, 437–510. There are some discrepancies in these two sources

concerning the history of the Valdés and Abadiano y Valdés printing businesses. Mathes asserts that Luis Abadiano joined Valdés as a partner in the 1820s and took over the establishment upon Valdés's death, but he does not cite his sources. Guilot cites notarial sources dealing with Abadiano's purchase of the business in 1838, but this does not foreclose the possibility that he was previously working with his uncle and cashed out his heirs at a later date. On colonial-era Jesuit printers and printing in the eighteenth century, see Martha Ellen Whittaker, "Jesuit Printing in Bourbon Mexico City: The Press of the Colegio de San Ildefonso." (PhD diss., University of California, Berkeley, 1998).

33. Addresses often appear on the title page of pamphlets and other publications. They also appear in published compendiums of information about the city known as Guías de forasteros. Thus both Manuel F. Redondas and Abadiano appear in Mariano Galván Rivera, *Guía de Forasteros en la ciudad de Mégico para el año 1854* (Mexico City: Imprenta de Santiago Pérez y Compañía, 1854), 318–19. This publication lists 13 bookstores and 11 printers. See also Juan N. del Valle, *El viajero en México: completa guía de forasteros para el año 1864* (Mexico City: Imprenta de Andrade y Escalante, 1864). This text listed fourteen bookstores, fourteen printers, and seven lithography shops, although in some cases they are essentially the same business. The Abadiano bookstore appears under the direction of Francisco Abadiano on Santo Domingo, and the press appears under management of his brother Juan Abadiano at Escalerillas. There were many other small printers and myriad small-time vendors of books and printed materials. The Guías only listed the well-known establishments. For more information and helpful maps showing the locations of specific printers and booksellers, see Nicole Giron Barthe, "El entorno editorial de los grandes empresarios culturales," in *Empresa y cultura*, ed. Suárez de la Torre and Castro, 51–64; and Lilia Guiot de la Garza, "El competido mundo de la lectura," in *Constructores*, ed. Suárez de la Torre, 437–510.

34. For an insightful discussion of the career and business practices of perhaps the most successful printer of the era, Ignacio Cumplido; see María Esther Pérez Salas, "Los secretos de una empresa exitosa: la imprenta de Ignacio Cumplido," in *Constructores*, ed. Suárez de la Torre, 101–82.

35. On the ups and downs of press laws at this time, see Gerald L. McGowan, *Prensa y poder, 1854–1857: la Revolución de Ayutla, el Congreso Constituyente* (Mexico City: El Colegio de México, 1978). See also Pablo Piccato, *The Tyranny of Opinion: Honor in the Construction of the Mexican Public Sphere* (Durham, NC: Duke University Press, 2010).

36. Laura Suárez de la Torre, "Presentación," in *Empresa y cultura*, eds. Suárez de la Torre and Castro, 7–11.

37. Girón, "El entorno editorial de los grandes empresarios culturales," in *Empresa y cultura*, eds. Suárez and Castro, 51–64. Tables listing estimated annual pamphlet printing appear on pages 62–64.

38. Ibid. Girón lists the Abadiano shop as a second-tier printer. The top printers, those producing more than two hundred pamphlets per year, represent only a handful of the many printing establishments.

39. Hundreds of the Librería Abadiano's receipts from the 1830s and 1840s provide evidence of diverse print business; SL, Mexicana Collection, SMMS HG10.

40. The SL's Mexican book and pamphlet collection and the Abadiano's papers housed therein offer dramatic testimony to the diversity of this business venture. The inventories or valuations of private libraries are themselves a remarkable source on the printed word in Mexico. For inventories, see Balance y entrega que hizo don Francisco Antonio Santiago a don Alexandro Valdéz de la imprenta, librería y demas anexos pertenecientes a la testamentaría de Doña María Fernández de Jáuregui en calidad de traspaso según convenio entre dichos señores y dio principio en 3 de enero de 1817 . . . a saver, SL, SMMS HG1:13. For additional book lists and valuations, see SL, SMMS HG1: 5 and SMMS HG1: 6.

41. Several essays in Empresa y cultura, eds. Suárez de la Torre and Castro; and Constructores, ed. Suárez de la Torre, attest to the dynamics of collaboration and rivalry among Mexico's printing establishments during this era.

42. Donald F. Stevens, "Temerse la ira del cielo," in El conservadurismo mexicano, eds. Fowler and Morales Moreno, 87–102. See also Donald F. Stevens, "Eating, Drinking, and Being Married: Epidemic Cholera and the Celebration of Marriage in Montreal and Mexico City, 1832–1833," The Catholic Historical Review 92, no. 1 (2006): 74–94. In the second of these essays Stevens focuses on issues related to personal impieties. For those inclined to think of cholera as a celestial scourge, it was impious political reform in addition to loose morals and disorderly behavior that brought on righteous punishment.

43. Jacinto María Remusat, Carta de un canónigo a un amigo suyo sobre la procsimidad del fin del mundo (Mexico City: Ignacio Cumplido, 1841).

44. Los frailes se han pronunciado contra el congreso malvado y a la faz de la nación, hoy hacen ver [sic] lo que son (Mexico City: Imprenta testamentaria del finado Valdés a cargo de José María Gallegos, 1834), 9. At the time of publication Valdés was dead and Gallegos was running the business before it turned completely over to Abadiano y Valdés in the late 1838. This was a common practice after a printer's passing. The SL's collection of the Abadiano's receipts contains many signed by Gallegos during the transition.

45. Michael P. Costeloe, "The Mexican Church and the Rebellion of the Polkos," The Hispanic American Historical Review 46, no. 2 (May 1996): 170–78.

46. On the bleak fears of national disintegration at this time, see Antonia Pi-Suñer Llorens, "Introducción," in En busca de un discurso integrador de la nación, 1848–1884: historiografía mexicana, vol. 4, eds. Ortega y Medina and Camelo (Mexico City: Universidad Nacional Autónoma de México, 1996), 9–30.

47. Ibid. See also Terry Rugeley, *Rebellion Now and Forever: Mayas, Hispanics, and Caste War Violence in Yucatán, 1800–1880* (Stanford, CA: Stanford University Press, 2009); and Rugeley, *The River People in Flood Time: The Civil Wars in Tabasco, Spoiler of Empires* (Stanford, CA: Stanford University Press, 2014).

48. Pi-Suñer Llorens, "Introducción" in *En busca*, eds. Ortega y Medina and Carmelo.

49. Charles A. Hale, "The War with the United States and the Crisis in Mexican Thought," *The Americas* 14, no. 2 (October 1957): 153–73.

50. A detailed and actually touching testimony in this regard is Manuel Payno's essay explaining his role in the Comonfort administration and the start of the Three Years War. See Payno, *Memoria sobre la revolución de diciembre de 1857 y enero de 1858* (Mexico City: Imprenta de Ignacio Cumplido, 1860).

51. Costeloe, "The Mexican Church and the Rebellion of the Polkos," 170–78.

52. Brian Hamnett, "The Comonfort Presidency, 1855–1857," *Bulletin of Latin American Research* 15, no. 1 (1996): 81–100.

53. For a general history of the period, see Jan Bazant, "Mexico from Independence to 1867," in *The Cambridge History of Latin America*, vol. 3, ed. Leslie Bethell (Cambridge: Cambridge University Press, 1986), 423–70.

54. Pani, *Para mexicanizar*, remains the most detailed portrait of Maximilian's rule and many Mexicans' collaboration in his administration.

55. Robert J. Knowlton, *Church Property and the Mexican Reform, 1856–1910* (DeKalb: Northern Illinois University Press, 1976).

56. For example, see José J. González, "Alerta, a los hombres religiosos y los liberales," *El Monitor Republicano*, 24 June 1857. See also the trepidation pervading *El Siglo Diez y Nueve*'s coverage throughout the summer and fall of 1857, where the increasing likelihood of civil war was discussed frequently.

57. Michael P. Costeloe claimed that *El Siglo Diez y Nueve* printed 2,200 copies per day and compares these figures to the *New York Daily Herald* of the same era with a daily circulation of 23,000. See Costeloe, *The Central Republic*, 12.

58. For a description of the eccentric Adolph Sutro's book and manuscript collecting, see Russ Davidson, "Adolph Sutro as Book Collector: A New Look," *Bulletin of the California State Library Foundation* 75 (2003): 2–25. See also Gary Kurutz, "The Sutro Library," *California History* 59, no. 2 (Summer 1980), 173–78.

59. Ana Cecilia Montiel Ontiveros, "Nuevas lecturas en prensas viejas," in *Publicistas, prensa, y publicidad en la Independencia de hispanoamérica*, ed. Moisés Guzmán Pérez (Michoacán: Instituto de Investigaciones Históricas, Universidad de San Nicolás de Hidalgo, 2011), 123–52. Montiel Ontiveros lists the Spaniard Bernardo Calderón as the seventeenth-century founder of the bookstore and press ultimately owned by María Fernández de Jáuregui, a descendent, in the early nineteenth century.

60. The family link between Rivera and Jáuregui was discovered by Kenneth Ward, the curator of Latin American books at the John Carter Brown Library (pers. comm., 17 January 2014). Incidentally prior to 1647 the Rivera family spelled their name "Ribera."

61. Here I am synthesizing information gleaned from Montiel, "Nuevas lecturas en prensas viejas," 123–52; and Mathes, "Origins of the Sutro Library and the Mexican Collection," v–xiii.

62. Balance y entrega que hizo Don Francisco Antonio Santiago a don Alexandro Valdez de la Ymprenta, Librería y demas anexos pertenecientes a la testamentaria de Doña María Fernandez de Jauregui en calidad de traspaso segun convenio entre dichos señores y dío principio en 3 de enero de 1817 . . . a saver, SL, SMMS HG1:13. The entire lot, including equipment, stores of paper, tools, and furniture, came to a whopping 47,770 pesos and change, although Valdés appears to have paid only about 29,663 pesos.

63. The transition remains somewhat murky. The Abadiano press officially opened its doors as an independent business in 1835 at the address of Tacuba 4, but it would still be a few years before the Librería de Valdés officially changed names. Announcements celebrating its opening can still be consulted: Luis Abadiano y Valdés, En el día del estreno de su imprenta, en la calle de Tacuba número 4, dedico las siguientes hendechas á su patrona María Santísima de Guadalupe, 1835; Box 9, Item 45, Collection of Mexican Pamphlets, no. 1365, UCLA. It is not clear exactly when the printing press moved to Escalerillas, but it was not long after 1838.

64. SL, SMMS HG10, envelopes 1835–1845. A sampling of religious print jobs include: Cuenta de la impressión del Cuadernillo de Religiosos de la Merced, 24 November 1836, envelope 1836; Cuenta de Sonetos para el Santuario de N. Sra. De Guadalupe, 15 December 1836, envelope 1836; Cuenta de la impresión de las comuniones es-pirituales para el Convento de las Sras. Religiosas de N.M. Santa Brigida, 25 February 1842, envelope 1842; Cuenta de las impresión de Nuestra Señora de las Lágrimas para el pueblo de Tetepango, 10 July 1844, envelope 1844; and Cuenta de la impresión de la novena del Señor del Noviciado del Convento de N.P. Sto. Domingo, 13 July 1844, envelope 1844. These documents coincide with the period of transition as Luis Abadiano took full control of the Valdés printing business, with first receipts occasionally noting "Imprenta testamenatria de Valdés" and from 1837 on "Imprenta Abadiano."

65. Examples of nonreligious print jobs include Cuenta de la impresión de la Representacion del Ayuntamiento al Soberano Congreso sobre los fondos de Cárceles, 25 Februrary 1837, SL, SMMS HG10; and also Cuenta de la Mainfestacion que hace el Ayuntamiento de esta Capital sobre las constestaciones originadas por la exposición que elevó al Soberano Concreso Nacional el 11 del presente, 28 March 1837, SL, SMMS HG10. In this latter case the printers listed their costs at 114 pesos and 3 reales and they charged 200 pesos and 4 reales, a markup of 75 percent.

Margins on individual orders are frequently noted and varied widely. Very rarely were they below 20 percent, and on a couple of occasions they topped 300 percent. A 40–80 percent markup was standard.

66. On Cumplido, see Pérez Salas, "Los secretos de una empresa exitosa," in *Constructores*, ed. Suárez de la Torre, 101–82.

67. SL, SMMS HG1: 12.

68. SL, SMMS HG1: 3.

69. SL, SMMS HG1: 3 and HG1: 4.

70. See Manuel Ceballos Ramírez, *El catolicismo social: un tercero en discordia* (Mexico City: El Colegio de México, 1991), 27–40. Ceballos Ramírez stresses the importance of the Jesuits in several aspects of the Catholic revitalization during the late nineteenth century.

71. In a manner revelatory of the abrupt changes Mexico went through during this period, the Jesuits returned to Mexico only to face dispersal a few times prior to the order's definitive reestablishment in the early twentieth century. See "The Jesuits after the Restoration (1814–1912)," *The Catholic Encyclopedia*, accessed 15 March 2012, www.newadvent.org/cathen/14100a.htm.

72. Whittaker, "Jesuit Printing in Bourbon Mexico City."

73. Tranquilino de la Vega, *Los jesuitas y la constitución, ó sea, colección de los fundamentos legales que obran en favor del restablecimiento de la Compañía de Jesús en la República Mexicana* (Mexico City: Imprenta de Luis Abadino y Valdés, 1850); SL, Mexican Pamphlet Collection, vol. 380.

74. *Diálogo entre un barbero y su marchante, ó, contestación a los libelos publicados contra la Compañía de Jesús: con motivo de su restablecimiento decretado por la legislatura de Querétaro* (Mexico City: Imprenta de Luis Abadino y Valdés, 1851); SL, Mexican Pamphlet Collection, vol. 380.

75. *Voto de Gracias al Exmo. Sr. Presidente de la República. D. Antonio López de Santa Anna por el Restablecimineto de la Sagrada Compañia de Jesus*, 30 September 1853 (Mexico City: Imprenta Luis Abadiano y Valdés, 1853); SL, Mexican Pamphlet Collection, vol. 380.

76. José Sánchez, *Sermón que en la insigne colegiata de María Santísima de Guadalupe pronunció el 6 de febrero de 1859 el R. P. Fr. José Sánchez, predicador y lector de sagrada teología en el Convento de Churubusco, en la solemne acción de gracias que por las victorias obtenidas mandó celebrar el Exmo. Sr. General de División y Presidente sustituto de la República Mexicana, D. Miguel Miramón* (Mexico City: Imprenta de Abadiano, 1859), 5–6.

77. Ibid., 7.

78. SL, SMMS HG15.

79. See *Reglamento de la Sociedad Católica de señoras y deberes de estas* (Mexico City: Imprenta de José Fernández de Lara, 1870).

80. See Adame Goddard, *El pensamiento político y social de los católicos mexicanos* (Mexico City: Universidad Autónoma de México, 1981), 17–29.

81. *La Sociedad Católica*, año primero, tomo I, cuaderno 8, 16 October 1869.

82. SL, SMMS HG15. The transactions with Duarte are not dated, but from entries on previous pages they appear to be from the 1860s. In addition to his writings on religion and the prophecies, Duarte also produced materials for primary schools, most notably for reading. The Librería Abadiano purchased one hundred of his *cartillas* (alphabet booklets) and 200 syllabaries. Incidentally these records also show the famous novelist and moderate liberal Manuel Payno also maintained an account at the Librería Abadiano.

83. See *Almanaque católico e histórico para el año bisiesto 1884* (Mexico City: Antigua Librería de Abadiano, Viuda de Abadiano é hijos).

84. Lucás Alamán, *Historia de Méjico*.

85. See Moisés González Navarro, *El pensamiento político de Lucas Alamán* (Mexico City: El Colegio de México, 1952); and Luis Martin, "Lucas Alamán Pioneer of Mexican Historiography," *The Americas* 32, no. 2 (October 1975): 239–56.

86. For detailed discussions of his career see Manuel Olimón Nolasco, "Clemente de Jesús Munguía y el incipiente liberalismo de estado en México (PhD diss., Universidad Iberoamericana, 2005); and Pablo Mijangos y González, "The Lawyer of the Church: Bishop Clemente de Jesús Munguía and the Ecclesiastical Response to the Liberal Revolution in Mexico" (PhD diss., University of Texas, 2009).

87. Mijangos, "Lawyer of the Church," 16–65.

88. Ibid., 165–72.

89. Clemente de Jesús Munguía, *Del derecho natural en sus principios comunes y en sus diversas ramificaciones, ó sea, curso elemental de derecho natural y de gentes público, político, constitucional, y principios de legislación* (Morelia: Imprenta de Ignacio Arango, 1849). For and extensive discussion of this text, see Mijangos, "Lawyer of the Church," 123–72.

90. For example, see SL holdings: Clemente de Jesús Munguía, *Del culto considerado en sí mismo y en sus relaciones con el individuo, la sociedad y el gobierno, o sea, tratado completo de las obligaciones para con Dios* (Morelia: Imprenta de Ignacio Arango, 1847); Clemente de Jesús Munguía, *Los principios de la Iglesia Católica: comparadas con los de las escuelas racionalistas en sus aplicaciones a la enseñanza pública* (Morelia: Imprenta de Ignacio Arango, 1849); and Clemente de Jesús Munguía, *Exposición del Illmo. Sr. Obispo de Michoacán Lic. D. Clemente de Jesús Munguía y su M. I. y venerable cabildo con motivo del decreto de 25 de junio de este año sobre expropiación eclesiástica, pidiendo su derogación, y en caso necesario protestando contra el* (Guanajuato: Juan E. Oñate, 1856). The SL also includes two copies of the bishop's influential pastoral instructions republished by different presses in Mexico City in 1857: *Instrucciones pastorales del licenciado Clemente de Jesús Munguía, Obispo de Michoacán, a los fieles de su diócesis* (Mexico City: Andrés Boix, 1857); and Clemente de Jesús Munguía, *Instrucciones pastorales del licenciado Clemente de Jesús Munguía, Obispo de Michoacán, a los fieles de su diócesis* (Mexico City: Vicente Segura, 1857). The latter publication was produced

specially for the conservative newspaper *Diario de Avisos* run by Segura, a well-known conservative printer.

91. Mijangos, *Lawyer of the Church*, 242.

92. For an overview of the newspaper's history and editorial evolution see Guadalupe Gómez-Aguado and Adriana Gutiérrez Hernández, "El pensamiento conservador en los periódicos *La Cruz* y *El Pájaro Verde*," in *Conservadurismo y derechas*, vol. 1, ed. Pani, 214–66.

93. Andrade had long been Munguía's agent and his establishment essentially hosted a conservative salon for decades. For background on Andrade see Miguel Ángel Castro, "José María Andrade, del amor al libro," in *Constructores*, ed. Suárez de la Torre, 381–435. Mexico's AGN preserves many issues of *La Sociedad* from early December 1855 through mid-1856.

94. "Prospecto," *La Cruz*, 1 November 1855.

95. *La Cruz*, 14 May 1857; and José Joaquín Pesado, "Reflexiones sobre la iglesia y el estado," *La Cruz*, 2 July 1857.

96. Ibid. See also "Cuestiones sociales y religiosas," *La Cruz*, 20 August 1857.

97. "Salmo VI. Oración en la desgracia," *La Cruz*, 14 May 1857.

98. José Mariano Dávila, "La eucaristía símbolo de unión," *La Cruz*, 11 June 1857. For a careful discussion of the sociopolitical significance of the Blessed Sacrament, see Brian Connaughton, *Dimensiones*, chapter 5. For an English-language treatment of the issue, see Connaughton, "Conjuring the Body Politic from the Corpus Mysticum: The Post-Independent Pursuit of Public Opinion in Mexico, 1821–1854," *The Americas* 55, no. 3 (1999): 459–79.

99. José Mariano Dávila, "La eucaristía símbolo de union, *La Cruz*, 11 June 1857.

100. ¿Para que hay revoluciones?" *La Cruz*, 6 August 1857.

101. "Perpetuidad de la religión contra las tentativas de sus enemigos," *La Cruz*, 13 August 1857.

102. José Joaquín Pesado, "Sucesos de Coahila y Nuevo Leon," *La Cruz*, 8 October 1857.

103. For an insightful overview of the conservative press at this time see Erika Pani, "Una ventana sobre la sociedad decimonónica: los periodicos católicos, 1845–1857," *Secuencia*, nueva época, 36 (1996): 67–88.

104. Miguel Ángel Castro, "La prensa mexicana de 1857 a 1967: dos ejemplos," in *La definición del estado mexicano*, ed. Esther Acevedo (Mexico City: Secretaría de Gobernación, Archivo General de la Nación, 1999), 537–55.

105. McGowan, *Prensa y poder*, 117–23.

106. See Castro, "La prensa mexicana de 1857 a 1967."

107. For commentary on Comonfort's acendency, see "Nueva situación," *La Sociedad*, 10 December 1855. In truth, criticism of the Ayutla Revolt and the emergent liberal regime appears in nearly every issue from this period.

108. An unvarnished sense of fear and revulsion concerning the masses and their participation in politics comes through in several articles. For example, see "La

democracia en América," *La Sociedad*, 8 December 1855; and Antenor (José María Roa Bárcena), "El pueblo,—La plebe,—El vulgo," *La Sociedad*, 10 December 1855.

109. The disappointment with Comonfort and the warnings of inexorable radicalization appear in an article serialized over two days at the end of year: "¿Cual vendra a ser la suerte de la república?" *La Sociedad*, 24 and 25 December 1855. The statement quoted here appeared on the latter day.

110. *La Sociedad*, 21 January, 4 and 5 February 1856.

111. For the full text of the law see *Ley sobre arreglo de la libertad de imprenta* (Puebla: Imprenta de José María Macías, 1856). The law is dated 28 December 1855 in this text.

112. See, "¡¡¡El gobierno que se llama liberal suprime la libertad de imprenta!!!" *La Sociedad*, 31 December 1855. Complaining intensified further as enforcement actions occured. For the moderate liberal perspective, see G. Alfaro, "Preferimos la censura previa," *La Patria*, 13 February 1856. For a discussion of press legislation and press juries see Piccato, *The Tyranny of Opinion*, chapter 1.

113. Francisco Vera, "Terrible desenfreno de ideas," *La Sociedad*, 8 March 1856.

114. For example, see G. Alfaro, "Revista de Periódicos," *La Patria*, 8 March 1856.

115. Luis Villard, "Revista de periódicos," *La Patria*, 15 January 1856. A month later G. Alfaro revisited the issue, faulting *El Monitor Repúblicano* for trying to hastily implant liberal utopia. Religious change, he suggested, had to be implemented very gradually and with marked prudence (a quality lacking among radicals). See Alfaro, "Revista de periódicos," *La Patria*, 15 February 1856.

116. Luis Villard, "Revista de periódicos," *La Patria*, 29 January 1856. For a thorough, clear presentation of the radical liberal critique of the Catholic Church's role in society and the rationale behind the Laws of the Reform, see E. J. Ríos, "Soberanía del Pueblo," *El Monitor Repúblicano*, serialized 1–5 January 1857. In a nutshell, Ríos argued that a true, deeply democratic Christianity had been highjacked by a clerical cabal when Gregory VII (circa 1020–1085) secured papal domination of the Church. Afterward corrupt churchmen amassed wealth, cynically blinded the populace with superstitious beliefs and practices, and systematically blocked popular sovereignty.

117. See *La Patria*, 20 March 1856. See also Florencio M. del Castillo, "La Cruz y la libertad," *El Monitor Repúblicano*, 9 April 1857; and José J. Gonzalez, "Viernes Santo," *El Monitor Repúblicano*, 10 April 1857.

118. Luis Villard, "Revista de periódicos," *La Patria*, 6 February 1856. The impetus behind this article was two of Vera's essays, "Males y peligros," printed two days before Villard's editorial, and "La demagogia es enemiga del órden y de la nacionalidad," cited above. On 24 January he had explicitly summarized and responded to Vera's "Los estremos se tocan."

119. Payno, *Memoria*, 77–78.

120. G. Alfaro, "Otro jucio de imprenta," *La Patria*, 26 February 1856.

121. G. Alfaro, "Revista de Periodicos, *La Patria*, 26 February 1856.

122. J. García de la Huerta, "Rumores," *El Monitor Repúblicano*, 29 January 1857.

123. For examples, see issues of *El Siglo Diez y Nueve* throughout the fall of 1857.

124. "Al fin del mundo," *El Siglo Diez y Nueve*, 2 July 1857. Apparently mystical narratives were in style. An eccentric prophetic pamphlet also appeared in 1863 that criticized both liberals and conservatives, but in this case the author declared himself the "Emmanuel of Mexico"; see José Manuel Teodocio Alvírez, *Manifiesto a los fieles de Jesucristo* (Morelia: Imprenta de O. Ortiz, 1863). This text appears in a bound collection of ephemera at the BN, Fondo Lafragua, RLAF 348 LAF. Incidentally, a copy of the Matiana prophecies from the *Calendario nigromántico para el año 1858* is in this same volume.

125. Manuel M. de Zamacona, "Falsas Alarmas—La prensa reaccionaria," *El Siglo Diez y Nueve*, 18 February 1861.

126. See Costeloe, *The Central Republic*, 12.

127. These figures come from Milda Bazant, "Lecturas del Porfiriato," in *Historia de la lectura en México* (Mexico City: El Colegio de México, 1988), 206. Not surprisingly, rates varied by sex: only 11 percent of women compared to 17 percent of men could read in 1895; and by 1910 these rates rose to an estimated 17 percent and 22 percent, respectively. Indeed, literacy rates were quite low until the twentieth-century educational reforms accompanying the revolution took hold. Thus by 1930 some 61 percent of the populace could read and by 1960 over 80 percent were literate: see Linda King, *Roots of Identity: Language and Literacy in Mexico* (Stanford, CA: Stanford University Press, 1994), 101–2.

128. Originally the novel was published under his pseudonym, Antenor. For more on this author see Begoña Arteta, "José María Roa Bárcena," in *En busa*, ed. Pi-Suñer Llorens, 241–56. See also Leticia Algaba, "Prólogo;" and Jorge Ruffinelli, "Epílogo," in José María Roa Bárcena, *Novelas y cuentos* (Mexico City, Factoría: 2000), ix–xii and 303–14, respectively. The novella appears on pages 95–198. See also John Hays Hammond, "José María Roa Bárcena: Mexican Writer and Champion of Catholicism," *The Americas* 6, no. 1 (1949): 45–55; and John S. Brushwood, "The Literary Personality of José María Roa Bárcena," *The Americas* 8, no. 2 (October 1951): 203–8.

129. Hammond, "José María Roa Bárcena," 51.

130. Erika Pani, "'Ciudadana y muy ciudadana'? Women and the State in Independent Mexico, 1810–1930," *Gender and History* 18, no. 1 (April 2006): 5–19. See also Pani, "Una ventana sobre la sociedad decimonónica: los periodicos católicos, 1845–1857," 67–88.

131. *Representación que algunas señoras morelianas eleven al soberano congreso constituyente contra la tolerancia de cultos* (Morelia: Imprenta Ignacio Arango, 1856), SL, Mexican Pamphlet Collection.

132. Pani, "'Ciudadana y muy ciudadana'?"

133. For an extensive discussion of the liberal and conservative press clashing over this issue and others, see McGowan, *Prensa y Poder*, 157–74.

134. Payno, *Memoria*, 48.

135. Pani, "'Ciudadana y muy ciudadana'?"
136. The topic had been debated previously, although not as hotly. Hence some petitions from earlier moments in the debate merit mention. One of these was published by the Abadiano press warned of encroaching Protestantism in 1835; José María de Jesús, *Segunda carta pastoral que dirige a su clero y diosesanos* (Mexico City: Luis Abadiano y Valdés, 1835). See also *Representación que la Congregación de San Pedro de esta capital dirige á las agustas cámaras de la unión, contra el proyecto de establecer en la república la tolerancia de cultos* (Mexico City: Tipografía de R. Rafael, 1849); For evidence of the 1856 petition campaign, see *Esposición que el Ilustrísimo Señor Obispo, el señor provisor y vicario general; y el venerable cabildo de la diocesis de Chiapas, dirijen al soberano congreso general consituyente contra el proyecto de tolerancia de cultos en la república* (Mexico City: Establecimiento Tipográfico de Andrés Boix, 1856); *Esposición que varios vecinos de Morelia eleven al soberano congreso constituyente pidiéndole se digne reprobar el artículo 15 del proyecto de constitución sobre tolerancia de cultos* (Morelia: Imprenta de Ignacio Arango, 1856); *Representación al soberano congreso contra el artículo 15 del proyecto de constitución sobre tolerancia religiosa* (Mexico City: Imprenta Andrade y Escalante, 1856); *Representación que eleven al soberano congreso los vecinos de las municipalidades de Cuautitlán, Tepotzotlán, Huehuetoca, San Miguel, Tultepec, Tultitlán, y Teoloyucán pidiendo se repuebe el artículo XV del proyecto de constitución sobre tolerancia religiosa* (Mexico City: Imprenta de Vicente Segura, 1856); and *Representación que los habitantes de Zamora dirigen al soberano congreso constituyente pidiendo que no se permita en la república la libertad de cultos que establece el artículo 15 del proyecto de constitución, presentado por la commission resprectiva de día 16 de junio de 1856* (Mexico City: Imprenta de M. Murguía, 1856).
137. See Stafford Poole, Our Lady of Guadalupe: The Origins and Sources *of a Mexican National symbol, 1531–1797*. (Tucson: University of Arizona Press, 1995).
138. Margaret Chowning, *Rebellious Nuns*, 254.

CHAPTER 3

1. Guilot de la Garza, "El competido mundo de la lectura," in *Constructores*, ed. Suárez de la Torre, 437–510.
2. "*Selectos calendarios para 1858*," *Diario de Avisos*, 11 November 1857, 4. Emphasis is present in the original.
3. For example, see *La Pata de Cabra*, 4 October, 1855; *Diario de Avisos*, 30 November 1857; and *Diario de Avisos*, 22 November 1859. According to Esther Pérez Salas, every October during this period *El Siglo Diez y Nueve* began running advertisements for calendarios, particularly those of Ignacio Cumplido (the printer and editor of the newspaper): see "Los secretos de una empresa existosa," in *Constructores*, ed. Suárez, 101–182. Extant receipts from the Librería Abadiano

preses also attest to this: see, SL, SMMS HG10, 1836 folder, Impresión del *Calendario de don Martin Rivera para el año 1837*, 19 October 1836. The following year they were also producing the next issue: see, SL, SMMS HG10, 1837 folder, *Calendario del Sr. don Martin Rivera para el año 1838*, 31 December 1837.

4. *Calendario nigromántico para el año 1858* (Mexico City: Imprenta de Manuel Murguía). Sadly, the extent versions lack the illustrations.

5. For example, see Suárez de la Torre, "Prosperidad y quiebra un vivencia en la vida de Mariano Galván Rivera." in *Empresa y cultura*, ed. Suárez de la Torre and Castro (Mexico City: Instituto de Investigaciones Dr. José María Luis Mora, 2001), 109–22

6. In the *Diario de Avisos*, 11 November 1857, the Librería Blanquel listed 30 distinct almanacs; including Mexico's oldest calendario, the famed *Calendario de Galván*; several of Manuel Murguía's almanacs; a self-titled *Calendario de Blanquel*; and others produced by Nabor Chávez's presses for exclusive sale at the Blanquel bookstore.

7. In 1859 the Librería Blanquel advertised calendarios at this price; see *Diario de Avisos*, 11 November 1859.

8. Costeloe, *The Central Republic*, 20. In this instance, Costeloe cites advertisements from the 1830s and 1840s.

9. *Diario de Avisos*, 11 November 1857. As expected, this almanac featured anecdotes from the life of Saint Francis and the history of the Franciscan order. For a single almanac, 1 real seems to have been a common price for many years. In the 1830s, the *Calendario de Galván* apparently sold for this price, and the same was true for the *Calendario de Cumplido* in the 1850s. In 1856 the Librería Blanquel sold the *Calendario de los polvos de la madre Celestina para el año 1857* for 1 real as well. The advertisement also notes that 1000 copies could be bought for 75 pesos; a gross for 12 pesos; and a dozen for 1 peso and 1 real. See Isabel Quiñonez, *Mexicanos en su tinta: calendarios* (Mexico City: Instituto Nacional de Antropología e Historia, 1994), 55, 62, and 100.

10. For a portrait of different shops see Guilot de la Garza, "El Portal de Agustinos," in *Empresa y cultura*, eds. Suárez de la Torre and Castro, 233–43.

11. Quiñonez, *Mexicanos en su tinta*, 100. One of the illustrations reproduced in this work features an advertisement placed by Simon Blanquel's bookstore on the back page of one of its 1858 almanacs. It states that in addition to his store in Mexico City, copies would be available at the festival of the Virgin of San Juan de los Lagos in Jalisco (January 25 to February 2 each year).

12. *Calendario de la Madre Matiana para el año 1867*. As stated on the title page, this almanac, although produced at Boix's shop, was commissioned for Simón Blanquel's bookstore.

13. *Diccionario Porrúa de historia, biografía y geografía de México* (Mexico City: Editorial Porrúa, 1995), vol. 3: 2400.

14. For a description of their origin and the collection in Mexico's National Library,

see Adalberto Lamadrid Lusarreta, "Guías de forasteros y calendarios mexicanos de los siglos XVIII y XIX, existentes en la Biblioteca Nacional de México," *Boletín del Instituto de Investigaciones Bibliográficas* 6 (1971): 9–135, particularly 9–11. For a general discussion of the genre, see Quiñónez, *Mexicanos en su tinta*.

15. See Erica Segre, *Intersected Identities: Strategies of Visualisation in Nineteenth- and Twentieth-Century Mexican Culture* (New York: Berghahn Books, 2007), 5–58.

16. Ibid., 1–4.

17. Ibid., 5–58.

18. For a detailed discussion of these texts see María Esther Pérez Salas, *Costumbrismo y litografía en México: un nuevo modo de ver* (Mexico City: Universidad Nacional Autónoma de México, 2005), 211–64.

19. Hence the magazine *El Daguerreotipo*. For a discussion of the daguerreotype metaphor, see Segre, *Intersected Identities*, 26–33.

20. Enrique Pupo-Walker, "The Brief Narrative in Spanish America," in *The Cambridge History of Latin American Literature*, eds. González Echevarría and Pupo-Walker (Cambridge: Cambridge University Press, 1996), 490–535.

21. J. Decaen et.al., *México y sus alrededres* (Mexico City: Establecimiento Litográfico de Decaen: 1855 and 1856). See also Hilarión Frías y Soto et. al., *Los mexicanos pintados por sí mismos*, facisimile edition (Mexico City: Librería Porrúa, 1974). The original text was first sold in installments in October 1854 and later offered as a single volume in 1855; see Pérez Salas, *Costumbrismo y litografía*, 278.

22. There are many examples of this custom. For example, the *Calendario de Juan Navarro para el año 1849* (Mexico City: Imprenta Navarro) reprinted excerpts on folkloric dress from *El Museo Mexicano o miscelánea pintoresca de amenidades curiosas e instructivas*, 4 volumes (Mexico City: Ignacio Cumplido, 1843–1844). At least three different almanacs published by Manuel Murguía published sketches and images from *Los mexicanos pintados por sí mismos* in the late 1850s: for example, the *Calendario de López, Calendario universal,* and *Calendario de Murguía*.

23. A classic example of this is the career of Guillermo Prieto; see Begoña Arteta, "Guillermo Prieto," in *En busca*, ed. Pi-Suñer Llorens, 35–54.

24. For example, see the recent facsimile edition; J. Decaen et.al., *México y sus alrededores: colección de vistas, trajes y monumentos* (Mexico City: Inversora Bursátil, 1989).

25. Ibid., 7. For example, Francisco González Bocanegra's entry, "El Sagrario Metropolitano," goes on at length about the profoundly devout sentiments of the populace, the religious zeal of priests, and waxes nostalgic about parish life. He relates intense feelings among the populace for the temples where they are baptized and become members of the Catholic Church. As a result, it is reminiscent of the editorializing of conservative newspapers and their claims of the nation's Catholic character. In a similar vein Nicieto Zamacois praises the colonial legacy

of Catholic architecture and its symbolic testimony to a lost social wellbeing; see "Convento de San Francisco," 21. In contrast, Florencio M. del Castillo's entries, "Trajes de indios mexicanos," 17–18, and "Trajes mexicanos," 19–20, reproduces the anticlerical criticisms common in liberal newspapers. He also alludes to new laws (liberal reforms) addressing these "problems."

26. Decaen et.al., *México y sus alrededores*, 1854 and 1855.

27. For a description of *Los mexicanos pintados*, see Pérez Salas, *Costumbrismo y litografía*, 277–323.

28. José María Rivera, "La china," in *Los mexicanos pintados*, 89–98.

29. See José María Rivera, "La chiera,"; Ignacio Ramírez, "La estanquillera"; and Pantaleón Tovar, "La recamarera," in *Los mexicanos pintados*, 7–12, 177–82, 99–108, respectively.

30. Juan de Dios Arias, "La partera," in *Los mexicanos pintados*, 267–71.

31. Niceto de Zamacois, "La casera," in *Los mexicanos pintados*, 227–36.

32. Manuel Gutiérrez Nájera, "El calendario de Galván," in *Obras*, edited by José Luis Martínez (Mexico City: Fondo de Cultura Económica, 2003): 506–7. This text was originally published on 27 December 1894.

33. Fidel (Guillemo Prieto), "San Lunes de Fidel," *El Siglo Diez y Nueve*, 16 December 1878.

34. See Quiñónez, *Mexicanos en su tinta*, 49–66.

35. For example, see *Almanak de la chocolatería española por José Juan Torremocha, 1878* (Mexico City: Imprenta Políglota).

36. Prieto is referring to one of the staple almanacs sold at the bookstore of Simon Blanquel: such as the *Calendario del negrito poeta para en año bisiesto de 1860* (Mexico City: Imprenta Nabor Chávez). These featured stories about a poor black colonial resident of Mexico City famed for his humorous verses.

37. See "Magic Lantern," *The Grove Encyclopedia of Materials and Techniques in Art* (Oxford: Oxford University Press, 2008).

38. See Rafael Barajas, "El país de 'El llorón de Icamole'" (Mexico City: Fondo de Cultura Económica, 2007), 45. Mexicans, apparently, appropriated the image of the devil figure as a dandified lanternist from French satire of the 1840s; see Segre, *Intersected Identities*, 44.

39. See José Tomás de Cuellar, *La linterna mágica*, ed. Mauricio Magdaleno (Mexico City: Universidad Aútonoma de México, 1973).

40. Segre, *Intersected Identities*, 42.

41. For example, the *Calendario jocoso y divertido del telégrafo para el año 1861* (Mexico City: Imprenta de Manuel Castro).

42. *Calendario de la democracia dedicado al Pueblo Mexicano, 1852* (Mexico City: Imprenta de Leandro Valdés).

43. *Calendario manual para el año del Señor de 1780* (Mexico City: Imprenta de Zúñiga y Ontiveros).

44. For example see José Mariano de Zúñiga y Ontiveros, *Calendario manual y guía de forasteros de México para el año de 1803* (Mexico City: Imprenta de Zúñiga y Ontiveros).

45. For example, see Mariano Galván Rivera, *Guía de forasteros* This text still contained classic santoral-centered front matter for the first 30 pages or so. In contrast, Juan N. del Valle, *El viajero en México*, abandoned the classic almanac material and offered an impressive 700-page compendium of information on the city.

46. See advertisement in *Calendario burlesco para el año 1861* (Mexico City: J.M. Aguilar y Compañía). Similar announcements appear in many Aguilar almanacs.

47. *Calendario de la Madre Matiana para el año 1867* and *Calendario de la Perla de México para el año 1867* (Mexico City: Imprenta A. Boix a cargo de M. Zornoza).

48. For example a copy of the Matiana prophecies from the *Calendario nigromántico* appears in such a volume, BN, Fondo Lafragua, RLAF 348 LAF. The SL contains several bound collections of almanacs. One in particular includes many different texts separated from the santoral and collected around 1870: such as recipes from the *Calendario curioso*, a history of Rome from the *Calendario universal*, a discussion of symbolism and flowers from the *Calendario de los amantes*, and stories about apparitions and ghosts from the *Nigromántico*. Of course, with the front matter removed accurate publication information is missing. However, as was customary, a footer on every second page lists the name of the calendario, such as "Amantes," or "Profético."

49. Benedict Anderson, *Imagined Communities: Reflections on the Origin and Spread of Nationalism*, rev. ed. (London: Verso, 2006).

50. For example, see *Tercer Calendario Portatil de Juan N. del Valle* (Mexico City: Imprenta Juan N. del Valle, 1844); and *Calendario para el año 1871* (Merida: Imprenta y litografía de J. D. Espinosa é Hijos), likely authored by María del Carmen Espinosa.

51. *Calendario protestante de los amigos cristianos para el año de 1868*, ed. José Parra y Álvarez (Mexico City: Tipografía de M. Castro).

52. See *Calendario de la Sociedad de San Vicente de Paul para el año 1867* (Mexico City: Imprenta de José María Andrade y Felipe Escalante, 1866).

53. *Diccionario Porrúa de historia*, vol. 1,1036.

54. *Calendario de Cumplido para el año de 1846*. Tegovita is more commonly known in the present-day as Kateri Tekakwitha (1656–1680). She was beatified by John Paul II in 1980 and canonized by Pope Benedict XVI in 2012. See "Blessed Kateri Tekakwitha," in *Catholic Online*, www.catholic.org/saints/saint.php?saint_id=154 (accessed 27 December 2011). See also Sharon Otterman, "Complex Emotions Over the First American Indian Saint," *The New York Times*, 24 July 2012.

55. For example, see *Calendario económico para el año 1861* (Mexico City: Imprenta de Manuel Murguía y Companía,). Issues for 1862, 1864, 1867, 1869, and 1870 reveal the same minimalist formula.

56. For example, see *Calendario de las niñas para el año 1861* (Mexico City: Tipografía de Manuel Murguía,). See also issues from 1862, 1864, 1867, and 1869.

57. *Calendario de las niñas para el año 1862* (Mexico City: Tipografía de Manuel Murguía). The section is titled "Maximas y pensamientos morales."

58. See *Calendario de los niños para el año 1859* and *Calendario de los niños para el año 1861* (Mexico City: Tipografía de Manuel Murguía). These issues offer essentially the same texts, but the latter has more attractive illustrations. Perhaps with civil war raging the press decided to reuse the same material within a few short years. The religion and race articles appeared in the 1861 issue.

59. *Calendario enciclopédico de la juventud para el año de 1865* (Mexico City: Imprenta Literario). Segura was the owner and editor of press until his murder in 1860. Like others it produced several almanacs every year. Most likely his sons or widow ran the business afterward. Segura's biography reveals how small the printing world of this era was in Mexico. He was a poet and had cofounded the influential satirical newspaper *Don Simplicio* with Guillermo Prieto and Ignacio Ramírez, and he was a collaborator in Cumplido's *El Museo Mexicano*. Incidentally he was the editor of the conservative *Diario de Avisos* when the Librería Abadiano purchased advertisements in the newspaper to announce the sale of the Madre Matiana pamphlets in 1857. See *Diccionario Porrúa de historia*, vol. 4: 3252.

60. See *Calendario universal para 1859* (Mexico City: Tipografía de Manuel Murguía). The 1861 issue is very similar but offers a different sketched character. From 1864 into the 1870s the *Calendario universal*'s specialty was world history with a mix of stories and social commentary.

61. For example, see *Calendario de Murguía para 1855*.

62. See *Calendario de Murguía para 1858* and *Calendario de Murguía para 1861*.

63. See *Calendario de la democracia dedicado al pueblo mexicano para 1851* and *Calendario de la democracia dedicado al pueblo mexicano para 1852*. It is not clear if there were any kinship ties between Luis Abadiano y Valdés and this printer.

64. The most caustically partisan calendario I have seen espouses the conservative cause and derides liberal leaders as a thieving, murderous cabal of traitors delivering Mexico into the clutches of the United States; see *Calendario reaccionario para el año de 1861* (Mexico City: Imprenta de Vicente Segura, 1860).

65. On Andrade, see Miguel Ángel Castro, "José María Andrade, del amor al libro," in *Constructores*, ed. Suárez de la Torre, 381-436.

66. *Calendario católico para el año 1861*.

67. *Calendario católico para el año 1863*.

68. *Calendario de la Sociedad de San Vicente de Paul para el año 1867*.

69. See the *Almanaque católico e histórico para el año bisiesto 1884*. The publication information states that this is the eighth edition, suggesting that their first almanac by this title emerged in 1876. The 1886 issue followed essentially the same structure and offered the same kinds of texts as the 1884 edition, including another very detailed santoral.

70. By 1884 both Luis Abadiano and his son and successor Francisco were dead. The press was now in the hands of the latter's widow and his sons.

71. *Calendario burlesco para el año 1861* and *El primer calendario impolítico y justiciero para el año 1853* (Mexico City: Imprenta de Navarro).

72. In a similar vein some almanac's offered plays or comic operas that incorporated costumbrista social types as characters. For example, see *Calendario nigromántico para el año 1856* (Mexico City: Tipografía Manuel Murguía); and *El calendario del Tío Caniyitas para el año 1858* (Mexico City: Imprenta Vicente Segura, 1857). The former features a mash up of Mexican costumbrista figures and Greek gods. The latter represents an example where the literary material is clearly a separate publication appended to the standard almanac material. It even features different publication information.

73. *Calendario profético para el año 1859* (Mexico City: Tipografía M. Murguía).

74. "Los profetas en política," *Calendario profético.* This text was removed from the original almanac and bound with several other calendario excerpts. The title page is missing so its exact date cannot be determined. However, several other almanacs bound alongside it reveal dates ranging from 1868 to 1870.

75. Other publishers also targeted this niche. For example, see *Calendario de los duendes y aparecidos para 1864* (Mexico City: Imprenta A. Boix a cargo de M. Zornoza).

76. For example, see *Calendario nigromántico para el año 1861* as well as the *Nigromántico*'s 1864 issue. Interestingly the former featured a lithograph of a typical wizard inspired by European folklore. He appears in his alchemist's laboratory. The latter offered an image of a shirtless African, or Afro-Latin, sorcerer wearing a grass skirt and wielding his wand as he dances outdoors.

77. *Calendario nigromántico para el año 1867.*

78. This was particularly the case for *Calendario de los duendes y aparecidos para 1864* and the *Calendario de los cuentos de aparecidos para 1867* (Mexico City: Imprenta A. Boix a cargo de M. Zornoza).

79. Boix had died and Zornoza ran the press for his heirs.

80. Blanquel also carried almanacs published by Nabor Chávez such as the *Calendario mágico y de suertes para el año de 1861* (Mexico City: Tipografía Nabor Chávez).

81. In another ironic twist of fate, Maximilian and his wife Carlota became fixtures of the almanac genre in subsequent years. Apparently the reading audience enjoyed the tragic story of the ill-fated European prince and his wife's desperate attempts to save him. For example, see *Calendario histórico de Maximiliano para el año 1869* (Mexico City: Imprenta de Murguía); *Calendario histórico de Carlota para 1869* (Mexico City: Imprenta de Juan N. del Valle); and *Calendario histórico de la Emperatriz Carlota Amalia para 1871* (Mexico City: González y Compañía).

82. *La Sombra*, 24 July 1866. Here the newspaper poked fun of Toluca, whose literary culture allegedly revolved around such things as the prophecies.

83. *El Siglo Diez y Nueve*, 9 July 1861. The paper in question was called *El Lazo Verde*.

84. "La reacción," *La Patria*, 30 October 1879.

85. "A la altura de nuestra causa," *El Libre Pensador*, 5 May 1870.

86. Juan A. Mateos, "Editorial: La Voz de México," *El Siglo Diez y Nueve*, 13 March 1875. For biographical information on Mateos, see *Diccionario Porrúa de historia*, vol. 3, 2359.

87. "Profecías, descubrimientos y opinions opuestas," *El Boquiflojo*, 17 March 1870. The reference here is to apocalyptic predictions associated with Anabaptism during the Reformation. See "Anabapitists," *The Oxford Dictionary of the Church*, 3rd ed., eds. F. L. Cross and E. A. Livingston (Oxford: Oxford University Press, 2005).

88. See "El congreso obrero," *El Hijo del Trabajo*, 22 May 1876. On newspapers and their political allegiances, see José Bravo Ugarte, *Periodistas y periódicos mexicanos* (Mexico City: Editorial Jus, 1966), 71.

89. "El congreso obrero," *El Hijo del Trabajo*, 22 May 1876.

90. See *La Metralla*, 7 September 1876; 10 September 1876; and 28 September 1876.

91. La Madre Matiana, "Otro consejo al Sr. Lerdo," *La Metralla*, 7 September 1876. The emphasis is present in the original source.

92. Interestingly, the author of *El Siglo*'s attacks was Juan A. Mateos, the liberal congressman and writer who made earlier reference to Madre Matiana in regard to Catholic education. The faux Matiana explicitly responded to his accusations; see *La Metralla*, 28 September 1876. According to Catholic historian Mariano Cuevas, Mateos repented on his deathbed, performing a full confession. See Cuevas, *Historia de la Iglesia en México*, 5th ed., vol. 5 (Mexico City: Editorial Patria, 1947): 413n9.

93. La Madre Matiana, "Juicio," *La Metralla*, 10 September 1876.

94. "Todavía lo de Sierra Mojada," *La Libertad*, 15 October 1879. See also *La Libertad*, 10 June 1880.

95. "La madre Matiana," *La Libertad*, 23 November 1880.

96. See "El profeta Juvenal," *La Libertad*, 7 August 1884.

97. "Felicitación por el año de 1898," *El Contemporáneo*, 5 January 1898.

98. Agustín Rivera, "El fanatismo: un artículo del sabio sacerdote y notable historiador D. Agustín Rivera," *El Contemporáneo*, 22 June 1908.

99. Previously Rivera criticized a pamphlet published by Mexico's Círculo Católico in 1887 that characterized liberalism as heresy. He was also very critical of efforts to distribute the offending pamphlet among the poor and middle classes. See Adame Goddard, *El Pensamiento*, 110–11.

100. Rivera, "El fanatismo," *El Contemporáneo*, 22 June 1908.

CHAPTER 4

1. Biographical information on Méndez Pérez Gil comes primarily from three books on the foundress of Adoratrices Perpetuas Guadalupanas: Vicente M.

Méndez, *Memorias de la Madre Mercedes de la Santísima Trinidad* (Merida: Díaz Massa, 1952); María Teresa Sánchez Velázquez, *Admirable es Dios en sus obras: madre María de las Mercedes, su vida, sus virtudes, su obra* (Mexico City: Instituto de Religiosas Adoratrices Perpetuas Guadalupanas, 1981); and *El Sí de María de las Mercedes de la Santísima Trinidad* (Mexico City: Instituto de Religiosas Adoratrices Perpetuas Guadalupanas, 1996). The founderess's nephew, then a priest in Merida, wrote the first of these. He claimed to have consulted documents provided by members of the APG. The latter lists no author and is written in first person as if it were an autobiography, even though Méndez never penned such a text. It was likely aimed at postulants, functioning as an expanded update of the previous books. None of these texts footnote their sources. A condensed biography appears online: http://adoratricesperpetuasguadalupanas.org. mx/Vida.html (accessed 18 May 2012). *Admirable es Dios* (20–21) and the online biographical sketch mentioned Madre Matiana's prophecies. In fact, the online text appears to be a summary of the 1981 publication.

2. Sánchez Velázquez, *Admirable es Dios*, 20–21. A first cousin, Maclovia Pérez, also joined the sisters' spiritual quest and became a member of the APG.

3. Méndez, *Memorias*, 15–49.

4. Adame Goddard, *El pensamiento político*, 76–94.

5. Pope John Paul II canonized the Siervas' founder, Father José María Yermo y Parres, in 2000 alongside dozens of Catholic martyrs of revolutionary church-state conflict. For more on this order see the founder's 1903 memoir: José María Yermo y Pares, *Memorias de la fundación, principios y progresos de la sociedad de las Siervas del Sagrado Corazón de Jesús y de los Pobres* (Puebla: Siervas del Sagrado Corazón de Jesús y los Pobres, 1969).

6. Méndez, *Memorias*, 72–73.

7. Present-day members of the group describe their order's move into education somewhat differently. Apparently the exclusive focus on devotion to the Blessed Sacrament was not producing hoped-for results. The APG added teaching in hopes that education would promote devotion to the Eucharist. Interview with Madre María de la Paz Zedillo, 24 July 2007.

8. *Profecías completas de madre Matiana* (Mexico City: Imprenta Gutemburg, 1914).

9. Dionisio A. de Jesus María to J. Reyes Velasco, 14 December 1883. AHAM, Base de Pelagio Antonio de Labastida y Dávalos, Secretaría Arzobispal, Correspondencia: caja 222, exp. 31, 1883.

10. For example, Abate Orsini, *Vida de la Santísima Virgen y explicación del Ave María* (Mexico City: Imprenta de José Reyes Velásco, 1874); *Reglamento interior del colegio fundado por la Comisión del Asilo de Criadas de la Sociedad de Ruth* (Mexico City: Tipografía de José Reyes Velásco, 1875); Ambrosio Lara, *Sermón de la Santísima Virgen de Guadalupe predicado en su insigne colegiata por Monseñor Dr. D. Ambrosio Lara, Protonotario Apostólico de su Santidad y Provisor del Arzobispado el día 12 de diciembre de 1893* (Mexico City: Imprenta Guadalupana

de Reyes Velásco, 1893); and Mateo C. Palazuelos, *Observaciones de un lector imparcial a la carta del Sr. D. Joaquín García Icazbalceta contra la aparición Guadalupana* (Mexico City: Imprenta Guadalupana de Reyes Velásco, 1896).

11. AHAM, Base de Pelagio Antonio de Labastida y Dávalos, Secretaría Arzobispal, Censura: caja 168, exp. 63; and caja 171, exp. 62, respectively.

12. AHAM, Base de Pelagio Antonio de Labastida y Dávalos, Secretaría Arzobispal, Censura: caja 188, exp. 57. Reyes did not mention the novel's author, but he included the title *La voz de la conciencia.* It seems likely that he was referring to Spanish writer Juan Cortada's mid-nineteenth-century novel *La voz de la conciencia, ó, el libro de familia: colección de ejemplos morales.* Reyes also published Laura Mantecón de González's testimony of her scandalous divorce from Porfirian henchman, as well as president from 1880 to 1884, General Manuel González. The long description of Gonzalez's boorish behavior and brusque treatment of Mantecón undoubtedly embarrassed a member of President Díaz's inner circle. See Laura Mantecón de Gonzalez, *Información producida por la señora Laura Mantecón de González ante la Tercera Sala del Tribunal Superior, en el jucio de divorcio que sigue contra su esposo el señor general don Manuel González* (Mexico City: J. Reyes Velásco, 1886).

13. Dionisio A. de Jesus María to J. Reyes Velasco, 14 December 1883, AHAM, Secretaría Arzobispal, Correspondencia: caja 222, exp. 31, 1883.

14. For examples, see Blackbourn, *Marpingen*; and Kselman, *Miracles and Prophecies.*

15. Ceballos Ramírez, *El catolicismo social.*

16. Interview with Madre María de la Paz Zedillo, 24 July 2007.

17. For a short biographical sketch see *Diccionario Porrúa de historia*, vol. 2, 1118–19.

18. See also "Rectificación," *La ilustración católica*, 19 February 1879. This notice was a response to a mistake this newspaper made concerning the school of law in Mexico City. They had confused the younger Duarte with his father and he corrected them, providing biographical information on the elder Duarte.

19. "Defunción," *La Voz de México*, 12 March 1897.

20. *La Sociedad*, 6 July 1863.

21. *La Sociedad*, 17 November 1863. The newspaper lists imperial officials, including Duarte, on this date. On his private practice, see del Valle, *El viajero en México*, 328. Duarte appears among the working lawyers in the city.

22. On these types of issues, see Pani, "Dreaming of a Mexican Empire," 1–5.

23. Adame Goddard, *El pensamiento político*, 17–29.

24. Ibid., 17–34.

25. *Diccionario Porrúa de historia*, vol. 2, 1118–19.

26. In *La Revista Universal*, 17 December 1868, Duarte is listed as the secretary of a school called Ateneo México. The texts are Duarte's *Silabario: dispuesto con un nuevo metodo para la mejor y más pronta enseñanza de la lectura* (Mexico City Imprenta Económica, 1865), and *Cartilla, o compendio teórico práctico de los*

primeros conocimientos necesarios para la buena lectura (Mexico City: Imprenta Económica, 1865). These were the same texts the Librería Abadiano received from him, as noted in chapter 2: SL, SMMS HG15; Duarte provided them one hundred *Cartillas* and two hundred *Silabarios*. The date is not recorded, but most of the previous pages list dates from the late 1860s. He continued publishing primary education materials in the 1870s, such as Duarte, *De las sílabas irregulares: lecciones dispuestas* (Mexico City: Imprenta del Cinco de Mayo, 1874); and *Silabario preparatorio* (Mexico City: Imprenta del Cinco de mayo, 1876).

27. Luis G. Duarte, *Argumentos sobre la Divina Providencia* (Mexico City: Imprenta de la Viuda é hijos de Murguía, 1874).

28. Luis G. Duarte, *Diccionario de dudas ortográficas* (Mexico City: Imprenta Católica, 1881.) Despite his political affiliations the government saw fit to purchase one hundred subscriptions of this text for public schools: AGN, GD 125, Instrucción Pública y Bellas Artes, vol. 233, exp. 39, 1881.

29. *La Voz de México*, 17 May 1887.

30. The Catholic press recommended Duarte's *Argumentos sobre la Divina Providencia*, and noted its official ecclesiastical approval; see *La Voz de México*, 4 July 1874. According to *El Correo del Comercio*, 28 September 1876, in that year his reading primers were being used by the municipal schools of Tacubaya. Advertisements from the late 1870s and 1880s promoted Duarte's bookstore and its selection of religious books, but Mexicans could also purchase images of conservative icon Agustín de Iturbide there; see *La Ilustración Católica*, 5 July 1879 and *La Patria*, 26 September 1883. Not surprisingly Catholic newspapers from the provinces, such as Puebla's *Amigo de la Verdad*, could be purchased at his store; see *El Tiempo*, 5 July 1884.

31. Luis G. Duarte, *Profecías de Matiana*.

32. The first of Duarte's "Opúsculos Guadalupanos" resides at the UCBL: *Impugnación a la memoria de D. Juan Bautista Muñoz contra la gloriosa aparición de Nuestra Señora de Guadalupe y breve respuesta á las objeciones de los editores de Madrid sobre el mismo asunto en el denominado "Libro de Sensación,"* ed. Salvador Gutiérrez (Mexico City: Imprenta del Sagrado Corazón de Jesús, 1892). The back-page adverstisement for the series noted that each pamphlet sold at the press for 25 cents. Duarte's basic argument centers on the infallibility of the Catholic Church and the pope.

33. For example, see Luis G. Duarte to Secretario del Arzobispado, 31 May 1882, AHAM, Base de Pelagio Antonio de Labastida y Dávalos, Secretaría Arzobispal, Censura: caja 144, exp. 36. Here Duarte requests permission to publish two Marian devotional texts. Notations on the page indicate he was successful. He also mentions a third forthcoming publication addressing the practice of worshiping the Blessed Sacrament, the devotion at the center of the Matiana prophesies. Interestingly he also sought permission to sell books banned by the Church; see Luis G. Duarte to Secretario del Arzobispado, 1883, AHAM, Base de Pelagio

Antonio de Labastida y Dávalos, Secretaría Arzobispal, Censura: caja 149, exp. 60. Documents regarding eccleisatical approval of Duarte's examination of the Madre Matiana prophecies reside at the archdiocesan archive: AHAM, Base de Pelagio Antonio de Labastida y Dávalos, Secretaría Arzobispal, Censura: caja 208, exp. 64, 1889. Duarte also included the texts announcing eccleisastical approval in the front matter of the book.

34. See, "Coincidencia," *El Tiempo*, 20 June 1890; and *El Tiempo*, 26 April 1898.

35. *El Cruzado*, 28 January 1894. Sánchez contributed to numerous Catholic papers in the 1890s. He later became the founder and editor of *El País*, perhaps the most important conservative daily of the early twentieth century. He gained fame as a champion of social Catholicism and critic of liberal development in Mexico: see Richard Weiner, "Trinidad Sánchez Santos: Voice of Catholic Opposition in Porfirian Mexico,"*Mexican Studies/Estudios Mexicanos* 17, no. 1 (2001): 321–49.

36. His editor, Antonio Martínez del Cañizo spoke of this tiff in a letter to the provisor of the archdiocese requesting that Solé be recused from ruling on *Profecías*: Cañizo to Provisor de la Mitra, 4 October 1889, AHAM, Base de Pelagio Antonio de Labastida y Dávalos, Secretaría Arzobispal, Censura: caja 208, exp. 64. Apparently Solé had previously run *El Tiempo*.

37. *El Tiempo*'s coverage in early 1889 was particularly shrill about the previous century's anticlericalism, impiety, and revolutionary excesses and the need for a new Christian century under the guidance of the pope. See for example, Francisco Flores Alatorre, "El Papa es rey de la asociación internacional," *El Tiempo*, 1 January 1889; "Irreligión," *El Tiempo*, 8 January 1889; and "Centenario de la guillotina," *El Tiempo*, 20 January 1889. See also a later essay with the same title: Bonifacio Correa, "El centenario de la guillotina," *El Tiempo*, 27 February 1889.

38. "Fijad la atención," *Hoja quincenal dedicada a la propaganda católica*, 15 August 1888. Here they stressed the need for Mexico to follow the example of France and England by building new churches and monuments dedicated to expiation and energetically contesting heresies. Incidently, the issues of the *Hoja* cited here reside along other requests for archdiocesan censor's approval: see AHAM, Base de Pelagio Antonio de Labastida y Dávalos, Secretaría Arzobispal, Censura: caja 202, Exp. 31, 1889.

39. "La propaganda," *Hoja quincenal dedicada a la propaganda católica*, 15 July 1888.

40. "Petición," *Hoja quincenal dedicada a la propaganda católica*, 15 December 1888.

41. Antonio Martínez del Cañizo to Provisor de la Mitra, 24 September 1889, AHAM, Secretaría Arzobispal, Censura, caja 208.

42. Cañizo to Provisor de la Mitra, 4 October 1889, AHAM, Secretaría Arzobispal, Censura: caja 208, exp. 64; and Vito Cruz, 8 November 1889, AHAM, Secretaría Arzobispal, Censura: caja 208, exp. 64.

43. José de Jesús Mota, Prosecretario del Señor Provisor y Vicario General Gobernador de la Mitra, 11 November 1889, AHAM, Base de Pelagio Antonio de Labastida y Dávalos, Secretaría Arzobispal, Censura: caja 208, exp. 64.

44. "Publicaciones," *El Tiempo*, 24 October 1889.
45. "Las profecías de Matiana VINDICADAS," *El Tiempo*, 23 November 1889.
46. Duarte, *Profecías*, 1–8.
47. Ibid., 1.
48. Ibid., 1–2.
49. The book was originally titled *Voix prophétiques*. Duarte did not specify which edition he consulted, however his citations match a Spanish translation of the fifth edition almost exactly: Jean-Marie Curicque, *Voces proféticas ó signos, apariciones y prediccioines modernas concernientes á los grandes acontecimientos de la cristiandad en el siglo XIX, y hacia la aproximación del fin de los tiempos*, 5th ed., trans. Pedro González de Villaumbrosia, vols. 1 and 2 (Barcelona: Imprenta y Librería Religiosa y Científica, 1874). In volume 1 many chapters tell the stories of different miraculous signs or apparitions. Others discuss mysterious calamities and enigmatic happenings during different revolutions. All of these portents took place between 1789 and 1874, and almost all of them occurred in Europe. The second volume offers a 500-page collection of prophecy narratives. Most of them address the lives and revelations of Early Modern and Modern prophets, the majority of whom were women.
50. See Kselman, *Miracles and Prophecies*, 84–120. Kselman discusses Curcique's contributions on 116, 123–24, and 132.
51. On this issue in Europe, see Christian, *Visionaries*, 350–51. In Mexico an anonymous Matiana reinterpreter in 1917 published a booklet called *Las verdaderas profecías de Matiana* that drew freely on Curicque, Duarte, and Spanish writers of the same ilk. The author, however, presented these texts as independent analyses of prophetic phenomenon when, in reality, *Voces proféticas* was the foundational source text for the others.
52. For example, Duarte reprints the story of Isabel Canori Mora and how she offered up her life in recompense for Rome's impieties. Apparently God accepted her sacrifice and she died in 1825 having forestalled celestial retribution. See Duarte, *Profecías*, 20–30. See also *Voces proféticas*, 232–40.
53. The decades surrounding the French Revolution offer a veritable case study of modern conspiracy theory trends from both the political right left and the right; see Brian Coward and Julian Swann, "Introduction," in *Conspiracy and Conspiracy Theory in Early Modern Europe: From the Waldesians to the French Revolution*, eds. Coward and Swann (Burlington, VT: Ashgate, 2004), 1–12. The paradigmatic case of left-wing conspiracy theory involved elaborate stories of international Jesuit machinations; see Geoffrey Cubitt, *The Jesuit Myth: Conspiracy Theory and Politics in Nineteenth-Century France* (Oxford: Clarendon Press, 1993). For a thorough discussion of right-wing conspiracy theory, see Darrin M. McMahon, *Enemies of the Enlightenment: The French Counter-Enlightenment and the Making of Modernity* (Oxford: Oxford University Press, 2001).
54. Amos Hofman, "Opinion, Illusion, and the Illusion of Opinion: Barruel's Theory of Conspiracy," *Eighteenth-Century Studies* 27, no. 1 (1993): 27–60, particularly 27–37.

55. Augustín de Barruel, *Memorias para servir a la historia del jacobinismo* (Mexico City: Impreso por Agustín Contreras, 1837). Editions published in Spain in 1813–1814 and 1827 were quite likely in circulation in Mexico. Mexican printers also published Barruel's *Historia del clero en tiempo de la revolución francesa* (Mexico City: Mariano Joseph de Zúñiga y Ontiveros, 1800). Clearly his conspiracy theories were circulating in Mexico by the late 1830s. Notes accompanying the Mexican edition of his memoir reveal that it is merely a reprint of an edition previously published in Spain.

56. Some of these were in the Librería Abadiano's holdings: For example, SL, Mexican Monograph Collection, Joseph de Marie Maistre, *El principio regenerador de toda sociedad, traducido del francés por un mejicano amante sincero de su nación* (Mexico City: Imprenta de Galván a cargo de Arévalo, 1835).

57. Hofman, "Opinion, Illusion, and the Illusion of Opinion," 55.

58. McMahon, *Enemies of the Enlightenment*, 10–15.

59. Ibid., 75–79.

60. Ibid., 154–88.

61. Duarte, *Profecías*, 3–5; see also 72–91 and 133–36 where Duarte identifies "aberrations" introduced by Madre Guerra.

62. Vito Cruz, AHAM, 8 November 1889, Secretaría Arzobispal, Censura: caja 208, exp. 64.

63. Duarte, *Profecías*, 5–6. In this translation I modernized the punctuation in hopes of greater clarity.

64. Duarte, *Profecías*, 1–14.

65. Duarte, *Profecías*, 14–20. Here the author builds on conservative interpretations of world history to describe societal rebellion against God, beginning with the Reformation and deepening in subsequent centuries. The nineteenth-century manifestation of this revolt was liberalism. Some Catholic thinkers who were widely read among conservatives in Mexico deemed socialism to be the next phase of this sacrilegious uprising. For a synthesis of these writings see Adame Goddard, *El pensamiento político*, 34–44.

66. Curicque, *Voces proféticas*, vol. 2, 363–88.

67. Duarte, *Profecías*, 20–30.

68. Ibid., 30–44.

69. Curicque, *Voces proféticas*, vol. 2, 80–92. Duarte also reprints passages related to the visions of a Parisian nun named María de Jesús (1797–1854); see Curicque, *Voces proféticas*, vol. 2, 278–83.

70. For this portrayal of the devil, see Duarte, *Profecías*, 172.

71. Ibid., 45–48. Cañizo's notes stress that U.S. constitutional principles are preparing the way of the Anti-Christ.

72. Ibid., 44.

73. Ibid., 45.

74. Ibid., 43–106.

75. Ibid., 106–56.

76. He was particularly drawn to the apocalyptic revelations attributed to Saint Catherine of Siena, Ana Maria Taigi, madre María de Agreda, Sor Natividad of Brittany, Ana Catalina Emmerich, Isabel Canori-Mora, María Lataste, and La Pequeña María de Terreaux. See Curicque, *Voces proféticas*, 54–60, 119–34, 162–73, 208–32, 232–40, 301–3, and 487–502.

77. Duarte, *Profecías*, 133–56.

78. Ibid., 138.

79. Ibid., 140.

80. On this topic, see Patrick W. Carey, "American Catholic Romanticism, 1830–1888," *The Catholic Historical Review* 74, no. 4 (1988): 590–606.

81. Duarte, *Profecías*, 142.

82. Ibid.

83. Ibid., 142–43.

84. Ibid., 150. Belial is a Hebrew name for the spirit of evil personified. It has also been used as a name for the Devil or one of his principle fiends. See *Oxford English Dictionary*, Online edition, www.oed.com (accessed 11 May 2012). See also *The Catholic Encyclopedia*, www.newadvent.org/cathen/02408a.htm (accessed 11 May 2012). By saying "*amigos del mundo*," Duarte was speaking in terms of that which is worldly or profane versus the pure and celestial.

85. This is the point of much of chapter 8 where Duarte warns Mexico not to be tempted by the material success of Protestant nations, or as he calls them, the devil's "concubines." See *Profecías*, 54–72. Duarte also appends a separate 12-page treatise at the end of *Profecías* to detail the U.S. threat. In his view, Mexico's neighbor is the anti-Rome: a de-Christianizing, anti-Catholic, bastard nation. See "La grandeza de los Estados Unidos es una tentación pasajera contra la union católica en todo el mundo," 1–12 (page numbering begins anew with this text, but it corresponds to pages 185–97 of *Profecías*).

86. For example, "Publicaciones," *El Tiempo*, 24 October 1889; and "Las profecías de Matiana VINDICADAS," *El Tiempo*, 23 November 1889.

87. "Coincidencia," *El Tiempo*, 20 June 1890.

88. "Las profecías de Matiana," *El Amigo de la Verdad*, 29 August 1891.

89. For example, *El Tiempo*, 26 April 1898.

90. See "La Prensa," *El Siglo Diez y Nueve*, 3 September 1890; and "Predicciones de la madre Matiana," *La Patria*, 6 September 1891.

91. For example, "El evolucionismo según El Tiempo," *El Siglo Diez y Nueve*, 25 January 1892; and "El tiempo perdido los ángeles lloran," *La Patria*, 2 February 1896. See also "El Nuncio de Copal," *El Hijo del Ahuizote*, 23 July 1899; and "Tolle lege," *La Patria*, 11 November 1903.

92. For example, see "Lo de China," *La Gaceta Comercial*, 2 July 1900. Here an article references Madre Matiana as it mocks North American coverage of events in China. The essay argues that U.S. imperialism and capitalist interests in Asia distort reportage into quasi-millenarian hysteria.

93. Antonio Ferrer, "Corona á la Santísima Virgen: revelación de una indita," *El Tiempo*, 15 May 1904.

94. *Profecías verdaderas*, 57–68.

95. See Ceballos Ramírez, *El catolicismo social*, 133–53.

96. Luis Santaella, *Las profecías de Matiana* (Oaxaca: Imprenta "La Voz de la Verdad," 1910); and "Las profecías de madre Matiana," *Boletín Oficial y Revista Ecclesiástica de Antequera*, 1 April 1910.

97. The archdiocese of Oaxaca was a hotbed of innovative religious institution building and pious militancy under Eulogio Gillow y Zalvalza; see Wright-Rios, *Revolutions in Mexican Catholicism*, 60–65.

98. The biography accompanying his obituary in the *Boletín* attests to his prominence: see "Muerte del Señor Cura don Luis Santaella," *Boletín* 8, no. 9, 1 September 1911.

99. See Wright-Rios, *Revolutions in Mexican Catholicism*, 105–6. The archdiocesan secretary and dean of the cathedral in the early twentieth century was Anastacio Santaella, who was most likely related to Luis and María in some fashion; see AHAO, folletería 1900–1910, *Estadística del venerable clero de la arquidiócesis de Oaxaca y alugnas noticias históricas* (Oaxaca: La Voz de la Verdad, 1905).

100. Eulogio Gillow, "Edicto," *Boletín*, 1 March 1901.

101. "Muerte del Señor Cura don Luis Santaella," *Boletín* 8, no. 9, 1 September 1911. In 1905 he served as Defensor del Oficio within the Provisoriato (the disciplinary arm of the archdiocesan curia) in addition to being Jalatlaco's curate: see AHAO, folletería 1900–1910, *Estadística del venerable clero de la arquidiócesis de Oaxaca y alugnas noticias históricas*, 1905.

102. For reportage on his sermons, see *La Voz de la Verdad*, 14 June 1896 and 20 February 1910. One of them was published in the *Boletín*, 1 February 1907. It offered typical militant Marian boilerplate: Mary as the great defender of the faith will bolster the Mexican nation's resistance to heresy and foil Catholicism's enemies, foreign and domestic. He also wrote a doctrinal column under the title "Noticia de algunas curiosidades pertenecientes a la ciencias sagradas": for example, see *Boletín*, 1 October 1905 and 1 November 1905.

103. Santaella, *Las profecías de Matiana*. The author goes on at length about the significance of October (the month dedicated to the Rosary) and the number eight (allegedly a reference to 8 December, the Feast of the Immaculate Conception).

CHAPTER 5

1. *La Madre Matiana*, 9 September 1917.

2. "Se aproxima el fin del mundo: las profecías se cumplen," May 1914, UHJC. Posada died in 1913, making this broadside an early posthumous publication. However, as was common in the popular press, images were frequently used

multiple times to illustrate distinct events. For example, this lithograph appeared in an 1894 broadside about an earthquake in Mexico City: see Ron Tyler, ed., *Posada's Mexico* (Washington, D.C.: Library of Congress and the Amon Carter Museum of Western Art, 1979), 180. Web searching reveals that the image had been reused a number of times. For example, see "Corrido: 'El Fin del Mundo,'" circa 1895–1900" (accessed 28 July 2011) www.artoftheprint.com/artistspages/ posada_jose_guadalupe_corrido_elfindelmundo.htm. Additionally it graced another broadside about earthquakes in 1912; (accessed 28 July 2011) see www. flickr.com/photos/posada/5214548257/in/set-72157625357117465/.

3. Respectively, *Profecías completas de madre Matiana* (Mexico City: Imprenta Gutemburg, 1914); and *Las verdaderas profecías de Matiana*.

4. "Unas profecías falsas," *Ecos*, 30 May 1914.

5. Ibid. The author did not provide an actual date, but he made this comment while criticizing the pre-Revolutionary history of the prophecies.

6. "Notas editoriales," *El Abogado Cristiano*, 26 November 1914.

7. Alan Knight, *The Mexican Revolution*, vol. 2 (Lincoln: University of Nebraska Press, 1986), 411–15.

8. J. Sauza González, "En casa ajena mentiras piadosas," *El Informador*, 3 March 1920.

9. "Prosas Dominicales," *El Porvenir*, 23 March 1920.

10. "Las profecías de madre Matiana," *El Porvenir*, 26 May 1920.

11. *El Porvenir*, 7 July 1927.

12. Wright-Rios, *Revolutions in Mexican Catholicism*, chapter 7.

13. See Ricardo Arizti, "Pedro Hagelstein fue uno de los periodistas más valientes y sufridos," in Comité Pro-Homenaje a Precursores se la Revolución, *Biografías Sintéticas: Félix C. Vera, Fernando Celada, Pedro Hagelstein. Contribución a la velada celebrada en el Teatro Hidalgo, del sindicato de trabajadores de los talleres gráficos de la nación, sindicato de ferrocarrileros de la república mexicana y 'tribuna obrera,' el periódico de la clase productora* (23 March 1935), Unpublished program, BN, G 908 MIS.30, exp. 11: 10-13.

14. *La Metralla*, 7 September 1876, 10 September 1876, and 28 September 1876.

15. Manuel Payno, *Los bandidos de Río Frío*, 20th ed.[originally 1889–1891] (Mexico City: Porrúa, 2000). Matiana is not a common name by any stretch; hence I interpret Payno's use of it as a reference to the prophecies. In the novel his Matiana is called on to resolve an exceptionally late pregnancy. She tells her patroness that the Virgin of Guadalupe requires a sacrificial victim, and she kidnaps an illegitimate, upper-class child. Ultimately she just abandons the infant in a garbage dump, and his subsequent fate propels the narrative. Ironically the patient goes into labor due to the shock caused by the notion of child sacrifice. In short, Payno mocks belief in miraculous cures. In this case, it "succeeds" but not because of the alleged magic.

16. See Rebecca Earle, *Return of the Native: Indians and Mythmaking in Spanish America, 1810–1930* (Durham, NC: Duke University Press, 2007); and Juan Pablo Dabove, *Nightmares of the Lettered City: Banditry and Literature in Latin America, 1816–1929* (Pittsburgh, PA: University of Pittsburgh Press, 2007). For an analysis that incorporates religion and nationalist examinations of indigenous culture in Mexico, see Edward Wright-Rios, "Indian Saints and Nation-States," *Mexican Studies/Estudios Mexicanos* 20 (2004): 47–68.

17. See Guillermo Bonfil Batalla, *México Profundo: Reclaiming a Civilization* (Austin: University of Texas Press, 1996). See also Alan Knight, "Racism, Revolution, and Indigenismo in Mexico, 1910–1940," in *The Idea of Race in Latin America, 1870–1940*, ed. Richard Graham (Austin: University of Texas Press, 1990), 71–114.

18. For the general characteristics of satire, see Rubén Quintero, "Introduction: Understanding Satire," in *A Companion to Satire: Ancient and Modern*, ed. Rubén Quintero (Malden, MA: Blackwell, 2007), 1–12.

19. Amy Wiese Forbes, *The Satiric Decade: Satire and the Rise of Republican Political Culture in France, 1830–1940* (Lanham, MD: Lexington Books, 2010). For colonial Latin America, Julie Greer Johnson argues that Creole satirists' portrayal of multiracial society and ineffective imperial administration laid the groundwork for Spanish American self-definition: see *Satire in Colonial Spanish America: Turning the New World Upside Down* (Austin: University of Texas Press, 1993).

20. On the broader complexities of nationalism, popular culture, and national identity in Mexico relevant to the period under consideration here, see Claudio Lomnitz-Adler, *Deep Mexico, Silent Mexico: An Anthropology of Nationalism* (Minneapolis: University of Minnesota Press, 2001); Ricardo Pérez Montfort, *Estampas de nacionalismo popular mexicano: diez ensayos sobre cultura popular y nacionalismo* (Mexico City: Centro de Investigaciones y Estudios Superiores en Antropología Social, 1994); and William H. Beezley, *Mexican National Identity: Memory, Innuendo, and Popular Culture* (Tucson: University of Arizona Press, 2008).

21. For an overview of anticlericalism at this time see Ben Fallaw, "Varieties of Mexican Revolutionary Anticlericalism: Radicalism, Iconoclasm, and Otherwise, 1914–1935," *The Americas* 65, no. 4 (2009): 481–509.

22. For basic biographical information see Humberto Muscacchio, *Milenios de México* (Mexico City: Hoja Casa Editorial, 1999), vol. 2, 1270; and *Diccionario Porrúa: historia, biografía, y geografía*, 6th ed., vol. 2: 1636. There is some discrepancy about the year of Hagelstein's death. The above sources list the year as 1933. However, the program from a *velada* (memorial featuring poetry, speeches, and music) dedicated to *La Madre*'s editor and a pair of his collaborators listed specific days for his birth and death (4 December 1877–30 November 1932). This specific information provided by Hagelstein's colleagues seems more

reliable. See Arizti, "Pedro Hagelstein, " Unpublished program, BN, G 908 MIS.30, exp. 11: 13.

23. Ariziti, "Pedro Hagelstein," Unpublished program, BN, G 908 MIS.30, exp. 11: 10–13.

24. Ibid.

25. On Mexico City's university students and a discussion of their dissipation via urban nightlife, liaisons with lower-class women, and journalism, see Piccato, *The Tyranny of Opinion*, 63–100.

26. "D. Francisco Bulnes y su libro sobre Juárez," *El Tiempo*, 30 August 1904.

27. In the mid and late 1890s Dorotea Hagelstein appears frequently in announcements and advertisements for musical performances. *The Mexican Herald* explicitly identified her as Pedro's sister; see "Theatrical Trouble: Interchange of Compliments between Messrs. De Bengardi and Hagelstein," 6 July 1897. A decade later newspapers announced Ms. Hagelstein's wedding, noting Pedro Hagelstein's attendance; see "Matrimonio," *El Popular*, 27 July 1907. Hagelstein's efforts as a stage actor are documented in advertisements and reviews: see, "El centro dramático en Arbeu," *El Popular*, 15 March 1899; "El centro dramático," *El Popular*, 19 March 1899; and "El centro dramático," *El Popular*, 19 May 1899. The latter commented on his singing.

28. "Club Dramático," *El Tiempo Ilustrado*, 19 August 1901.

29. See "Mechanics to Celebrate," *The Mexican Herald*, 29 August 1901. For another example, see "Velada en Arbeu," *La Voz de México*, 20 September 1901.

30. On Hagelstein's involvement with the Compañía de Opera Mexicana; see, "Información del día," *La Voz de México*, 26 November 1901; and announcements "La Compañía de Opera Mexicana," *El Popular*, 25 March 1902, 14 April 1902, and 19 April 1902.

31. On the newspaper's founding, see "El Estudiante," *La Voz de México*, 2 April 1896. On the paper's legal troubles, see "Denuncia," *El Tiempo*, 29 May 1896.

32. "Nuevo periodico," *La Voz de México*, 7 November 1896.

33. "Solemne coronación de la Sma. Virgen de la Luz en León," *La Voz de México*, 12 October 1902.

34. On El País, see Ugarte, *Periodistas y periódicos*, 84. Ugarte stressed the unblemished integrity of the newspaper's director, Catholic intellectual Trinidad Sánchez Santo (1859–1912), and the impressive print runs of 200,000 issues per day in the early 1900s. In some instances Hagelstein attended functions as Sánchez Santos's personal representative; see "En Honor de Samuel Hanneman," *El País*, 11 April 1901.

35. Ibid. *La Voz* in particular often referred to him as *"nuestro particular amigo"* or *"antiguo compañero"* ("our particular friend" or "longtime colleague").

36. "*La Voz de México* desde el mes próximo: reformas radicales," *La Voz de México*, 22 March 1904.

37. "Gran escándalo en la cámara de diputados," *La Patria*, 5 May 1911.

38. "Riñeron Lozano y Hagelstein," *El Tiempo*, 10 April 1912. Lozano faced charges, but ultimately was absolved of guilt; see "Congressman is Taken by Police," *The Mexican Herald*, 10 April 1912; and "Se absuelve á Lozano," *El Tiempo*, 30 April 1912.

39. Piccato, *Tyranny of Opinion*, particularly 63–100 and 188–221. In fact, Hagelstein's biography in many respects echoes the array of issues analyzed by Piccato.

40. "Reunión animada," *El Popular*, 1 July 1898.

41. On his role as a founder and leader of journalistic institutions, see, for example, "La agrupación mejicana de periodistas," *El País*, 5 June 1901; "La agrupación de periodistas," *El País*, 13 June 1901; "El festival de reporteros," *El Popular*, 30 January 1903; "Junta de Reporters [sic]" *La Voz de México*, 20 September 1903; and "Una junta de periodistas importantes," *El País*, 22 April 1911. For evidence of his charity activism, see "En favor de las víctimas de Mazatlán," *El Popular*, 21 January 1903; "La semana," *La Patria*, 25 November 1906; and "Junta del Comité Ejecutivo," *El Diario del Hogar*, 24 July 1911.

42. For example, see "El baile ofrecido á la Sra. Romero Rubio de Díaz," *El Diario del Hogar*, 5 December 1900; "Solemne ceremonia," *El Popular*, 27 February 1901; and "En Honor de Samuel Hanneman," *El País*, 11 April 1901.

43. "Matrimonio elegante," *El Popular*, 25 September 1902; and "Ball Given in French Casino," *The Mexican Herald*, 15 July 1903.

44. "Agreeable Banquet," *The Mexican Herald*, 21 December 1902.

45. Arizti, "Pedro Hagelstein," Unpublished program, BN, G 908 MIS.30, exp. 11: 10–13.

46. See "La degradación de la prensa," *La Patria*, 30 October 1911. This article included a letter signed by Luis C. Hagelstein, who apparently administered *Los sucesos*'s finances, but rejected the paper's politics. He claimed that the editors had been subsidized by *reyistas* and *vazquiztas* (the followers of Bernardo Reyes and Emilio Vázquez Gómez, opponents of President of Francisco Madero).

47. On *reyismo*, see Knight, *The Mexican Revolution*, vol. 1: 47-55.

48. Musacchio, *Milenios de México*, vol. 2: 1270 claimed Hagelstein had been jailed twenty times. Bravo Ugarte, *Periodistas y periódicos*, 85, simply said "over eighteen."

49. Reporting on the case and Hagelstein's trial appeared in many newspapers during 1905 and 1906. For example, "Suspención de *Los Sucesos*," *El Tiempo*, 7 April 1905; "Se les negó la libertad caucional," *El Tiempo*, 15 April 1905; and "Pedro Hagelstein, sentenciado," *El Tiempo*, 8 June 1906.

50. On *Frégoli*, the newspaper, see Diccionario Porrúa, vol. 2: 1636. On aspects of Leopoldo Frégoli's career, see Erik Barnouw, *The Magician and the Cinema* (Oxford: Oxford University Press, 1981), 62–65.

51. Manuel Mañón, *Historia del teatro principal en México, 1753-1931* (Mexico City: Editorial "Cvltvra," 1932), 182–83.

52. "La degradación de la prensa," *La Patria*, 30 October 1911.

53. José Sánchez Somoano, *Modismos locuciones y términos mexicanos* (Madrid: Manuel Minuesa de los Ríos, 1892).

54. See *Diccionario de autoridades*, facsimile edition of 1726 original, 449–50. This early eighteenth-century Spanish dictionary defines *"salir de madre"* as "to exceed in superabundance in some action, be it good or bad."

55. See Linton H. Robinson, *Mexican Slang: A Guide* (Campo, CA: Bueno Books, 1992). Octavio Paz famously explores this dynamic's centrality in the national psyche in his disquisition on Mexicaness; see Paz, *The Labyrinth of Solitude* (New York: Grove Press, 1985), 74–88.

56. Robinson, *Mexican Slang*, 38–43; and José Martínez Pérez, *Dichos*, 30.

57. Martínez Pérez, *Dichos*, 154. A related expression fulfilling much the same function is *"¡Ni madre!"*; see *Diccionario de la lengua española*, 22nd ed. This dictionary published in Spain stipulates Mexican colloquial usage.

58. *Diccionario de la lengua española*, vol. 2, 1413–14.

59. Arturo Langle Ramírez, *Vocabulario, apodos, seudónimos, sobrenombres y hemerografía de la Revolución* (Mexico City: Universidad Nacional Autónoma de México Instituto de Investigaciones Históricas, 1966). See also *Diccionario de la lengua española*, vol. 2, 1413–14.

60. Robinson, *Mexican Slang*, 38–39. *"Romper la madre"* is a common equivalent phrase. Often these are deployed as threats, such as *"Te voy a partir la madre"* (roughly, I am going to break your face).

61. See Martínez Pérez, *Dichos*, 30. Although less common in some contexts *"no tiene madre"* is also used a superlative. In both cases they serve as the equivalent of English phrases like "off-the-charts" or "out-of-sight." See also Robinson, *Mexican Slang*, 38–39.

62. For the prefix *des-* see *Diccionario de la lengua española*, vol. 1, 755. For *desmadre*, see vol. 1, 790.

63. Langle Ramírez, *Vocabulario*, 37.

64. Martínez Pérez, *Dichos*, 94.

65. 3rd ed. s.v. "The Collins Spanish Dictionary."

66. A more polite way of calling someone shameless is *sinvergüenza*. It denotes a lesser degree of shamelessness. See *Diccionario de la lengua española*, vol. 2, 2072.

67. See Francisco Javier Santamaría and Joaquín García Icazbalceta, *Diccionario de mejicanismos* (Mexico City: Porrúa, 1959). In doing so it equates *"no tiene madre"* with being *chingado/a*: the product of violent sexual domination. An example of the lack of *madre* signifying a space beyond the pale of social norms appears in Juan Rulfo's short story, "Luvina." In this text, rustic peasants deadpan their deep suspicion of the Mexican government: "También nosotros lo conocemos [el gobierno] . . . De lo que no sabemos nada es de la madre del gobierno" ("We also know the government . . . But we know nothing about the government's mother"). See "Luvina," in Juan Rulfo, *Obras* (Mexico City: Fondo de Cultura Económica, 1987).

68. Here I use the colloquial term for a "formidable or domineering woman," because it carries sexist connotations similar to the Mexican uses of Madre Matiana. See *The Oxford English Dictionary Online*, 3rd edition (Oxford: Oxford University Press, 2010).

69. Quintero, *A Companion to Satire*, 3.

70. Ibid.

71. See Carmen Ramos-Escandón, ed., *Presencia y transparencia: la mujer en la historia de México* (Mexico City: Colegio de México, 2006); Elsa Muñiz, *Cuerpo, representación, y poder. México en los albores de la reconstrucción nacional, 1920–1934* (Mexico City: Universidad Autónoma Metropolitana, Miguel Angel Porrúa, 2002); Apen Ruiz Martínez, "Nacion y género en el México revolucionario: la India Bonita y Manuel Gamio," *Signos históricos* 5 (2001): 55–86; and Esperanza Tuñon Pablos, *Mujeres que se organizan: el Frente Único Pro Derechos de la Mujer, 1935–1938* (Mexico City: Porrúa, 1991). For a portrait of the field in Mexico, see María Teresa Fernández-Aceves, "Imagined Communities: Women's History and the History of Gender in Mexico," *Journal of Women's History* 19, no. 1 (2007): 200–205. For a broader portrait of the issues and theoretical approaches see William E. French and Katherine Elaine Bliss, eds., introduction to *Gender, Sexuality, and Power*, 1–31. Recent Anglophone works on the Revolutionary era include Jocelyn Olcott, *Revolutionary Women in Postrevolutionary Mexico* (Durham, NC: Duke University Press, 2005); Jocelyn Olcott, Mary K. Vaughan, and Gabriela Cano, eds., *Sex in Revolution: Gender, Politics, and Power in Modern Mexico* (Durham, NC: Duke University Press, 2006); Stephanie J. Smith, *Gender and the Mexican Revolution: Yucatan Women and the Realities of Patriarchy* (Chapel Hill: University of North Carolina Press, 2009); and Stephanie Mitchell and Patience Schell, eds., *The Women's Revolution in Mexico, 1910–1953* (Lanham, MD: Roman and Littlefield, 2007).

72. See Franco, *Plotting Women*. For the examination of the gendered nationalist implications of literary depictions of race, class, and romance, see Doris Sommer, *Foundational Fictions: The National Romances of Latin America* (Berkeley: University of California Press, 1993). For the depiction of women in film, see Julia Tuñon, *Mujeres de luz y sombra en el cine mexicano: la construcción de una imagen (1939–1952)* (Mexico City: Colegio de México, 1998). In the arena of painting Frida Kahlo has inspired almost a separate branch of gender studies. For an overview of important Frida books, see Salomon Grimberg, "Review: Thinking of Death," *Women's Art Journal* 14, no. 2 (1993–1994): 44–50. For useful essays addressing the various polemics see Elizabeth Barber, "Art Critics on Frida Kahlo," *Art Education* 45, no. 2 (1992): 42–48; Oriana Baddeley, "'Her Dress Hangs There: De-Frocking the Kahlo Cult,'" *Oxford Art Journal* 14, no. 1 (1991): 10–17. See also Sharyn R. Udall, "Frida Kahlo's Mexican Body: History, Identity, and Artistic Aspiration," *Women's Art Journal* 24, no. 2 (Autumn 2003–Winter 2004): 10–14.

73. Daniel Cabrera, the director of *El Hijo del Ahuizote*, represents an example of the heroic journalistic figure. See Margarita Espinosa Blas, "El Hijo Del Ahuizote: un Periódico Americanista," in *La prensa decimonónica en México*, eds. Adriana Pineda Soto and Celia del Palacio Montiel (Morelia: Universidad Michoacana de San Nicolás de Hidalgo, 2003), 245-62.

74. Pablo Piccato, *The Tyranny of Opinion*. For the conceptualization of public opinion, and efforts by factions to control it; see McGowan, *Prensa y poder*. For the religious dimensions, see Brian F. Connaughton, "Conjuring the Body Politic from the Corpus Mysticum," and "A Most Delicate Balance," *Mexican Studies / Estudios Mexicanos* 17, no. 1 (2001): 41-69. For the Catholic press in the mid-nineteenth century, see Pani, "Una ventana sobre la sociedad decimonónica," 67-88.

75. For example, Anderson, *Imagined Communities*; Craig J. Calhoun, *Nationalism* (Minneapolis: University of Minnesota Press, 1997); and Ernest Gellner, *Nations and Nationalism* (Malden, MA: Blackwell, 2005). For a summary of approaches to identity formation see Karen A. Cerulo, "Identity Construction: New Issues, New Directions," *Annual Review of Sociology* 23 (1997): 385-409.

76. See Nira Yuval-Davis, "The Bearers of the Collective," *Feminist Review*, no. 4 (1980): 15-27; Nira Yuval-Davis, *Gender and Nation* (London: Sage Publications, 1997).

77. Yuval-Davis, "The Bearers of the Collective," 15.

78. Calhoun, *Nationalism*, 1-7.

79. Yuval-Davis, *Gender and Nation*, 43-44.

80. Yuval-Davis, *Gender and Nation*. This kind of representation of women in nationalist discourse appears in Paz, *Labyrinth of Solitude*, 35-40.

81. Jill Lane, *Blackface Cuba, 1840-1895* (Philadelphia: University of Pennsylvania Press, 2005).

82. See Adrian Bantjes, "Mexican Revolutionary Anticlericalism: Concepts and Typologies," *The Americas* 65, no. 4 (2009): 467-80. See also Alan Knight, "The Mentality and Modus Operandi of Revolutionary Anticlericalism," in *Faith and Impiety in Revolutionary Mexico*, ed. Matthew Butler (New York: Palgrave MacMillan, 2007), 21-56.

83. Although male, the Cuban blackface character most reminiscent of Madre Matiana is the *negrito catedrático* (little black professor). A fictional invention, he mocks black attempts to master high culture and act educated. The character constantly assumes a preposterous air of grandeur while making a mess of erudite Spanish. In a similar fashion the fanatical Matiana is a stereotyped female fool who imagines herself enlightened but only succeeds in broadcasting her ignorance. Coincidentally, such was the popularity of the Cuban figure that a newspaper called *Los Negros Catedráticos* specialized in political satire in the voice of this character. See Lane, *Blackface Cuba*, 71-86 and 96.

84. María del Carmen Ruiz Castañeda et al., *El periodismo en México: 450 años de historia* (Mexico City: Editorial Tradición, 1974).

85. For an entertaining baptism in these publications, see Rafael Barajas, *El país de "El Ahuizote"*; Barajas, *El país de "El Llorón de Icamole"*; and Barajas, *La historia de un país en caricatura* (Mexico City: Consejo Nacional para la Cultura y las Artes Dirección General de Publicaciones, 2000).

86. See Barajas, *El país de "El Llorón de Icamole,"* 45.

87. Interestingly a French satirical newspaper, *La Caricature*, employed the slogan "*castigat ridendo mores*" (one chastises character or habits by laughing) in the 1830s. For this publication the point was to discipline political leaders through ridicule, conceived of as a tool to broaden political participation during monarchical rule. See Forbes, *The Satiric Decade*, xiii. The Latin motto used in this French newspaper was also in use in the Brazilian satirical press. Brazilians also employed a subtitle similar to Mexico's joco-serio (*sério-moleque*). See Marco Aurélio Ferreira da Silva, "'Corrige os costumes rindo:' Humor, vergonha e decoro na sociabilidade mundana de Fortaleza (1850–1890)" (PhD diss., Universidade Federal de Pernambuco, 2004), 101. Ferreira da Silva stresses the phrase's complex meaning. It connotes punishment and correction via censure, but it also suggests moralizing through humor the habits seen as deviant or subversive to the social order. He argues that in its Brazilian usage it also targeted customs deemed irrational or ridiculous from an elite perspective. Mid-nineteenth-century satirical publications in Spain also called themselves joco-serio: see José Pijoán et. al. eds., *Summa artis: historia general del arte, vol. XXXII: el grabado en España, siglos XIX–XX* (Madrid: Espasa-Calpe, 1988), 326 and 411.

88. Pani, "'Ciudadana y muy Ciudadana'?" In some ways Mexican conservatives' recourse to ethically pure female figures was to echo notions of womanhood and morality that had animated the strategic feminization of abolitionism in Brazil. See Roger A. Kittleson, "Women and Notions of Womanhood in Brazilian Abolitionism," in *Gender and Slave Emancipation in the Atlantic World*, eds. Pamela Scully and Diana Paton (Durham, NC: Duke University Press, 2005), 99–120.

89. For Mexico, the classic picaresque character is Pedro Sarmiento, more commonly known by his nickname "el Periquillo Sarniento." See Fernández de Lizardi, *El periquillo sarniento* (Madrid: Cátedra, 1997); and Luis Leal, "Aspects of the Mexican Novel from Lizardi to Elizondo," 53–64. For the nation-building import of the novel, see Antonio Benítez-Rojo, "José Joaquín Fernández de Lizardi and the Emergence of the Spanish American Novel as National Project," *Modern Language Quarterly* 57, no. 2 (1996): 325–39.

90. Examples include *El Ahuizote* and *El Hijo del Ahuizote*. On the former see Barajas, *El país de "El Ahuizote."* Because the latter focused on criticism of the Díaz government and involved legendary artists, like José Guadalupe Posada, its articles and cartoons have been widely reproduced: see Armando Bartra and Ricardo Flores Magón, *Regeneración, 1900–1918: la corriente más radical de la Revolución de 1910 a través de su periódico de combate* (Mexico City: Hadise,

1972); and Manuel González Ramírez, *La caricatura política* (Mexico City: Fondo de Cultura Económica, 1974). See also Espinosa Blas, "El Hijo Del Ahuizote."

91. Aside from journalistic figures, a good example of these types of characters can be found in nineteenth-century puppet theater. The staff of *La Madre* was probably very familiar with El Negrito and Vale Coyote; see Beezley, *Mexican National Identity*. The news clown Brozo (Víctor Trujillo) carried on this tradition in the 1990s and early 2000s. Brozo is a vulgar, lecherous social critic. His character is deliberately inappropriate street humorist, enjoying sexual puns (*albures*) as he comments on events and politics. His television show, El Mañanero, also parodied the santoral. A cursory search on www.youtube.com for *"el mañanero brozo"* turns up a host of video clips.

92. R. M. Price, "On Religious Parody in the Buscón, *Modern Language Notes* 82, no. 2 (1971): 273–79. The novels often cited in this regard are Mateo Alemán's *Guzmán de Alfarache* (1599); and Francisco de Quevedo's *Historia de la vida del Buzcón, llamado Don Pablos, ejemplo de vagamundos y espejo de tacaños* (1626).

93. Barajas, *El país de "El Ahuizote,"* 86–91. In this particular case it is also a tongue-and-cheek reference to the nationalist overtones of the Virgin of Guadalupe apparition narrative.

94. See Barajas, *El país de "El Ahuizote,"* 78; and Barajas, *El país de "El Llorón de Icamole,"* 32.

95. Frías y Soto, *Los mexicanos pintados por sí mismos*, 227.

96. *La Casera*, 1 June 1879 in *El país de "El Llorón de Icamole,"* 169–73.

97. For more on the Padre Cobos character, see Barajas, *El País de "El Ahuizote,"* 94–103. In the context of liberal hero worship, invoking notions of Miguel Hidalgo (and José María Morelos) made Cobos a potent nationalist symbol.

98. Few know of this saint, but he is the patron of the city of Comitán, Chiapas; see Carlos Navarrete, *Documentos para la historia del culto a San Caralampio, Comitán, Chiapas* (Chiapas: Gobierno del Estado de Chiapas, Consejo Estatal de Fomento a la Investigación y Difusión de la Cultura, and Instituto Chiapaneco de Cultura, 1990).

99. See Santamaría and García Icazbalceta, *Diccionario*, 735. Although it is interesting to consider, I do not perceive any allusions to Afro-Mexican origins in the texts or cartoons featuring doña Caralampia, beyond her surname. It is perhaps best seen as a reference to the mixed-race nature of the urban working class that she represents. In addition, as with the word *naco*, words mocking the lower-class taste, style, or intelligence often have racist origins: see Santamaría and García Icazbalceta, *Diccionario*, 750.

100. Franco, *Plotting Women*, 79–102.

101. *Profecías completas*, 14–15.

102. Ibid.

103. Carlos M. de Heredia S. J., *Historietas y leyendas*, vol. 7 (Buenos Aires, Argentina: Editorial Difusión, 1946), 65–70.

104. *Las Verdaderas profecías de Matiana*, 1.

105. To this end he cited Curicque and Duarte. However, he also includes information from Antonio Martínez Sacristán, *El Antecristo y el fin del mundo según revelaciones divinas, y muy especialmente el Apocalipsis* (Astorga: Establecimiento Tipográfico de L. López, 1890); Rafael Pijoan, *El siglo XX y el fin del mundo* (Barcelona, Librería "La Hormiga de Oro," 1914).

106. *La Revista Mexicana*, 8 July, 1917.

107. I have only been able to locate one issue of the first era from 1917: *La Madre Matiana*, 9 September, 1917. The newspaper appears to have at least published from July to September. The newspaper reemerged in the mid-1920s and 15 issues from 1923 reside in the collection of BUS.

108. Nicolás Kanellos and Helvetia Martell, *Hispanic Periodicals in the United States, Origins to 1960: A Brief History and Comprehensive Bibliography* (Houston, TX: Arte Público Press, 2000), 70–72.

109. *La Revista Mexicana*, 16 April 1916.

110. "La situación mexicana," *La Revista Mexicana*, 16 April 1916.

111. For the former, see *La Revista Mexicana*, 19 November 1916. For the jests about shaving, see *La Revista Mexicana*, 8 July 1917. This theme also appears in "La situación de Venus," 16 March 1919.

112. "Tópicos del día," *La Revista Mexicana*, 29 October 1916. See also "Una disputa de enterradores," 28 October 1917.

113. "Elecciones," *La Revista Mexicana*, 13 August 1916. Here they claimed that most of the population hoped for an outcome like that predicted by Matiana.

114. "Carta sin sobre al dizque presidente Venustiano Carranza," *La Revista Mexicana*, 21 July 1918.

115. "Carta sin sobre a la madre Matiana," *La Revista Mexicana*, January 5, 1919.

116. A caiman is a crocodilian native to Central and South America.

117. *Trashumante* means migratory or peripatetic. However, the pun here relies on its roots, *tras* (meaning after, following, or in continuation of) and *humo* (smoke). The origins of the compound word appear to come from the vivid, visual depiction of cattle drivers (i.e., smoke or dust chasers), and thus applicable to individuals that live "on the move." The author is playing with the fact that the congress was literally "mobile" during the Revolution and hence labeled "*trashumante*." Given the context of the lines immediately following this word in the satirical poem, though, it is more appropriate to translate this word in English as "smoke-passers," in the sense of liars or those who, in colorful English, "talk out their ass."

118. *Tlachique* is technically the maguey sap (*aguamiel*) prior to fermentation. Afterward it is called *pulque*, the indigenous alchoholic beverage associated with lower-class drunken proclivities and immorality. However, in this case tlachique serves as the metaphorical stand-in for the intoxicating beverage much in the same way corn can function as a synonym for moonshine in American English. See Santamaría, *Diccionario de mejicanismos*, 1057.

119. Colonche is another popular alcoholic drink; in this case it is made from fermented prickly pear juice.

120. Here the author employs a somewhat ribald expression: the "it'll shrink on you" is a phallic reference denoting a loss of valor.

121. "Una interview con la madre Matiana," *La Revista Mexicana*, 12 December 1917. The original text appeared in a newspaper called *El Pueblo* with a pseudonym, "El Licenciado Verdad, Hijo."

122. In addition, exactly two weeks after *La Madre Matiana*'s initial publication, a different Mexico City newspaper commented on the prophecies. It kept them at arm's length, addressing the visions within an essay on popular myths, but nonetheless promised to republish the "sensational prophecies of madre Matiana." See *Confeti*, 14 July 1917. I have not been able to find a copy of this version of the prophecies.

123. *La Madre Matiana*, 9 September 1917, mentioned agents in Orizaba, Veracruz, Córdoba, and Nogales. In addition, extant issues from 1923 are housed at BUS, suggesting that *La Madre* reached this northern state.

124. "Nuevo Jefe Militar en Potrero del Llano," *El Demócrata*, 29 August 1924.

125. In this case *La Madre* employed the Spanish saying: *"Para que la cuña apriete, tiene que ser del mismo palo"* (roughly, for the wedge to hold tightly, it must be from the same wood). A colloquial English saying that approximates this expression is the commonly used hair of the dog that bit you comment in reference to a metaphorical antidote. The implication of this turn-the-tables phrase is clear. Matiana was the clergy's creature in the newspaper's estimation, but now she would attack her one-time masters.

126. The reference here is to the distinctive hat traditionally worn by Mexican and Spanish clergymen: the four-cornered *bonete*.

127. Excerpts from *La Madre Matiana*, in *La Revista Mexicana*, 8 July 1917.

128. Ibid.

129. In its original meaning a beata is a female member of a lay order. However, in common usage it refers to women who make a show of their Catholic piety and their allegiance to the Catholic Church. The term often connotes a sanctimonious prude and a clerical sycophant. Nonetheless, it also can mean simply "churchy." When used with the augmentative suffix -*ona* to make *beatona* it is always pejorative. By extension beatería refers to the useless pious actions or expressions of conservative actors. See *Diccionario de la lengua española*, v.1, 304. See also Smith, *The Collins Spanish Dictionary*, 93. For an example of its sarcastic and misogynist usage in liberal texts, see "Milagros de la Reforma: La beata," 1858, Bilbioteca Pública de Jalisco, miscelánea 376, no. 5. This pamphlet pretends to be a zoological tract analyzing the beata as one of the nation's "animals."

130. For *metiche* see Santamaría and García Icazbalceta, *Diccionario de la lengua española*, 720. As evident in the examples provided in this reference work, the word is frequently used to describe women and gossip.

131. For a definition of *marimacha*, see Smith, *The Collins Spanish Dictionary*, 465. There it is translated as a mannish or butch woman. According *Diccionario de la lengua española*, vol. 2, 454, it refers to a woman who due to excessive weight or actions appears to be male. This fits the image on the 1917 masthead of *La Madre*.

132. See John Lear, *Workers, Neighbors, and Citizens: The Revolution in Mexico City* (Lincoln: University of Nebraska Press, 2001), 341–50.

133. For a discussion of Carrancista politics, administration, and the political climate in Mexico between 1916 and 1920, see Knight, *The Mexican Revolution*, vol. 2, 435–93.

134. *La Revista Mexicana*, 22 July 1917.

135. *La Madre Matiana*, 9 September 1917.

136. *La Madre Matiana*, 24 May 1923 and 3 June 1923, respectively.

137. *La Madre Matiana*, 9 September 1917.

138. Lear, *Workers*, 341–58.

139. *La Madre Matiana*, 28 June 1923.

140. On Carranza's efforts from 1916 to 1920 and prevailing attitudes toward governance and corruption, see Knight, *Mexican Revolution*, vol. 2, 478–90.

141. Knight, *The Mexican Revolution*, vol. 2, 493–494. See also Jaime Tamayo, *El obregonismo y los movimientos sociales: la conformación del estado moderno en México (1920–1924)* (Guadalajara: Universidad de Guadalajara, 2008).

142. "Tampico en calzones," *La Madre Matiana*, 28 June 1923.

143. "Desmadres: Agraristas y rancheros," *La Madre Matiana*, 28 June 1923.

144. "Concurso de hembras modernistas," *La Madre Matiana*, 24 May 1923; and "Desmadres," *La Madre Matiana*, 31 May 1923.

145. Among those in attendance were well-organized Yucatecan women led by radical feminist Elvia Carrillo. These women shocked many Mexicans with their call for sexual freedom, sex education, and contraception; see Ana J. Lau, "Las luchas por transformar el estatus civil de las mexicanas," in *Integrados y marginados en el México posrevolucionario*, eds. Nicolas Cardenas Garcia and Enrique Cuerra Manzo (Mexico City: Universidad Autónoma Metropolitana, Xochimilco, 2009), 297–348. Lau specifically analyzes the impact of this congress (325–332).

146. Féliz Ramos y Duarte, *Diccionario de mejicanismos; colección de locuciones i frases viciosas, con sus correspondientes críticas i correcciones fundadas en autoridades de la lengua; máximas, refranes, provincialismos i remoques populares de todos los estados de la república mejicana* (Mexico City: Imprenta de Dublan, 1895); see also Santamaría, *Diccionario de mejicanismos*, 554–55.

147. Cabeza Pelada, "Viva el amor libre y la nivelación de los 'secsos:' mi Gata se va . . . se va . . . se fué," *La Madre Matiana*, 31 May 1923.

148. "Lo que vio, oyó, olfateó, y gustó 'Cabeza Pelada' en el último combate de flores," *La Madre Matiana*, 24 May 1923.

149. Romulo Díaz, S. J., "Calamidades sociales," *La Madre Matiana*, 28 June 1923. It is interesting to note that the author was ostensibly a Jesuit priest.

150. See Robert Buffington, "Homophobia and the Mexican Working Class, 1900–1910" in *The Famous 41: Sexuality and Social Control in Mexico, c. 1901*, eds. Robert McKee Irwin et al. (New York: Palgrave, 2003), 193–226.

151. See Jorge Mejía Prieto, *Albures y refranes de México* (Mexico City: Panorama Editorial, 1985), 14. According to this author, *La Madre* excelled at the *albur* (racy double entendre) and represents a historical model of this expressive genre.

152. Carlos Monsiváis, *Amor perdido* (Mexico City: Ediciones Era, 1977), 342. Monsiváis here comments on vulgar commentary of 1960s-era publications, and he criticizes them as boorish and predictable, but emphasizes the successful nature of this crass kind of Mexican identity formation. In journalism he traces the tradition to *La Madre*. Monsiváis describes a kind of general reveling in the notion that Mexicans are particularly ingenious when it comes to scatological humor and synonyms for sexual intercourse.

153. *La Madre Matiana*, 7 June 1923.

154. *Lengua* (tongue) and its derivations have rich and varied connotations. See Santamaría and García Icazbalceta, *Diccionario* , 659–60; *Diccionario de la lengua española*, vol. 2, 1362–1363; and Smith, *The Collins Spanish Dictionary*, 436. Here *La Madre* is working from a large number of expressions, such as *lengua larga*, *mala lengua*, and *lenguón*, which all refer to foolishly talkative, being verbose, malicious speech, or impertinent gossip.

155. Monsivás, *Amor perdido* (342) also provided these additional examples from *La Madre*. For a discussion of the Nahuatl-derived 'petaca,' see Santamaría and García Icazbalceta, *Diccionario*, 837–38.

156. I owe this idea to John Lear, personal communication, 14 March 2014.

157. Calhoun, *Nationalism*, 1–7.

158. Beezley, *Mexican National Identity*.

159. John Charles Chasteen, *National Rhythms, African Roots: The Deep History of Latin American Popular Dance* (Albuquerque: University of New Mexico Press, 2004).

160. For example, the cartoon from *El Ahuizote*, 5 February 1884, where the Constitution of 1857 is depicted as a bold Athena-like figure, "how she was," but by 1874 appears a ravaged wench "after what they have done to her." See Barajas, "*El país de 'El Ahuizote*,'" Image 55, 150, and 284.

CHAPTER 6

1. Carlos Monsiváis, *Amor Perdido*, 342.

2. Juan Almagre, "Con la brocha de aire," *El Nacional*, 3 September 1947.

3. Matthew Butler, *Popular Piety and Political Identity in Mexico's Cristero Rebellion: Michoacán, 1927–29* (Oxford: Oxford University Press, 2004).

4. See Jean Meyer, *La Cristiada*, 3 vols. (Mexico City: Siglo Veintiuno, 1973).

5. Ibid.; and Adrian Bantjes, *As if Jesus Walked the Earth: Cardenismo, Sonora, and the Mexican Revolution* (Wilmington, DE: Scholarly Resources, 1998).

6. Leopoldo Méndez, *En nombre de Cristo* (Mexico City: Editorial Gráfica Popular, 1939).

7. As far as I can tell, *Las verdaderas profecías de Matiana* (1917) represents the last published attempt to describe the visions in their entirety.

8. For a detailed examination of the Ixpantepec apparitions, see Wright-Rios, *Revolutions in Mexican Catholicism*, 206–70.

9. Ibid.

10. Lola Álvarez Bravo, *Recuento fotográfico* (Mexico City: Editorial Penélope, 1982), 18–19.

11. For background on the artist and discussions of her impact on Mexican art see Debroise, *Lola Álvarez Bravo*; and Ferrer, *Lola Álvarez Bravo*.

12. Lola Álvarez Bravo, *Recuento fotográfico*, 93–117, describes her network of friends and activities from the late 1920s through the 1940s.

13. Ferrer, *Lola Álvarez Bravo*, 14–17.

14. Ibid., 13–21.

15. See Helen Delpar, *The Enormous Vogue of Things Mexican: Cultural Relations Between the United States and Mexico, 1920–1935* (Tuscaloosa: University of Alabama Press, 1995).

16. See Rick A. López, *Crafting Mexico: Intellectuals, Artisans, and the State After the Revolution* (Durham, NC: Duke University Press, 2010).

17. Álvarez Bravo, *Recuento fotográfico*, 116.

18. Ibid., 12–13.

19. Ibid., 20–21. This is how she described producing two of her more famous images, *Entierro en Yalalag* and *Unos suben y otros bajan*.

20. Ibid., 17.

21. Carlos Monsiváis, "Y ahora, con su venia, conversaré de usted mi luciente señora (y no menos admirable fotógrafa)," in Álvarez Bravo, *Recuento fotográfico*, 187–90.

22. Álvarez Bravo, *Recuento fotográfico*, 117.

23. CCP, AG 154: 21, Reportaje: Caballos Fabricos.

24. Álvarez Bravo's recourse to irony may have, in part, stemmed from the influence of her ex-husband Manuel Álvarez Bravo. To break with the clichés of typical previous photographers of Mexican popular culture, like Hugo Brehme, he emphasized the ironic. This was noted by contemporaries and is stressed by scholars today: see John Mraz, *Looking for Mexico: Modern Visual Culture and National Identity* (Durham, NC: Duke University Press, 2009), 85–91.

25. See also *Saliendo de la Ópera*, ca. 1950, in Ferrer, *Lola Álvarez Bravo*, frontispiece.

26. See William H. Beezley, *Judas at the Jockey Club and Other Episodes of Porfirian Mexico* (Lincoln: University of Nebraska Press, 1987), 3–4 and 89–124.

27. For example, see Diego Rivera, "Burning the Judases," in Leonard Folgarait, *Mural Painting and Social Revolution in Mexico, 1920-1940: Art of the New Order* (Cambridge: Cambridge University Press, 1998), plate VII. The original mural adorns a wall in the courtyard of the Secretariat of Education.

28. For a depiction of the crowds during a Judas burning, see Lola Álvarez Bravo, "Sábado de Gloria 2," 1955, in Ferrer, *Lola Álvarez Bravo*, Plate 62, 97.

29. CCP, AG154:15, Judas, negatives, 1–4.

30. For a similar image of Judas in transit, see Lola Álvarez Bravo, *Judas*, taken in Mexico City, 1942, as shown in Ferrer, *Lola Álvarez Bravo*, plates 63, and 98–99.

31. Lola Álvarez Bravo apparently took note of this tradition as well. Among her unpublished negatives are a series of seven photographs of the Virgin Mary holding the baby Jesus Christ in regal attire. In these images, most likely a representation of the popular Virgen de los Remedios, both Mary and Christ wear oversized crowns. Although it is impossible to tell in the negatives these outsized adornments that seem to defy gravity by remaining perched on the figures' heads may be what attracted the artist to this image in the first place: see CCP, AG 154: 5, Santos.

32. CCP, AG 154: 5, Santos. This image is the third negative of fifteen placed together in an envelope.

33. See Ferrer, *Lola Álvarez Bravo*, 46–47.

34. Real Academia Española, *Diccionario de la lengua española*, 22nd ed., http://buscon.rae.es/draeI (accessed 18 November 2011).

35. CCP, AG 154: 26, Reportaje: santeros muñecas "santorio," CCP_ag154_bneg_26_reportaje_1_.

36. See Lola Álvarez Bravo, *El ruego*, 1946, in Ferrer, *Lola Álvarez Bravo*, plate 60, 95; and *Entierro en Yalalag*, 1946, in Ferrer, *Lola Álvarez Bravo*, plate 58, 92–93.

37. For comparison, see *El Duelo*, State of Mexico, ca. 1950, in Ferrer, *Lola Álvarez Bravo*, plates 43, 74.

38. The emphasis on conformity and blind collective anonymity is even more marked in an unpublished variant of *Entierro at Yalalag*. Here the procession is about to enter a building, probably the church. A mass of women completely covered by their shawls fills the center of the photograph. Again, a line of men hems them in. In this image they are clearly male pall bearers and musicians (individuals with specific tasks). CCP, AG 154: 54, Negatives—The Favorites of Lola, Box B, Albums, part 1 and 2, folder 13, 1/6, *Entierro en Yalalag*, variant, 1946.

39. For example, see *Marion Greenwood*, ca. 1935, plate 21; *María Izquierdo*, 1946, plate 91; and *Frida Kahlo*, ca. 1944, plates 98, 99, and 100, in Ferrer, *Lola Álvarez Bravo*.

40. For numerous negatives focusing on masked male performers see CCP, AG 154:8, D2 Box A, 2/3, Danzantes, *Jalisco: Sonajeros* and *Zacatecas: Santiagos*,

Matachines, Moros y Cristianos. These images feature many figures on hobby-horses and donning elaborate masks. See also the negatives in the same box, but in a different envelope: "Papantla–Danzantes, Negritos, Voladores, Huahuas, Queztals." This series includes masked individuals and others in blackface (a different kind of mask, as it were).

41. See David F. Martin, "On Portraiture: Some Distinctions," *The Journal of Aesthetics and Art Criticism* 20 (1961): 61–72.

42. Metepec's celebration of San Isidro Labrador on 15 May, and its famous procession called Defile de los Locos de San Isidro, was renowned for its extravagant masks and revelry in the 1930s and continues today, although much changed. For a description of the 1936 event, see Rodney Gallop, "A Mexican 'Plough Monday,'" *Folklore* 49, no. 4 (1938): 394–99. The devotion originated in Spain, where the saint allegedly lived during the eleventh and twelfth centuries. He is the patron of farmers, peasants, and day laborers. The banners were traditionally part of decorated yolks and carts born by oxen, which themselves were decorated and blessed as part of the ceremonies. In the procession many pairs of men appear attired as the farmer and his *tlacualera* (the woman tasked with bringing food to the fields). There were also numerous men dressed as rancheros on hobbyhorses. Many of the masks, however, depicted grotesquely distorted human faces and others represented stylized animals. Álvarez Bravo's photograph, although not dated, was undoubtedly taken during this festival. In fact, her negatives reveal many more images of the celebration; see CCP, AG 154:15, D3, Box C, pt.1, Metepec—Bendicion de Animales.

43. See also, *La manda,* 1946, in Ferrer, *Lola Álvarez Bravo,* plate 61.

44. For other pictures taken at the same time and some different negatives taken of these same statues, see CCP, Lola Álvarez Bravo Collection, AG 154: 54, The Favorite Pieces of Lola, Box B, Albums part 1 and 2, Folder 42, 3/3, Figures of Santos. Another negative in this folder also appears to have been a satirical image. It features a male and a female saint in what appears to be a corridor. Removed from sanctified space, the couple appear to be energetically attempting to communicate via gesture. However, like the published image their frozen gesticulations appear foolish in their unchanging intensity.

45. Leonard Folgarait, *Seeing Mexico Photographed: The Work of Horne, Casasola, Modotti, and Álvarez Bravo* (New Haven, CT: Yale University Press, 2008), 1–2.

46. On these issues see Martin, "On Portraiture," 61–72.

47. On the *carte de visite* and depictions of social types, see Deborah Poole, *Vision, Race, and Modernity: A Visual Economy of the Andean Image World* (Princeton, NJ: Princeton University Press, 1997), chapter 5. See also Mraz, *Looking for Mexico,* 22–35.

48. See Bantjes, *As if Jesus Walked the Earth,* 6–18.

49. Lola Álvarez Bravo, *La Madre Matiana,* 1935, CCP, 93.6.42.

50. I owe this observation to anthropologist and linguist Sergio Romero; personal communication, 20 October 2010.

CHAPTER 7

1. Yáñez, *Las tierras flacas*, 80–95, 180–85; for English, see Yáñez, *The Lean Lands*. In these passages the author resorts to italicized interior monologues to convey characters', including Madre Matiana's, thoughts and feelings.
2. "La doctrina de la Madre Matiana," UCBL. A printed date does not appear on this broadside, but an archival stamp records 26 April 1938. It is misidentified as a Revolutionary corrido (ballad) when in fact it is a mock catechism.
3. For example, see F. Tejedor, "Los espantos y la credulidad," *Sucesos para todos*, 14 December 1937; Carlos González Peña, "Empezamos a pagar," *El Universal*, 24 July 1946; and Cándido Mirón, "Carnet dominical," *El Porvenir*, 4 December 1949. The first article fits within longstanding critiques of superstition as a trait of Mexican culture. The author links Madre Matiana to the tradition of prediction at year's end and equates her with street-corner ghost stories. The second refers to recent power outages in Mexico City and quips that many residents were living by candlelight, as in "the times of Madre Matiana." The latter appears ignorant of the prophecies' origins, claiming that before the Revolution, Madre Matiana made yearly predictions regarding such things as comets and plagues, before disappearing mysteriously.
4. Heredia, *Historietas y leyendas*, vol. 7: 2, 65–70. These pages feature a short synopsis of the Matiana prophecies drawn largely from Duarte's 1889 *Profecías de Matiana*. The Jesuit Heredia, however, does not simply support the book's thesis. Instead he approaches the prophecies as but one of many legends from a previous period in Church history when many women reported mystical experiences and the credulous *vulgo* (rabble) was often willing to accept them simply because said women enjoyed saintly reputations.
5. Frances Toor, *A Treasury of Mexican Folkways* (New York: Crown Publishers, 1947), 538. Toor lists Madre Matiana among the humorous names given to Mexican bars.
6. See also José Paniagua Arrendondo, "El asesinato de Jaramillo. ¡México pide justicia!," *Impacto*, 27 July 1962. This article deploys Matiana in a statement of frustration about a political murder.
7. "Futurísmo presidencial," *La Crítica*, 1 February 1955.
8. Lucio Mendieta y Núñez, "Lo que no hará el Consejo Nacional de Economía," *El Universal*, 24 July 1946.
9. Catarino Gómez Bravo, "Puebla cuna de la Revolución maderista," *El Universal*, 24 July 1946; and P. Lussa (clearly a comedic pseudonym, *pelusa* means fluff and is also a slur for those of middling class—not middle-class—origins), "Profetas a

la carta," *El Porvenir*, 29 October 1954. For the definition of *pelusa* see Santamaría, *Diccionario de mejicanismos*, 827.

10. For some reason the special Thursday supplement of the Mexico City newspaper *Excelsior* included a number of these kinds of articles. See L. F. Bustamante, "Cuando y como se acabará en mundo," *Jueves de Excelsior*, 21 March 1946; and L. F. Bustamante, "El hombre de la túnica morada," *Jueves de Excelsior*, 18 April 1946. The first of Bustamante's essays represents a debunking overview of end-of-times predictions. He states that Mexicans are very familiar with Madre Matiana, and he lists happenings such as the Revolution of 1910 and the Cristero Revolt as events seemingly predicted by the prophetess. In the second article, published about a month later, Bustamante critiques a popular healer in one of Mexico City's poor neighborhoods, noting that he invokes Madre Matiana and predicts the end of the world in 2000. See also "Cómo será el fin," *Jueves de Excelsior*, 14 June 1951. The newspaper included a photograph of a painting that featured a nun and claimed it represented Madre Matiana Francisca del Señor San José. Most likely this is one of many colonial *monja coronada* (crowned nun) images with no relation to the prophecies.

11. For example, P. Lussa, "Profetas a la carta," *El Porvenir*, 29 October 1954; and P. Lussa, "El día del Juicio Final," *El Informador*, 2 August 1961. These articles may be by the same author, but they could also be by different individuals using the same pseudonym. The former paper is from Monterrey and the latter is from Guadalajara, which makes the possibility of different authors seem more likely. In the first instance the author relates an anecdote about his late aunt's claims that the world will end in 2000. He described her as *"muy beatita"* ("very pious") and hence given to reading Madre Matiana's prophecies and other similar *fuentes* (sources). In the second essay, the author quipped that the Villista insurgency inspired long debates among *"las comadres"* (roughly, the old ladies).

12. See "Las nuevas profecías de la madre Matiana," *La Crítica*, 1 June 1951, 1 February 1955, 1 July 1955, 1 August 1962, 1 September 1962, and 1 October 1962.

13. Enrique Aceves, "Ráfagas," *El Informador*, 12 November 1961.

14. For a distilled biography of Yáñez, see Roderic Ai Camp, *Mexican Political Biographies, 1935–1993*, 3rd ed. (Austin: University of Texas Press, 1995), 744–45. For a useful biological sketch particularly sensitive to understandings of his career and writings in Jalsico: see Leandro Limón Gómez, "Agustín Yáñez: genio y figura," in *Acto preparatorio*, eds. Agustín Vaca and Antonio Gómez Robledo (Gudalajara: El Colegio de Jalisco, 2003), 33–38.

15. See Jaime Olveda, "La Yahualica de Agustín Yáñez," in *Acto preparatorio*, eds. Vaca and Gómez, 61–68.

16. Gómez Limón, "Agustín Yáñez" in *Acto preparatorio*, eds. Vaca and Gómez, 33–38. See also Jaime Olveda, "La obra histórica de Agustín Yáñez," in *Acto preparatorio*, ed.Vaca and Gómez, 46–51.

17. See Meyer, *La Cristiada*, vol.1: 50–78; and Robert Curley, "'The First Encounter': Catholic Politics in Revolutionary Jalisco, 1917–19," in *Faith and Impiety in Revolutionary Mexico*, ed. Matthew Butler (New York: Palgrave, 2007), 131–48.

18. Roderic Ai Camp, "An Intellectual in Mexican Politics: The Case of Agustín Yáñez," *Mester* 12, no. 1 and 2 (1983): 3–17. This special journal issue was dedicated to Yáñez in the wake of his death in 1980.

19. José Luis Martínez, "La formación literaria de Agustín Yáñez y *Al filo del Agua*." *Mester* 12, nos. 1 and 2 (1983): 26–40.

20. For a detailed study of the Secretariat of education, see Mary K. Vaughan, *Cultural Politics in Revolution: Teachers, Peasants, and Schools in Mexico, 1930–1940* (Tucson: University of Arizona Press, 1997).

21. Antonio Gómez Robledo, an associate from his editorial activities in the 1920s who accompanied Yáñez to Mexico City and the UNAM, suggests that the author's transformation took shape during his studies with Alfonso Caso; see Antonio Gómez Robledo, "Cuando todo se ha dicho," in *Acto preparatorio*, eds. Vaca and Gómez, 17–32.

22. For a basic biography of Bassols, see Camp, *Mexican Political Biographies*, 66–67.

23. Yáñez, *Al Filo del Agua*, 2nd ed., ed. Arturo Azuela (Nanterre, France: Signatarios Acuerdo Archivos ALLCA XX Université Paris X, 1996). On the novel's importance, see Randolph Pope, "The Spanish American Novel from 1950 to 1975," in *The Cambridge History of Latin American Literature*, vol. 2, eds. González Echevarría and Pupo-Walker, 226–78.

24. Camp, "An Intellectual in Mexican Politics."

25. Luis Leal, "Agustín Yáñez y la novella Mexicana," *Mester* 12, nos. 1 and 2 (1983): 18–25. For Yáñez's unwavering emphasis on social criticism, see Christopher Harris, *The Novels of Agustín Yáñez: A Critical Portrait of Mexico in the 20th Century* (Lewiston, NY: Edwin Mellen Press, 2000). As Harris demonstrates, at numerous points in his career the author reiterated his insistence that the Mexican novel must entail unflinching social criticism, 135–36.

26. Martínez, "La formación literaria de Agustín Yáñez."

27. For an overview of scholarly examinations of caciquismo, see Alan Knight, "Introduction," in *Caciquismo in Twentieth-Century Mexico*, eds. Alan Knight and Wil Pansters (London: Institute for the Americas, 2005), 1–50. For the rather pedantic statist critique of caciquismo in film, see *Rio Escondido*, directed by Emilio "El Indio" Fernández, original release 1948 (Thousand Oaks, CA: Excalibur Media Group, 2004), DVD.

28. For an extensive discussion of this issue, particularly in *La tierra pródiga*, see Jean Franco, *Lectura sociocrítica de la obra novelística de Agustín Yáñez* (Guadalajara: Gobierno de Jalisco, 1988). Franco stresses the author's presentation of modern statist developmentalism, displacement, and rural clientalism as transparently positive advancements.

29. See Knight, "Introduction," in *Caciquismo*, eds. Knight and Pansters, 1–50.

30. See Carlos Alonso, "The *Criollista* Novel," in *The Cambridge History of Latin American Literature*, vol. 2, eds. González Echevarría and Pupo-Walker: 195–212. In a sense, Madre Matiana is Yáñez's doña Barbara.

31. For examples of *Al filo*'s glowing assessment among English-language scholars see Walter M. Langford, *The Mexican Novel Comes of Age* (Notre Dame, IN: University of Notre Dame Press, 1971), 71–87; and John S. Brushwood, *Mexico in Its Novel: A Nation's Search for Identity* (Austin: University of Texas Press, 1966), 7–12.

32. For example, see "Agenda de Cultura," *El Informador*, 16 December 1962; and "Hondura y fuerza de *Las tierras flacas*," *El Libro y el Pueblo*, 1 May 1963.

33. On the critical appraisal of his work, see Gómez Limón, "Agustín Yáñez" in *Acto preparatorio*, ed.Vaca and Gómez, 33–38. Some critics mused that he would have been a better writer if he had avoided politics.

34. For example, see Agustín Vaca, "Introducción," in *Acto preparatorio*, eds. Vaca and Gómez. See also Olveda, "La obra histórica de Agustín Yáñez" in the same collection.

35. In the most extreme cases, scholars have shown how Revolutionary actors sought to extirpate popular Catholicism. On this topic, see Adrian Bantjes, *As if Jesus Walked the Earth*; and Ben Fallaw, *Religion and State Formation in Postrevolutionary Mexico* (Durham, NC: Duke University Press, 2013).

36. Agustín Yáñez, *Llama de amor viva: cuentos de amor* (Guadalajara: Tipografía S. R. Velásquez, 1925). A note at the back of the book claims that stories were actually written in 1923 when the author was only 19.

37. Agustín Yáñez, *Divina floración: miscelánea de caridad* (Guadalajara: Tipografía S. R. Velásquez, 1925).

38. Yáñez, *Llama de amor viva*, 33–34.

39. Ibid., 35–36.

40. Ibid., 43–55

41. Ibid., 68–69.

42. Ibid., 56–75.

43. Ibid., 56–75.

44. Ai Camp, "An Intellectual in Mexican Politics." Camp bases this contention on interviews with individuals who knew Yáñez at the time. See also Gómez Limón, "Agustín Yáñez" in *Acto preparatorio*, eds. Vaca and Gómez, 33–38.

45. For the epigraph, see Yáñez, *Al filo*, 3. On the importance of Yahualica in his works, see Ignacio Díaz Ruiz, "Al filo del agua en la historia personal de Agustín Yáñez y el itinerario de su obra," in Yáñez, *Al filo del agua*, 2nd ed., 275–84. See also John Flasher, *México contemporáneo en las novelas de Agustín Yáñez* (Mexico City: Porrúa, 1969), 39.

46. For an overlaping interpretation, see José María Muriá, "En torno *Al filo del Agua*," in *Acto preparatorio*, eds. Vaca and Gómez, 69–75. Muriá argues that the

author is not so much trying to capture historical reality, but rather to reproduce the feeling of brusque change experienced in Los Altos.

47. Margo Glantz interprets the novel as a complex struggle of the internal spiritual, mental, and emotional conflicts that are unleashed by the corrosive, liberating functions of the written word. In her view, the book becomes a mosaic of tabloid-like stories as its characters live out their personal stories of sin, crime and calamity. See Margo Glantz, "Yáñez y *Al filo del agua*," in *Acto preparatorio*, eds. Vaca and Gómez, 93–103.

48. For parish formation in Jalisco and its political ramifications related to the Cristero Revolt, see Ramón Jrade, "Counterrevolution in Mexico" (PhD diss., Brown University, 1980). On these issues in Michoacán, see Jennie Purnell, *Popular Movements and State Formation in Revolutionary Mexico: The Agraristas and Cristeros of Michoacán* (Durham, NC: Duke University Press, 1999); and Matthew Butler, *Popular Piety*.

49. See the quarterly reports housed in Guadalajara's archdiocesan archive: for example, AHAG, Gobierno, Secretaría, Correspondencia con Parroquias, 1911–1917, caja 16, exp. 1911–1914, Presbiterio Agapito Ramírez, Informe Cuatrimestral de Tepatitlán, 1 May 1910. At this time Tepatitlán, a relatively large town in Los Altos, employed twelve priests, five of which worked in the parish seat. Ramírez's glowing appraisal of attendance at Mass, lay access to priestly services, and expanding sacramental frequency is extraordinary. He also described new Catholic associations as "florescent." For numerous additional reports, many of which are also very upbeat about lay religiosity and institutional participation, see AHAG, Gobierno, Secretaría, Correspondencia con Parroquias, 1897–1911, caja 15, exp. 1911–1913. Some describe the endurance of effervescent priest-centered Catholic practice despite the Revolution. For example, see Ildefonso B. Gutierrez to Archbishop José de Jesús Ortiz, Mezquital de Oro (Zacatecas), 30 April 1912. Gutierrez gushes about the impact of spiritual excercises similar to the encierro portrayed by Yáñez in *Al filo*. He also speaks gleefully of the "*obedencia suma*" ("total obedience") and "*subordinación absoluta*" ("absolute subordination") of the faithful. For another example of burgeoning Catholic life during the Revolution, see also Dionisio María Gómez to Archbishop Francisco y Jiménez, San Diego de Alejandría, 11 May 1914, AHAG, Gobierno, Secretaría, Correspondencia con Parroquias, exp. 1912–1918.

50. See Wright-Rios, *Revolutions in Mexican Catholicism*, particularly chapters 3 and 4.

51. A good picture of religious practice in the area near Yahualica appears in the documentation from neighboring Cuquío, the municipal seat to which it historically was subject: AHAG, Gobierno, Parroquias, Cuquío, 1887–1938, caja 5. For example in exp. 1908, see Plutarco Contreras to Archbishop of Guadalajara, 4 September 1908. See also in exp. 1914–1917, Justino Orcona, Informe 31 August 1920 and 31 December 1920. Also in the same *expediente* (folder), see Orocona

to Cathedral Dean Manuel Alvarado, 20 July 1918; the author describes a trip to Yahualica for encierro exercises.

52. See Ceballos Ramírez, *El catolicismo social.*

53. Yáñez, *Al filo*, 139.

54. Ibid., 142.

55. Ibid., 148.

56. Ibid., 142–44.

57. Ibid., 11.

58. Carlos Monsiváis, "'Pueblo de mujeres enlutadas:' el programa descriptivo en *Al filo del agua*," in Yáñez, *Al filo del Agua* (1996), ed. Arturo Azuela, 369–82.

59. On this aspect, see Glantz, "Yáñez y *Al filo del agua*" in *Acto preparatorio*, eds. Vaca and Gómez, 93–103.

60. For example, *El Sol*, a newspaper from Guadalajara published in 1899, debated and critiqued end-of-the-world predictions related to the Biela comet. See Juvenal, "Faz sombría del sol," *El Sol*, 3 November 1899; "El cometa Biela y otros cometas" and "El fin del mundo," *El Sol*, 8 November 1899; and "El fin del mundo: falso pronóstico de un terrible cataclismo," and J. Jover, "La próxima lluvia de estrellas y el fin del mundo," *El Sol*, 14 November 1899. In general these articles criticize superstitious ignorance they perceived in the end-of-the-world fears linked to astronomical events. The issue with the Biela comet was largely due to ideas about comet-Earth collisions. Biela was a small comet discovered in 1826; it reappeared every 6.6 years and traveled relatively near the Earth. This led to questions about what would happen if the Earth's orbit brought it directly into the comet's path. In 1846 Biela broke in two, and the distinct parts could be seen again in 1852. Subsequently in 1872, 1885, 1892, and 1899 magnificent meteor showers occurred when the Earth passed through the remains of the broken-up astral body. The possibility of numerous large meteors hitting the Earth during these events became the grist for end-of-the-world scenarios. See "The Return of Halley's Comet," *Bulletin of the American Geographical Society* 42, no. 4 (1910): 261–65; Dorrit Hoffleit, "What Falls from Heaven," *The Scientific Monthly* 60, no. 1 (1945): 30–36; and James Stokley, "Falling Meteors Might Wipe out Cities, *The Science News-Letter* 16, no. 432 (20 July 1929): 27–29.

61. Mercurio López Casillas, *Manilla* (Mexico City: Editorial RM, 2005), 177.

62. See Julian Rothenstein, ed., *Posada: Messenger of Mortality* (London: Redstone Press, 1989), 68–9, plates 68 and 71; and Tyler, ed., *Posada's Mexico*, 189, plates 144 and 145. The former reproduces the comet images from broadsides from 1889 and 1899. The latter includes broadsides using the same engravings in 1910. Naturally, the accompanying texts have changed. For the prevalence of these fears related to comets in neighboring Michoacán during both 1899 and 1910, see José Gonzalez y Gonzalez, *Pueblo en vilo: microhistoria de San José de Gracia* (Mexico City: El Colegio de México, 1968), 133–34, 170, and 176.

63. The rough number comes from figures quoted in *La Gaceta*. They claimed twenty-three quakes occurred between 7 and 8 May, and a total of sixty-four within the three following weeks. The paper reported that a government seismic station recorded another sixty in July. See "La Ciudad se encuentra en una expectación dolorosa," *La Gaceta, 8 May 1912*; Ezequiel Ordóñez, "Nota sobre los temblores recientes de Guadalajara y su causa probable," *La Gaceta*, 9 June 1912; and "Se ha iniciado un nuevo period de actividad sísmica," *La Gaceta* 30 July 1912.

64. On the exodus from Guadalajara, see *La Gaceta*, 10 August 1912. On merchant responses, see the advertisement entitled "No tema los temblores," *El Regional*, 12 May 1912. The operators of the city's tram lines also tried to stoke ridership claiming that the shaking was not felt on their cars and making them safer than walking; see advertisement "Tiembla en todas partes, menos los tranvías," *La Gaceta*, 10 May 1912. See also advertisement titled "Oscilador sísmico," *La Gaceta*, 26 July 1912. Allegedly, this device woke up the owner with flashing lights at the slightest tremor.

65. Both periodicals also covered strong quakes in Mexico City during June of the previous year. They raised eyebrows because they coincided with Francisco Madero's arrival in the capital after Porfirio Díaz's ousting. Some Mexicans, apparently, interpreted this coincidence as evidence of divine disapproval.

66. "La ciudad se encuentra en una expectación dolorosa," *La Gaceta, 8 May 1912*. *El Regional*, 8 May 1912 offered very similar coverage of the happenings and the scene in Guadalajara.

67. "La Virgen se mueve," *La Gaceta*, 8 May 1912. These events prompted Mexico City's archdiocesan authorities to investigate: see AHAM, Fondo Ecclesiastico, Secrertaría, Serie Parróquias, caja 38, exp. 9, Decreto, 23 May 1912; and Decreto, 5 June 1912.

68. For example, see *La Gaceta*, 14 May 1912.

69. "Los temblores que han sucedido durante el día," *La Gaceta*, 11 May 1912.

70. "La mano de Dios," *El Regional*, 12 May 1912. In fact, this argument had been aired earlier as evident in an announcement signed by the members of the Vela Perpetua del Santísimo Sacramento. See "Misa de desagravios," *El Regional*, 11 May 1912. The Vela's members stressed that society had been committing tremendously sinful acts of late, and hence it was to be expected that God would punish the entire city. A few days later the paper followed with another essay outlining the biblical "history" of divine retribution. The Italian earthquake at Messina in 1908 was held up as an example of celestial punishment. See Jasso S. Cimella, "Sobre el mismo tema," *El Regional*, 14 May 1912. The same issue also discussed how the Guadalajara's Virgin of Soledad had a history of protecting the city from earthquakes, and hence merited devotion.

71. Jerónimo Hijar, "No se debe exagerar el miedo de temblores," *La Gaceta*, 14 May 1912.

72. See "Triduos muy solemnes en la Santa Iglesia catedral: en desagravio de las blasfemias que han vertido últimamente los impios," *El Regional*, 21 May 1912.

73. "A pesar de que han cesado los temblores, no se ha disipado el pánico," *La Gaceta*, 18 May 2012. In July a new theory pointed to a peculiar alignment of the stars that caused atmospheric perturbations that shook the Earth. See "Los temblores han seguido sembrando pánico," *La Gaceta*, 21 July 1912. In addition, a publication from Queretaro alleged that Guadalajara resided precariously upon a subterranean volcano. See Antonio Olvera y Gilmes, "Guadalajara encima de un volcán," *La Gaceta*, 11 June 1912.

74. José G. Aguilera, Director of the Mexican Institutoe of Geology, to Governor of Jalisco, 14 May 1912, Archivo Histórico del Estado de Jalisco (AHEJ), fomento, fenomenos naturales, F-18–912–3318. This file includes reports from building inspectors and various officials on damages and commentary on different temblors and their intensity. Several reports comment on geologists' activities in the region. See also "Una comisión científica," *La Gaceta*, 16 May 1912; and "La comisión de geólogos," *La Gaceta*, 17 May 1912.

75. See "¿Otro Erasmo Ruiz?" *La Gaceta*, 11 May 1912. See also "La nota cómica de los temblores, 'El Calor'"; and "Causa de los sismos, habla Centeno," *La Gaceta*, 27 May 1912.

76. Vicente Michel, S. Pedro Tlaquepaque, to Vicario Capitular Antonio Gordillo, Guadalajara, 17 July 1912, AHAG, Gobierno, Secretaría, Correspondencia con Parroquias, 1912, caja 18. The files in this box are not numbered, although they are labeled by the year and appear to be in chronological order. This letter resides in the fourth file from 1912.

77. Artemio Rodríguez, ed., *José Guadalupe Posada: 150 años/150 years* (Los Angeles, CA: La Mano Press, 2003), 60; and Tyler, ed., *Posada's Mexico*, 176. The latter reproduces a small image of the original broadside.

78. "Fuertes temblores registrados a noche, causaron horrible pánico en la ciudad," *La Gaceta*, 26 May 1912.

79. "La Providencia Divina y los temblores," *El Regional*, 29 June 1912. The Catholic newspaper blamed a masonic plot for the anonymous effrontery.

80. *La Gaceta*, 21 July 1912. The interim governor (Alberto Robles Gil) attacked Arreola and Díaz publically for sewing terror and inspiring accusations against the state government.

81. "El sabio geólogo Presbiterio José María Arreola predice los temblores que tendremos hasta á principios de agosto," *La Gaceta*, 22 July 1912. See also *La Gaceta*, 23 July 1912.

82. *La Gaceta*, 25 July 1912. Apparently Arreola based his predictions on a combination of astronomy, meteorology, and the notion that the rash of quakes followed previous patterns. According to the government geologist, Arreola simply mapped the past events over the summer of 1912, even though the epicenters were completely different. More quakes, he assured, would occur, but it was impossible

that they would match up with Arreola's predictions unless by coincidence. Alongside this missive, another letter appeared from a local engineer who rejected attempts to connect the Guadalajara happenings to the devastating earthquakes in Messina in 1908, stressing the very different geology of Italy.

83. "Mil pesos de apuesta á que no se cumplirán las predicciones de P. Arreola." *La Gaceta*, 24 July 1912.

84. "Las nuevas predicciones del sabio geólogo Sr. D. José María Arreola," *El Regional*, 23 July 1912; "Los fenómenos," *El Regional*, 30 July 1912; and "Opina el Señor Arreola sobre el temblor de próximo día seis," *El Regional*, 31 July 1912. In the first article, they printed photographs of both Díaz and Arreola. On the processions, see Francisco J. Zavala, "Una opinion autorizada," *El Regional*, 1 August 1912.

85. "Consejas que alarman á la población," *La Gaceta*, 27 July 1912. Apparently rumors claimed that Arreola had been silenced by the government or jailed.

86. "Se ha iniciado un nuevo periodo de actividad sísmica," *La Gaceta*, 30 July 1912. See also "Los moradores de Guadalajara esperan los anunciados sismos en jardines y plazuelas," *La Gaceta*, 31 July 1912.

87. "Ni ahora, ni nunca he llegado a creer que haya motivo para temer que nuestra hermosa ciudad sea destruida por estos temblores," *La Gaceta*, 1 August 1912.

88. "No ha habido temblores," *La Gaceta*, August 5, 1912; "Guadalajara se dispone á recibir el temblor fuertísimo anunciado para hoy" and "El pánico y el fanatismo," *La Gaceta*, August 6, 1912; and "Desafiando la fatalidad de los pronósticos, Guadalajara está de pie," 7 August 1912. For the Catholic critique of *La Gaceta's* treatment of Arreola, see "La Gaceta desmentida," *El Regional*, 7 August 1912.

89. See Zenaido Michel Pimenta, "Infundados temores al terminar el Siglo de 'Las Luces,'" *El Informador*, 9 January 1977. Pimenta recounted his memories as a teenager in 1900, and he explicitly noted the role of Matiana's prophecies.

90. See Enrique Francisco Camarena, "Hace Cincuenta Años," *El Informador*, 4 April 1965; and "Los 50 años de vida periodística de El Informador," *El Informador*, 5 October 1967.

91. Carlos Fuentes, *La muerte de Artemio Cruz* (Mexico City: Fondo de Cultura Económica, 1962).

92. Gilbert Joseph, *Revolution from Without: Yucatán, Mexico, and the United States, 1880–1924* (Cambridge: Cambridge University Press, 1982).

93. See Butler, *Popular Piety*. See also Christopher Boyer, *Becoming Campesinos: Politics, Identity, and Agrarian Struggle in Postrevolutionary Michoacán, 1920–1935* (Stanford, CA: Stanford University Press, 2003).

94. Yáñez, *Las tierras flacas*, 1–23.

95. Yáñez also writes a section in the voice of Merced; ibid., 115–18.

96. Ibid., 60–61.

97. Ibid., 23–25.

98. San Ramon Nonato (1204–1240) is the patron saint of childbirth, midwives, and

pregnant women. See "Saint Raymond Nonnatus," *Catholic Online*, www.catholic. org/saints/saint.php?saint_id=314 (accessed 24 June 2013).

99. Yáñez, *Las tierras flacas*, 24–25.

100. Ibid., 80–95.

101. Ibid., 82–93. In the original text these remembrances span several pages. I have translated and linked these excerpts in a single quotation to give a full sense of their revelatory function in the most economical fashion possible.

102. Ibid., 95.

103. Ibid., 180–82.

104. Ibid., 183–84.

105. Ibid., 184.

106. Part II of the novel charts the return of Miguel Archangel/Jacobo. Through various characters' thoughts and memories, his backstory is exposed; ibid., 99–127.

107. Ibid., 186–98.

108. Ibid., 332–37.

CONCLUSION

1. See announcements published in *El Informador*, 2 November 1976 and 11 November 1976. The content of this talk was not revealed to the newspapers. Most of the other conference sessions address health issues in Mexico.

2. Antonio de Ríus Facius, "La madre Matiana," *El Porvenir*, 7 April 1971. The author in this case offers a sketch of the seer's legend and origins paraphrased from a nineteenth-century collection of historical vignettes. See Manuel Rivera Cambas, *México pintoresco, artístico, y monumental: vistas, descripcion, anecdotas y episodios de los lugares mas notables de la capital y de los estados, aun de las poblaciones cortas, pero de importancia geográfica ó histórica: las descripciones contienen datos científicos, históricos y estadísticos*, facsimile of 1882 edition, (Mexico City: Editora Nacional, 1957), vol. 2, 221–22. Ríus Facius refers to Matiana in a mocking tone and repeats the stranger aspects of her alleged visions, such as the prediction of a miraculous well of oil that materialed in the Jeronymite convent. In keeping with his source, he presents her as an actual historical figure—in this case, an Indian convent servant of the colonial era who imagines she has miraculous experiences.

3. Eduardo Aldama, "Maddox sigue sorprendiendo," losdodgers.com (accessed 8 August 2006).

4. Armando Fuentes Aguirre, "La otra historia de México," *El Informador*, 11 January 1993. Fuentes accepted without question that the seer was an actual eighteenth-century historical personage. He claimed that after the 1850s Matiana was largely forgotten only to be mysteriously republished in the twentieth century. Citing their similarity to the sermons of the day he surmises that the Catholic Church was responsible for her reemergence.

5. According to his website, de Luna's wares are available at many bookstores and shops around the nation. In press coverage Madre Matiana occasionally appears on the Lotería game pieces. See Mireya Ballesteros, "Completa Erik de Luna su Lotería de los 100 nombres que los mexicanos le dan a la muerte," *Tribuna de Querétaro*, 23 September 2005, www.calakitas.com.mx/prensa/prensa4.html.

6. See Claudio Lomnitz-Adler, *Death and the Idea of Mexico* (Brooklyn, NY: Zone Books, 2005), 26. Lomitz-Adler makes no mention of the Matiana legacy, but his source (see footnotes 8 and 9) does: see Juan M. Lope Blanch, *Vocabulario mexicano relativo a la muerte* (Mexico City: Dirección General de Publicaciones, 1963), 24n24, 24n26. Lomnitz-Adler asserts that Matiana is a derivation of *matar* (to kill). Lope Blanch, however, doubts this connection. He emphasizes Madre Matiana's role as a legendary figure and claims that she had become a symbol of antiquity, witchcraft, and sorcery. He did not elaborate on when these associations emerged. In the nineteenth-century and early twentieth-century texts that I have analyzed here she is not depicted as a personification of death, although in some sources, like the newspaper *La Madre Matiana*, she is sometimes portrayed as having returned from the dead.

7. Heredia, *Historietas y leyendas*, 65–70.

Bibliography

Archival Collections

Archivo General de la Nación	AGN
Archivo Histórico del Arzobispado de Guadalajara	AHAG
Archivo Histórico del Arzobispado de México	AHAM
Archivo Histórico del Arzobispado de Oaxaca	AHAO
Archivo Histórico del Estado de Jalisco	AHEJ
Archivo Histórico Distrito Federal	AHDF
Biblioteca de la Universidad de Sonora	BUS
Biblioteca Miguel Lerdo de Tejada	BMLT
Biblioteca Nacional de España	BNE
Biblioteca Nacional de México	BN
Biblioteca Pública de Jalisco	BPJ
California State University–Sutro Library	SL
Center for Creative Photography	CCP
Centro de Estudios Históricos de México	CEHM
Hemeroteca Nacional de México	HN
University of California, Berkeley, Bancroft Library	UCBL
University of California, Los Angeles Library, Special Collections	UCLA
University of Hawaii at Manoa Library, Jean Charlot Collection	UHJC
University of Texas at Arlington Library, Special Collections	UTAL
University of Texas at Austin Library, Benson Collection	UTBC
Yale University Sterling Memorial Library	YSML

Newspapers

Boletín Oficial y Revista Ecclesiástica de Antequera, Oaxaca
Círculo Católico, Mexico City
Confeti, Mexico City
Diario de Avisos, Mexico City

Diario de la República Mexicana, Mexico City
Ecos, Mexico City
El Abogado Cristiano, Mexico City
El Amigo de la Verdad, Puebla
El Boquiflojo, Mexico City
El Buscapié, Mexico City
El Contemporáneo, San Luis Potosí
El Cruzado, Mexico City
El Demócrata, Veracruz
El Diario del Hogar, Mexico City
El Hijo del Ahuizote, Mexico City
El Hijo del Trabajo, Mexico City
El Imparcial, Mexico City
El Informador, Guadalajara
El Libre Pensador, Mexico City
El Libro y el Pueblo, Mexico City
El Monitor Republicano, Mexico City
El Nacional, Mexico City
El País, Mexico City
El Pájaro Verde, Mexico City
El Popular, Mexico City
El Porvenir, Monterrey
El Regional, Guadalajara
El Siglo Diez y Nueve, Mexico City
El Tiempo, Mexico City
El Tiempo Ilustrado, Mexico City
El Universal, Mexico City
Hoja quincenal dedicada a la propaganda católica, Mexico City
Impacto, Mexico City
Jueves de Excelsior, Mexico City
La Casera, Mexico City
La Crítica, Mexico City
La Cruz, Mexico City
La Gaceta Comercial, Mexico City
La Gaceta de Jalisco, Guadalajara
La Ilustración Católica, Mexico City
La Libertad, Mexico City
La Madre Matiana, Mexico City
La Metralla, Mexico City
La Pata de Cabra, Mexico City
La Patria, Mexico City
La Revista Mexicana, San Antonio, TX
La Revista Universal, Mexico City

La Sociedad, Mexico City
La Sociedad Católica, Mexico City
La Sombra, Mexico City
La Voz de la Verdad, Oaxaca
La Voz de México, Mexico City
The Mexican Herald, Mexico City
Sucesos para Todos, Mexico City

Calendarios and Almanaques

Note: Unless noted, all the titles were published in Mexico City. Most Mexican almanacs included at the end of their title the year for which they were prepared (e.g. "... para el año 1858") without actually listing a true publication date. In almost every case they would have been printed and promoted in the months prior to the year they were prepared, just as calendars are today. Hence, in the strictest sense their publication date would be the year before what appears on the title page. However, this is not how they are cataloged in libraries and archival collections. The years listed below represent the years for which the calendars were prepared, unless the publisher actually listed a publication date (for the most part these were produced by Andrade and Escalante).

Almanak de la chocolatería española por José Juan Torremocha (Imprenta Poliglota, 1878)
Almanaque católico e histórico (Antigua Librería de Abadiano, 1884 and 1886)
Calendario agrícola (Imprenta Literaria, 1867)
Calendario burlesco (J. M. Aguilar y Compañía, 1861, 1862, 1864, 1867)
Calendario católico (Andrade y Escalante, 1861 and 1863; published in 1860 and 1862, respectively)
Calendario curioso (Imprenta de M. Murgía, 1861, 1862, 1863,1864, 1867, and 1871)
Calendario curioso dedicado a las señoritas (Imprenta de M. Murgía, 1851, 1853 and 1855)
Calendario de adivinanzas (Imprenta Literaria, 1867)
Calendario de Cumplido (Imprenta de Ignacio Cumplido, 1844, 1845, 1846, and 1848)
Calendario de Juan Navarro (Imprenta Navarro, 1849)
Calendario de la democracia dedicado al pueblo mexicano (Imprenta de Leandro Valdés, 1851 and 1852)
Calendario de la Madre Matiana (Imprenta de A. Boix a cargo de M. Zornoza, 1867)
Calendario de la Perla de México (Imprenta A. Boix a cargo de M. Zornoza, 1867)
Calendario de las musas (Imprenta Literaria, 1867)
Calendario de las niñas (Tipografía de Manuel Murguía, 1862, 1862, 1864, 1867, and 1869)
Calendario de la Sociedad de San Vicente de Paul (Imprenta de Andrade y Escalante, 1867; published in 1866)

Calendario del negrito poeta (Imprenta Nabor Chávez, 1860–1862 and 1864)

Calendario de López (Tipografía de M. Murgía, 1861, 1862, 1864)

Calendario de los agricultores (Tipografía de Manuel Murgía, 1862, 1864, and 1867)

Calendario de los amantes (Imprenta de Manuel Murgía, 1861 and 1862)

Calendario de los cuentos de aparecidos (Imprenta A. Boix a cargo de M. Zornoza, 1867)

Calendario de los duendes y aparecidos (Imprenta A. Boix a cargo de M. Zornoza, 1864)

Calendario de los enamorados (Imprenta A. Boix a cargo de M. Zornoza, 1867)

Calendario de los jóvenes (Imprenta Tipografía de Nabor Chávez, 1867)

Calendario de los niños (Tipografía de Manuel Murguía, 1859 and 1861)

Calendario de los polvos de la Madre Celestina (Tipografía de Rivera y Murgía, 1857)

Calendario de Murguía (Imprenta de M. Murgía y Compañía, 1855, 1858, 1861, 1867, and 1876)

Calendario dramático (Imprenta Aguilar y Ortiz, 1864)

Calendario económico (Imprenta de Manuel Murguía y Compañía, 1861, 1862, 1864, 1867, 1869, and 1870)

Calendario enciclopédico de la juventud (Imprenta Literario, 1865)

Calendario histórico de Carlota (Imprenta de Juan N. del Valle, 1869)

Calendario histórico de la Emperatriz Carlota Amalia (González y Compañía, 1871)

Calendario histórico de Maximiliano (Imprenta de Murguía, 1869)

Calendario joco-serio (Imprenta A. Boix a cargo de M. Zornoza, 1867)

Calendario jocoso y divertido del telégrafo (Imprenta de Manuel Castro, 1861)

Calendario mágico y de suertes (Tipografía Nabor Chávez, 1861)

Calendario manual (Imprenta de Zúñiga y Ontiveros, 1780)

Calendario manual y guía de forasteros de México (Mexico City: Imprenta de Zúñiga y Ontiveros)

Calendario nigromántico (Imprenta de Manuel Murguía, 1858, 1861, 1862, 1864, 1867, 1869–1871, and 1876)

Calendario para el año 1871 (Merida: Imprenta y litografía de J. D. Espinosa é Hijos)

Calendario profético (Tipografía M. Murguía, 1859)

Calendario protestante de los amigos cristianos, edited by José Parra y Álvarez (Tipografía de M. Castro, 1868)

Calendario reaccionario (Imprenta de Vicente Segura, 1861; printed in 1860)

Calendario universal (Tipografía de M. Murgía, 1859, 1861, 1862, 1864, 1867, and 1874)

El calendario del Tío Caniyitas (Imprenta Vicente Segura, 1858)

El primer calendario impolítico y justiciero (Mexico City: Imprenta de Navarro, 1853).

Tercer calendario portátil de Juan N. del Valle (Imprenta Juan N. del Valle, 1844)

Published Primary Sources

Alamán, Lucas. *Historia de Méjico desde los primeros movimientos que prepararon su independencia en el año 1808, hasta la* época *presente.* 5 vols. Mexico City: Imprenta de José María Lara, 1849–1852.

Alvírez, Manuel Teodicio. *Manifiesto a los fieles de Jesucristo*. Morelia: Imprenta de O. Ortiz, 1863.

Arias, Juan de Dios, "La Partera." In Frías y Soto et al., *Los mexicanos pintados por sí mismos*, 267–71.

Curicque, Jean-Marie. *Voces proféticas ó signos, apariciones y predicciones modernas-concernientes á los grandes acontecimientos de la cristiandad en el siglo XIX, y hacia la aproximación del fin de los tiempos*. Barcelona: Imprenta y Librería Religiosa y Científica, 1874.

de Barruel, Agustín. *Historia del clero en tiempo de la revolución francesa*. Mexico City: Mariano Joseph de Zúñiga y Ontiveros, 1800.

———. *Memorias para servir a la historia del jacobinismo*. Mexico City: Impreso por Agustín Contreras, 1837.

Decaen, J. et.al. *México y sus alrededores: colección de vistas, trajes y monumentos*. Mexico City: Ejecutado en el establecimiento litografía de Decaen Portal del Coliseo Viejo, 1855 and 1856.

———. *México y sus alrededores: colección de vistas, trajes y monumentos*. Facismile of the second edition. Mexico City: Inversora Bursátil, 1989

de la Pasión de Jesús, María Josefa. *Profecías de Matiana, sirvienta que fue en el convent de San Gerónimo de México, sobre los sucesos que han de acontecer en esta capital*. Mexico City: Valdés y Redondas, 1847.

———. *Profecías de Matiana, sirvienta que fue en el convento de San Gerónimo de México, sobre los sucesos que han de acontecer en esta capital*. Mexico City: Imprenta Abadiano, 1857.

———. *Profecías de Matiana, sirvienta que fue en el convento de San Gerónimo de Mexico, sobre los sucesos que han de acontecer en al [sic] espresada capital*. Mexico City: Imprenta de la calle del Cuadrante de Santa Catarina, 1861.

de la Vega, Tranquilino. *Los jesuítas y la constitución, ó sea, colección de los fundamentos legales que obran en favor del restablecimiento de la Compañía de Jesús en la República Mexicana*. Mexico City: Imprenta de Luis Abadino y Valdés, 1850.

del Valle, Juan N. *El viajero en México: completa guía de forasteros para 1864*. Mexico City: Imprenta de Andrade y Escalante, 1864.

Diálogo entre un barbero y su marchante, ó, contestación a los libelos publicados contra la Compañía de Jesús: con motivo de su restablecimiento decretado por la legislatura de Querétaro. Mexico City: Imprenta de Luis Abadino y Valdés, 1851.

Día quinze: exercicio en honra de la admirable virgen, seráfica doctora, y madre Santa Teresa de Jesús. Mexico City: Imprenta Nueva Madrileña de los herederos del Lic. D. Joseph de Jáuregui, 1783.

Duarte, Luis G. *Argumentos sobre la Divina Providencia*. Mexico City: Imprenta de la Viuda é hijos de Murguía, 1874.

———. *De las sílabas irregulares: lecciones dispuestas*. Mexico City: Imprenta del Cinco de Mayo, 1874.

———. *Diccionario de dudas ortográficas*. Mexico City: Imprenta Católica, 1881.

———. *Impugnación a la memoria de D. Juan Bautista Muñóz contra la gloriosa aparición de Nuestra Señora de Guadalupe y breve respuesta á las objeciones de los editores de Madrid sobre el mismo asunto en el denominado "Libro de Sensación."* Edited by Salvador Gutiérrez. Mexico City: Imprenta del Sagrado Corazón de Jesús, 1892.

———. *Profecías de Matiana acerca del triunfo de la iglesia: expurgadas, defendidas y corrobadas con respetabilísimos y muy notables vaticinios de santos, de personas canónicamente beatificadas y de otras que han muerto en olor de santidad.* Mexico City: Imprenta del Círculo Católico, 1889.

———. *Silabario: dispuesto con un nuevo metodo para la mejor y más pronta enseñanza de la lectura.* Mexico City: Imprenta Económica, 1865.

———. *Silabario preparatorio.* Mexico City: Imprenta del Cinco de Mayo, 1876.

El camino verdadero. Coloquio entre el dulcísimo Jesús y la alma su esposa, deseosa de agradarle y servile y ansiosa por amarle y gozarle en su divina unión. Mexico City: Imprenta de Luis Abadiano y Valdés, 1851.

El Museo Mexicano o miscelánea pintoresca de amenidades curiosas e instructivas. 4 volumes, (Mexico City: Ignacio Cumplido, 1843–1844).

El sí de María de la Mercedes de la Santísima Trinidad. Mexico City: Instituto de Religiosas Adoratrices Perpetuas Guadalupanas, 1996.

Esposición que el Ilustrísimo Señor Obispo, el señor provisor y vicario general; y el venerable cabildo de la diócesis de Chiapas, dirijen al soberano congreso general consituyente contra el proyecto de tolerancia de cultos en la república. Mexico City: Establecimiento Tipográfico de Andrés Boix, 1856.

Esposición que varios vecinos de Morelia eleven al soberano congreso constituyente pidiéndole se digne reprobar el artículo 15 del proyecto de constitución sobre tolerancia de cultos. Mexico City: Imprenta de Ignacio Arango, 1856.

Fernández de Lizardi, José Joaquín. *El Periquillo Sarniento.* Madrid: Cátedra, 1997.

Frías y Soto, Hilarión et al. *Los mexicanos pintados por sí mismos.* Facimile of the 1855 edition. Mexico City: Librería de M. Porrúa, 1974.

Galván Rivera, Mariano. *Guía de forasteros en la ciudad de Mégico para el año 1854.* Mexico City: Imprenta de Santiago Pérez y Compañía, 1854.

García Cubas, Antonio. *El libro de mis recuerdos.* Mexico City: Secretaría de Educación Pública, 1946.

González, Laura Mantecón de. *Información producida por la señora Laura Mantecón de González ante la Tercera Sala del Tribunal Superior, en el ejuicio de divorcio que sigue contra su esposo el señor general don Manuel González.* Mexico City: J. Reyes Velásco, 1886.

Gutiérrez Nájera, Manuel. "El calendario de Galván." In *Obras*, edited by José Luis Martínez, 506–7. Mexico City: Fondo de Cultura Económica, 2003.

———. "El ministerio de Hacienda y las profecías de la Madre Matiana." In *Escritos inéditos de sabor satírico: "Plato del día.,"* edited by Mary Eileen Carter and Boyd G. Carter, 120–121. Columbia: University of Missouri Press, 1972.

Himnos para dar gracias por la mañana y noche: y letrilla de Santa Teresa de Jesús. Mexico City: Imprenta de las Escalerillas á cargo de Agustín Guiol, 1831.

Jesús, José Manuel de. *Sermón de la seráfica madre y doctora Santa Teresa de Jesús: predicado en el día 15 de octubre de 1820 en la iglesia del Convento de Carmelitas Descalzas de esta ciudad de México.* Mexico City: Imprenta de Alejandro Valdés, 1820.

Jesús, José María de. *Segunda carta pastoral que dirige a su clero y diosesanos.* Mexico City: Luis Abadiano y Valdés, 1835.

Lara, Ambrosio. *Sermón de la Santísima Virgen de Guadalupe predicado en su insigne colegiata por Monseñor Dr. D. Ambrosio Lara, Protonotario Apostólico de su Santidad y Provisor del Arzobispado el día 12 de diciembre de 1893.* Mexico City: Imprenta Guadalupana de Reyes Velásco, 1893.

Las verdaderas profecías de Matiana: comparadas y coordinadas con otras profecías semejantes de este y del antiguo continente acerca del triunfo final de la Iglesia y del Fin del Mundo. Mexico City: Tipografía "La Catalana," 1917.

Ley sobre arreglo de la libertad de imprenta. Puebla: Imprenta de José María Macías, 1856.

Los frailes se han pronunciado contra el congreso malvado y a la faz de la nación, hoy hacen ver [sic.] lo que son. Mexico City: Imprenta testamentaria del finado Valdés a cargo de José María Gallegos, 1834.

Maistre, Joseph de Marie. *El principio regenerador de toda sociedad, traducido del francés por un mejicano amante sincero de su nación.* Mexico City: Imprenta de Galván a cargo de Arévalo, 1835.

Martagón, Fernando. *Manual de ejercicios espirtuales para practicar los santos desagravios de Cristo Señor Nuestro.* Mexico City: Tipografía de M. Torner y Companía, 1874.

Martínez Sacristán, Antonio. *El Antecristo y el fin del mundo según revelaciones divinas, y muy especialmente el Apocalipsis.* Astorga: Establecimiento Tipográfico de L. López, 1890.

Méndez, Leopoldo. *En nombre de Cristo.* Mexico City: Editorial Gráfica Popular, 1939.

Munguía, Clemente de Jesús. *Del culto considerado en sí mismo y en sus relaciones con el individuo, la sociedad y el gobierno, o sea, tratado completo de las obligaciones para con Dios.* Morelia: Imprenta de Ignacio Arango, 1847.

———. *Del derecho natural en sus principios comunes y en sus diversas ramificaciones, ó sea, curso elemental de derecho natural y de gentes público, político, constitucional, y principios de legislación.* Morelia: Imprenta de Ignacio Arango, 1849.

———. *Exposición del Illmo. Sr. Obispo de Michoacán Lic. D. Clemente de Jesús Munguía y su M. I. y venerable cabildo con motivo del decreto de 25 de junio de este año sobre expropiación eclesiástica, pidiendo su derogación, y en caso necesario protestando contra el.* Guanajuato: Juan E. Oñate, 1856.

———. *Instrucciones pastorales del licenciado Clemente de Jesús Munguía, Obispo de Michoacán, a los fieles de su diócesis.* Mexico City: Andrés Boix, 1857.

———. *Los principios de la Iglesia Católica: comparadas con los de las escuelas racionalistas en sus aplicaciones a la enseñanza pública.* Morelia: Imprenta de Ignacio Arango, 1849.

———. *Instrucciones pastorales del licenciado Clemente de Jesús Munguía, Obispo de Michoacán, a los fieles de su diócesis* Mexico City: Andrés Boix, 1857.

Museo Mexicano o miscelánea pintoresca de amenidades curiosas e instructivas. 4 vols. Mexico City: Ignacio Cumplido, 1843–1844.

Nepuen, Francisco. *Método facil, que se propone á los que practican los ejercicios espirituales, para que puedan formar santos propositos, en orden al nuevo arreglo de vidas.* Mexico City: Imprenta de Luis Abadiano, 1840.

Orsini, Abate. *Vida de la Santísima Virgen y explicación del Ave María.* Mexico City: Imprenta de José Reyes Velásco, 1874.

Palazuelos, Mateo C. *Observaciones de un lector imparcial a la carta del Sr. D. Joaquín García Icazbalceta contra la aparición Guadalupana.* Mexico City: Imprenta Guadalupana de Reyes Velásco, 1896.

Payno, Manuel. *Los bandidos de Río Frío.* 20th ed. Mexico City: Porrúa, 2000.

———. *Memoria sobre la revolución de diciembre de 1857 y enero de 1858.* Mexico City: Imprenta de Ignacio Cumplido, 1860.

Pijoán, Rafael. *El siglo XX y el fin del mundo.* Barcelona: Librería "La Hormiga de Oro," 1914.

Profecías completas de la madre Matiana: según documento histórico auténtico, de las cuales muchas se han cumplido , otras estan cumpliéndose, y otras por cumplir : juicio crítico acerca de sus vaticinios aún no cumplidos : copiado y arreglado de los calendarios de la madre Matiana y del nigromántico, el uno editado por Blanquel en 1867 y el otro en 1858, que existen en la Biblioteca Nacional. Mexico City: Imprenta Gutemburg, 1914.

Ramírez, Ignacio. "La estanquillera." In Frías y Soto et al., *Los mexicanos pintados por sí mismos,* 177–82.

Ramos y Duarte, Féliz, *Diccionario de mejicanismos; colección de locuciones i frases viciosas, con sus correspondientes críticas i correcciones fundadas en autoridades de la lengua; máximas, refranes, provincialismos i remoques populares de todos los estados de la república mejicana.* Mexico City: Imprenta de Dublan, 1895.

Reglamento de la Sociedad Católica de señoras y deberes de estas. Mexico City: Imprenta de José Fernández de Lara, 1870.

Reglamento interior del colegio fundado por la Comisión del Asilo de Criadas de la Sociedad de Ruth. Mexico City: Tipografía de José Reyes Velásco, 1875.

Remusat, Jacinto María. *Carta de un canónigo a un amigo suyo sobre la procsimidad del fin del mundo.* Mexico City: Ignacio Cumplido, 1841.

Representación al soberano congreso contra el artículo 15 del proyecto de constitución sobre tolerancia religiosa. Mexico City: Imprenta Andrade y Escalante, 1856.

Representación que algunas señoras morelianas eleven al soberano congreso constituyente contra la tolerancia de cultos. Morelia, Mexico: Imprenta Ignacio Arango, 1856.

Representación que eleven al soberano congreso los vecinos de las municipalidades de Cuautitlán, Tepotzotlán, Huehuetoca, San Miguel, Tultepec, Tultitlán, y Teoloyucán pidiendo se repuebe el artículo XV del proyecto de constitución sobre tolerancia religiosa. Mexico City: Imprenta de Vicente Segura, 1856.

Representación que la congregación de San Pedro de esta capital dirige á las agustas cámaras de la unión, contra el proyecto de establecer en la república la tolerancia de cultos. Mexico City: Tipografía de R. Rafael, 1869.

Representación que los habitantes de Zamora dirigen al soberano congreso constituyente pidiendo que no se permita en la república la libertad de cultos que establece el artículo 15 del proyecto de constitución, presentado por la commisión respectiva de día 16 de junio de 1856. Mexico City: Imprenta de M. Murguía, 1856.

Rivera, José María. "La chiera." In Frías y Soto et al., *Los mexicanos pintados por sí mismos*, 7–12.

———. "La china." In Frías y Soto et al., *Los mexicanos pintados por sí mismos*, 89–98.

Rivera Cambas, Manuel. *México pintoresco, artístico y monumental: vistas, descripcion, anecdotas y episodios de los lugares mas notables de la capital y de los estados, aun de las poblaciones cortas, pero de importancia geográfica ó histórica: las descripciones contienen datos científicos, históricos y estadísticos.* 3 vols. Facimile edition. Mexico City: Editora Nacional, 1957.

Roa Bárcena, José María. *La quinta modelo.* In *Novelas y cuentos.* Mexico City: Factoría, 2000, 95–198.

Sánchez, José. *Sermón que en la insigne colegiata de María Santísima de Guadalupe pronunció el 6 de febrero de 1859 el R. P. Fr. José Sánchez, predicador y lector de sagrada teología en el Convento de Churubusco, en la solemne acción de gracias que por las victorias obtenidas mandó celebrar el Exmo. Sr. General de División y Presidente sustituto de la República Mexicana, D. Miguel Miramón.* Mexico City: Imprenta de Abadiano, 1859.

Santaella, Luis. *Las profecías de Matiana.* Oaxaca: Imprenta "La Voz de la Verdad," 1910.

Sigüenza y Góngora, Carlos de. *Parayso occidental: plantado y cultivado por la liberal benefica mano de los muy catholicos y poderosos reyes de España, nuestros señores, en su magnifico Real Convento de Jesus Maria de Mexico.* 1684. Facimile of the first edition. Mexico City: Facultad de Filosofía y Letras Centro de Estudios de Historia de México Condumex, 1995.

Tovar, Pantaleón. "La recamarera." In Frías y Soto et al., *Los mexicanos pintados por sí mismos*, 99–108.

Voto de gracias al Exmo. Sr. Presidente de la República. D. Antonio López de Santa Anna por el restablecimineto de la sagrada Compañía de Jesús. Mexico City: Imprenta Luis Abadiano y Valdés, 1853.

Yáñez, Agustín. *Al Filo del Agua.* Edited by Arturo Azuela. Nanterre, France: Signatarios Acuerdo Archivos ALLCA XX Université Paris X, 1996.

———. *Divina floración: miscelánea de caridad.* Guadalajara: Tipografía S. R. Velásquez, 1925.

———. *The Edge of the Storm*. Austin: University of Texas Press, 1963.

———. *The Lean Lands*. Translated by Ethel Brinton. Austin: University of Texas Press, 1968.

———. *Las tierras flacas*. Mexico City: Editorial Joaquín Mortiz, 1962.

———. *Llama de amor viva: cuentos de amor*. Guadalajara: Tipografía S.R. Velásquez, 1925.

Yermo y Pares, José María. *Memorias de la fundación, principios y progresos de la sociedad de las Siervas del Sagrado Corazón de Jesús y de los Pobres*. Puebla: Siervas del Sagrado Corazón de Jesús y los Pobres, 1969.

Zamacois, Nicieto de. "La casera." In Frías y Soto et al., *Los mexicanos pintados por sí mismos*, 227–36.

Zúñiga y Ontiveros, José Mariano de. *Calendario manual y guía de forasteros de México para el año de 1803*. Mexico City: Imprenta de Zúñiga y Ontiveros.

Secondary Sources

Acevedo, Esther, ed. *La definición del estado mexicano*. Mexico City: Secretaría de Gobernación and Archivo General de la Nación, 1999.

Adame Goddard, Jorge. *El pensamiento político y social de los católicos mexicanos*. Mexico City: Universidad Nacional Autónoma de México, 1981.

Aguilar Mora, Jorge. *Una muerte sencilla, justa, eterna: cultura y guerra durante la Revolución mexicana*. Mexico City: Ediciones Era, 1990.

Ahlgren, Gillian T. W., ed. and trans. *The Inquisition of Francisca: A Sixteenth-Century Visionary on Trial*. Chicago, IL: University of Chicago Press, 2005.

———. *Teresa de Avila and the Politics of Sanctity*. Ithaca, NY: Cornell University Press, 1996.

Algaba, Leticia, "Prólogo," In *Novelas y cuentos*, ix–xii. Mexico City, Factoría: 2000.

Alonso, Carlos. "The Criollista Novel." In *The Cambridge History of Latin American Literature*, edited by Roberto González Echevarría and Enrique Pupo-Walker, vol. 2, 195–212. Cambridge: Cambridge University Press, 1996.

Álvarez Bravo, Lola. *Recuento fotográfico*. Colección de arte Fotografía. Mexico City: Penélope, 1982.

Anderson, Benedict. *Imagined Communities: Reflections on the Origin and Spread of Nationalism*. Rev. ed. London: Verso, 2006.

Andrews, Cartherine. "Sobre conservadurismo e ideas conservadoras en la primera república federal 1824–1835." In Pani, *Conservadurismo y derechas en la historia de México*, 86–134.

Annino, Antonio. "Soberanías en lucha." In *De los imperios a las naciones*, edited by François-Javier Guerra et. al., 229–53. Zaragoza: Ibercaja, 1994.

———. "The Two-Faced Janus: The Pueblos and the Origins of Mexican Liberalism." In *Cycles of Conflict, Centuries of Change: Crisis, Reform, and Revolution in Mexico*, edited by Elisa Servín et. al., 60–90. Durham, NC: Duke University Press, 2007.

Annino, Antonio, and Francois-Javier Guerra, eds. *Inventando la nación: Iberoamérica siglo XIX*. Mexico City: Fondo de Cultura Económica, 2003.

Annino, Antonio, Luis Castro Leiva, and François-Javier Guerra, eds. *De los imperios a las naciones: Iberoamérca*. Zaragoza: IberCaja, 1994.

Apolito, Paolo. *Apparitions of the Madonna at Oliveto Citra: Local Visions and Cosmic Drama*. State College: Pennsylvania State University Press, 1998.

Armancanqui-Tipacti, Elia. "La propia escritura y la re-escritura de un transcriptor de 'Vida de la Madre María Manuela de la Ascensión Ripa," In *Diálogos Espirituales*, edited by Asunción Lavrin and Rosalva Lorreto, 228–42. Puebla: Instituto de Ciencias Sociales y Humanidades de la Benemérita Universidad Autónoma de Puebla, 2006.

Arrom, Silvia Marina. *The Women of Mexico City, 1790–1857*. Stanford, CA: Stanford University Press, 1985.

Arteta, Begoña. "José María Roa Bárcena," In *En busca de un discurso integrador de la nación, 1848–1884: historiografía mexicana*, vol. 4, edited by Antonia Pi-Suñer Llorens, 241–56. Mexico City: Universidad Nacional Autónoma de México Instituto de Investigaciones Históricas, 1996.

Baddeley, Oriana. "'Her Dress Hangs There': De-Frocking the Kahlo Cult." *Oxford Art Journal* 14, no. 1 (1991): 10–17.

Banner, Lois W. "Review: Women's History: Culture and Feminization." *Reviews in American History* 6, no. 2 (1978): 155–62.

Bantjes, Adrian. *As If Jesus Walked the Earth: Cardenismo, Sonora, and the Mexican Revolution*. Wilmington, DE: Scholarly Resources, 1998.

———. "Burning Saints, Molding Minds: Iconoclasm, Civic Ritual, and Failed Cultural Revolution." In *Rituals of Rule, Rituals of Resistance: Public Celebrations and Popular Culture in Mexico*, edited by William Beezley, Cheryl English Martin, and William E. French, 261–306. Wilmington, DE: Scholarly Resources Inc., 1994.

———. "Mexican Revolutionary Anticlericalism: Concepts and Typologies." *The Americas* 65, no. 4 (2009): 467–80.

Barajas, Rafael. *El país de "El ahuizote": la caricatura mexicana de oposición durante el gobierno de Sebastián Lerdo de Tejada (1872–1876)*. Mexico City: Fondo de Cultura Económica, 2005.

———. *El país de "El llorón de Icamole": caricatura mexicana de combate y libertad de imprenta durante los gobiernos de Porfirio Díaz y Manuel González (1877–1884)*. Mexico City: Fondo de Cultura Económica, 2007.

———. *La historia de un país en caricatura: caricatura mexicana de combate 1829–1872*. Mexico City: Consejo Nacional para la Cultura y las Artes Dirección General de Publicaciones, 2000.

Barber, Elizabeth. "Art Critics on Frida Kahlo." *Art Education* 45, no. 2 (1992): 42–48.

Barnouw, Erik. *The Magician and the Cinema*. Oxford: Oxford University Press, 1981.

Bartra, Armando, and Ricardo Flores Magón. *Regeneración, 1900–1918: la corriente más radical de la Revolución de 1910 a través de su periódico de combate*. Mexico City: Hadise, 1972.

Bazant, Jan. "Mexico from Independence to 1867." In *The Cambridge History of Latin America*, edited by Leslie Bethell, 423–70. Cambridge: Cambridge University Press, 1986.

Bazant, Milda. "Lecturas del porfiriato." In *Historia de la lectura en México*, 205–42. Mexico City: El Colegio de México and Ediciones El Ermitaño, 1988.

Beezley, William H. *Judas at the Jockey Club and Other Episodes of Porfirian Mexico*. Lincoln: University of Nebraska Press, 1987.

———. *Mexican National Identity: Memory, Innuendo, and Popular Culture*. Tucson: University of Arizona Press, 2008.

———, Cheryl English Martin, and William E. French, eds. *Rituals of Rule, Rituals of Resistance: Public Celebrations and Popular Culture in Mexico*. Wilmington, DE: SR Books, 1994.

Benítez-Rojo, Antonio. "José Joaquín Fernández de Lizardi and the Emergence of the Spanish American Novel as National Project." *Modern Language Quarterly* 57, no. 2 (1996): 325–39.

Blackbourn, David. *Marpingen: Apparitions of the Virgin Mary in Nineteenth-Century Germany*. New York: Alfred A. Knopf, 1994.

Bonfil Batalla, Guillermo. *México Profundo: Reclaiming a Civilization*. Translated by Philip A. Dennis. Austin: University of Texas Press, 1996.

Bost, David H. "Historians of the Colonial Period: 1620–1700." In *The Cambridge History of Latin American Literature*, edited by Roberto González Echevarría and Enrique Pupo-Walker, vol. 1, 143–90. Cambridge: Cambridge University Press, 1996.

Boyer, Christopher R. *Becoming Campesinos: Politics, Identity, and Agrarian Struggle in Postrevolutionary Michoacán, 1920–1935*. Stanford, CA: Stanford University Press, 2003.

Brading, David A. *Church and State in Bourbon Mexico: The Diocese of Michoacán, 1749–1810*. Cambridge: Cambridge University Press, 1994.

———. *The First America: The Spanish Monarchy, Creole Patriots and the Liberal State, 1492–1866*. New York: Cambridge University Press, 1991.

———. *Mexican Phoenix: Our Lady of Guadalupe: Image and Tradition across Five Centuries*. Cambridge: Cambridge University Press, 2001.

Bravo Ugarte, José. *Periodistas y periódicos mexicanos, hasta 1935; selección*. Mexico City: Editorial Jus, 1966.

Brittsan, Zachary. "In Faith or Fear: Fighting with Lozada." Ph D diss., University of California, San Diego, 2010.

Brushwood, John. S. "The Literary Personality of José María Roa Bárcena." *The Americas* 8, no. 2 (1951): 203–8.

———. *Mexico in Its Novel: A Nation's Search for Identity*. Austin: University of Texas Press, 1966.

Buck, Sarah A. "Constructing a Historiography of Mexican Women and Gender." *Gender and History* 20, no. 1 (2008): 152–60.

Buffington, Robert. "Homophobia and the Mexican Working Class, 1900–1910." In *The Famous 41: Sexuality and Social Control in Mexico, c. 1901*, edited by Robert McKee Irwin, Ed McCaughan, and Michelle Rocío Nasser, 193–226. New York: Palgrave, 2003.

Butler, Matthew. *Faith and Impiety in Revolutionary Mexico*. New York: Palgrave Macmillan, 2007.

———. *Popular Piety and Political Identity in Mexico's Cristero Rebellion: Michoacán, 1927–29*. Oxford: Oxford University Press, 2004.

Bynum, Caroline Walker. ". . . And Woman his Humanity: Female Imagery in Religious Writing of the Later Middle Ages." In *Gender and History: On the Complexity of Symbols*, edited by Caroline Walker Bynum, Stevan Harell, and Paula Richman, 257–88. Boston, MA: Beacon Press, 1986.

———. "The Complexity of Symbols." In *Gender and Religion: On the Complexity of Symbols*, edited by Caroline Walker Bynum, Stevan Harell, and Paula Richman, 1–22. Boston: Beacon Press, 1986.

———. *Holy Feast and Holy Fast: The Religious Significance of Food to Medieval Women*. Berkeley: University of California Press, 1987.

Calhoun, Craig. *Nationalism*. Minneapolis: University of Minnesota Press, 1997.

———. "Nationalism and Ethnicity." *Annual Review of Sociology* 19 (1993): 211–39.

Camp, Roderic Ai. "An Intellectual in Mexican Politics: The Case of Agustín Yáñez." *Mester* 12, nos. 1 and 2 (1983): 3–17.

———. *Mexican Political Biographies, 1935–1993*. 3rd ed. Austin: University of Texas Press, 1995.

Cárdenas García, Nicolás, and Enrique Guerra Manzo. *Integrados y marginados en el México posrevolucionario: los juegos de poder local y sus nexos con la política nacional*. Las ciencias sociales Tercera década. Mexico City: Universidad Autónoma Metropolitana M. Á. Porrúa, 2009.

Carey, Patrick W. "American Catholic Romanticism, 1830–1888," *The Catholic Historical Review* 74, no. 4 (1988): 590–606.

Castellanos, Rosario. "La novela mexicana contemporánea y su valor testimonial." *Hispania* (1964): 223–30.

Castro, Miguel Ángel. "José María Andrade, del amor al libro." In *Constructores de un cambio cultural*, edited by Laura Suárez de la Torre, 381–436. Mexico City: Instituto de Investigaciones Dr. José Luis Mora, 2003.

———."La prensa mexicana de 1857 a 1967: dos ejemplos." In *La definición del estado mexicano*, edited by Esther Acevedo, 537–55. Mexico City: Secretaría de Gobernación, 1999.

Castro Gutiérrez, Felipe. "Profecías y libelos subversivos contra el reinado de Carlos III." *Estudios de Historia Novohispana* 11 (1991): 85–96.

Ceballos Ramírez, Manuel. *El catolicismo social: un tercero en discordia*. Mexico City: El Colegio de México, 1991.

Cerulo, Karen A. "Identity Construction: New Issues, New Directions." *Annual Review of Sociology* 23 (1997): 385–409.

Chasteen, John Charles. *National Rhythms, African Roots: The Deep History of Latin American Popular Dance.* Albuquerque: University of New Mexico Press, 2004.

Chowning, Margaret. "The Catholic Church and the Ladies of the Vela Perpetua: Gender and Devotional Change in Nineteeth-Century Mexico." *Past and Present* 221, no. 1 (November 2013): 197–237.

——. *Rebellious Nuns: The Troubled History of a Mexican Convent, 1752–1863.* Oxford: Oxford University Press, 2005.

Christian, William A. *Moving Crucifixes in Modern Spain.* Princeton, NJ: Princeton University Press, 1992.

——. *Visionaries: The Spanish Republic and the Reign of Christ.* Berkeley: University of California Press, 1996.

Coakley, John Wayland. *Women, Men, and Spiritual Power: Female Saints and their Male Collaborators.* New York: Columbia University Press, 2006.

Connaughton, Brian. "Agio, clero y bancarrota fiscal, 1846–1847." *Mexican Studies/ Estudios Mexicanos* 14, no. 2 (1998): 263–85.

——. "Conjuring the Body Politic from the Corpus Mysticum: The Post-Independent Pursuit of Public Opinion in Mexico, 1821–1854." *The Americas* 55, no. 3 (1999): 459–79.

——. *Dimensiones de la identidad patriótica: Religión, política y regiones en México, siglo XIX.* Mexico City: Universidad Autónoma Metropolitana Unidad Iztapalapa, 2001.

——. "The Enemy Within: Catholicism and Liberalism in Independent Mexico, 1821–1860." In *The Divine Charter: Constitutionalism and Liberalism in Nineteenth-Century Mexico,* edited by Jaime E. Rodriguez, 183–204. Lanham, MD: Rowman & Littlefield Publishers, 2005.

——. *Ideología y sociedad en Guadalajara (1788–1853).* Mexico City: Dirección General de Publicaciones del Consejo Nacional para la Cultura y las Artes, 1992.

——. "A Most Delicate Balance: Representative Government, Public Opinion, and Priests in Mexico, 1821–1834." *Mexican Studies / Estudios Mexicanos* 17, no. 1 (2001): 41–69.

——, ed. *Prácticas populares, cultura política y poder en México, siglo XIX.* Mexico City: Universidad Autonoma Metropolitana Unidad Iztapalapa, 2008.

——, Carlos Illades, and Sonia Pérez Toledo, eds. *Construcción de la legitimidad política en México en el siglo XIX.* Mexico City: El Colegio de Michoacán, 1999.

Corrigan, John. *Business of the Heart: Religion and Emotion in the Nineteenth Century.* Berkeley: University of California Press, 2002.

Costeloe, Michael P. *The Central Republic in Mexico, 1835–1846: Hombres de Bien in the Age of Santa Anna.* Cambridge: Cambridge University Press, 1993.

——. "Church-State Financial Negotiations in Mexico during the American War, 1846–1847." *Revista de Historia de América,* no. 60 (1965): 91–123.

———. "Federalism to Centralism in Mexico: The Conservative Case for Change, 1834–1835." *The Americas* 45, no. 2 (1988): 173–85.

———. "Mariano Arista and the 1850 Presidential Election in Mexico." *Bulletin of Latin American Research* 18 (1999): 51–70.

———. "The Mexican Church and the Rebellion of the Polkos." *The Hispanic American Historical Review* 46, no. 2 (1966): 170–78.

———. "Santa Anna and the Gómez Farías Administration in Mexico, 1833–1834." *The Americas* 31, no. 1 (1974): 18–50.

Covo, Jacqueline. "La idea de la revolución francesa en el congreso constituyente de 1856–1857." *Historia Mexicana* 38, no. 1 (1988): 69–78.

Coward, Barry, and Julian Swann. *Conspiracies and Conspiracy Theory in Early Modern Europe: From the Waldensians to the French Revolution*. Aldershot, UK: Ashgate, 2004.

Cubitt, Geoffrey. *The Jesuit Myth: Conspiracy Theory and Politics in Nineteenth-Century France*. Oxford: Clarendon Press, 1993.

Cuéllar, José Tomás de. *La linterna mágica*. Edited by Mauricio Magdaleno. 3rd ed. Mexico City: Universidad Nacional Autónoma de México Dirección General de Publicaciones, 1973.

Cuevas, Mariano. *Historia de la Iglesia en México*. 5th ed. Mexico City: Editorial Patria, 1946.

Curcio-Nagy, Linda Ann. *The Great Festivals of Colonial Mexico City: Performing Power and Identity*. Albuquerque: University of New Mexico Press, 2004.

Curley, Robert. "'The First Encounter': Catholic Politics in Revolutionary Jalisco, 1917–19." In *Faith and Impiety in Revolutionary Mexico*, edited by Matthew Butler, 131–48. New York: Palgrave, 2007.

Dabove, Juan Pablo. *Nightmares of the Lettered City: Banditry and Literature in Latin America, 1816–1929*. Pittsburgh, PA: University of Pittsburgh Press, 2007.

Davidson, Russ. "Adolph Sutro as Book Collector: A New Look." *Bulletin of the California State Library Foundation*, no. 75 (2003): 2–25.

Deanda, Elena. "El Chuchumbe te he de soplar: sobre obscenidad, censura y memoria oral en el primer 'son de la tierra' novohispano." *Mester* 36 (2007): 53–71.

Debroise, Olivier. *Lola Álvarez Bravo: In Her Own Light*. Tucson: Center for Creative Photography at the University of Arizona, 1994.

de Heredia, Carlos M. *Historietas y leyendas*. Vol. 8. Obras completas de Carlos M. de Heredia, S.J. Buenos Aires: Editorial Difusión, 1946.

Della Cava, Ralph. *Miracle at Joaseiro*. New York: Columbia University Press, 1970.

Delpar, Helen. *The Enormous Vogue of Things Mexican: Cultural Relations Between the United States and Mexico, 1920–1935*. Tuscaloosa: University of Alabama Press, 1992.

Díaz Ruiz, Ignacio. "Al filo del agua en la historia personal de Agustín Yáñez y el itinerario de su obra." In Agustín Yáñez, *Al filo del agua*, edited by Arturo Azuela, 275–84. Mexico: ALLCA XX, 1996.

Diccionario de autoridades. 1726. Facimile of the first edition. Real Academia Española. Madrid: Gredos, 1963.

Diccionario de la lengua española. 22nd ed. 2 vols. Real Academia Española. Madrid: Espasa Calpe, 2001.

Diccionario de la lengua española. Online edition. Real Academia Española. www.rae.es.html.

Diccionario Porrúa de historia, biografía y geografía de México. 6th ed. 4 vols. Mexico City: Editorial Porrúa, 1995.

Douglas, Ann. *The Feminization of American Culture.* New York: Noonday Press, 1998.

Earle, Rebecca. *The Return of the Native: Indians and Myth-Making in Spanish America, 1810–1930.* Durham, NC: Duke University Press, 2007.

Eich, Jennifer Lee. *The Other Mexican Muse: Sor María Anna Agueda de San Ignacio, 1695–1765.* New Orleans, LA: University Press of the South, 2004.

Escalante Gonzalbo, Fernando. *Ciudadanos imaginarios: memorial de los afanes y desventuras de la virtud y apología del vicio triunfante en la República Mexicana— tratado de moral pública.* Mexico City: Colegio de México, 1992.

Espinosa Blas, Margarita. "El Hijo del Ahuizote: un periódico americanista." In *La prensa decimonónica en México: objeto y sujeto de la historia,* edited by Adriana Pineda Soto and Celia del Palacio Montiel, 245–62. Morelia: Universidad Michoacana de San Nicolás de Hidalgo, 2003.

Falcón, Romana. "El arte de la petición: rituales de obedencia y negociación, México, segunda midad del siglo XIX." *Hispanic American Historical Review* 86, no. 3 (2006): 467–500.

Fallaw, Ben. *Cárdenas Compromised: The Failure of Reform in Postrevolutionary Yucatán.* Durham, NC: Duke University Press, 2001.

———. *Religion and State Formation in Postrevolutionary Mexico.* Durham, NC: Duke University Press, 2012.

———. "Varieties of Mexican Revolutionary Anticlericalism: Radicalism, Iconoclasm, and Otherwise, 1914–1935." *The Americas* 65, no. 4 (2009): 481–509.

Fernández, Emilio ("El Indio"). *Río Escondido.* Los Angeles: Mexicinema Video Corp., 1986.

Fernández-Aceves, María Teresa. "Imagined Communities: Women's History and the History of Gender in Mexico." *Journal of Women's History* 19, no. 1 (2007): 200–205.

Fernández de Lizardi, José Joaquín. *El Periquillo Sarniento.* Madrid: Cátedra, 1997.

Ferreira da Silva, Marco Aurélio. "Corrige os costumes rindo:' Humor, vergonha e decoro na sociabilidade mundana de fortaleza (1850–1890)." PhD diss., Universidade Federal de Pernambuco, 2004.

Ferrer, Elizabeth. *Lola Álvarez Bravo.* New York: Aperture Foundation, 2005.

Ferrer Benimeli, José Antonio. "Los jesuitas y los motines en la España del siglo XVIII." In *Coloquio internacional Carlos III y su siglo: actas,* vol. 1, 453–84. Madrid: Universidad Complutense, 1990.

Flasher, John J. *México contemporáneo en las novelas de Agustín Yáñez*. Mexico City: Editorial Porrúa, 1969.

Florescano, Enrique. "Patria y nación en la época de Porfirio Díaz." *Signos históricos*, no. 13 (2005): 153–87.

Folgarait, Leonard. *Mural Painting and Social Revolution in Mexico, 1920–1940: Art of the New Order*. Cambridge: Cambridge University Press, 1998.

———. *Seeing Mexico Photographed: The Work of Horne, Casasola, Modotti, and Álvarez Bravo*. New Haven, CT: Yale University Press, 2008.

Forbes, Amy Wiese. *The Satiric Decade: Satire and the Rise of Republican Political Culture in France, 1830–1940*. Lanham, MD: Lexington Books, 2010.

Ford, Caroline C. *Divided Houses: Religion and Gender in Modern France*. Ithaca, NY: Cornell University Press, 2005.

Fowler, Will. "Dreams of Stability: Mexican Political Thought During the 'Forgotten Years.' An Analysis of the Beliefs of the Creole Intelligentsia (1821–1853)." *Bulletin of Latin American Research* 14, no. 3 (1995): 287–312.

———. "El pensamiento político de los moderados, 1838–1850." In *Construcción de la legitimidad política en México en el siglo XIX*, edited by Brian C. Connaughton, Carlos Illades, and Sonia Pérez Toledo, 275–302. Zamora: El Colegio de Michoacán, 1999.

———. *The Liberal Origins of Mexican Conservatism, 1821–1832*. Glasgow, UK: University of Glasgow, Institute of Latin American Studies, 1997.

———. *Mexico in the Age of Proposals, 1821–1853*. Contributions in Latin American Studies. Westport, CT: Greenwood, 1998.

———. "Valentín Gómez Farías: Perceptions of Radicalism in Independent Mexico, 1821–1847." *Bulletin of Latin American Research* 15, no. 1 (1996): 39–62.

Fowler, Will, and Humberto Morales Moreno, eds. *El conservadurismo mexicano en el siglo XIX*. Puebla: Benemérita Universidad Autónoma de Puebla, 1999.

Franco, Jean. *Lectura sociocrítica de la obra novelística de Agustín Yáñez*. Guadalajara: Gobierno de Jalisco, 1988.

———. *Plotting Women: Gender and Representation in Mexico*. New York: Columbia University Press, 1989.

French, William E., and Katherine Elaine Bliss. *Gender, Sexuality, and Power in Latin America Since Independence*. Lanham, MD: Rowman and Littlefield, 2007.

Fuentes, Carlos. *La muerte de Artemio Cruz*. Mexico City: Fondo de Cultura Económica, 1962.

Gallop, Rodney. "A Mexican 'Plough Monday.'" *Folklore* 49, no. 4 (2012): 394–99.

Garber, Elizabeth. "Art Critics on Frida Kahlo: A Comparison of Feminist and Non-Feminist Voices." *Art Education* 45, no. 2 (1992): 42–48.

García Gutiérrez, Blanca Estela. "La comomisión política de nación conservadora en México a mediados del siglo XIX. Una retrospectiva a través de la prensa." *Iztapalapa* 43 (1998): 27–50.

———. "La experiencia cultural de los conservadores durante el México independiente: un ensayo interpretativo." *Signos históricos* 1, no. 1 (1999): 127–48.

Gellner, Ernest. *Nations and Nationalism*. Malden, MA: Blackwell Pub., 2005.

Girón, Nicole. "El entorno de los grades empresarios culturales." In *Empresa y cultura en tinta y en papel, 1800–1860*, edited by Laura Súarez de la Torre and Miguel Ángel Castro, 51–64. Mexico City: Instituto de Investigaciones Dr. José Luis Mora, 2001.

———."La idea de 'cultura nacional' en el siglo XIX: Altamirano y Ramírez." In *En torno a la cultura nacional*, edited by Héctor Aguilar Camín, 53–81. Mexico City: Instituto Nacional Indigenista, 1976.

Glantz, Margot. "Yáñez y *Al filo del agua*." In Vaca and Gómez Robledo, *Acto preparatorio*, 93–103.

Gómez-Aguado, Guadalupe and Adriana Gutiérrez Hernández, "*El pensamiento conservador en los periódicos La Cruz y El Pájaro Verde*." In Pani, *Conservadurismo y derechas en la historia de México*, 214–66.

Gómez de Silva, Guido. *Diccionario breve de mexicanismos*. Mexico City: Academia Mexicana and Fondo de Cultura Económica, 2001.

Gómez Robledo, Antonio. "Cuando todo se ha dicho." In Vaca and Gómez, *Acto preparatorio*, 17–32.

González, María del Refugio. "El pensamiento de los conservadores mexicanos." In *Mexican and Mexican American Experience in the Nineteenth Century*, edited by Jaime E. Rodriguez, 55–67. Tempe: Arizona Bilingual Press, 1989.

González Echevarría, Roberto. *Myth and Archive: Toward a Theory of Latin American Narrative*. Cambridge: Cambridge University Press, 1990.

González Echevarría, Roberto, and Enrique Pupo-Walker, eds. *The Cambridge History of Latin American Literature*. 3 vols. Cambridge: Cambridge University Press, 1996.

González Navarro, Moises. *El pensamiento político de Lucas Alamán*. Mexico City: El Colegio de México, 1952.

González Ramírez, Manuel. *La caricatura política*. Mexico City: Fondo de Cultura Económica, 1974.

González y González, Luis. *Pueblo en vilo: microhistoria de San José de Gracia*. Mexico City: El Colegio de México, 1968.

Graham, Richard, ed., with Thomas E. Skidmore, Aline Helg, and Alan Knight. *The Idea of Race in Latin America, 1870–1940*. Austin: University of Texas Press, 1990.

Gravier, Marina Garone, and Albert Brandt. "Nineteenth-Century Mexican Graphic Design: The Case of Ignacio Cumplido." *Design Issues* 18, no. 4 (2002): 54–63.

Graziano, Frank. *Cultures of Devotion: Folk Saints of Spanish America*. New York: Oxford University Press, 2006.

———. *Wounds of Love: The Mystical Marriage of Saint Rose of Lima*. Oxford: Oxford University Press, 2004.

Grimberg, Saloman. "Review: Thinking of Death." *Women's Art Journal* 14, no. 2 (1993–1994): 44–50.

Guardino, Peter F. *Peasants, Politics, and the Formation of Mexico's National State: Guerrero, 1800–1857.* Stanford, CA: Stanford University Press, 1996.

——. *The Time of Liberty: Popular Political Culture in Oaxaca, 1750–1850.* Durham, NC: Duke University Press, 2005.

Guerra, François-Javier. *Las revoluciones hispánicas: independencias americanas y liberalismo español.* Cursos de verano de El Escorial. Madrid: Editorial Complutense, 1995.

——. "Mexico from Independence to Revolution: The Mutations of Liberalism." In *Cycles of Conflict, Centuries of Change: Crisis, Reform, and Revolution in Mexico,* edited by Elisa Servín et. al., 129–52. Durham, NC: Duke University Press, 2007.

——. *Modernidad e independencias: ensayos sobre las revoluciones hispánicas.* Madrid: Editorial Mapfre, 1992.

Guilot de la Garza, Lilia. "El competido mundo de la lectura: librerías y gabinetes de lectura en la ciudad de México, 1821–1855," In *Constructores de un cambio cultural,* edited by Laura Suárez de la Torre, 437–510. Mexico City: Instituto de Investigaciones Dr. José Luis Mora, 2003, 437–510.

——."El portal de los agustinos: un corredor cultural en la ciudad de México," In *Empresa y cultura en tinta y en papel,* edited by Laura Súarez de la Torre and Ángel Castro. Mexico City: Instituto de Investigaciones Dr. José Luis Mora, 2001, 233–44.

Gunnarsdóttir, Ellen. *Mexican Karismata: The Baroque Vocation of Francisca de los Angeles, 1674–1744.* Lincoln: University of Nebraska Press, 2004.

Gutiérrez Nájera, Manuel. "El calendario de Galván." In *Obras,* edited by José Luis Martínez. Mexico City: Fondo de Cultura Económica, 2003.

——. "El ministerio de Hacienda y las profecías de la Madre Matiana." In *Escritos inéditos de sabor satírico: "Plato del día.,"* edited by Mary Eileen Carter and Boyd G. Carter, 120–21. Columbia: University of Missouri Press, 1972.

Guzmán Pérez, Moisés. *Publicistas, prensa y publicidad en la independencia de Hispanoamérica.* Morelia: Comisión Institucional para la Conmemoración del Bicentenario de la Independencia y el Centenario de la Revolución Mexicana, 2011.

Hageneder, Fred. *The Meaning of Trees: Botany, History, Healing, Lore.* San Francisco, CA: Chronicle Books, 2005.

Hale, Charles A. "The War with the United States and the Crisis in Mexican Thought." *The Americas* 14, no. 2 (1957): 153–73.

Hammond, John Hays. "José María Roa Bárcena: Mexican Writer and Champion of Catholicism." *The Americas* 6, no. 1 (1949): 45–55.

Hamnett, Brian. "The Comonfort Presidency, 1855–1857." *Bulletin of Latin American Research* 15, no. 1 (1996): 81–100.

——. "El partido conservador en México, 1858–1867: La lucha por el poder." In *El conservadurismo mexicano en el siglo XIX,* edited by Will Fowler and Humberto

Morales Moreno, 313–37. Puebla: Benemérita Universidad Autónoma de Puebla, 1999.

———. "Mexican Conservatives, Clericals, and Soldiers: The 'Traitor' Tomás Mejía through Reform and Empire, 1855–1867." *Bulletin of Latin American Research* 20, no. 2 (2001): 187–209.

Harris, Christopher. *The Novels of Agustín Yáñez: A Critical Portrait of Mexico in the 20th century*. Lewiston, NY: Edwin Mellen Press, 2000.

Historia de la lectura en México. Mexico City: Ediciones del Ermitaño and Colegio de México, 1988.

Hoffleit, Dorrit. "What Falls from Heaven." *The Scientific Monthly* 60, no. 1 (1945): 30–36.

Hofman, Amos. "Opinion, Illusion, and the Illusion of Opinion: Barruel's Theory of Conspiracy." *Eighteenth-Century Studies* 27, no. 1 (1993): 27–60.

Ibsen, Kristine. *Women's Spiritual Autobiography in Colonial Spanish America*. Gainesville: University Press of Florida, 1999.

Irwin, Robert McKee, Ed McCaughan, and Michelle Rocío Nasser, eds. *The Famous 41: Sexuality and Social Control in Mexico, c. 1901*. New York: Palgrave Macmillan, 2003.

Jaffary, Nora E. *False Mystics: Deviant Orthodoxy in Colonial Mexico*. Lincoln: University of Nebraska Press, 2004.

———."María Josefa de la Peña y la defense de la legitimidad mística." In *Diálogos Espirituales*, edited by Asunción Lavrin and Rosalva Loreto López, 120–33. Puebla: Instituto de Ciencias Sociales y Humanidades de la Benemérita Universidad Autónoma de Puebla, 2006.

Jesús, Ursula de, and Nancy E. Van Deusen. *The Souls of Purgatory: The Spiritual Diary of a Seventeenth-Century Afro-Peruvian Mystic, Ursula de Jesús*. Albuquerque: University of New Mexico Press, 2004.

Johnson, Julie Greer. "Feminine Satire in Concolorcorvo's "El Lazarillo de ciegos caminantes." *South Atlantic Bulletin* 45, no. 1 (1980): 11–20.

———. *Satire in Colonial Spanish America: Turning the New World Upside Down*. Austin: University of Texas Press, 1993.

Jonas, Raymond Anthony. *France and Cult of the Sacred Heart: An Epic Tale for Modern Times*. Berkeley: University of California Press, 2000.

Joseph, Gilbert. *Revolution from Without: Yucatán, Mexico, and the United States, 1880–1924*. Cambridge: Cambridge University Press, 1982.

Jrade, Ramón. "Counterrevolution in Mexico: The Cristero Movement in Sociological and Historical Perspective." PhD diss., Brown University, 1982.

Kagan, Richard L. *Lucrecia's Dreams: Politics and Prophecy in Sixteenth-Century Spain*. Berkeley: University of California Press, 1990.

Kanellos, Nicolás, and Helvetia Martell. *Hispanic Periodicals in the United States, Origins to 1960: A Brief History and Comprehensive Bibliography*. Houston, TX: Arte Público Press, 2000.

King, Linda. *Roots of Identity: Language and Literacy in Mexico*. Stanford, CA: Stanford University Press, 1994.

Kittleson, Roger A. "Women and Notions of Womanhood in Brazilian Abolitionism." In *Gender and Slave Emancipation in the Atlantic World*, edited by Pamela Scully and Diana Paton, 99–120. Durham, NC: Duke University Press, 2005.

Knight, Alan. "The Mentality and Modus Operandi of Revolutionary Anticlericalism." In *Faith and Impiety in Revolutionary Mexico*, edited by Matthew Butler, 21–56. New York: Palgrave MacMillan, 2007.

———. *The Mexican Revolution*. 2 vols. Lincoln: University of Nebraska Press, 1986.

———. "Racism, Revolution, and Indigenismo in Mexico, 1910–1940." In *The Idea of Race in Latin America, 1870–1940*, edited by Richard Graham, 71–114. Austin: University of Texas Press, 1990.

Knight, Alan, and Wil Pansters, eds. *Caciquismo in Twentieth-Century Mexico*. London: Institute for the Study of the Americas, 2005.

Knowlton, Robert J. *Church Property and the Mexican Reform, 1856–1910*. DeKalb: Northern Illinois University Press, 1976.

Kristof, Jane. "The Feminization of Piety in Nineteenth-Century Art." In *Reinventing Christianity: Nineteenth-Century Contexts*, edited by Linda Woodhead, 165–91. Burlington, VT: Ashgate, 2001.

Kselman, Thomas. *Miracles and Prophecies in Nineteenth-Century France*. New Brunswick, NJ: Rutgers University Press, 1983.

Kurutz, Gary F. "The Sutro Library." *California History* 59, no. 2 (1980): 173–78.

Lagos, Ramona. "Tentación y penitencia en Al filo del agua de Agustín Yáñez." *Atenea* 166, no. 419 (1968): 105–21.

Lamadrid Lusarreta, Adalberto. "Guías de forasteros y calendarios mexicanos de los siglos XVIII y XIX, existentes en la Biblioteca Nacional de México." *Boletín del Instituto de Investigaciones Bibliográficas*, no. 6 (1971): 9–135.

Lane, Jill. *Blackface Cuba, 1840–1895*. Philadelphia: University of Pennsylvania Press, 2005.

Langford, Walter M. *The Mexican Novel Comes of Age*. Notre Dame, IN: University of Notre Dame Press, 1971.

Langle Ramírez, Arturo. *Vocabulario, apodos, seudónimos, sobrenombres y hemerografía de la Revolución*. Mexico City: Universidad Nacional Autónoma de México, Instituto de Investigaciones Históricas, 1966.

Larkin, Brian. *The Very Nature of God: Baroque Catholicism and Religious Reform in Bourbon Mexico City*. Albuquerque: University of New Mexico Press, 2010.

Lau, Ana J. "Las luchas por transformar el estatus civil de las mexicanas." In *Integrados y marginados en el México posrevolucionario*, edited by Nicolas Cárdenas Garcia and Enrique Cuerra Manzo, 297–347. Mexico City: Universidad Autónoma Metropolitana, Xochimilco, 2009.

Lavrin, Asunción. El más allá en el imaginario de las religiosas novohispanas." In *Muerte y vida en el más allá: España y América*, edited by Gisela Von Wobeser and Enriqueta Vila Vilar, 181–201. Mexico City: UNAM, 2009.

———. "La madre María Magdalena Lorravaquio y su mundo visionario." *Signos histórico* 13 (2005): 22–41.

———. "María Marcela Soria: una capuchina queretana," In *Diálogos Espirituales*, edited by Asunción Lavrin and Rosalva Lorreto, 74–93. Puebla: Instituto de Ciencias Sociales y Humanidades de la Benemérita Universidad Autónoma de Puebla, 2006.

———."Review: The Church: Institution and Spirituality in New Spain." *Mexican Studies / Estudios Mexicanos* 17, no. 2 (2001): 403–12.

———. "Unlike Sor Juana? The Model Nun in the Religious Literature of Colonial Mexico." In *Feminist Perspectives on Sor Juana Inés de la Cruz*, edited by Stephanie Merrim, 61–86. Detriot, MI: Wayne State University Press, 1991.

Lavrin, Asunción, and Rosalva Loreto López, eds. *Diálogos espirituales: manuscritos femeninos hispanoamericanos, siglos XVI–XIX*. Puebla: Instituto de Ciencias Sociales y Humanidades de la Benemérita Universidad Autónoma de Puebla, 2006.

———, eds. *Monjas y beatas: la escritura femenina en la espiritualidad barroca novo- hispana siglos XVII y XVIII*. Mexico City: Universidad de las Américas-Puebla and Archivo General de la Nación, 2002.

Leal, Luis. "Agustín Yáñez y la novela Mexicana." *Mester* 12, no. 1 (May 1983): 18–25.

———. "Aspects of the Mexican Novel from Lizardi to Elizondo." *Arizona Quarterly* 24, no. 1 (1968): 53–64.

Lear, John. *Workers, Neighbors, and Citizens: The Revolution in Mexico City*. Lincoln: University of Nebraska Press, 2001.

Lester, Rebecca J. "Embodied Voices: Women's Food Asceticism and the Negotiation of Identity." *Ethos* 23, no. 2 (1995): 187–222.

———. *Jesus in Our Wombs: Embodying Modernity in a Mexican Convent*. Berkeley: University of California Press, 2005.

Lewis, Laura A. *Hall of Mirrors: Power, Witchcraft, and Caste in Colonial Mexico*. Durham, NC: Duke University Press, 2003.

Limón, Graciela. "Madre Matiana: Agustín Yáñez's 'Sapienta' in Revolutionary Mexico." *Américas* 31, no. 10 (1979): 25–27.

Limón Gómez, Leandro. "Agustín Yáñez: genio y figura." In Vaca and Gómez Robledo, *Acto preparatorio*, 33–38.

Lombardo García, Irma. *El siglo de Cumplido: la emergencia del periodismo de opinón, 1832–1857*. Mexico City: Universidad Nacional Autónoma de México, 2002.

Lomnitz-Adler, Claudio. *Death and the Idea of Mexico*. Brooklyn, NY: Zone Books, 2005.

———. *Deep Mexico, Silent Mexico: An Anthropology of Nationalism*. Minneapolis: University of Minnesota Press, 2001.

Lope Blanch, Juan M. *Vocabulario mexicano relativo a la muerte*. Mexico City: Direccion General de Publicaciones, 1963.

López, Rick A. *Crafting Mexico: Intellectuals, Artisans, and the State After the Revolution*. Durham, NC: Duke University Press, 2010.

López Casillas, Mercurio. *Manilla*. Mexico City: Editorial RM, 2005.

Loreto López, Rosalva. *Una empresa divina: las hijas de Santa Teresa de Jesús en América, 1604-2004*. Puebla: Universidad de las Américas, 2004.

Mañon, Manuel. *Historia del teatro principal en México, 1753-1931*. Mexico City: Editorial "Cvltvra," 1932.

Martin, David F. "On Portraiture: Some Distinctions." *The Journal of Aesthetics and Art Criticism* 20, no. 1 (1961): 61–72.

Martin, Luis. "Lucas Alamán Pioneer of Mexican Historiography: An Interpretative Essay." *The Americas* 32, no. 2 (1975): 239–56.

Martínez, Jose Luis. ""La formación literaria de Agustín Yáñez y Al filo del agua." *Mester* 12, nos. 1 and 2 (1983): 26–32.

Martínez Pérez, José. *Dichos, dicharachos y refranes mexicanos: colección moderna con interpretación*. Mexico City: Editores Mexicanos Unidos, 1977.

Mathes, W. Michael. "Origins of the Sutro Library and the Mexican Collection." In *Latin American History and Culture: Series 4, The Mexican Rare Monograph Collection, 1548-1861*, v–xiii. Woodbridge, CT: Primary Source Microfilm, 2003.

Matute, Alvaro, Evelia Trejo, and Brian Francis Connaughton Hanley. *Estado, Iglesia y sociedad en México, siglo XIX*. Mexico City: Facultad de Filosofía y Letras UNAM: Grupo Editorial M. A. Porrúa, 1995.

McGowan, Gerald L. *Prensa y poder, 1854-1857: la Revolución de Ayutla, el Congreso Constituyente*. Mexico City: El Colegio de México, 1978.

McMahon, Darrin M. *Enemies of the Enlightenment: The French Counter-Enlightenment and the Making of Modernity*. Oxford: Oxford University Press, 2001.

Mejía Prieto, Jorge. *Albures y refranes de México*. Mexico City: Panorama Editorial, 1985.

Méndez, Vicente M. *Memorias de la madre Mercedes de la Santísima Trinidad*. Merida: Diaz Massa, 1952.

Meyer, Jean. *Esperando a Lozada*. Mexico City: El Colegio de Michoacán, 1984.

———. *La cristiada*. 3 vols. Mexico City: Siglo Veintiuno, 1973.

Mijangos y González, Pablo. "The Lawyer of the Church: Bishop Clemente de Jesús Munguía and the Ecclesiastical Response to the Liberal Revolution in Mexico." PhD diss., University of Texas, 2009.

Mitchell, Stephanie, and Patience Schell, eds. *The Women's Revolution in Mexico, 1910-1953*. Lanham, MD: Roman and Littlefield, 2007.

Monsiváis, Carlos. *Amor perdido*. Mexico City: Ediciones Era, 1977.

———. "Y ahora, con su venia, conversaré de usted mi luciente señora (y no menos admirable fotógrafa)." In Lola Álvarez Bravo, *Recuento fotográfico*, 187–90. Mexico City: Penélope, 1982.

Montiel Ontiveros, Ana Cecilia "Nuevas lecturas en prensas viejas." In *Publicistas, prensa, y publicidad en la independencia de hispanoamérica*, edited by Moisés Guzmán Pérez, 123–52. Morelia: Instituto de Investigaciones Históricas, Universidad de San Nicolás de Hidalgo, 2011.

Mörner, Magnus, ed. *The Expulsion of the Jesuits from Latin America*. New York: Knopf, 1965.

Mraz, John. *Looking for Mexico: Modern Visual Culture and National Identity*. Durham, NC: Duke University Press, 2009.

Muñiz, Elsa. *Cuerpo, representación y poder: México en los albores de la reconstrucción nacional, 1920–1934*. Mexico City: Universidad Autónoma Metropolitana, 2002.

Muriá, José María. "En torno *Al filo del Agua*." In Vaca and Gómez Robledo, *Acto preparatorio*, 69–75.

Muriel, Josefina. *Conventos de monjas en la Nueva España*. Mexico City: Editorial Santiago, 1946.

———. *Cultura femenina novohispana*. 2nd ed. Mexico City: Universidad Nacional Autónoma de México Instituto de Investigaciones Históricas, 1994.

Muscacchio, Humberto. *Milenios de México*. 2 vols. Mexico City: Hoja Casa Editorial, 1999.

Myers, Kathleen A."Crossing Boundaries: Defining the Field of Female Religious Writing in Colonial Latin America." *Colonial Latin American Review* 9, no. 2 (2000): 151–65.

Navarrete, Carlos. *Documentos para la historia del culto a San Caralampio, Comitán, Chiapas*. Chiapas: Gobierno del Estado de Chiapas; Consejo Estatal de Fomento a la Investigación y Difusión de la Cultura; and Instituto Chiapaneco de Cultura, 1990.

Navarete Maya, Laura. "El Gil Blas Cómico, publicación satírica y de humor." In *La prensa decimonónica en México: objeto y sujeto de la historia*, edited by Adriana Pineda Soto and Celia del Palacio Montiel, 263–72. Morelia: Universidad Michoacana de San Nicolás de Hidalgo, 2003.

Noriega, Cecilia and Erika Pani, "Las propuestas 'conservadoras' en la década de 1840." In *Conservadurismo y derechas*, vol. 1, edited by Erika Pani, 175–213. Mexico City: Fondo de Cultura Económica, 2009.

O'Dogherty Madrazo, Laura. *De urnas y sotanas: el Partido Católico Nacional en Jalisco*. Mexico City: Consejo Nacional para la Cultura y las Artes, 2001.

Olcott, Jocelyn. *Revolutionary Women in Postrevolutionary Mexico*. Durham, NC: Duke University Press, 2005.

———, Mary K. Vaughan, and Gabriela Cano, eds. *Sex in Revolution: Gender, Politics, and Power in Modern Mexico*. Durham, NC: Duke University Press, 2006.

Olimón Nolasco, Manuel. "Clemente de Jesús Munguía y el incipiente liberalismo de Estado den México." PhD diss., Universidad Iberoamericana, 2005.

Otterman, Sharon, "Complex Emotions over the First American Indian Saint." *The New York Times*, 24 July 2012.

The Oxford Dictionary of the Church. Oxford Reference Online. Oxford: Oxford University Press, 2005. www.oxfordreference.com.

Pagden, Anthony, ed. *Hernán Cortés: Letters from Mexico*. New York: Grossman, 1971.

Pani, Erika. "'Ciudadana y muy ciudadana'? Women and the State in Indpendent Mexico, 1810–1930." *Gender and History* 18, no. 1 (2006): 5–19.

——, ed. *Conservadurismo y derechas en la historia de México.* Mexico City: Fondo de Cultura Económica, 2009.

——."Dreaming of a Mexican Empire: The Political Projects of the 'Imperialistas.'" *The Hispanic American Historical Review* 82, no. 1 (2002): 1–31.

——. *El segundo imperio: pasados de usos múltiples.* Mexico City: Fondo de Cultura Económica; and Centro de Investigación y Docencia Económicas, 2004.

——. "Entre transformar y gobernar: la Constitución de 1857." *Historia y Política* 11 (2004): 65–86.

——. "Las fuerzas oscuras." In *Conservadurismo y derechas en la historia de México,* vol. 1, edited by Erika Pani, 11–92. Mexico City: Fondo de Cultura Económica, 2009.

——. *Para mexicanizar el Segundo Imperio: el imaginario político de los imperialistas.* Mexico City: Colegio de México Centro de Estudios Históricos, 2001.

——. "Una ventana sobre la sociedad decimonónica: los periodicos católicos, 1845–1857." *Secuencia,* nueva época, no. 36 (1996): 67–88.

Paz, Octavio. *The Labyrinth of Solitude.* New York: Grove Press, 1985.

Pérez Montfort, Ricardo. *Estampas de nacionalismo popular mexicano: ensayos sobre cultura popular y nacionalismo.* Mexico City: Centro de Investigaciones e Estudios Superiores en Antropología Social, 1994.

Pérez Salas, María Esther C. *Costumbrismo y litografía en México: un nuevo modo de ver.* Mexico City: Universidad Nacional Autónoma de México, 2005.

——. "Genealogía de Los mexicanos pintados por sí mismos." *Historia Mexicana* 48, no. 2 (1998):167–207.

——. "Los secretos de una empresa exitosa: la imprenta de Ignacio Cumplido." In *Constructores de un cambio cultural,* edited by Laura Suárez de la Torre, 101–82. Mexico City: Instituto de Investigaciones Dr. José Luis Mora, 2003.

Piccato, Pablo. *The Tyranny of Opinion: Honor in the Construction of the Mexican Public Sphere.* Durham, NC: Duke University Press, 2010.

Pijoán, José et al., eds., *Summa artis: historia general del arte, vol. XXXII: el grabado en España, siglos XIX–XX.* Madrid: Espasa-Calpe, 1988.

Pineda Soto, Adriana, and Celia del Palacio eds. *La prensa decimonónica en México: objeto y sujeto de la historia.* Guadalajara: Universidad de Guadalajara, Centro Universitario de Ciencias Sociales y Humanidades, 2003.

Pi-Suñer Llorens, Antonia ed. *En busca de un discurso integrador de la nación, 1848–1884: historiografía mexicana.* Vol. 4. Mexico City: Universidad Nacional Autónoma de México Instituto de Investigaciones Históricas, 1996.

Poole, Deborah. *Vision, Race, and Modernity: A Visual Economy of the Andean Image World.* Princeton, NJ: Princeton University Press, 1997.

Poole, Stafford. *Our Lady of Guadalupe: The Origins and Sources of a Mexican National Symbol, 1531–1797.* Tucson: University of Arizona Press, 1995.

Pope, Barbara Corrado. "A Heroine Without Heroics: The Little Flower of Jesus and Her Times." *Church History* 57, no. 1 (1988): 46–60.

Pope, Randolph D. "The Spanish American Novel from 1950 to 1975." In *The Cambridge History of Latin American Literature*, vol. 2, edited by Roberto González Echevarría and Enrique Pupo-Walker, 226–78. Cambridge: Cambridge University Press, 1996.

Price, R. M. "On Religious Parody in the Buscón." *Modern Language Notes* 86, no. 2 (1971): 273–79.

Pupo-Walker, Enrique. "The Brief Narrative in Spanish America." In *The Cambridge History of Latin American Literature*, vol. 1, edited by Roberto González Echevarría and Enrique Pupo-Walker, 490–535. Cambridge: Cambridge University Press, 1996.

Purnell, Jennie. *Popular Movements and State Formation in Revolutionary Mexico: The Agraristas and Cristeros of Michoacán*. Durham, NC: Duke University Press, 1999.

Quiñónez, Isabel. *Mexicanos en su tinta: calendarios*. Mexico City: Instituto Nacional de Antropología e Historia, 1994.

Quintero, Ruben, ed. *A Companion to Satire*. Malden, MA: Blackwell, 2007.

Rama, Angel. *The Lettered City*. Durham, NC: Duke University Press, 1996.

Ramos-Escandón, Carmen, ed. *Presencia y transparencia: la mujer en la historia de México*. 2nd ed. Mexico City: Colegio de México, Programa Interdisciplinario de Estudios de la Mujer, 2006.

———. "Women and Citizenship in Nineteenth-Century Mexico: Three Entangled Perspectives." *Gender and History* 18, no. 1 (2006): 1–4.

Reina, Leticia. *Las rebeliones campesinas en México, 1819–1906*. Mexico City: Siglo Veintiuno Editores, 1980.

"The Return of Halley's Comet." *Bulletin of the American Geographical Society* 42, no. 4 (1910): 261–65.

Reynolds, David S. "The Feminization Controversy: Sexual Stereotypes and the Paradoxes of Piety in Nineteenth-Century America." *The New England Quarterly* 53, no. 1 (1980): 96–106.

Rivera Ayala, Sergio. "Lewd Songs and Dances from the Streets of Eighteenth-Century New Spain." In *Rituals of Rule, Rituals of Resistance: Public Celebrations and Popular Culture in Mexico*, edited by William H. Beezley, Cheryl English Martin, and William E. French, 27–46. Wilmington, DE: Scholarly Resources Books, 1994.

Robe, Stanley L. "Yáñez y el regionalismo." *Mester* 12, nos. 1 and 2 (1983): 53–77.

Robinson, Linton H. *Mexican Slang: A Guide*. Campo, CA: Bueno Books, 1992.

Rodríguez, Artemio, ed. *José Guadalupe Posada: 150 años/150 years*. Los Angeles, CA: La Mano Press, 2003.

Rodríguez, Jaime E., ed. *The Divine Charter: Constitutionalism and Liberalism in Nineteenth-Century Mexico*. Lanham, MD: Rowman and Littlefield Publishers, 2005.

————. *Down from Colonialism: Mexico's Nineteenth Century crisis*. Los Angeles: Chicano Studies Research Center Publications, University of California, 1983.

Rodríguez Piña, Javier. "Rafael de Rafael y Vilá: el conservadurismo como empresa." In *Constructores de un cambio cultural*, edited by Laura Suárez de la Torre, 318–19. Mexico City: Instituto de Investigaciones Dr. José Luis Mora, 2003.

Rosaldo, Renato. "A List of Slang and Colloquial Expressions of Mexico City." *Hispania* 31, no. 4 (1948): 437–45.

Ross, Kathleen. *The Baroque Narrative of Carlos de Sigüenza y Góngora: A New World Paradise*. Cambridge: Cambridge University Press, 1993.

————. "Historians of the Conquest and Colonization of the New World: 1550–1620." In *The Cambridge History of Latin American Literature*, vol. 1, edited by Roberto González Echevarría and Enrique Pupo-Walker, 101–42 Cambridge: Cambridge University Press, 1996.

Rothenstein, Julian. *Posada: Messenger of Mortality*. London: Redstone Press, 1989.

Rubial García, Antonio. *La santidad controvertida: hagiografía y conciencia criolla alrededor de los Venerables no canonizados de Nueva España*. Sección de obras de historia. Mexico City: Universidad Nacional Autónoma de México Facultad de Filosofía y Letras, 1999.

Ruffinelli, Jorge, "Epílogo." In José María Roa Bárcena, *Novelas y cuentos*, 303–14. Mexico City, Factoría: 2000.

Rugeley, Terry. *Rebellion Now and Forever: Mayas, Hispanics, and Caste War Violence in Yucatán, 1800–1880*. Stanford, CA: Stanford University Press, 2009.

————. *The River People in Food Time: The Civil Wars in Tabasco, Spoiler of Empires*. Stanford, CA: Stanford University Press, forthcoming.

Ruiz Castañeda, María del Carmen, *El periodismo en México: 450 años de historia*. Mexico City: Editorial Tradición, 1974.

Ruiz Martínez, Apen. "Nación y género en el México revolucionario: la India Bonita y Manuel Gamio." *Signos históricos* 5 (2001): 55–86.

Rulfo, Juan. *Obras*. Mexico City: Fondo de Cultura Económica, 1987.

Salomon, Grimberg. "Thinking of Death." *Woman's Art Journal* 14, no. 2 (1993): 44–50.

Sánchez Somoano, José. *Modismos locuciones y términos mexicanos*. Madrid: Manuel Minuesa de los Ríos, 1892.

Sánchez Velázquez, María Teresa. *Admirable es Dios en sus obras: madre María de las Mercedes, su vida, sus virtudes, su obra* Mexico City: Instituto de Religiosas Adoratrices Perpetuas Guadalupanas, 1981.

Santamaría, Francisco Javier, and Joaquín García Icazbalceta. *Diccionario de mejicanismos*. Mexico City: Editorial Porrúa, 1959.

Schwartz, Stuart B. *All Can be Saved: Religious Tolerance and Salvation in the Iberian Atlantic World*. New Haven, CT: Yale University Press, 2008.

Scully, Pamela, and Diana Paton. *Gender and Slave Emancipation in the Atlantic World*. Durham, NC: Duke University Press, 2005.

Seeley, Paul. "O Sainte Mere: Liberalism and the Socialization of Catholic Men in Nineteenth-Century France." *The Journal of Modern History* 70, no. 4 (1998): 862–91.

Segre, Erica. *Intersected Identities: Strategies of Visualisation in Nineteenth- and Twentieth-Century Mexican Culture.* New York: Berghahn Books, 2007.

Servín, Elisa, Leticia Reina, and John Tutino, eds. *Cycles of Conflict, Centuries of Change: Crisis, Reform, and Revolution in Mexico.* Durham, NC: Duke University Press, 2007.

Sieber, Harry. *Language and Society in La vida de Lazarillo de Tormes.* Baltimore, MD: Johns Hopkins University Press, 1978.

Slade, Carole. *Saint Teresa of Avila: Author of a Heroic Life.* Berkeley: University of California Press, 1995.

Smith, Colin. *The Collins Spanish Dictionary.* New York: Harper Collins, 1992.

Smith, Stephanie J. *Gender and the Mexican Revolution: Yucatan Women and the Realities of Patriarchy.* Chapel Hill: University of North Carolina Press, 2009.

Sommer, Doris. *Foundational Fictions: The National Romances of Latin America.* Berkeley: University of California Press, 1991.

Stepan, Nancy Leys. "Race and Gender: The Role of Analogy in Science." In *Anatomy of Racism*, edited by David Theo Goldberg, 38–57. Minneapolis: University of Minnesota Press, 1990.

Stevens, Donald F. "Eating, Drinking, and Being Married: Epidemic Cholera and the Celebration of Marriage in Montreal and Mexico City, 1832–1833." *The Catholic Historical Review* 92, no. 1 (2006): 74–94.

———. "Lo revelado y lo oscurecido: la política popular desde los archivos parroquiales." In *Construcción de la legitimidad política en México en el siglo XIX*, edited by Brian C. Connaughton, Carlos Illades, and Sonia Pérez Toledo, 207–26. Mexico City: El Colegio de Michoacán, 1999.

———. *Origins of Instability in Early Republican Mexico.* Durham, NC: Duke University Press, 1991.

———. "Patriots, Poverty, Taxes, and Death: Recent Work on Mexican History, 1750–1850." *Latin American Research Review* 40, no. 2 (2005): 150–65.

———. "Temerse la ira del cielo," In *El conservadurismo mexicano en el siglo XIX*, edited by Will Fowler and Humberto Morales Moreno, 87–102. Puebla: Benemérita Universidad Autónoma de Puebla, 1999.

Stokley, James. "Falling Meteors Might Wipe out Cities." *The Science News-Letter* 16, no. 432 (1929): 27–29.

———. "Forecasting Meteors." *The Science News-Letter* 20, no. 552 (1931): 294–303.

Suárez de la Torre, Laura, ed. *Constructores de un cambio cultural: impresores-editores y libreros en la ciudad de México, 1830–1855.* Mexico City: Instituto de Investigaciones Dr. José María Luis Mora, 2003.

———. "Prosperidad y quiebra: un vivencia en la vida de Mariano Galván Rivera." In *Empresa y cultura en tinta y papel, 1800–1860*, edited by Laura Súarez de la Torre and Miguel Ángel Castro, 109–22. Mexico City: Instituto de Investigaciones Dr. José María Luis Mora, 2001.

———, and Miguel Angel Castro, eds. *Empresa y cultura en tinta y papel, 1800–1860.* Mexico City: Instituto de Investigaciones Dr. José María Luis Mora, 2001.

Tamayo, Jaime. *El obregonismo y los movimientos sociales: la conformación del Estado moderno en México (1920–1924).* Guadalajara: Universidad de Guadalajara, 2008.

Taves, Ann. "Context and Meaning: Roman Catholic Devotion to the Blessed Sacrament in Mid-Nineteenth-Century America." *Church History* 54, no. 4 (1985): 482–95.

———. *The Household of Faith: Roman Catholic Devotions in Mid-Nineteenth-Century America.* Notre Dame, IN: University of Notre Dame Press, 1986.

Thomson, Guy P. C. "La contrareforma en Puebla, 1854–1886." In *El conservadurismo mexicano en el siglo XIX,* edited by Will Fowler and Humberto Morales Moreno, 239–64. Puebla: Benemérita Universidad Autónoma de Puebla, 1999.

Thomson, Guy P. C., and David G. LaFrance. *Patriotism, Politics, and Popular Liberalism in Nineteenth-Century Mexico: Juan Francisco Lucas and the Puebla Sierra.* Wilmington, DE: Scholarly Resources, 1999.

Toor, Frances. *A Treasury of Mexican Folkways.* New York: Crown Publishers, 1947.

Toro Pascua, María Isabel. "Milenarismo y profecía en el siglo XV: La tradición del libro de Unay en la Península Ibérica." *Península,* no. 0 (2003): 29–37.

Tuñón, Julia. *Mujeres de luz y sombra en el cine mexicano: la construcción de una imagen (1939–1952).* Mexico City: Colegio de México, Instituto Mexicano de Cinematografía, 1998.

Tuñón Pablos, Esperanza. *Mujeres que se organizan el Frente Único pro Derechos de la Mujer, 1935–1938.* Colección Las ciencias sociales. Mexico City: Coordinación de Humandidaes: M. A. Porúa, 1992.

Tutino, John. *From Insurrection to Revolution in Mexico: Social Bases of Agrarian Violence, 1750–1940.* Princeton, NJ: Princeton University Press, 1986.

Tyler, Ronnie C. *Posada's Mexico.* Washington, D.C.: Library of Congress, 1979.

Udall, Sharyn R. "Frida Kahlo's Mexican Body: History, Identity, and Artistic Aspiration." *Woman's Art Journal* 24, no. 2 (2003): 10–14.

Vaca, Agustín, and Antonio Gómez Robledo, eds. *Acto preparatorio: Agustín Yáñez a cien años.* Zapopán: El Colegio de Jalisco, 2003.

Van Young, Eric. *The Other Rebellion: Popular Violence, Ideology and the Mexican Struggle for Independence, 1810–1821.* Stanford, CA: Stanford University Press, 2001.

Vaughan, Mary K. *Cultural Politics in Revolution: Teachers, Peasants, and Schools in Mexico, 1930–1940.* Tucson: University of Arizona Press, 1997.

Vázquez, Josefina Zoraida. "Los años olvidados." *Mexican Studies/Estudios Mexicanos* 5, no. 2 (1989): 313–26.

Velasco Toro, José. "Matiana, mística del imaginario y 'voz de ultratumba.'" *Ulúa* 10 (June–December 2007), 39–71.

Viqueira Albán, Juan Pedro. *Propriety and Permissiveness in Bourbon Mexico.* Translated by Sonya Lipsett-Rivera and Sergio Rivera Ayala. Wilmington, DE: Scholarly Resources Inc., 1999.

Voekel, Pamela. *Alone Before God: The Religious Origins of Modernity in Mexico.* Durham, NC: Duke University Press, 2002.

Walker, Charles F. *Shaky Colonialism: The 1746 Earthquake-Tsunami in Lima, Peru, and its Long Aftermath.* Durham, NC: Duke University Press, 2008.

Ward, Gerald. *The Grove Encyclopedia of Materials and Techniques in Art.* Oxford: Oxford University Press, 2008.

Weber, Alison. *Teresa of Avila and the Rhetoric of Femininity.* Princeton, NJ: Princeton University Press, 1990.

Weiner, Richard. "Trinidad Sánchez Santos: Voice of the Catholic Opposition in Porfirian Mexico." *Mexican Studies/Estudios Mexicanos* 17, no. 2 (2001): 321–49.

Welter, Barbara. *Dimity Convictions: The American Woman in the Nineteenth Century.* Athens: Ohio University Press, 1976.

Whittaker, Martha Ellen. "Jesuit Printing in Bourbon Mexico City: The Press of the Colegio de San Ildefonso." PhD diss., University of California, Berkeley, 1998.

Wright-Rios, Edward. "Indian Saints and Nation-States: Ignacio Manuel Altamirano's Landscapes and Legends." *Mexican Studies/Estudios Mexicanos* 20, no. 1 (2004): 47–68.

———. *Revolutions in Mexican Catholicism: Reform and Revelation in Oaxaca, 1887–1934.* Durham, NC: Duke University Press, 2009.

Yuval-Davis, Nira. "The Bearers of the Collective: Women and Religious Legislation in Israel." *Feminist Review*, no. 4 (1980): 15–27.

———. *Gender and Nation.* London: Sage Publications, 1997.

Index

Page numbers in italic text indicate illustrations.